PROFESSIONAL COURAGE

PROFESSIONAL COURAGE

*My Journey in Military Intelligence
Through Peace, Crisis, and War*

MAJOR GENERAL JACK LEIDE USA (RET)

Copyright © 2023 Major General Jack Leide USA (Ret). All rights reserved.

All rights reserved. No part of this publication may be reproduced, distributed, or transmitted in any form or by any means, including photocopying, recording, or other electronic or mechanical methods, without the prior written permission of the publisher, except in the case of brief quotations embodied in critical reviews and certain other noncommercial uses permitted by copyright law.

To request permission, contact jaleide@aol.com

The views expressed in this book are those of the author and do not reflect the official policy or position of the Department of Defense or the US Government.

ISBN: 979-8-89109-353-9 (paperback)
ISBN: 979-8-89109-582-3 (hardcover)
ISBN: 979-8-89109-354-6 (ebook)

These are my memories, from my perspective, and I have tried to represent events as faithfully as possible.

DEDICATION

To Ann, the love of my life, who was with me through thick and thin. I cannot think of my life or military career without her. She was my true inspiration, always, and the perfect army wife and mother. With her at my side throughout, I was truly blessed.

CONTENTS

Acknowledgements..xvii
Foreword..xxi
Prolepsis xxv
Preface xxvii

Chapter 1: From the Beginning..1
   The Infantry Is Really Basic..3
      I Must Learn to Listen to My Instincts 5
      Advanced Infantry Training, Fort Benning, Georgia 8
   Becoming a Paratrooper: Airborne Qualification
   Course, Fort Benning, Georgia February-24 April 1964 9
   82nd Airborne Division: Fort Bragg, North Carolina,
   March 1964 13
   Bravo Company, 3rd Battalion (Airborne), 325th Infantry.....16
   Operation Power Pack: Dominican Republic 19
      My First Combat Experience: Dominican Republic...............22
   A New Job: Aide de Camp..27
   Into the Unknown with the 173rd Airborne Brigade 32

Chapter 2: Sky Soldier 35
   173rd Airborne Brigade (Separate), Bien Hoa,
   Republic of Vietnam, April 1966 36
      Taking Command of Charlie Company 2nd
      Battalion, 173rd Airborne Brigade..................................38

Heliborne Assault Into Vung Tau..39
Company Ambush Mission, Xuan Loc 41
    Tactical Planning for the Ambush Mission..........................43
    Moving Again Toward the Unknown...............................49
    The Ambush Begins 53
    Moving into a Company-Level Ambush/Defensive Position ...57
Out Of The Crab Trap: Moving Back To Base Camp............67
Saying Goodbye To Charlie Company....................................72
II Field Force: Long Binh, South Vietnam, December
1966–April 1967...76
    Talking Strategy: My Time with Harry G. Summers, Jr...........78
    Red's Promise...81
Assessing The "Unpitied Sacrifice": Transferring To
The Military Intelligence Branch 83

Chapter 3: My First Experiences in the World of
      Intelligence **86**
    My First Knock on the Green Door 92
    The Call of the Eagles..93
A Screaming Eagle: 101st Airborne Division, Camp
Eagle, Phu Bai, Vietnam...94
    The G-2 Plans and Order of Battle Section.........................97
    Operational Missions..98
    Facing that Damned Green Door, Again!.........................100
    Khe Sanh Revisited?..102
    Degradation of Combat Unit Capability 104
    Time for a Cigar...105
Taking Command Of The 101st Military
Intelligence Company..106
    The Importance of Military Interrogators........................107
    Sensors: A Look Into the Future...................................111
    Ripcord: A Last Hurrah 112
Leaving Camp Eagle 113

**Chapter 4: Invaluable Career-Expanding
 Experiences: 1971-1980..............................118**

My Experience With Chinese Language Begins:
United States Army Language School, Monterey,
California: November 1970-December 1971 119
Entering the Joint Arena: The Armed Forces Staff
College, Norfolk, VA: December 1971-June 1972 120
Advanced Language and Area Study 122
    Back to School: Survival of the Fittest 123
    A Year of Many Countries.. 125
    Republic of China Army Command and Staff College......... 128
Directorate for Estimates Defense Intelligence
Agency: January-July 1975 131
Hong Kong Soldier.. 133
    My Time with the Joint Services Intelligence Staff 135
    Creating a Unique Collection Program 138
A Special Forces Soldier 141
    My Green Beret: Smoke Bomb Hill 143
    One Special Soldier... 146
    My Return to the 82nd Airborne Division 148

Chapter 5: All-American! All the Way! 151

Back to the All Americans 152
    Master Blaster On-Call... 154
    An Exercise in Actual Crisis Planning 157
    The Beginnings of Army SERE....................................... 160
    The Red Beret Caper 163
    Developing a Linguist Database 164
A Blueprint for the Future 166

Chapter 6: To the Pentagon and Back, and a Whole World in Between 169

    Chief, China/Far East Division, Directorate for Estimates, Defense Intelligence Agency, Washington, DC: June 1982–January 1983 171

    Office Of The Secretary Of Defense, Washington, Dc: January 1983–July 1984 173

        Terrorism and Counterterrorism 175
        Worldwide Counterterrorism Units 177
        Reforming Our Special Operations Forces 180
        Onward, Ever Onward 183

    500th Military Intelligence Group, United States Army Intelligence and Security Command: Camp Zama, Japan: July 1984–July 1986 183

        A Mission and Its People 184
        Six Phases of Afterburner 188
        Off to the Cold North 190

    Office of the United States Army, Deputy Chief of Staff for Intelligence, the Pentagon, Washington, DC: July 1986–March 1988 194

Chapter 7: Into the Middle Kingdom 198

    The Beginnings in the Middle Kingdom 199
        The Family Plan 202
    An Unprecedented Trip to the United States 203
    An Airborne Adventure 205
    The Internal Situation in China Becomes Serious 208
        Inside the Command Center 215
    The Crisis Goes Red 216
        A Quick Run to the Airport 223
    The City Quiets 224

Chapter 8: Post Tiananmen: Destroying Classified and Evacuating Citizens 227
    Fang Lizhi 229
  The Jinguomenwai Incident 229
  Destroying Classified 233
  The Evacuation Challenge 234
  Beyond Tiananmen 239
  Back to Beijing 240
    A Date with the Russian 241
    A Special Relationship 242
    Another Presidential Visit 244
    Fang Lizhi Revisited 245
  My Time in China Winds Down 246

Chapter 9: Into the Gathering Storm: Operation Desert Shield 253
  United States Central Command, MacDill Air Force Base, July 1990 254
    Exercise Internal Look: July 1990 255
    Fine Tuning Our Working Relationships 259
    A Prediction Fulfilled: WATCHCON 1 264
    Preparing to Deploy 268
  Preparing for War: Riyadh, Saudi Arabia 270
    Our Diplomatic Partner 272
    The Scud Threat 273
    A Report Conundrum 275
    Blood Chits 276
  Preparing for Battle: Our Arab Allies 277
    Our Saudi Connection 277
    General Schwarzkopf's Arab "Counterpart" 281
    An Important Relationship with the Egyptians 283
  The Saga of JSTARS 284
  Lead-Up to the Air Campaign 290

Chapter 10: We Are At War: Operation Desert Storm ...293

   The Dynamic Development of BDA 296
   Intelligence: An Integral Part of the Operational Effort 303
   Planning to Meet the Terrain: Maps, Trafficability,
   and Weather 307
      The Fire Trenches 310
      A Trip to Cairo 310
   Working with the National Intelligence Agencies 312
      Challenging Tank Kills: An Unwarranted CIA Challenge 313
      A Bright CIA Light 317
   Conducting the Collection Management Orchestra 317
      Unique Cultural Challenges 321
      Keeping Israel out of the War 324
      Scud Hunters 325
   Moving Toward the Final Phase: Planning the
   Ground Campaign 327
   Iraq's Aborted Strike 332
   The Battle for Khafji 333
   The Landing That Never Was 337
   G-Day-2: February 22, 1991 339
   G-Day-1: February 23, 1991 341
      EMCON Suicide 341
   The Final Briefings 343

Chapter 11: The 100 Hour War 347

   Final Preparations for Operation Desert Spear: The
   Ground Campaign 347
   G-Day: February 24, 1991 348
      In the War Room 348
      In the KTO 350
      In the War Room 351
      In the KTO 353
   G-Day +1: February 25, 1991 353
      In the War Room 353

 In the KTO..357
 In the War Room: The Republican Guard Enters the
 EMCON Suicide Trap..358
 In the KTO..359
 In the War Room...359
G-Day +2: February 26, 1991 359
 In the KTO..359
 In the War Room: Iraq's Republican Guard Falls into
 the EMCON Suicide Trap...360
 In the KTO..361
G-Day +3: February 27, 1991 363
 In the War Room...363
 In the KTO..364
G-Day +4: February 28, 1991 365
 In the War Room: Cease-Fire..365
Arranging the Cease-Fire 367
Safwan: An Attempt at Peace 368
A Visit into the Abyss 371
The Shia-Kurd Uprisings 373
After-Action Report...375
 Weapons of Mass Destruction: The Aftermath......................376
 The Iraqi Combat Forces..378
 Iraqi Casualty Assessment..382
From Victory to MacDill..385

Chapter 12: Finishing What I Started **392**
My Final Days at CENTCOM 392
 Celebrating Victory and Sharing Honors.............................395
 A Change of Command...397
Director for Operations, DIA: Washington, DC, June
1992–August 1995 398
Director, National Military Intelligence Collection Center.....400
Director, Defense HUMINT Service 401
 Our HUMINT Blueprint..403

The Potential of the DAS 404
Director, Central MASINT Office 405
Becoming a Harvard Fellow 407
Visits to Operational Organizations and Areas 408
Back to My Roots 411
My Final Days at the DIA and in the Army 415

Glossary 419
About the Author 425

ACKNOWLEDGEMENTS

Ann- My everything

John, Jeff, Mei- For putting up with the constant turmoil and ultimately becoming the wonderful spouses and parents that make us so proud.

Mom- Who gave me, not only a wonderful life growing up, but also instilled in me the values that guided me throughout my life. I Love you Mom.

Dad- He instilled in me-family first. He loved, and sacrificed for my sister and me without limits. He had a special place in his heart for his grandchildren. I love you dad.

Mary Ann- as a wonderful sister she has been always there for me, even cleaning popcorn pans.

Renee Ergazos- My faithful editor, who asked all the right questions, guided me throughout, and kept me focused on writing this book for everyone.

Lieutenant General H.R. McMaster- For his faith in me and what I accomplished and for his gracious effort to write the foreword to this book.

Lieutenant General Pat Hughes, Bill Spracher and Chris Bailey for believing enough in the value of imy manuscript to write professional reviews

Lieutenant General Tom Weinstein- My mentor, hero and, most importantly, dear friend.

Captain Larry Britten- My early alter ego who was taken from us all too soon. May he rest in peace.

Sergeant Major Charlie "Catfish" Bryant-Instilled in me a great respect for service and the incredible value of NCO's

Colonel Butch Kendrick- Had faith in a young first lieutenant to give me a command of a rifle company in the 82nd Airborne Division. A great troop commander.

Colonel Woodrow J. Schrawder- Taught me how to treat subordinates with respect and always ask for, listen to and respect their views.

Lieutenant Colonel John J. "Chris" Christensen- Instilled in me the value of the study of foreign nations and languages.

CWO Mike Fried- My invaluable fellow Screaming Eagle. A wonderful lifetime friend and great tribute to the military intelligence corps.

Colonel Lynne Murray- Instilled in me the value of being a contributing military attaché.

Major General Sandy Meloy- The best commander I ever had. A legend in the 82nd Airborne Division who encouraged me to be the best combat intelligence officer I could be.

Colonel Larry Wortzel- My right hand in Beijing. Promoted him to sergeant and to colonel.

General H Norman Schwarzkopf- For believing in me during the most challenging of times. For trusting and using our intelligence during Desert Storm.

Lieutenant General Ed Soyster- A great boss and an unflinching, dynamic supporter of our efforts during Desert Storm.

Colonel Harry Fukuhara- A legendary Japanese-American who was a priceless national asset during his incredibly long career. He served as my "teacher" during my tour in Japan.

EdValentine- An invaluable right hand during the entirety of Desert Shield and Desert Storm. Always had a great supply of "pogey bait" which he readily shared with me.

Major General Bill Harmon- A brilliant colleague, who guided and encouraged me on my quest from start to finish.

Ray Starmann- A cavalry friend who has supported me throughout.

Last, but certainly not least, the wonderful troops and civilians from all services- They were critical to any successes I may have had.

FOREWORD

I once asked a professor of mine, historian Don Higginbotham, if he had read a book published in his field, to which he replied, "Historians do not read books, we use them." Major General Jack Leide's Professional Courage however is a book to be both read and used. Historians, students of the art of war, and general readers will appreciate Jack's unique career and wide range of experiences in the airborne infantry, intelligence organizations, and special operations. Professional Courage is a story of service to nation and commitment to fellow soldiers. Jack Leide dedicated his entire professional life to supporting troops. I benefitted directly from Jack's tireless efforts to provide timely and accurate intelligence as a cavalry troop commander during the Battle of 73 Easting in Operation Desert Storm and during multiple combat tours in Iraq and Afghanistan during the first two decades of this century.

Jack's recount of leading soldiers in combat balances humanity with the challenges of two combat tours in Vietnam and should be read and discussed by today's officers and sergeants. His trenchant analysis of the flawed strategy under which that war was fought provides an invaluable on-the-ground perspective on how Vietnam War decision-making was mainly based on fantasy in Washington rather than reality in the field. A key theme throughout the book is developing the moral courage to resist telling a boss only what they want to hear by having the constant fortitude to be candid and forthright. Jack's 33-year army career provides a unique window from which to view the last half of the 20th century. He provides an action-packed, first-hand account of his experiences as an airborne infantry company commander, from the firefights in the sniper-infested streets in the war-torn barrios of Santo Domingo to intense combat in the triple-canopy jungles of Vietnam. From a soldier's perspective, he describes in gripping detail the dangers and hardships of close combat with Vietnamese Communist Forces and the daily pressures of commanding an infantry company in the heat of battle.

Jack provides a vivid account of his experiences as the defense and army attaché to China, especially as he bore witness to the Tiananmen massacre and oversaw the evacuation of American citizens out of China. He highlights the essential elements of crisis response including the importance of anticipating key requirements and the criticality of collecting and reporting time-sensitive intelligence to enable decisions at the highest levels of government.

As General Schwarzkopf's Director for Intelligence, he invites readers into the daily crucible of the intense war room during Desert Storm. He emphasizes the challenges and necessity of telling the commander what he needs to know, despite the consequences. He describes how he organized successful collection management, analysis, and reporting of predictive, actionable intelligence that contributed to the coalitions stunning victory against the world's fourth largest army. Jack also describes the need to combine skills of a soldier with those of a diplomat while working within large, diverse international coalitions in combat. He candidly illustrates how departmental and service parochialism, especially during combat operations, can be counter-productive, impede decision-making, and undercut capabilities.

Professional Courage reveals the lessons that we seem to relearn in every conflict, including the value of human intelligence, foreign languages, and special operations forces. And he exposes the moral dimensions of war with first-hand accounts of the valor and emotions of soldiers at war as well as the sacrifices and strains their families endure. Jack describes his experiences and relationships with world leaders with detailed appreciation and great humility. His lifelong love of learning languages and immersing himself in cultures will inspire younger generations to follow the path of service and experience the rewards of contributing to significant military and political endeavors. Jack was often personally selected by our top military leadership for the most challenging assignments. His accomplishments remain relevant to the most significant political challenges we face today, especially his deep understanding of China.

From one end of the world to the other, Jack Leide was on the razor's edge of US national security and policy. His Professional Courage is a uniquely valuable contribution to history and learning.

H.R. McMaster, Lieutenant General, USA (Ret)

PROLEPSIS

THE WAR ROOM: RIYADH, SAUDI ARABIA
0200 HRS JANUARY 17, 1991

On this fateful night, there are 38 minutes before the Air Campaign is scheduled to begin in all its potential fury, signaling the highly anticipated launch of Operation Desert Storm. As I sit in the pressure-packed war room, scanning through mounds of current intelligence reporting, I know that I must be prepared to provide the latest pertinent intelligence or to respond to any questions from my boss, the US Central Command Commander-in-Chief (CINC), General H Norman Schwarzkopf. As his wartime director for Intelligence, J-2, I will have to provide the CINC with the accurate intelligence, in useable formats, and at the right time to help him make crucial decisions during the offensive phases of the battle that would be joined this night. Mission success, the lives of 541,000 coalition forces, and the American national interest are all at stake. Our 35-country coalition's primary objective is the defeat of Saddam Hussein's large Iraqi military forces arrayed before us and to force him to withdraw from his illegal occupation of Kuwait. During the leadup to the war, my intelligence staff and I have done all that we could to prepare what we called "the intelligence battlefield." From now on, we will be challenged to the fullest while playing a crucial role in the CINC's decision-making processes as he leads the coalition into the largest conventional battle since World War II. My role during the looming conflict will challenge every fiber of my mind, body, and soul, and as I sit, I know I cannot waiver under the inevitable pressures to come.

I realize that challenges to the estimates and conclusions of my intelligence support mission will likely occur. I have previously delt with various versions of such challenges during my previous combat experiences and during the leadup to this final phase of the war. Intelligence processes are more art than science. Experience has shown that I will encounter individual, bureaucratic, and parochial detractors critical of certain portions of our efforts, procedures, conclusions, and recommendations. I will constantly have to rely on a positive personal quality that I have assiduously, consciously, and subconsciously developed over my 30-year Army career: professional courage. My personal priority will be to consistently provide General Schwarzkopf with unvarnished, useable, timely, and predictive intelligence analysis and recommendations, so he can make learned combat decisions, no matter the consequences.

PREFACE

Following my retirement from the Army, I occasionally gathered and loosely organized unclassified and declassified papers, reports, charts, and briefings describing the United States' efforts during Desert Shield and Desert Storm. I used those archives to begin the writing of an embryonic historical memoir of my firsthand experiences, observations, and especially lessons learned during that campaign. Shortly thereafter, I put it all into a holding file. At the time, the thought of writing a book had never entered my mind. Some years later, after a futile attempt at tracing my own ancestral roots, I decided, in frustration, to do a historical picture book of my military career for my grandkids. The book ended up as a 62-page photo documentary. Many of my family and friends paged through that book, and all recommended that I should provide some written context to the historical photos and events. I decided to begin crafting a memoir starting at the very beginnings of my 33-year army career. The writing progressed slowly as I recalled the details of my incredible experiences, the places I had been, the people that I had met and, most importantly, the lessons I had learned. I thought, more and more, that it could be a worthwhile effort to document some of those experiences and to pass on as much historical insight and lessons as I could to those that follow. As I sent selected draft chapters to former military colleagues, whom I highly respected, they suggested that what I was collating was important enough to continue to describe fully in a manuscript, not only for use by our military but also for historians, veterans, scholars, and the public at large. What follows is the result.

Having personally experienced four combat tours—the first as an airborne rifle company commander during the U.S. intervention in the Dominican Republic, two Vietnam tours as an airborne rifle company commander and as an intelligence staff officer and company commander and, finally, as General Schwarzkopf's J-2, director for Intelligence during Desert Shield/Desert Storm, I am convinced that firsthand combat experiences are valuable incubators of lessons learned. Military combat inevitably causes one to become a potential historian and, most importantly, a chronicler of important critical observations and conclusions to be passed on to future generations. The main personal theme throughout this book is a constant development and continued reliance on an important inner quality that I describe as professional courage. One should always do and say what they think is right, and tell it like it is, no matter what the eventual consequences. This invaluable precept was first instilled in me by my mom and then reinforced from constant experience. Based on knowledge and awareness in a variety of situations, self-discipline, and, eventually, confidence in my own learned ability to determine what is right and true, professional courage became my credo.

My basic career philosophies were seared into my psyche during my first tour in Vietnam as a rifle company commander with the 173rd Airborne Brigade. We Vietnam veterans have been deeply scarred by our experiences during that horrific conflict. We witnessed, firsthand, the ill-conceived, faulty, or ill-timed political and military decisions that cost the precious lives of brave men and women. Many strategic, operational, and tactical decisions were based, not only on some false premises, but also followed by inaccurate and warped data. During that travesty, 58,220 American military heroes were killed, over 150,000 wounded, and some 1600 are still missing in action. Additionally, large numbers of the almost three million veterans who served in that combat zone have been adversely affected over their lifetimes, both physically and psychologically. Once the Vietnam war had finally ended, those of us who remained on active duty developed and followed an almost religious zeal to fix what had become our tragically broken military. I personally vowed that I would devote myself, through my new career in intelligence to help prevent the situation that occurred in Vietnam from ever happening again. The result of our almost herculean decade and a half's worth of effort, was the spectacular, highly trained, equipped, and motivated volunteer force that totally decimated the world's fourth largest army in 100 hours during Operation Desert Storm.

In this manuscript, I included the experiences from my wide-ranging tours, during combat and peacetime. I learned from each and every one. I have included my four combat tours and tried to provide clear and realistic lessons from each, especially the immense difficulty the infantry soldier endures in combat. I show how the proven value of unvarnished, useable, timely, and predictive intelligence analysis and recommendations is the key to victory during any conflict. I describe my challenging and career-enhancing years in the Far East in places such as Taiwan, Hong Kong, Japan, and China, especially during my intimate involvement in the Tiananmen incident. I explain how I came to appreciate the invaluable world of human intelligence collection and my admiration for the potential contribution of those that speak foreign languages. I describe the continuous rapid development of technical intelligence systems and the breaking down of barriers to some of its use. I demonstrate my increasing admiration and support for our special operations forces and their ever-increasing need, development, and contributions to our nation's defense. Most importantly, I describe in detail how all that I had previously experienced and learned was put to the ultimate test as General Schwarzkopf's director for Intelligence, J-2, during Operation Desert Storm. The proudest moment in my career was when General Schwarzkopf remarked while pinning a medal on my chest: "Jack, I could not have done it without you." Even during large combat operations like Desert Storm, dissimilar national and international objectives, departmental and service parochialism, and cultural differences between members of a coalition can create crucial, unforeseen cracks in an all-important operational unity of command. During my final responsibilities in the Defense Intelligence Agency, I was able to use, influence, promote, and effect much of the intelligence efforts and initiatives I had fiercely advanced throughout my career. I hope that this manuscript will help our children, their children, and beyond to appreciate the importance of what came before them and how our story may eventually fit into their own hopes and dreams. Finally, I pray that today's soldiers and those to come will not have to witness the horrors of war, but we must remain constantly vigilant and aware of what a sage once said: "Only the dead have seen the end of war."

CHAPTER 1

FROM THE BEGINNING

I grew up in a wonderful, nurturing Italian family in Auburn, New York. My mom was my rock. She instilled in me the ethics, morals and patriotism that shaped my life. Once I had graduated from high school, I was scheduled to attend Marquette University in Milwaukee in the fall of 1954. Earlier that spring, my three best high-school buddies had all been accepted at my first choice, Georgetown, but I had missed the deadline for my application. As I entered Marquette's academic auditorium to select my initial college courses, I made a beeline for the ROTC table. I always had been interested in military history, so I initially signed up for ROTC and then filled in my schedule with other required academic courses. After the first academic quarter, my grades were just plain terrible, except for an A in ROTC. My hopes of transferring to Georgetown were close to being dashed. While in ROTC, I became fascinated with military history and enjoyed the challenging leadership and discipline requirements that were basic to the course. After those horrific first quarter grades, I remember sitting on my bed thinking about my future and decided that I needed to dedicate myself to excelling in all of my studies. I knew that my study habits were terrible, but in high school I got away with it. I knew I had to change my priorities drastically from sports, music, and social activities to strictly academics, or my plans for a bright future and joining my friends at Georgetown would be dashed. As I sat on that bed, I set not only the present but my life's priorities in this order: learning, learning, and learning. This was a critical juncture in my life that would become a big influence on my future. Those priorities would guide me through the rest of my life.

Once I decided that I was all in, I studied like I had never done before. As a result, I did great for the remainder of the first semester and even better during the final semester. I now felt confident that my improved grades would give me a good chance at Georgetown. Following my year at Marquette, I went back home to Auburn for the summer, worked on a construction job, and applied for a transfer to Georgetown. Later that summer, I got the wonderful news that I was accepted into the social science program at Georgetown for my sophomore year.

Mom and dad drove me to Washington, DC for my initial year. In those days, Georgetown was a very small, all-male school with a few women in the Foreign Service School. Along with the basic social sciences courses, we were required to achieve at least a minor in philosophy, which included the Jesuit tried-and-true, but also an esoteric curriculum such as epistemology, cosmology, ontology, and logic. These courses were valuable for mind development and character building, with logic probably having the most merit. Later in my career, I would even use variations of the ontological processes for culling specific value from huge databases. Throughout my time at Georgetown, I remained in the army ROTC and gravitated toward an almost devout interest in the military. I got all A grades in ROTC for all years combined and decided that a career in the military might be for me. I was selected for advanced ROTC for my third and fourth years at Georgetown and graduated as a

Distinguished Military Graduate. During my ROTC summer camp at Fort Meade, Maryland, I had greatly admired the training cadre from the 82nd Airborne Division, and I kept thinking how great it would be to be part of that famous "All-American" division.

During spring break of my senior year at Georgetown, I returned home to Auburn, and a close bud, Bill Cuddy, introduced me to his sister's friend, Ann Harmon Searing. I swear, she was the prettiest girl I had ever seen, and I quickly became totally, without question, smitten. I then returned to school, studied hard, and finished what was one of the greatest experiences of my life. I will always be proud to be known as a "Gentleman of Georgetown." My mom, dad, and sister Mary Ann drove down for the graduation and for my commissioning as a second lieutenant in the United States Army. Ann and I dated often that summer, but when I considered a possible long-term relationship, I knew that her young age could be a problem. In July I was scheduled to go on active duty as an infantry second lieutenant, first to the Infantry Basic Course at Fort Benning, Georgia and then on to the 3rd Basic Training Regiment at Fort Dix, New Jersey. I had a reserve commission in the infantry, but as a Distinguished Military Graduate, was given the opportunity to apply for a regular army commission. At that time, reserve officers were only scheduled to spend six months on active duty. I applied for a regular commission in the infantry branch since I believed that the only way to be in the army was as an infantryman.

THE INFANTRY IS REALLY BASIC

My first real experience with the army at a major army base was in the Infantry Officer's Basic Course at Fort Benning, Georgia, July 1958. The challenging course curricula and physical training taught me the first lesson that would carry throughout my career: Only the fittest survive, not only physically, but mentally. We were taught the basic tenets of platoon-level combat leadership, how to identify certain highly challenging combat situations, how to react to those situations, and how to convert those reactions into tactical orders and actions. I quickly learned that the life of an infantryman is very challenging but satisfying in many ways and is not for the faint of heart.

In the course, we were taught how to use and maintain various weapons such as individual weapons, machine guns, and mortars, how to call in artillery fire, and the art of land navigation. In addition to basic survival skills, we also learned basic vehicle and equipment maintenance requirements and how to cope with and treat combat casualties. In the end, the course taught me the challenges of leading an infantry platoon, especially in combat. I enjoyed being part of the active army and the camaraderie involved. We would roleplay during dynamic military situations. One day I would be a basic soldier grunting through a challenging patrol with a heavy pack and the next day I might be a squad leader or a platoon leader. I quickly learned that each individual was an integral part of each unit and was critical to unit mission cohesion. I graduated with honors, and I learned that being an infantry combat leader was what I wanted to do. After the course and before I signed in to my first real assignment as a platoon leader in a basic-training regiment at Fort Dix, NJ, I went back to Auburn for a short leave.

Before my trip back south, my dad gave me a beat-up 1950 Ford with a bad paint job. I bought some black paint at the car parts store and asked my uncle if he would spray it for me. We were in a hurry because I was leaving for Fort Dix in two days, so he sprayed it without any masking. He just blasted the whole car, including the windshield and bumpers. It looked like a damned bat mobile. Ann and I did a lot of scraping that Sunday morning, and then on Monday, I said my goodbyes to mom, dad, Mary Ann, and the beautiful Ann.

I began my drive south to New Jersey early Monday morning. Once I arrived at Fort Dix, I signed into the training center and was assigned to the 3rd Basic Training Regiment as a platoon leader. I oversaw basic infantry training for about 200 recruits per each three-week training cycle. The recruits for each cycle also came under the wing of my platoon sergeant, a seemingly grizzled but fairly sharp veteran. I was incredibly surprised that he and several other platoon sergeants had been, at one time, infantry officers during the Korean War. The army was downsizing, and those officers decided to remain in the army as noncommissioned officers (NCOs) in order to get to their twenty years in so they could retire at their highest pay grade. Since they were all former infantry unit commanders, with combat experience, there was no course, anytime, anywhere that could be more valuable than the discussions I had with them in the field, on breaks, or in the barracks. They were patient with me as I asked questions, particularly on proven leadership traits, along with situational unit leader actions and orders. I applied much of what I learned during those discussions during the rest of my career. Throughout my time in the regiment, I lead a total of 2,000 recruits through the challenging basic infantry training course. My platoon was rated as the best in the regiment for all five training cycles for which I was responsible. As the year stretched into the winter months, the outdoor training became more difficult and very uncomfortable, especially when we were at the firing range. The Korean War veterans would describe the brutal winters that they had endured, and some of the horrendous experiences while fighting in the bitter cold, ice, and snow. In January of 1959, as I was coming to the end of my mandated six-month tour I received an offer of a regular army commission, but in artillery, not infantry. It was decision time.

I Must Learn to Listen to My Instincts

While in the US Army, I had been doing what I enjoyed, and I flourished. But, since I wanted to be a career infantryman, I now had the choice to accept the regular army commission in artillery or get out of the army and go home. My mom and dad didn't really understand the army or my dedication to it. Mom was pressing me to rid myself of "this craziness," and to come back home and get a job in the Auburn area or go to law school at Syracuse. I agonized over pleasing my mom or going into the artillery branch. Another reason for getting out and going home was that Ann was there. Against my better instincts, I turned down the artillery branch assignment, signed out from the army and returned to Auburn. I then applied for and was accepted at Syracuse Law School. Once I began attending classes, I quickly realized that I had made a catastrophic mistake. I found my interest in the law paltry and was dwindling with each day. Ann and I dated, but infrequently. I was living in Syracuse and we both felt like she didn't fit comfortably into my "present environment." For the remainder of my time at Syracuse, if we saw each other, it was only by accident. While in law school, I had joined the National Guard infantry unit in Auburn where, after a while, I was promoted to first lieutenant. I found that I had more interest in my duties there and spent a much more satisfying time at the armory than I did studying the law.

During my third year of law school, I clerked for a law firm doing title searches. My hard work probably made them a ton of money. But, undoubtedly thinking that they were doing me a favor, they treated me badly. I began to realize that if I had to constantly deal with this type of colleague in my chosen profession, I would pass. However, from that experience, I learned a valuable life lesson: **how not to treat subordinates.** Not being a quitter, I eventually persevered and in fact did finally graduate from law school.

While I was seriously rethinking about the law as a profession, a very close friend, Tom Viscardi, came home on leave. He was then in the 82nd Airborne Division, and when we got together, he was wearing his khakis with the AA ("All Americans") patch, airborne cap, jump wings, and jump boots. During our visit, I mentioned to Tom about how I had admired the 82nd Airborne Division NCOs who were the cadre for training at my ROTC summer camp at Fort Meade in 1957. That short visit with Tom became like a religious experience: It brought some clarity and eagerness to what I wanted to do with my life.

After I graduated from law school, I received orders through the National Guard to attend the Infantry Officers Advanced Course at Fort Benning, Georgia. While on my way to Benning, I stopped in the Washington, DC, area to talk to assignment officers in the army's personnel center. When I approached the infantry desk officer, he asked me what I wanted to do. I told him that I wanted to return to active duty and apply for a regular army commission in the infantry. He asked what I had been doing recently, and I told him that I had just graduated from law school. He looked utterly surprised and sputtered, "Are you sure you're not looking for the Judge Advocate General Branch?" I replied, "No sir, I want to be a regular army airborne infantry officer, assigned to the 82nd Airborne Division, jump out of airplanes, kick ass, and take names." He looked at me with a huge grin and said, "You're wacky enough to fit beautifully into the 82nd." He would cut orders for my return to active duty, then to jump school, and on to the 82nd. He also said that he would recommend approval for my regular army commission in the infantry. I was stoked. In the meantime, I was off to attend the Infantry Officers Advanced Course.

As a result of my decision to return to active duty, I knew that my mom and dad would be disappointed, even devastated. But they also now knew how much I had felt uncomfortable in law school and how happy and productive I was during my time in the local National Guard. I basically told them that I would not be successful in life if I was not doing something that I was interested in and dedicated to. They had always been supportive in what I wanted to do with my life up to that point, as long as I was happy. I loved them both very much and I hoped that I would eventually make them proud. Since they really had little understanding of the military, I would dedicate my life not only to the service to my country but also to hopefully help them appreciate that I had made the right decision. In the end, they were very proud of my career.

Advanced Infantry Training, Fort Benning, Georgia

During the summer 1963, I attended the Infantry Officer's Advanced Course at Fort Benning. The course represented the next step in school progression for an infantry officer, following the Infantry Officer Basic Course. The advanced course built on the initial platoon leader responsibilities I learned in the basic course into two basic phases: the company command-level phase and the battalion/ brigade staff-level phase. The first phase basically included army doctrinal command responsibilities during company command. Tenets that I would later call on when commanding airborne infantry and intelligence companies during peacetime and in combat. The second phase of the course focused service on battalion or brigade staff, which would, again, would serve me well. We were provided various scenarios and took part in exhaustive role-playing in both the company-level command and the battalion/brigade staff levels. The school cadre constantly observed and graded our "actions and orders" (our decision-making processes). I was delighted when I received orders as a regular army infantry officer and was directed to report first to airborne school at Fort Benning, Georgia, and then on to the 82nd Airborne Division at Fort Bragg, NC.

I have two distinct recollections during this period at Fort Benning. The barracks complex next to mine housed many veteran officers from the Bay of Pigs who were now being enlisted and integrated into our army. They were part of the Cuban military resistance to Castro's revolution and had escaped to the US. I thought of them as possible future assets both for their area expertise and the language capability and to augment any future operations we may have in the Latin America area. Native linguists with such valuable combat experience could be extremely beneficial. Toward the end of the course, on November 22, 1963, I was in the barracks when I heard on the radio about the assassination of President John F. Kennedy. Every person of my generation is said to remember where they were on that terrible day in history. I was in the barracks at Fort Benning, Georgia.

BECOMING A PARATROOPER: AIRBORNE QUALIFICATION COURSE, FORT BENNING, GEORGIA FEBRUARY-24 APRIL 1964

As I drove from Fort Benning to Auburn, I had time to think of all I needed to do before I headed to active duty at jump school and then to the 82nd Airborne Division. I finally was going to be part of the elite unit I previously had only dreamed about. The weather in Auburn was really cold and snowy, so I began a strict physical training regimen at the National Guard armory. I diligently worked out and ran lap after lap in jump boots around the large indoor formation area. I had endured tough physical training during the advanced course, but I knew that the airborne course was going to be even more physically and mentally challenging. I was excited but I kept thinking, Am I doing the right thing? And, Damn I'll be jumping out of a perfectly good airplane! After a few weeks, some close friends organized going-away parties for me. Ann and I had seen each other a couple of times while I was home, and she came to one of my farewell parties. I could not help but wonder that since I would be out of the Auburn area indefinitely if our relationship could ever be possible. The finality of my upcoming move hurt when I thought that this may spell the end of our relationship. I finally packed up my car with virtually everything I owned, which was not much, and said my emotional goodbyes to mom and dad.

As I drove through the gates at Fort Benning, the "Home of the Infantry" and the airborne school, I felt strangely alone and naturally wondered how I would react to the challenges that lay ahead in the "real army." Two days later, we were awakened abruptly from our bunks and herded into an early morning formation. Right from the beginning, we were being treated like raw meat. In elite army schools like airborne, ranger, and special forces, a demeaning process is meant to tear down self-esteem in order to root out individual weaknesses and then, through time-tested training methods, build up one's self-confidence and physical endurance into a new, stronger soldier in mind and body.

We were subjected to exhaustive physical training. I could handle most everything pretty well, but the long runs were devastating. The school cadre, the "black hats," were hand-picked NCOs mostly from the active airborne units. They all wore black baseball caps adorned with coveted master parachutist jump wings and drove us mercilessly. They were the sharpest soldiers I had ever seen. I will never forget the times, as we were running our miles, gagging and struggling to stay in formation, those magnificent bastards would be running alongside, backwards. In those days, we ran in jump boots, which was pretty stupid, but that's the way it was in the entire military. (Several years later, we smartened up and used running shoes.) During the first week, we did what seemed like a million parachute landing falls (how to hit the ground and roll on our sides) from high stands, until it became second nature. Because there is little time to react to circumstances that could be life threatening, the sequences and procedures we learned in jump school had to become rote and ingrained into our psyche.

We next moved to jumping from the 34-foot tower. As I stood in the door of the tower and looked down, I was hoping that I would not freeze in place and say, "To hell with this." Fortunately, I pushed myself to the door opening, took a deep breath, and jumped. I was a bit shocked by the incredible jerk when I was stopped by the cable, and then I rode that cable all the way to a large mound at the far end. My anxieties were being overcome with a feeling of exhilaration and confidence as I thought, "Maybe I really can do this." Each jump from that tower felt better and better. The next challenge was the 250-foot tower. We were pulled to the top of the tower with a fully deployed chute and then dropped. We then had to react to similar challenges that we would have during an actual jump. I had never experienced a feeling of the great unknown like that before.

Once we finished "tower week," we had a weekend of relaxation before we would begin "jump week," when we would be required to make five qualification jumps before receiving our coveted jump wings. We were scheduled to jump twice on the first day, twice on the second day, and once on the third day, with the pinning of our jump wings on the drop zone soon after that final jump. We would be jumping from the twin tail Fairchild C-119 "Flying Boxcar," which was originally designed with airborne operations in mind.

As we were trucked to the airfield on the first morning, hardly anyone said a word. After we donned our chute and reserve, the black hats gave each of us a jumpmaster equipment check. We then waddled onto the C-119 and sat in two rows along each of the outside bulkheads. I was fifth from the front in my stick (line of troopers down one side of the aircraft). As the plane roared for takeoff, I said to myself, What in the hell are you doing here? I then breathed a response, Because this is what you want to do with your life. The aircraft droned on its inevitable course into a seeming abyss. When the jumpmaster barked "10 minutes!" the tension rose. As the jumpmaster growled through his jump-commands, "Get ready" and "Stand up," we rose with weak-kneed apprehension. Then came "Hook up," and as I hooked up my static line, I wondered how that small line could be my lifeline. Next came "Check equipment," and we all gave what equipment we could see or feel a once-over; that of our own and the fellow trooper to our front. Then, "Sound off for equipment check," each jumper from back to front yelled "Okay!" and slapped the backside of the trooper in front of him until the last jumper shouted, "All okay." Then after a slight pause, the jumpmaster gave us a one-minute mark, which sounded like a death sentence. Once the jump door was yanked open, the roar of the prop blast (the rearward force of the wind from the propellers) sounded and felt like the end of the world. The jumpmaster then shouted while pointing to the first jumper, "Stand in the door." The red light beside the door was still on, but the pilot immediately changed it to green. After the jumpmaster barked, "Go," it was like all hell broke loose. The first jumper bounded out, and one by one, our jump boots banged on the metal floor as we shuffled towards that beckoning door. After a split-second hesitation and a quick prayer, I leaped out and felt like a rag doll in the whirlwind of the prop blast. After about three or four seconds, I felt the jerk of the parachute opening and deploying fully. I apprehensively looked up saw that the chute had deployed in good shape and that my static lines were not tangled. As I drifted down, the relative dead silence was wonderful and as I saw the "welcoming" sight of the drop zone below, I began to prepare for my parachute landing fall. I rode the wind, slammed into the ground, and rolled just like we were trained to do. After being dragged for a short distance, I ran toward the billowing parachute, grabbed it, and quickly rolled it, so that the wind could not get to it and drag me further along the ground. The next four jumps were practically the same, except during the third jump, I was the first trooper in the stick and stood in the door waiting for the command to go. During the scores of jumps I made over my career, I always had that fleeting but anxious fear as I stood in the door preparing to jump. Fear is not a weakness, but a normal human reaction to possible imminent danger. However, a combat leader must be able to control that fear, not only within himself, but within his subordinates.

After our final jump, we all stood at proud attention on the drop zone waiting to have our jump wings pinned on our chests. The senior black hat placed my jump wings on my chest then pushed the pins into my skin, which painfully introduced me to the traditional "blood wings" (those pins pushed into the chest drew some blood). I was as proud as I had ever been. Once I looked down on my chest and saw those wings, I was in a daze—a proud, wonderful daze. As I walked off the drop zone as a US army paratrooper,

I anxiously looked forward to being proud member of the famous and elite 82nd Airborne Division.

82ND AIRBORNE DIVISION: FORT BRAGG, NORTH CAROLINA, MARCH 1964

As I drove towards the entrance to the post and saw the sign, "Fort Bragg, North Carolina, Home of the Airborne" my heart raced with excitement and anticipation. I thought that this is what I had always wanted to do, and where I wanted to be, without even knowing what it was really all about. There are units in the US Army and then there are units. The 82nd Airborne has a history filled with sacrifice and heroism. They fought as a "leg" (nonairborne) infantry unit in World War I, and because it was comprised of soldiers from every state in the union, it earned the nickname The All-American Division. In 1942, the 82nd was reconstituted as an airborne division. During World War II, the 82nd parachuted into Sicily in 1943, and they fought so valiantly that the German soldiers described them as "those devils in baggy pants." On D-Day, the division jumped into Normandy and then participated in the massive parachute operation into Holland in September of 1944 as part of the ill-fated Operation Market Garden. During the Battle of the Bulge in December of 1944, the 82nd fought magnificently despite overwhelming odds against the numerically superior and fanatical Waffen-SS.

I signed into the bachelor officer quarters, and a couple of lieutenants recommended that I should visit the 82nd Airborne Officers' Club. It was on the other side of the railroad tracks that passed through the post and looked to be in an old barracks building. As with the outside, the inside of the club was not elegant. It was filled with an eclectic combination of characters: guys with buzzcuts and gals of every shape and size, all drinking heavily and trying to outdo each other by seeing who could tell the biggest lie, in the most convincing way. I wiggled my way through a group of dancing forms and finally reached the immense bar. I sidled up next to a an impressively large, bald guy who asked if I was new on post. I told him that I had just arrived and was being assigned to the division. Everyone just called the 82nd the division.

He responded in a slow southern drawl, "Ha, I'm Butch Kendrick and hell, let me buy ya a cold beer." He stuck out a burly hand and squeezed mine so hard that I was about to cry. After he bought me the beer, he clinked my bottle with his and said, "Great to meet ya Jack, see ya around. Airborne." As he left the bar and was disappearing into the morass of gyrating bodies I yelled back, "All the way and thanks Butch." I had another cold one, shot the breeze with a couple other guys and gals, and finally started for the door when I heard a loud commotion. Two guys over by the juke box were arguing over the unconditional love of some gal and started pummeling each other with airborne vigor. It all ended abruptly when they were pulled apart. Judging by the under-reaction to the scene by the other patrons, I surmised that this was a just another normal happening. Gals would come from near and far to snag a paratrooper officer for the evening, if not possibly longer. I had never seen a club like that before or since.

Early Monday morning, after going through the normal division administrative paperwork, I was ordered to report to Echo Company, 325th Airborne Battle Group. As I walked into the company headquarters, I was all spit and polish, in starched fatigues with my jump boots gleaming, enough to see my face in the reflection. I walked down the hallway and met an impressive vision of an airborne soldier with about a million stripes and a diamond in the middle (representing a company first sergeant). I gingerly walked over to him and told him who I was, and he said, "Hi sir, welcome, we've been expecting you." Holy crap! This guy just called me "Sir!" He was First Sergeant Charlie "Catfish" Bryant. Charlie and I hit it off right from the beginning and became close, lifelong friends. Charlie had a Combat Infantryman Badge and a Master Blaster (master parachutists) Badge with a gold star, which meant that he had made a combat jump. On his right shoulder (combat patch) was a 101st Airborne Division Screaming Eagles patch. He had jumped into Normandy as a private machine gunner. Charlie introduced me to the company commander, who seemed happy that I was reporting in as his executive officer. I was a first lieutenant and a little raw, but I began to feel right at home in Echo Company. After a few days into my job, I was scheduled to meet the battle group commander, a colonel. It felt like I was approaching a meeting with a Greek god. I nervously entered his large office, stood at attention in front of his desk, and barked, "Lieutenant Leide reporting as ordered, sir." I was staring straight ahead out the window behind him until he gave me an "at ease." I looked down and in the state of absolute shock I saw that it was my bar buddy, Butch Kendrick. He let out a big laugh and welcomed me with open arms. After he dismissed me, I saluted him with the normal, "All the way, sir," and he replied "Airborne." As I did my about-face, and walked out of his office door, I saw smiling faces throughout, as if they knew what had happened at the bar. This is what airborne comradeship is all about.

I worked hard in Echo Company, enjoyed the airborne atmosphere, and would take every chance to jump with the troops. Since I wasn't married, I had spent long days, nights, and weekends doing what I thought had to be done to help make Echo Company as competent and combat ready as possible. I loved working with the airborne soldiers. After I had been there several months, I learned that we were scheduled to transition our divisional organization from the battle group to a standard regimental formation with three infantry brigades and division artillery along with other support units such as Logistics, Signals, and Intelligence.

In July of 1964, Charlie Bryant told me in confidence that he was going to be assigned as the battalion sergeant major of the newly formed 3rd Battalion, 325th Parachute Infantry. Then, with a wry smile, he whispered that I had been selected to command Bravo Company in the same battalion. I was flabbergasted and quite shocked. Company command in the 82nd was the Holy Grail for captains, and there were a lot of captains in the division. But here I was, still a first lieutenant about to get a command.

BRAVO COMPANY, 3RD BATTALION (AIRBORNE), 325TH INFANTRY

A few days later, the new battalion commander and I walked over to the new 325th Brigade headquarters for a scheduled meeting with Colonel Butch. After I walked into his office, saluted, and barked "All the way Sir." He replied, "Airborne and stand at ease." After some small talk about how I was enjoying the 82nd, Colonel Butch bellowed, "Leide, I'm going to give you command of Bravo Company, the worst damned company in this division." Bravo Company was called the "Raleigh Roadrunners", and evidently poor leadership at the company command and senior NCO level had led to the worst record in nearly every negative category for which a company could be rated: AWOL, Article 15s (nonjudicial punishments), courts-martial, and the list went on. I thought that I could go down in flames if I didn't fix it, but on the other hand, the only way to go was up. I thanked Colonel Butch for his confidence in me and told him that I wouldn't let him down. As I walked back to the company area, I thought the challenge of being the only first lieutenant company commander in the division who is leading the worst company. As I look back on my whole career, some of the most important jobs were when I was taking over a command or position from someone who was not performing the way the commander expected.

I next had to assess the various challenges involved in my new company command. As usual, I sought Charlie Bryant's learned advice and counsel. He told me that the Bravo Company first sergeant wasn't worth a damn, but that I had one of the finest platoon sergeant E-7s in the battalion and that he had solid potential to be a terrific first sergeant. The first sergeant position is normally filled by an E-8 and is usually critical to the success or failure of a unit. With Charlie's help, we were able to get the first sergeant reassigned and make the E-7 my acting first sergeant until we could get him promoted. As Charlie had predicted, he would turn out to be a terrific first sergeant. During that period, a number of West Point graduates from the class of 1963 were being assigned to the division. Shortly after I took command, the finest officer I ever met, Second Lieutenant Larry Britten from that class was assigned as my executive officer. With the dedicated, rock-solid help of Larry and our new first sergeant, we slowly but surely moved the company forward with every passing week. We identified and met every challenge head on, then solved them methodically. Larry was married and just had a little girl, so I tried to give him some slack. He was totally dedicated to our mission and was loath to take time off.

During this period, the division was being put through what I call the Command Military Maintenance Inspection (CMMI) purges. For whatever reason, there was a push in the army to inspect every unit's supply and maintenance procedures and records in the most minute of details. Commanders were being relieved for the most mundane inspection faults. Maintenance inspection teams from all levels descended on us: We had courtesy inspections, real inspections, and even simulated inspections. Larry and I studied and were guided by Field Manual 38-750, The Army Maintenance Management System (TAMMS) User's Manual until the pages were totally dog-eared. After much hard work by each soldier in the company, we attained a "high satisfactory" on every inspection. The company was improving daily, and we were getting a reputation for being really good. However, a day after we had undergone our latest inspection, I got a call from battalion that the brigade commander wanted to see me and that I needed to bring the maintenance logbook for my command Jeep. I met the battalion commander, and we walked to the brigade headquarters with me holding the logbook like it was a case of the clap. As we entered Colonel Butch's office, he looked like he had a real case of the red ass. I stood at stiff attention and yelled "all the way sir" He quickly replied "airborne" and he glared up at me and said, "Give me that damned logbook." He looked at it intently, slammed it shut, and barked, "Leide, you little SOB, do you know what I'm going to do to you?" Every sinew in my body was twitching, and I said rather meekly, "No Sir." He then looked up at me, smiled, and said, "I'm going to promote you to captain." I just about passed out on the floor! I had made an unexpected, and somewhat unprecedented, accelerated promotion to captain. Colonel Butch then got up and pinned the captain's bars on my fatigues. He then patted me on the shoulders and said, "Now get out of here captain and do some work to earn those bars."

Larry, the first sergeant and I were on a roll and were moving the company in the right direction, while Charlie Bryant continued to give us some worthwhile insights and recommendations. As we brought the company along slowly but surely, Larry and I bonded like brothers. We took a much-needed couple days off and drove up to Philadelphia for the army-navy football game. One day, the division was scheduled to host an important visit from an assistant secretary of the army, and we in Bravo Company were chosen to represent the brigade. We set up a tour, created and delivered a briefing based on his primary interests, and hosted him for refreshments in our company mess hall. All went very well, and the assistant secretary said he had a great visit (he even sent a thank-you letter). Later that day, Colonel Butch came into our mess hall to congratulate me on the successful visit. Then, out of the blue, he told me that we had been rated as the best company in the division for the past quarter. He looked me square in the eye and said, "Jack you have taken Bravo Company from the worst company in this division to the best." He looked at me like a proud father. Although it was great news, I couldn't rest on my laurels. Once the maintenance inspections had finally subsided, we began to concentrate on our actual combat mission: jumping out of airplanes and being able to perform whatever important mission we were assigned.

OPERATION POWER PACK: DOMINICAN REPUBLIC

At 1200 hours on the April 23, 1965, the 1st Battalion of the 508th Infantry relieved us and assumed the duties as the Division Ready Force (DRF). A DRF is a unit that is charged with executing a strategic airborne forcible entry into any area of the world within 18 hours of notification. On April 27, 1965, I got a call from battalion that all company commanders needed to meet in the battalion conference room at 1300. As we all gathered, I could tell by the unusually hushed atmosphere that something important was up. The battalion commander told us that the division had been alerted for possible missions in the Dominican Republic (DR). We would eventually call it "Operation Power Pack". We then were told that the Dominican Revolutionary Party ("the rebels") and others had taken over the national palace and installed a provisional president. Loyalist forces were resisting the takeover and street violence was escalating. Our ambassador had warned that US citizens in the country were at risk and that "outside influences" (Cuba) were likely playing a role. As I look back on the times and situation, his description of outside influences was likely politically reflexive. We were seeing communists behind every bush. The Cuban missile crisis had occurred about two and a half years earlier and the 82nd reportedly had been alerted to jump into Havana had that been necessary. We were told that we were on call to deploy to the DR to protect US citizens and keep the warring factions separated so that peaceful negotiations could take place. President Johnson announced that our deployment would protect hundreds of citizens who remained in the Dominican Republic. But, supposedly, the chairman of the Joint Chiefs gave the 18th Airborne Corps commander two missions: "Your announced mission is to save US lives. Your unannounced mission is to prevent the Dominican Republic from going Communist."

After furiously rounding up all of the company troopers from wherever they were and identifying and loading all of our required rapid deployment gear, we started breaking out our weapons from the arms room. Then we were locked into the barracks. The next day, I overheard the first sergeant talking to someone on the phone and repeating, "No ma'am he cannot come to the phone right now. He's doing fine, thank you ma'am." It was my mother who had seen on TV that the 82nd had been alerted for possible deployment to quell the turmoil in the DR. Here I was, a fully trained, rock-hard paratrooper, and my mom is calling to see if I had brushed my teeth or something. But I really loved her for that.

A couple times, we loaded up, moved to Green Ramp (the parking ramp used to stage joint operations with the air force) on Pope Air Force Base (next to Bragg) and prepared to move out. Both times we sat around on the tarmac for a while and then were moved back to the barracks The DRF Battalion the 1st Battalion 508th Infantry from the 3rd Brigade was the first unit to take off for the DR and landed at the country's San Isidro Airbase at 0216 on April 30. They then secured the perimeter of the base. The 1st Battalion 505th Infantry flew next and assumed security of the airbase from the 1/508th, who at sunrise, moved 25 kilometers east to the Duarte Bridge, which spanned the Ozama River and led into the capital city of Santo Domingo. They then established a bridgehead.

Meanwhile, we again were moved to Green Ramp and this time the Korean vets in the company began breaking open the ammo boxes, gorging on the rounds of ammunition, and loading up on grenades. I knew this time was for real. I grabbed an adequate supply of ammo for my .45 caliber pistol, and we waited for the order to move on to our C-130s. We company commanders had received very basic briefings on the political situation in the DR and little on the all-important military situation. Every space on every ramp was filled with a mix of troopers, artillery, 106mm recoilless rifles, trucks, trailers, and all kinds of special equipment.

All necessary personnel, weapons, ammunition, and other items from all of our previous training exercises had been assiduously identified and organized into our company load plan. Everybody and everything were planned to be in a proper place, at a proper time, and loaded in a proper sequence. However, to our great surprise and consternation, the loadmasters were eclectically placing various troops and equipment together as they arrived at Green Ramp. Our meticulous load preplans went out the window. Troopers and equipment were just mashed together seemingly in any order to just get them aboard an aircraft and flying. When it comes to loading aircraft, the air force loadmaster is king and are considered the best of the best. I eventually was loaded on a C-130 with my Jeep, driver, and an engineer company 3/4-ton truck loaded with rolls of barbed wire. As we took off, I was wondering where the hell the rest of my company was and if and in what sequence they would arrive at our destination.

Despite the apparent turmoil, I would discover later that the loadmasters actually did a magnificent job under very challenging circumstances. As the Dominican crisis was developing, various units from around the country were preparing to take part in a major exercise called Blue Flag and there were aircraft in a number of different locations loaded for air-land, air-drop, and airborne operations. Our brigade hadn't been scheduled to take part in Blue Flag because we had been the previous DRF and had to be ready on a moment's notice to deploy anywhere in the world. The reason for the continuous false starts and apparent confusion at Green Ramp were due to all of the conflicts of loading and reloading a multitude of aircraft taking place throughout the country. I found out later that in that short period of time, at least 33 aircraft had to be unloaded and reloaded. However, on this day, I now had to concentrate on the problems involved with regaining company integrity after landing and how to react in this state of fragmented unit disorganization if we were met by some sort of armed opposing force.

My First Combat Experience: Dominican Republic

On the afternoon of May 1, 1965, I was airborne and enroute to the DR. As we approached Santo Domingo, the pilots invited me up to the cockpit to observe the city as we approached from the air. When I looked down, I saw pockets of fire and smoke in the city proper and knew that eventually we would probably have to get into the middle of that morass. As we landed at San Isidro, about 25 kilometers west of Santo Domingo, the aircraft came to a jarring halt, the as rear ramp came down, we peered out into the darkness and then made our way toward the perimeter of the runway. I did not know whether the rest of my company had landed, when they would land, or where they might be. When the first sergeant finally arrived, he was magnificent at locating and organizing our company back into a cohesive unit. As additional aircraft landed, we established a unit identification system that helped us finally reorganize the company into a capable and recognizable force.

Considering the vague political turmoil that brought us on this mission, I still did not know what the enemy looked like, where he was, or what his intentions and capabilities were. As far as I was concerned, this was unacceptable in a combat situation and was seared into my memory for future reference. To make it even worse, the "rebels" most likely had no identifiable uniform. Every step in a combat plan is difficult and often complicated, but it is made even more difficult when little usable intelligence is given, and no operational maps are available. The little pertinent intelligence we had was left behind at Fort Bragg. Using the little information we had, and with the help of some Esso gas station road maps, I created rough tactical sketches of our mission and the area involved.

By 0615 on May 2, we had reorganized, deployed, and completed the execution of our initial mission of perimeter security for the air base. Once the next battalion in the air flow arrived, we quickly passed that mission on to them and began our movement 25 kilometers westward toward Santo Domingo. After we, the leading battalions, had been organized into a cohesive bridgehead around the Duarte, we were then tasked to attack across the bridge into the heart of the city, clear, and occupy one of the main roads, the Calle San Juan Bosco, that meandered through the center of Santo Domingo. Controlling the entirety of that road would isolate the fighting Dominican factions, one to the north (loyalists) and one to the south (rebels). We attacked westward with infantry battalions passing through each other at night, clearing the buildings along that main road, with our forward elements linking up with the marines, who were securing the US embassy at the far end of the city. Even a linkup of friendly forces, especially at night, takes a great deal of professional expertise and courage, and our troopers and the marines did it magnificently.

The marines had landed 1,700 reinforcements at the Polo Field and were protecting the US embassy and other vulnerable diplomatic compounds. Their stated mission, as was ours, was the protection of American citizens, but we all knew that the "other" mission was to prevent the leftist rebels from gaining a foothold in the DR. During the early stages of the operation, each of the deploying companies was provided an attached linguist. Many of the linguists, including mine, were the very Bay of Pigs veterans who had been billeted in the barracks next to mine at Fort Benning, while I was in the Infantry Officers Advanced Course. The Cuban officer assigned to my company almost always accompanied me wherever I went. As we solidified control of our sector, he served as my translator, and provided information that he gleaned from chatting with the locals about the situation on the ground and helping to identify possible rebel positions. Having a knowledgeable interpreter was extremely worthwhile and made a deep positive impression on me, one that I carried throughout my career. I became convinced that language capabilities and training should be one of our highest of priorities. It would be invaluable in many operational scenarios, especially during overseas covert and clandestine operations.

The entire corridor, or in military terms "the line of communications," including our sector, through the center of the city was completed by daylight on May 3. We had therefore separated the two main warring factions: the loyalists to the north and the most strident armed rebels into the southeast, between us and the water of the Santo Domingo Basin.

Once the San Bosco sector had been secured, we began taking fire from snipers, mainly from local rooftops. For the next weeks, we constantly were involved in a number of small local firefights around the perimeter, resulting in an unacceptable number of our troopers being either killed or wounded. As time went on, I could tell that the troopers were getting frustrated and spoiling for a fight. I got my first taste of incoming fire when I was with my driver and interpreter riding in my Jeep, checking our positions along the San Bosco. Suddenly, I could hear the cracks of incoming fire from a rooftop to our left. Rounds were chipping the road around us, and one struck the fender of my Jeep. When a round is being fired, it has a tell-tale hollow-sounding crack as it breaks the sound barrier. I would experience those ominous resonant cracks in spades later in Vietnam and elsewhere. We bolted out of the Jeep and, along with some troopers behind us, began returning fire and maneuvering on foot to get a better angle on the snipers. We then saw two shadowy figures on a rooftop, and I directed our response onto them. I believe we may have hit one or both after the firing stopped. The situation in the DR became increasingly frustrating and dangerous. One of our troopers was shot squarely in the left butt cheek while in morning formation. Every day, we all felt that we were easy targets for those damned interminable snipers. We tried to develop some initial countermeasures. We conducted platoon-sized patrols in some suspect areas and some local house-to-house searches. A couple of our NCOs had brought along their own match M-1 rifles with high-powered scopes and would sit patiently in one spot for hours just to get an accurate shot at a sniper. We also employed the 106 recoilless rifle 50 caliber infra-red spotting round in the antisniper role with incredible accuracy. The dangerous and aggravating back-and-forth firefights went on for weeks with little apparent satisfactory conclusion.

The Organization of American States (OAS) was eventually put "in charge" of the entire operation in order to give it more political legitimacy and to quell a perception that the United States was occupying a Latin American nation. Troops from Honduras, Brazil, Nicaragua, and Costa Rica were added to the troop mix, and a Brazilian general was installed as the figurehead commander. However, the actual operational commander on the ground was Lieutenant General Palmer, the 18th Airborne corps commander. Under the OAS auspices, there were frustrating attempts at negotiating a settlement and reestablishment of a legitimate government. The papal nuncio was even brought in to help. All to no avail.

The "hurry up and wait" bane was rearing its ugly head. During the early part of May, there was some scuttlebutt of a unit withdrawal, but nothing really came of it. In mid-May, our company was ordered back to the San Isidro Air Base for 10 days of intensive combat training. On our return to Santo Domingo, we were given a week-long mission to protect the city's power plant. A couple days after we had rotated back to our original security sector along the San Bosco, the first sergeant told me that one of our troopers had been driving a Jeep during a resupply mission the previous night and got lost. He was captured by the rebels, who then published a picture of some of the armed rebels riding in our Jeep but provided no word about my trooper. The issue was elevated to the highest levels and negotiations began for his return. After many frustrating discussions, including an intervention by the papal nuncio, our trooper was finally released safely, but the rebels kept our Jeep. During this period, I also distinctly recall reading in the Stars and Stripes that on May 3, 1965, the 173rd Airborne Brigade (Separate) had been deployed from Okinawa to Vietnam.

Political negotiations continued throughout the late spring and early summer. The leadership continued to enlist the papal nuncio to help. Suddenly, after about six weeks of sporadic sniper attacks, and back and forth skirmishes, the rebels held a political rally on the 14th of June. From the reported tenor of the rally, they undoubtedly were feeling increasing pressure of being limited to their small portion of southern Santo Domingo. At 0800 on the 15th of June, they began shooting at some of our troopers on the outer perimeter ring facing the sea. After holding fire for thirty minutes, we were finally given the order to return fire. A frustrating back and forth lasted until about 1600 when we were finally ordered to mount a concerted attack with a vengeance. Each company was ordered to attack south down one or two assigned streets. We placed a supporting 106mm recoilless rifle on each street. The 1/505th was given the task to attack down Duarte Street, the main road into the rebel area. The remainder of the supporting companies moved south in a coordinated attack into the rebel zone for 30 blocks, clearing the barrios house-to-house, right down to the shoreline. The sounds of the 106's, machine guns and close-in fighting down those narrow streets were deafening. After a series of brutally conclusive firefights, the rebels finally surrendered. Our troopers performed magnificently. The untold hours or training and preparation had paid off when it counted. The combat elan of the US paratrooper is unmatched. The total US casualties during that attack on the 15th and 16th were 5 killed in action and 36 wounded. The rebels had incurred 80 dead, 80 wounded, and 350 captured. The total US casualties for the entire period of Operation Power Pack were 25 killed in action and 63 wounded.

After the combat operation and after-action cleanup, the crisis had basically subsided and we naturally anticipated a redeployment back to Fort Bragg. However, before we redeployed, we were scheduled to make a training parachute jump into a sugarcane field. The jump went great, and we all felt positive about our job well done. Interestingly, the cane field was one of the original two possible drop zones that corps had selected if we had been ordered parachute into the DR instead of air landing. Supposedly, President

Johnson decided that an airborne operation into a friendly country seemed a more strident way of arriving than landing at a "friendly" air base. As we found out later, the two drop zones that were initially selected were both fraught with incredible problems at the time. The cane field where we made our training jump would have been recently cut at the time of our original deployment in late April/ early May. It would have been like jumping into a field of spikes. We eventually rode over to look at the other originally recommended drop zone; it was strewn with rocks and boulders and would have been an equal disaster. Another lesson learned for me: Current and accurate intelligence is critical to ultimate mission accomplishment.

A NEW JOB: AIDE DE CAMP

During July 1965, I got a call from the battalion adjutant. He informed me that I was being considered for the position of senior aide-de-camp for the new division commanding general, Major General Joe S. Lawrie. Although I didn't look forward to leaving Bravo Company, I had been in command for 13 months and the situation in the DR had settled into a grinding, boring routine. I was ready for a new challenge and felt that I could learn a lot working for General Lawrie. Since the corps commander was remaining in the DR for an indefinite period, he would also be the 18th Airborne Corps rear commander. In August, I was informed that I had, in fact, been selected as General Lawrie's aide. I left Bravo Company in what I hoped were good hands, said my grateful goodbyes to everyone, and hopped on a C-130 back to Fort Bragg.

On my first day on the job, the division chief of staff warmly welcomed me aboard, showed me my little hovel of an aide's room, and had his deputy brief me on a typical daily routine in support of the commanding general. General Lawrie had been a battalion commander with the 503rd Airborne Regimental Combat Team when they made their legendary combat jump into Corregidor during the liberation of the Philippines in World War II. During my initial meeting with him, I felt that I would enjoy working for him and that I could learn a lot as his senior aide. My responsibility was to ensure that his schedule was solid, all arrangements were made ahead of time, that he knew who and what he was going to see and what was on the meeting or visit agenda. My tasks centered on helping him in the performance of all military and social responsibilities. He also had a sergeant who took care of his every need in his uniform and household requirements and a cook to prepare his daily meals and assist when he had to officially entertain, which he did often.

Since he was the acting 18th Airborne Corps commander as well, we would spend the morning at the division and the afternoon at corps. I learned a lot about organization, missions, and relationships of both the division and corps combat arms and support units. He also represented the division and corps at special occasions, both on post and in the political and business communities.

Being the commanding general's aide-de-camp had many benefits, including some interesting parachute jumps. For example, we took part in the first mass tactical jump from a Lockheed C-141 Starlifter jet aircraft. Once I jump-mastered the commanding general, we boarded the aircraft and took off for Sicily drop zone. As I sat next to General Lawrie, I wondered what and how he felt before he made that treacherous jump into Corregidor. In comparison, I knew this would have to be a piece of cake for him. He was the first out the door and I was right behind him. As I exited the door, I could hear the different sounds of the jet engines rather than the familiar roar and the initial blast of a propeller-driven aircraft. I previously had jumped out of various models of aircraft: the C-47, C-119, C-123, C-124, C-130, and the L-20 Beaver as well as some helicopters. But this was a jet, it was different, but it did provide a relatively smooth exit. As my chute jerked open, I looked around to locate General Lawrie and tried to steer close to his position so that after we landed, I could help him get out of his parachute. I landed with an expected thud, hand-rolled my chute, left it there for a truck to pick up, and ran over to General Lawrie. He was almost out of his chute, and I helped him remove the rest. We both smiled with satisfaction and had a relaxed small-talk ride back to division headquarters.

One day, the chief of staff told me that the assistant division commander for Operations was getting a new aide, and that he would like me to take him under my wing. When the new aide came into the aide's room, I was shocked but thrilled that it was my dear friend Larry Britten. I was excited to be working with Larry again and together we accomplished a lot and always seamlessly covered for each other. We spent many hours of most days together, and our conversations almost always seemed to turn to what was going on in Vietnam. Larry would often say, "Sir, I've got to get over there before this [war in Vietnam] ends." At the time, no one knew how long our involvement in the Vietnam conflict would last and many wanted to march to the sound of the guns while the opportunity existed. About mid-1965, Larry learned that his boss was being assigned to the 1st Cavalry Division in Vietnam and asked if he could go along as his aide. His boss agreed. Larry told me that he planned to go over as the aide and then, hopefully, get himself reassigned to a line unit. As time went on, and after Larry had left for Vietnam, I started to get antsy for the action myself.

In the early fall, I got an unexpected phone call from Ann. We hadn't seen each other or talked since I had left Auburn for the army. I was so surprised that I was almost speechless. We caught up for quite a while and our conversation was comfortable and familiar. As we were nearing the end of the call, I told her that all I wanted was for her to be happy with whatever life she chose to live. After we hung up, I thought that maybe, just maybe, there was a chance for us. In retrospect that phone call became the most important in my lifetime. The next day, I called her back and invited her to fly down to Fayetteville for a few days. I was pleasantly surprised when she agreed. When I met her at the airport, she looked as beautiful as ever. During her visit, I showed her around the post, we went to dinner at the Officers' Club, and we visited with Charlie Bryant and his family next door to my rented house. She slept in my bed, and I slept on the couch. I remembered she told me that the nuns at Mount Carmel said, "Leave room for the Holy Ghost." I wanted our relationship to develop out of mutual respect and love. After she returned to Auburn, we tried to stay in touch.

My desire to move on to Vietnam got a real push when General Lawrie and I visited the 101st Airborne Division at Fort Campbell, Kentucky. We were attending their major celebration of "Bastogne Day" in memory of the Screaming Eagles' heroic stand during the Battle of the Bulge in December 1944. I made the normal travel arrangements for General Lawrie. I saw that his greens were all set up and checked that his jump boots were appropriately spit-shined. When I showed him that everything was all set for the trip, he said, "No, we won't wear jump boots with our greens, we'll wear low quarters." I was totally horrified to think that we were going to visit another airborne division, especially the 101st, wearing those ghastly low quarters. I lightly and politely prodded him about reconsidering, but he would not back off. We flew to Fort Campbell wearing those damned low quarters, and as a proud paratrooper, I felt like crawling under a rock. As we were flying to Fort Campbell, I thought of the time when I was having lunch at the 82nd Officers Club and a leg (nonairborne qualified soldier) came in wearing jump boots with his greens. A bunch of young airborne lieutenants grabbed him, held him down, took off his boots, brought them in the kitchen and used a carving knife to cut them down to low quarters, threw them at him, and kicked his ass out of the club. Jump boots are an emotional topic.

As we walked down the steps of the plane at Fort Campbell, I wished I could have hidden those low quarters with something, anything. I saw the evident looks of amazement on those proudly wearing the Screaming Eagle patch. However, one of the most positive and memorable events during the visit was the opportunity for me to sit and talk with retired Lieutenant General Bob Sink, a legend in airborne lore. He supposedly had been in the original airborne test platoon and was the commander in the 506th Parachute Infantry Regiment when they jumped into Normandy on D-Day. His unit was memorialized by the HBO miniseries Band of Brothers. He was now physically ailing and had to use an oxygen tank to breathe, but he seemed interested and eager to talk with me. I'll never forget what he told me as we sat talking:"-Jack, never give up and always take care of your troopers." It was like being in the presence of an airborne god, and I have always remembered what he said. After an impressive division parade, with General Sink as the reviewing officer, our time at Fort Campbell came to an end. We then hopped on our plane and flew to Fort Bragg. Sadly, General Sink died shortly after in December 1965.

INTO THE UNKNOWN WITH THE 173RD AIRBORNE BRIGADE

That experience, my conversation with General Sink, and other career pressures were all precipitating my thinking about getting to Vietnam before it "ended." Since General Lawrie had commanded the 503rd Regimental Combat Team, and the battalions of the 173rd Airborne Brigade in Vietnam were designated as the 1st, 2nd, and 3rd Battalions of the 503rd Airborne Infantry, I began lobbying with him to see if he could help me get orders to the 173rd. The 173rd was nicknamed Tien Bing, or Sky Soldiers, by the Chinese Nationalist paratroopers back when the 173rd held training exercises in Changhua, Taiwan. After constant diplomatic begging, he finally made a call and my orders to join the 173rd were cut.

During this period, personnel requisitions to Vietnam were made against certain individual job positions. I would be initially assigned as the brigade's S-2 (Air) officer. I had a report date to the 173rd of April 7, 1966. My first responsibilities would include planning for and requesting aerial reconnaissance missions in support of brigade operations. To gain some expertise for that first job, I received orders for the Air-Ground Operations School at Eglin Air Force Base, Florida. The first two weeks were attended by both air force and army officers. We would learn how to plan for, identify requirements, request, and use aerial reconnaissance in support of field combat units. Fortunately, for whatever reason, I was the only army officer allowed to stay on for the third week. During that week we were taught how to plan for, request, and call in air strikes in support of ground combat units and then vector them in for the most effective results. That third week would later prove invaluable during my combat experiences as a rifle company commander with the 173rd Airborne in Vietnam. I would smoothly and effectively coordinate supporting air strikes with air force forward air controllers during some really life-threatening and complicated combat missions.

During the second and third week of November 1965, I read that a major fight had been raging between major elements of the 1st Cavalry Division, including the famed 7th Cavalry, and hard-core North Vietnamese units in Vietnam's Ia Drang Valley. There were reports that an unusually large numbers of US soldiers had been killed and I began to worry about Larry Britten. Had he gotten into the thick of it? I called the current aides at Fort Bragg and asked I asked if they could find out Larry's status through the aide grapevine. After they checked they called and told me that Larry had made it through unscathed. I hoped that he had not yet gotten down to a combat field unit. Still, the extended battle for the Ia Drang had me worried.

Once I completed the course at Eglin, I returned to Fort Bragg, cleared the division and post, and left for Auburn for two weeks of leave. I truly enjoyed that short, but precious time at home. On April 5, 1966, two days before I was to leave for Vietnam, I got a somber call from one of the aides at Fort Bragg. He told me that Larry Britten had been killed in action on March 30 and would be buried at West Point on April 6. Larry had indeed gotten down to a ground combat unit and was serving as a reconnaissance platoon leader when he was killed by small-arms fire. I was totally devastated and had to tell the aide that I was leaving for Vietnam the very next day so would not be able attend the funeral for my dear friend. In the years that followed, whenever I visited West Point, especially when our son John was a cadet there, I always visited Larry's grave. I would just kneel there and talk to him like we used to at night out in the bush at Fort Bragg. Our son Jeff's middle name is Britten and one of Jeff's son's first name is Britten. We have kept Larry in our hearts and thoughts to this day.

Before I left Auburn, Ann and I saw each other a few times, and our relationship seemed to be growing. On April 6, I went to where she worked, and we had tearful goodbyes. I was hoping that she would write to me often. If our relationship progressed, if only through the mail, and I returned home safely, I decided that

I would ask her to marry me. My mom and dad took me to the airport in Syracuse. After some parting thoughts and many tears from mom, I was off to whatever hellish adventure I would face in Vietnam.

CHAPTER 2

SKY SOLDIER

UNITED STATES ARMY, REPUBLIC OF VIETNAM, APRIL 1966–APRIL 1967

Someone recently asked a Vietnam Vet "When was the last time you were in Vietnam?" "Last night," he replied.

By January of 1966, the United States had 184,000 military personnel stationed in the Republic of Vietnam, also known as South Vietnam. The Republic of Vietnam's military forces totaled 514,000, while the North Vietnamese Army (NVA) numbered nearly 400,000. Most of the NVA troops were still in the Democratic Republic of Vietnam, although 50,000 North Vietnamese soldiers had infiltrated into the Republic of Vietnam. US military intelligence estimated that there were nearly 239,000 Viet Cong (VC) guerrillas in the Republic of Vietnam as well. The year before, the United States had conducted an extensive bombing campaign, codenamed Rolling Thunder, over the Democratic Republic of Vietnam. By the end of 1965, President Lyndon B.

Johnson announced a pause in the bombing to seek peace with the Democratic Republic of Vietnam. On the ground in 1965, General William Westmoreland had ordered a series of search and destroy operations, to engage the NVA and VC in a conventional battle. (The use of herbicides and riot control agents had started in 1962). On November 14–15, 1965, two battalions from the 7th Cavalry and elements from the 2nd and 3rd Brigades, 1st Cavalry Division fought two NVA regiments in the battle at Ia Drang, which was also the first major battle between the NVA and the US armed forces. Over 300 US soldiers died at Ia Drang. I arrived in South Vietnam in April of 1966. There was no end in sight to the fighting against an elusive and surprisingly competent enemy, and US casualties mounted every day.[1]

173RD AIRBORNE BRIGADE (SEPARATE), BIEN HOA, REPUBLIC OF VIETNAM, APRIL 1966

As I flew over the Pacific toward Vietnam, I closed my eyes and fitfully thought about three things. First, I recalled my experience in the 82nd Airborne Division and the dedicated troopers. My mind often went to my proud moments of receiving of the coveted Combat Infantry and Senior Parachutist Badges, and I knew that I was on my way to qualifying as a Master Parachutist. Second, I thought of Ann. Our relationship had grown in commitment and love, and I was hoping that we would have a future together. Last, I thought of the dangerous, unknown jungle that I was about to encounter in Vietnam.

The plane was filled with newbies, like me, and as it made its final approach into Saigon, I could see an incredible amount of military activity at Tan Son Nhut Airbase. We climbed down the

---

[1] "DCAS Vietnam Conflict Extract File record counts by incident or death date (as of April 29, 2008)," archives.gov, April 29, 2008, https://www.archives.gov/research/military/vietnam-war/casualty-statistics#date

steps and were immediately slapped in the face by a blast of heat and humidity and then met by a line of buses on the busy runway. All sorts of aircraft and helicopters were taking off and landing, and support vehicles and fuel trucks were being shepherded by scurrying ground crews. After a short ride to Camp Alpha, we were processed into the United States Army, Vietnam. We were then divided into groups and shown to our hot, almost rancidly musty, transient sleeping tents for our first night in 'Nam.

Early the following day, a ¾ ton truck from the 173rd Airborne Brigade arrived. The brigade was located near the Bien Hoa Airbase, about 27 kilometers away. I rode in the back of the truck with four other brigade troopers. As we drove past rice paddies, vegetable fields, and lush jungle areas, it all seemed so peaceful and serene. First impressions can be terribly wrong. We arrived later that morning at Camp Zinn, the base camp of the 173rd, and were escorted directly to the brigade mess hall for lunch and some initial orientation. A captain then escorted me over to the S-3 (Operations) tent where the S-2 (Intelligence) Section was located. I was slotted as the S-2 (Air) with the primary mission to plan for and request aerial reconnaissance in support of brigade plans and missions. It really wasn't a full-time job, so I eventually became just another S-2 action officer and spent a great deal of time with the Order of Battle Section. We researched and compiled important information about enemy units such as strengths, weaknesses, weapons, organization, tactics, capabilities, locations, and how they fight. I worked on the order of battle for both VC and the more capable NVA units. As I dug into existing data bases and researched others, I acquired a great interest in the art of enemy order of battle. I wrote in-depth estimates on the enemy situation and constantly updated the unit stickers on a large enemy situation map located in the operations tent. I tried to make the enemy situation on those maps as accurate and useful as I could to help those who were making operational decisions. Mission success and precious lives were at stake.

The 173rd was known as General Westmoreland's Fire Brigade. Evidently, any time he needed a special mission accomplished, he first looked to the 173rd. The brigade supposedly was the only unit that eventually would be deployed for action in all four corps areas. Therefore, we had to collate basic information on the enemy situation Vietnam-wide. I worked long, hard hours doing S-2 (Air) work. Using the training I received at the Air-Ground Operations School at Eglin, I planned and requested many aerial reconnaissance missions in support of planned and existing brigade operations. Due to my efforts, I was charged to write a Brigade Standing Operating Procedure for the S-2 (Air) Mission. My short but valuable time in the S-2 section was reinforcing what I had learned while in the 82nd: Intelligence, or lack thereof, could be crucial to the success or failure at any level of military operations.

I was scheduled to report to the 2nd Battalion, 503rd Parachute Infantry Regiment on April 29, 1966, to assume command of Charlie Company. Commanding an airborne infantry rifle company was the reason I volunteered for duty in Vietnam. At the time, the brigade had three airborne infantry battalions, an artillery battalion, and other normal support units such as Signal, Intelligence, and Engineer. While at brigade for that short period I gained a clearer idea how my future company command fit into the bigger scheme of the brigade operational tactics and strategy.

Taking Command of Charlie Company 2nd Battalion, 173rd Airborne Brigade

When the time arrived for my move to the 2nd Battalion, I was excited yet naturally pensive. I knew that commanding an airborne rifle company during combat, in triple-canopy jungle, would present significant leadership challenges. I would have to make the right decisions at the right time and in the right way to accomplish each dynamic tactical mission without taking an inordinate number of casualties. The survival and safety of my troopers was always front and center in my mind. On April 28, 1966, I moved to the 2nd Battalion and was warmly welcomed by the battalion commander, the executive officer, and the S-3. I then picked up the necessary field gear I would need for future combat operations.

Charlie Company was already deployed in the field. The next morning, I climbed aboard the UH-1 ("Huey") helicopter, along with the battalion commander and sergeant major, and we flew toward the Charlie Company bivouac area. Once we landed in the secured LZ, we were escorted to the company headquarters. The company was in a Michelin plantation, which was neatly lined with measured linear rows of rubber trees. The battalion commander and sergeant major conducted the change of command ceremony, passing the company guidon (flag) from the previous commander to me. The ceremony was very emotional. The battalion commander, the sergeant major, and the outgoing company commander gave me a quick ceremonial pat on the ass, wished me luck, and flew off into the eerie morning mist.

HELIBORNE ASSAULT INTO VUNG TAU

We had already received an order to prepare and conduct the first company-level nighttime heliborne assault during the Vietnam War the very next day. I had to hit the ground running! The Vung Tau-Ba Ria port area was a US resupply and troop rest and relaxation (R&R) area. The VC had been lobbing an increasing number of mortar and rocket propelled grenades from the nearby high ground into the US cantonment areas. After studying the mission order, I quickly gathered the platoon leaders, field first sergeant, and senior non-commissioned officers (NCOs) for a mission planning session that also included factoring in our pathfinders and incredible brigade chopper pilots. Well before dawn, we took off into the unknown darkness. With the help of the pathfinders, we landed in the right troop sequence, at the right time, and in the right area, at the base of the objective high ground. We then moved up the mountain, prepared to clear out any VC rat nests as we moved. Supposedly, no non-VC had ventured into that area in twenty-two years. The platoon and squad leaders competently led their troopers as planned. Each of us, loaded down with heavy combat gear, trudged up the steep, wet slope, clinging to trees, bushes, and vines as we pulled and climbed toward the summit.

Although we did not encounter many VC, we did run into some poorly constructed and placed booby traps tripped by our troopers on the point. Some of the booby traps were armed with dud 105mm artillery rounds that the VC had dug up. It was a physically and mentally tough mission, and the troops were performing superbly. We eventually had four minor contacts and, in the end, killed three residual VC who had been dug in awkwardly near the top of the mountainside and had two slightly wounded troopers. We eventually reached the top, located, cleared, and destroyed several VC firing positions that had been used to attack the Vung Tau area.

Since it was getting dark, and I was confident that our company medic could care for the wounded, I decided we should stay overnight on the summit and move down to the pickup zone the following day. At first light, we began to slip and slide back down the steep slope, again clinging to trees and undergrowth as we descended. When we reached the bottom, we loaded our wounded on a Dustoff (Callsign for medevac helicopters in Vietnam), and the remainder of the company boarded slicks (transport helicopters) for our trip back to base camp.

That relatively short mission would likely end like most search and destroy and other kinds of missions in Vietnam: We would physically leave the area we had just cleared and temporarily occupied and then the VC would just move back into the area again. How could this be called mission success? I would soon learn that gauging mission success in Vietnam was one of the most difficult but important problems during this war. In terms of simply accomplishing our assigned mission, that first mission was an initial success. During the mission, I gained an initial positive feel for the combat competency and toughness of the company and its leadership. I knew that more difficult missions would challenge them and me much further, and that tactical success would become our constantly fluid metric. During my time commanding Charlie Company, we were tasked to conduct seven different search and destroy missions in various areas of II and III Corps, each for a period of two to twelve days in duration. Each of those missions affected my thinking on the strategy and tactics during the Vietnam War. Since it would be repetitious to describe each mission, I will depict in detail one of the most representative and consequential missions.

COMPANY AMBUSH MISSION, XUAN LOC

After a couple of blustery, rainy late-June days, my company first sergeant poked his head in the door of my hooch and barked, as only first sergeants can do, that I needed to head down to the battalion command post and report to the S-3 (Operations officer). His gruff voice broke me from a numbed and bummed mood. I had just finished writing a couple of excruciatingly difficult letters of condolence to the families of some of our beloved Charlie Company troopers who had been recently killed in action during our latest search and destroy mission. Writing those letters was the most difficult and emotional task that I had been given up to that point in my life and, frankly, since. A company commander was required to personally write agonizing letters of condolence to the next of kin within ten days of the deadly incident and describe the action in which their beloved trooper was killed and how he had performed bravely. I recalled writing one of these letters, at night, out in the field, with a flashlight, the paper tucked under my poncho, while the wind and monsoon rain pelted loudly on my shelter half, producing a constant, thunderous rumble. I remember thinking, it was as if God was displaying an anger at the continuing travesty that was affecting our beloved troopers, this country, and its people.

Once the first sergeant left, I popped up from my ammo box seat, put on my fatigue jacket, and helmet and trudged out of my hooch. I splashed down onto the ever-present mud oozing through the pierced steel planking, which at least enabled us to stay somewhat above the constantly wet, muddy ground. As I splashed down the company street toward battalion, I could smell the overpowering, ever-present musty odor of the constantly wet tentage and sandbags. Our base camp was full of incongruent smells. The welcomed pungent aromas emanating from the mess tents were always comforting. The ever-grinding generators and the vehicles moving around the base produced a constant brash sound and a haze of fuel vapor that would suddenly catch in one's throat. In the bush, must, mold, mud, and death were ever-present, while incessant huge mosquitoes relentlessly gnawed at our necks, arms, and faces, causing welts and interminable itching.

I slapped through the flap of the battalion command tent, and, with a high level of apprehension, reported to the S-3, a major. He told me that II Field Force and brigade intelligence had identified some "VC hard-core units and high-speed logistic trails" in the Xuan Loc area, deep in the heart of what we called Indian Country. Our battalion, as part of Operation Yorktown, was ordered to deploy all three rifle companies on the 28th of June (eventually we would be further delayed until the 29th because of bad weather and again until the 30th due to enemy contact).

The battalion had been assigned the mission to plan an operation to ambush, search and destroy, and disrupt those key critical VC resupply routes. Charlie Company, along with our sister companies Alpha and Bravo, had been selected by the battalion commander to conduct a heliborne insert and conduct company-level ambush operations in a general area around Xuan Loc. Alpha Company was scheduled to be the first to deploy on the 29th near an area called LZ Brazil. We were scheduled to insert several hours later to their southeast near LZ Chile and Bravo Company would was to land to our southwest and operate near LZ Peru. I was told, almost proudly, that this would be the first company-level ambush mission in the Vietnam War. I thought, great, another first.

Ambush operations had been conducted in Vietnam in the past, but never at a combat infantry company level. The larger the unit, the more difficult it would be, not only to keep such an operation obscure, but to be able to conduct a truly effective ambush operation for an extensive period without precipitating a counterattack. I recalled from my time in the brigade S-2 section that the Xuan Loc area was a huge VC rat's nest and one of the nastiest areas in Vietnam. There was no precedent for such a large ambush operation, but an ambush primarily requires intricate planning, covert-style insert operations, and a continuous need for security and stealthy action until an eventual planned egress (movement back to base) is affected. I asked the S-3 how long he thought we would be conducting this ambush operation and how would we, after the mission was "completed," egress from the objective area? He told me, "As of now, everything is likely open-ended." That was not comforting. As I returned to my company area, I thought about the important tactical preparations and planning we would have to make. I also would break the bad news to the company troopers that their scheduled down time would be cut short again by a special mission that would certainly be difficult, dangerous, and probably deadly. I continued to wonder why company-level ambushes had not been attempted before in Vietnam, why it was being ordered now, and why the objective and the objective area warranted such a mission.

Tactical Planning for the Ambush Mission

An ambush is by definition "a surprise attack by people lying in wait in a concealed position." This mission would remain a true ambush only until the VC knew we were there, and that would occur after our first contact. I felt that the only way to at least hold off the VC's immediate response was to continuously confuse them about our strength, mission, disposition, and location. We needed to draw weapons, ammo, equipment, rations, and water for a flexible length of time. For this mission, we included special items such as shotguns, smoke grenades in a variety of colors, and as many Claymore mines as we could carry. Claymore mines were developed to defend against mass attacks. They consist of 700 steel balls embedded in C4 explosive. The mine is shaped like a curved rectangle, which allows for a horizontal full 60-degree pattern of deadly steel balls to be fired when activated. The blast can mow right through elephant grass. Used creatively in the defense, we would, at times, first detonate some Claymores shoulder high on trees and then, as the VC would drop to the ground for cover, a second or two later detonate additional mines at ground level. On the other hand, the VC learned to crawl toward our perimeter, wait until they saw the opportunity, then turn the Claymores around so that they faced us when we detonated them. We in turn painted a white stripe on the back of the Claymores and made sure we saw that stripe before detonating them. The VC made their own homemade Claymore-type mines, casting concrete, metal scraps, explosives, and detonators surrounded on the back by a metal pan to direct the metal scraps forward toward their intended target.

During this mission, we would have to survive for a period without the normal resupply missions by battalion and brigade. We always attempted to ensure a ready supply of our life's blood: potable water. While moving through the jungle, whether during the incessant rainy season or scorching heat and stifling humidity, we would become soaking wet. As we developed a tactical plan, we always looked for areas where we would have access to streams or ponds. In this case, we planned to increase our normal supply of water purification tablets along with salt tablets used to replace the salt lost by the body from constantly sweating. We normally carried a heavy supply of mosquito repellant, which we sloshed on liberally, and the pungent smell from the stuff was everywhere. We also had to ensure that we had taken our scheduled malaria tablets prior to our deployment.

As infantrymen carrying an onerously heavy load through the triple-canopy jungle, we carefully planned our individual loads, starting with our rations. We were provided C rations, which were left over from World War II and Korea. The meals were packed in actual cans that were not only heavy to carry through the bush, but the sharp edges of the cans carried in our rucksacks also cut into our shoulders and backs no matter how we tried to pad them. Those rations always included the infantryman's friend: cigarettes, nonfiltered Old Gold, Lucky Strike, Chesterfield, and Camels. Just smoking a cigarette seemed to relieve some of the constant pressure, bringing a momentary feeling of being almost human again. They were also useful for burning off ever-present parasites like leeches, chiggers, and ticks. I did not smoke normally, but both times I was in Vietnam, I smoked then quit each time I got back home.

While cutting and thrashing through the dense jungle quagmire, troopers would carry individual combat loads ranging anywhere from fifty to eighty pounds (at times more). Stuffed in their basic rucksack, they would carry gear and clothing (dry socks to the infantryman are like gold), varying combinations of rations, two collapsible two-quart water canteens (weighing about eight to ten pounds), trip flares, Claymore mines, ammunition magazines and belts, detonation chord, C-4 plastic explosives, blasting caps, smoke grenades, hand grenades, first-aid battle dressings, mosquito repellant, malaria pills, salt tablets, poncho, flashlight, entrenching tool, bayonet, M-16 or M-60 machine gun or shotgun, 81mm mortar, mortar rounds, grenade launcher, flashlight batteries, repelling rope, and possibly a radio. A radio-telephone operator would also carry a twenty-five-pound PRC-25 radio and could carry a total load of at least eighty pounds. Carrying those onerous loads while cutting through triple-canopy jungle was extremely uncomfortable and challenging I felt that during our initial tactical planning we should include a secondary LZ close enough to the objective but far enough away so that it would not divulge our surreptitious mission's location near the high-speed logistic trails. Once we reached the ambush objective area, we needed company plans for the ambush attacks, defense of our positions, and for an egress if the area turned "hot." I estimated that the VC would respond violently once we were ripping into their critical supply and resupply efforts. As for eventual exfiltration, I hoped that choppers would eventually get us out of there, but we would be well advised to have a solid plan to egress out on foot as well.

I next had to consider what artillery and close-air support we could call on during the mission. The S-3 told me that brigade would move at least one battery of M102-105mm airborne light artillery to a forward location to provide direct support of our mission if we were deployed in the area. He also said that the remaining two batteries would be positioned so they could move quickly and provide additional supporting fire for us and our sister companies while operating in the objective area. Although the brigade artillery batteries were competent, artillery support in many parts of Vietnam was problematic due to various limitations of range, firepower, and the degradation of effectiveness including possible pre-detonation of artillery rounds in the jungle. The S-3 also told me that corps artillery batteries were located at fire bases in the vicinity and could be moved forward if needed. As for close-air support the S-3 told me that aircraft such as A-1 Skyraiders, F-4 Phantoms, and F-100 Super Sabers could be on call. All were proven close-air support aircraft, but my favorite was the Skyraider, which was a powerful, radial-engine prop aircraft that could carry a fairly large bomb load and, most importantly, had the ability to stay "on station" for longer periods of time.

We then planned our heliborne assault into a LZ close to the objective area. A company-level helicopter assault into an LZ could take a dangerously extended period and attract some reaction from the VC. The first key issue in our planning was to avoid a "hot" LZ.

We, in the airborne, have a unique way of looking at an operation and do what we call backward planning. During an airborne or airmobile operation, the most vulnerable time is just after boots strike the ground and just before being able to set up an initial defensive perimeter.

Our loading plan for the air assault included a total of ninety-six troopers. In airborne operations, we at times cross loaded units so that if an aircraft went down, it would not take out a unit's total capability. But in an airmobile operation with a smaller number of personnel on board, we attempted to keep unit integrity within the loading plan. We planned on eight to ten fully loaded troopers plus the standard door gunner for each Huey or "Slick."

As I was finalizing our plans with company leadership, I was informed that Alpha Company, which had already deployed on their mission, became involved in a violent firefight on the 29th and it lasted into the 30th. They had killed thirty-three VC, but unfortunately had fifteen KIA and thirty-eight wounded. Battalion decided that the entire operation required a change of plans. For the companies to be mutually supportive during the operation, battalion delayed our and Bravo Company's air assault mission until the 30th. Our objective was changed to an area located between Alpha and Bravo's and toward an ultimate landing zone (LZ), designated as LZ Peru. To be stealthy and not give away our ultimate objective area, I chose to air assault into a more remote area some distance from the designated ambush site.

Once our mission area had been changed, I gathered the platoon leaders, artillery fire support officer, and the field first sergeant, and conducted a map, sketch, and photo reconnaissance of our newly assigned area. We selected a remote LZ with what looked like a reasonable line of march to the final objective area near LZ Peru. A reasonable line of march is a purely subjective term when it comes to moving through thick jungle and its attendant undergrowth, particularly the gnarly bamboo. We could not and would not travel along any roads or developed trails because the enemy could anticipate our route of movement and set up an ambush either along the route or at the objective. Mapping, charting, and geodesy support during the early years of the Vietnam conflict was not great. At times, we even used Michelin road maps. We were frustrated that we did not have access to accurate mapping for many geographical portions of some of our missions. I had already experienced this map problem in the Dominican Republic! We scoured all the available information from reports, sketch maps, and photos on VC activity and the supply trail complex in our new objective area.

One of the most challenging tactical problems would be surreptitiously deploying an infantry company (with a field strength of ninety-six paratroopers) along a highly traveled area that belonged to the enemy. As I saw it, the conundrum was that the more successful we were, as we hopefully hit them hard and often, they would be forced to react with a vengeance. To conduct a proper ambush and cover a large area with many high-speed trails (similarly, the much larger Ho Chi Minh Trail was not just a single road but a massive complex of intersecting pathways and trails), I decided to initially deploy smaller unit positions and plan how to protect them once they attacked the passing VC from their ambush positions. We also had to deploy so that fields of fire would not put fellow troopers in jeopardy from friendly crossfire.

During planning for positioning at the objective area with the platoon leaders and senior NCOs (I depended a great deal on senior NCOs during my career), I decided to initially deploy multiple ambush positions in section strength (there were two sections in a squad). In anticipation of a potential VC counterattack, each following day we would consolidate by deploying in increasing unit-level ambush positions. On the second day, we would consolidate the sections into integral squad positions and then the following day into platoon-sized ambush positions, and finally on the fourth day, when I felt we would be most vulnerable, we would deploy into a company-level ambush perimeter. The plan was like playing Russian Roulette: How long would we be able to redeploy into ever-stronger perimeters until we would face a counterattack? I hoped that when that happened, we would have moved into a mutually supporting, company-strength perimeter. Training, combat experience, and instinct were all at play during this stage of my tactical planning.

Anxiety increased the closer we got to the launching of the operation. The evening before the heliborne assault, we conducted our final operational and logistic checks and had our last "normal" meal, and maybe a beer. Each time soldiers approach a combat mission, every second, every minute, everyone feels differently; differently toward each other, toward the mission, toward family, and our country. Being hours and minutes away from the inevitable and dangerous unknown creates a distant and surreal world, but we continue to act and react out of a learned or innate animal instinct while running on a strange level of autopilot. Combat focuses a person to think in the basic tenets of life, death, and just plain survival.

Moving Again Toward the Unknown

We were now in the final throes of preparations for the air assault. As always in the hours before an impending operation our voices became almost muted. Many troopers tried to reduce the tension by telling jokes and stories. They would share dark advice such as how to die correctly when presented with the "opportunity," and had even written a tongue-in-cheek, official-looking directive on how to die with flair if combat photographers were present.

As a drizzly, wet dawn broke on June 30th, we arrived at the chopper loading area. The familiar "wop-wop" of the rotor blades was eerie and ominous, like a call beckoning us to move into an unknown abyss. As we loaded into the troop compartments, the door gunners greeted us like long-lost brothers and shouted, "Welcome aboard." The door gunner helped to suppress any enemy fire at the LZ; he was like a welcomed security blanket. We sat huddled as the chopper engine revved up and the forceful whoosh of the blade downdraft blew the wind and rain toward the faces of the troopers sitting on the floor's outer edge. Their legs were hanging down, feet on the skids, ready to spring. We could see the other choppers in the flight with their troopers' legs hanging down over the side. As I looked down at the thick jungle in the light misting rain, it felt like an out-of-body experience. Each time I flew close to the coastline or in the high hills and mountains along the spine of Vietnam, I stared in wonderment at what a beautiful country it would be when this horrific war was finally over.

As we approached the LZ, the thick, high elephant grass blew in violent patterns and the choppers nestled down into what resembled large bird's nests. The lead troopers snapped to the ground and bounded into a crouched running movement toward the edges of the LZ and set up an initial defensive perimeter. This was the critical time in any heliborne assault. Fortunately, there were no signs of VC activity. The other choppers arrived carrying the remainder of the company, and we became more confident that we could defend our new company perimeter. Once the initial cacophony of noise, movement, and apprehensive terror during the air landing had subsided, we broke from our temporary defensive perimeter and started moving through the dense, wet jungle on our planned azimuth, at a normal pace and with constant alertness. The 2nd Platoon was in the lead, followed by the 1st Platoon, Weapons Platoon, Company Headquarters, and the 3rd Platoon securing the rear of the column. We had to get to the objective area before dark to set up our initial ambush positions quickly, quietly, and effectively so we deployed minimal flank security.

Later that day, as we approached the objective area, we stopped temporarily to deploy a six-man scout patrol on a mission to provide the latest information on current VC activity in the objective area and assess the trail complex. Initially, it looked like the trails had been cut into the jungle with little apparent plan or reason, but the more we had studied them, the more we saw that they had some practical reasoning to them. A basic understanding of the trail patterns would help us plan the most effective tactical dispositions to accomplish the mission. Through our training and experience, we would always have the option to redeploy and reposition our unit areas of responsibility when the tactical situation evolved, even under fire. Our patrol returned and reported that there was no current VC activity in our objective area, and they gave us some additional information on the trail complex. We then calmly and smoothly moved into our designated line of march toward the staggered deployment positions in and around the objective area. Once we were about a half of a kilometer out, the designated rifle and support sections began to fan out from their parent squad and platoons and moved stealthily into their position on the sketched-out trail complex. Within thirty minutes of our arrival in the objective area, each individual unit was in position and ready for combat action and reaction. We had positioned our multiple small units on a varied trail complex, so the company was now deployed into a looser, more jagged perimeter than we would have normally used in a classic, mutually reinforcing, company-sized, defensive/attack position. We located our small company headquarters (field first sergeant, artillery forward observer, radio-telephone operator, and me) in the center of the deployed units. We had to continuously ensure that each unit was in the most tactically effective position and stealthy enough to spring its individual ambush task while positioning each unit to lessen friendly crossfire situations. I knew that this unique and complex mission would challenge the training and experience of every Sky Soldier and the combat dexterity of the entire company leadership.

Instead of walking portions of the perimeter and interacting with the company leaders and troopers, as I liked to do, I let the small unit leadership to do what they did best: lead. We had planned to arrive at the objective area just before last light hoping to find a possible time crease in the VC resupply activity and to give us enough light to dig into our assigned ambush positions. Normally, as we moved into an attack/defensive perimeter, we would immediately dig in to create small, individual foxhole-like fighting positions that we called spider holes. Unfortunately, we were in the middle of monsoon season, and the rains this year were especially intense, so the water table was high. As soon as we tried to dig a spider hole into the jungle floor, we would hit water at a few inches, filling the hole. If a trooper wanted to use the spider hole for protection he could continue to dig further and sit in a pool of bone-chilling, infested water all night and possibly into the next day. It was one of a myriad of unique and difficult decisions an infantryman makes in a combat environment: in this case, choose between being terribly uncomfortable and possibly getting ill or being more vulnerable to potential enemy fire. We completed our final deployment and preparations just as darkness fell on the thick, dripping triple-canopy jungle.

A critical aspect of the combat environment in Vietnam that took a heavy toll was sleep, or the lack thereof. Because the lives of our wonderful troopers and our mission success were dependent on my decisions, I was never able to have a semblance of a deep sleep. I constantly thought about unforeseen risks and felt an immense responsibility for the mission and the welfare of the troops. Additionally, the crackling hiss of the command radio nets was like a constant, but necessary, irritant that would startle me out of a nodding sleep. Lack of sleep is not only uncomfortable, but it is terribly debilitating physically and mentally. Also, during my time in the Charlie Company I lost quite a bit of weight. For some strange reason, I thought about that weight loss during that first night in Xuan Loc.

At the first signs of light on July 1st, I felt that the VC/North Vietnamese would soon attempt to move through the area with their daily supply and resupply loads. As the area continued to brighten, we tried to keep as much ancillary noise to a minimum, and I turned down that interminable squelch on the command radio. My ever-faithful radio-telephone operator and I learned how to communicate with each other by physical signs or just with our eyes. During the Vietnam conflict, it seemed that we were always waiting for the VC or the NVA to take the initiative. Although it may have seemed like we were the hunter at times, once we entered the bush, the VCs had an intimate knowledge of their jungle home and we quickly turned into the hunted. As we waited on this first day of the ambush, the lowest level of the infantry in the daily crucible of search and destroy missions, I envisioned us being drawn into the enemy's jungle home like crabs being lured into a crab trap.

The Ambush Begins

As the slivers of morning light were sifting down through the constantly dripping jungle, a sudden round of small arms fire led to a series of small firefights breaking out around the perimeter. After a couple minutes of sporadic fire, it all ended with a thunderous calamity of sound, then incongruent silence. On cue, I heard section, squad, platoon NCOs, and platoon leaders bark out loud, curt orders, including a final "cease fire" over many sectors of our ambush positions. Then again came an eerie silence. The platoon leaders reported that elements of second and first platoons had ambushed a line of VC, many on bicycles transporting various types of supplies, weapons, and ammunition. After those initial contact reports, the first sergeant and I crouched and moved to the sites of the reported contacts. We counted boxes of rifles, mortars, ammo, bags of rice, some bicycles, and several dead VC strewn along the trails that cut through the thick jungle along the perimeter of our defensive positions. I radioed battalion, told them of the contact and listed the type and number of weapons, supplies, and materials we had captured. They replied that choppers would be dispatched to pick up the captured equipment at the nearby LZ Peru.

Battalion then asked how many dead VC we had counted. We replied, "Five VC KIA." They then asked if we had found blood trails leading away from the contact area. Blood trails indicated that wounded VC limped, crawled, or were dragged away through the jungle with blood trailing from their wounds. We responded that we had not yet ventured beyond our outer perimeter. I thought that the VC may have planned this initial contact to draw us out of our defensive perimeter. Battalion then tasked us to report on the blood trails leading away from our perimeter. We cautiously complied. Shortly, the troops reported that they had counted six definitive blood trails, and I relayed the information back to the battalion. I would later learn that the battalion reported eight VC KIA during that initial contact. Perhaps some flexible policy on measuring body count had been formulated? They appeared to take half the number of blood trails counted and then would add that number to the actual KIA. Later, as I looked at various body count formulas more closely, I concluded that there was no hard and fast rule. It seemed that the body count figure at various headquarters was left up to some rotating number cruncher who used some sort of concocted formula for enemy contacts and resultant KIA, including those based on blood trails. Shortly after I had assumed command of the company in April, I had put out a hard and fast rule: Do not count a dead enemy body unless you can put a warm hand on a cold ass. Even as a young captain, I instinctively knew that inflating those numbers was wrong. The continued reliance on enemy body count as a methodology for determining progress in this war would eventually become a major problem and result in an eventual disaster.

After the contact was over, several choppers had landed at LZ Peru, which meant we had lost any chance at a further stealth operation. The initial contact and the hovering choppers would certainly tell the VC where we were located. This was no longer a standard, everyday ambush. We carried the materials out to the choppers, and they took away all the captured weapons and ammunition, but they left the bags of rice. Rice was a valuable commodity to the VC, and we were often forced to leave it behind. Bags of rice were not only heavy, but also very difficult to dispose of unless dumped in a pond or stream.

Now that some portions of our positions had been exposed, I had to assess our next move. I knew that our time had started to run out. If we could make it through this day, then we should keep to our plan and transition into a squad position strength defensive perimeter later that day, July 1st and into July 2. We conducted the preplanned repositioning during that day and set in to wait while the VC either restarted their resupply activities or attack us. I knew that the VC did not have a robust communications system and normally passed their intelligence reporting and operational planning by courier. Once we repositioned into our new ambush sites, we waited for the VC to make the next move, which was the frustrating norm in Vietnam. I thought that we might have one more day and night of success then we would begin to lose whatever tactical advantage we still had.

As darkness fell on our jungle "home," I chatted with one of our combat chaplains, Father (Captain) John McCullough. The chaplains in Vietnam were amazing and slogged it out with us, even during the most dangerous of missions. The very presence of the chaplains was comforting and reassuring, and they provided a great morale boost. They would comfort our wounded and perform religious services in the field, which were even attended by troopers who were not normally religious. (One of our chaplains, Father Watters, was awarded the Medal of Honor for his valor during the later battle of Dak To.) I had a long, hushed chat with Father John that night about the war and how great our troopers were.

At 0500 on the morning of the 2nd all hell broke loose. Two of the platoons had unleashed maximum firepower on a long column of VC passing just beyond our outer perimeter. The sound and experience of a close firefight is about as frightening and unique as anything one can experience on earth. The humidity and the density of the jungle keeps each sharp, earsplitting sound amplified and reverberating. I again heard the cacophony of gruff, loud orders coming from the platoon and squad leaders, and then almost on cue, everything fell into silence, in anticipation of the start of another eruption.

At first light, we reset the perimeter and I crouched and moved along the perimeter, talking to the troops and assessing the damage. We had two minor wounded that the company medic had already handled with his usual professionalism and care. We found six more VC KIA and a number of blood trails leading out of the area. (I don't know how many VC KIA were eventually reported from this contact, but I assume some formula was wisely devised.) This time, we had captured a larger number of military supplies including three more boxes of AK-47s, one box of SKS rifles, a few 82mm mortars, and many hand and rocket propelled grenades. I reported the contact, casualties, and the material we had captured to battalion. They sent choppers to pick up our wounded, resupply us with rations, water, and ammo and loaded up the material we had captured. That day, the 2nd, happened to have been my birthday, but I had never thought of it, until I got birthday wishes delivered on one of the resupply choppers. That unexpected letter was from the commanding general and triggered a myriad of thoughts. My thoughts focused on my beloved mother and fleeting memories of the wonderful life mom and dad had given me. I also had melancholy thoughts of Ann. I then wondered if I would live to see another birthday or even the rest of this day. Each time that I have looked at that letter, it brings back the same incongruent emotions of both hope and dread. During mid-day, I assembled the company leadership and planned a contingency retrograde movement when and if we were ordered to move back to base camp, either on foot or by chopper out of LZ Peru. Later in the day, I reported our latest tactical situation report to battalion and asked if there was a timeframe for our return to our base camp. The operation remained open-ended, and we were ordered to remain in position. Now I felt that the crab trap was set. I needed to hone our plan to defend against an increasingly probability of the springing of that trap.

I gathered the company leadership and told them that we would skip the next tactical phase. I told them to position their platoons close to known trails of ingress (approaching) and egress (leaving) so that we could call fire in on the VC as they approached, attacked, or retreated. Some of those trails could be used if we needed to quickly extricate ourselves. I again stressed the need to avoid the possibility of friendly crossfire. Experience, training, and instinct were now driving my tactical decisions. I observed the troops to gauge mental and physical health. They were unshaven, mud-smeared, and had sunken, staring eyes. Some of us had a Mohawk haircut, which was an old airborne tradition from yelling "Geronimo" while blasting through the door of an airplane on a combat jump. During combat, it does not take long to be worn down by the surrounding atmosphere. The intense pressure of close combat, the debilitating jungle, intense heat and humidity, the rain, the mosquitoes and other insects, the leeches, the common bouts of malaria and dengue fever, along with the lack of sleep all take an eventual toll, even on the best of the best. But as I looked hard at the company leaders and the troopers, I could see that they were still totally focused on the job at hand and still had plenty of fight in them. I recalled what General Sink had said to me Fort Campbell: "Jack, never give up and always take care of your troops."

Moving into a Company-Level Ambush/Defensive Position

During the remainder of July 2, we redeployed into a full, company-level defensive perimeter around the area of a figurative clock. We now had mutually reinforcing and integrated fields of fire that would be most effective during a perimeter defense. Finally, we would not have to split our unit integrity, which would reduce the possibility of friendly fire incidents. We now had the critical sinews of our company capability knitted together, and I felt we were best positioned to repel a possible attack. That night I fitfully dozed in my small hammock to the low crackle of the radio. During the early pre-dawn hours of the 3rd, I woke and looked up at the slim rays of the early sun fighting through the dark, dripping wet canopy. At about 0615 on that day, July 3, I checked in with battalion and the S-3 finally approved beginning our retrograde back to base camp early that morning. We would use the movement plan we had devised on the 2nd with a sound tactical egress, including the order of march and appropriate flank security. At 0635 I reported our plan to the battalion S-3 and requested a firefly mission be on standby until full daylight. A firefly was a UH-1 helicopter that could drop illumination (MK-24 flares) if we had to move or operate during periods of little light or no light. The firefly was normally accompanied by two helicopter gunships. (Later, the firefly would have powerful searchlights.) The firefly arrived on station and then left shortly once the sky began to brighten. Once we got approval from battalion to move out, I decided to move that day to a westerly map coordinate several kilometers away to get us out of the immediate danger. But we would still not fully be out of what I described as "the ring of fire," which I felt was a VC key defensive tactical zone of about 20 kilometers around Xuan Loc. We planned and prepared to begin our movement out at 0730. However, at 0715, as some of our lead elements began pulling out and moving toward their preplanned line of march, sporadic small firefights broke out along various sectors around the company perimeter, and then stopped as quickly as they had begun. The second platoon reported that they had "bloused" one VC, and the first platoon reported one minor wounded trooper. I had to quickly evaluate what these seemingly minor events meant for the company and our mission. These small VC contacts around the perimeter were either a feeble attempt to cause us some retributive casualties before we left the area, or they could be trying to hold us in place so that their supply columns could move through. However, I thought that these were most probably probing attacks attempting to determine our location, disposition, and strength. I told the platoons to stop any movement out of present positions. At 0733 I reported the enemy activity to the battalion Operations officer and told him that it may well have been a probing attack. He suggested that we delay any movement until we had a stabilized situation. I rogered his suggestion. Because we had one wounded trooper, I requested that a Dustoff stand by. At 0740 I requested that battalion prepare a sling load of ammunition but not to launch the chopper until I requested it.

At about 0745 I had a continuing gnawing feeling in my gut and told battalion that the initial contact could build into something significant and that we may eventually require reinforcements. At 0747, as I sat on my small hammock working on my sketch map, reassessing the situation and planning our next move, all hell broke loose around the entire perimeter. Large caliber machine gun fire was raking the perimeter, and I heard a series of violent explosions. On instinct, I rolled out of my hammock onto the mud below, and tried to get an assessment of what was happening. Large caliber rounds of grazing enemy fire raked over my head, chopping up trees and ripping holes in my hammock. Enemy fire was incoming but with more ominous sounds. I could hear the low-pitched, but very loud, slow bark of a 14.5 mm machine guns (equivalent to our 50-caliber machine gun) and the whoosh and blasts of rocket propelled grenades. The presence of those heavier weapons indicated that we were not facing a small VC platoon. This may be at least a company, a reinforced battalion, or God forbid, a full VC regiment. Having assessed that this had now become a serious and threatening attack, I let the platoon leaders do what they do best: lead the defense of their individual platoon areas. I quickly moved along the inner perimeter placing various company elements, which had been preparing to move out, back into their original positions. Now it was time to call in some heavy-duty artillery fire in there and fast. I told the artillery forward observer to request supporting fire from the on-call direct support standby 173rd Artillery Battery.

At first, I requested them to target areas and trails 200–300 yards beyond our perimeter in all directions. As I quickly determined that the enemy fire was coming primarily from the east and northeast, I redirected the forward observer to have the battery concentrate its fire on that area.

I barked to the forward observer, "Just get it in here." I hoped that our perimeter defenses would hold and that once the artillery rounds started raking the jungle, the VC would become discouraged and stop the attack. The brigade artillery was soon blasting holes in the jungle just beyond our defensive perimeter. Over time, I had developed a personal tactical policy that I would not send a trooper anywhere that I could send a bullet or a shell. The initial artillery fire did not deter the VC and they pressed their attack more fiercely. I knew that one artillery battery could only cover a portion of our outer attack perimeter, so I told the forward observer to request fire from additional artillery batteries. Again, I instructed their fire to be on the outer edges of the perimeter, concentrating on the east and northeast. The troopers of 173rd Artillery Battalion reacted magnificently. They put the remaining two forward prepositioned batteries of 105s into action, covering the additional areas around and beyond our perimeter. The firepower from the entire artillery battalion was devastating, and we could hear the screams of the VC outside the perimeter grow louder and more violent. The VC close-in attack, however, continued without let-up. We were now at about ten minutes into this contact. One minute of violent combat in a closed area like a jungle seems like an eternity. Thankfully, our perimeter positions were holding firmly, and it appeared that the VC had miscalculated the size, strength, and disposition of our defensive perimeter. We had moved into our company-level defensive perimeter at just the right time and place.

At 0758 I reported to battalion that the VC appeared to be pulling back or possibly regrouping. The firefight had ebbs and flows as we both made some tactical adjustments, but it continued like a nonstop nightmare. At 0800 I told battalion that the situation had again somewhat stabilized. But, at 0805, the VC reattacked our perimeter again, in earnest, especially from the north, northeast, and east. The continuous barking and cracking sounds emanating from the incoming and outgoing weapons were deafening. I quickly called battalion and requested that reinforcements be made available on call. As the VC pressed the attack, some of our positions reported that some VC had penetrated portions of our perimeter. I yelled for the platoons to eject them before hand-to-hand combat would be necessary. I then reported to battalion that we had stabilized our perimeter for the time being, and, as of that time, we had three friendly KIAs and four WIAs and that I thought that the VC main force was located mostly between us and the eastern side of LZ Peru. Fierce firefights continued unabated around the perimeter.

At 0817, battalion reported that an air force forward air controller along with close-air support aircraft armed with at least 500-pound bombs were moving on station. Air support was a great asset to have, but it needed to be closely controlled to prevent friendly fire incidents. I informed the forward air controller that when he was prepared to vector in strike aircraft, we would pop red smoke around our perimeter. I also asked him to look for targets of opportunity at least 400 to 500 meters outside of our perimeter, mainly in the area east/northeast of LZ Peru.

A short time later, the fighter bombers arrived on station and were revving overhead as the attacks on the ground continued. It was comforting to hear them, and I hoped that the VC would be reluctant to press the attack when they heard them as well. At 0822, I reported to battalion that we were maintaining contact with the VC, were employing Claymore mines, and we expected to be hit again. At 0845, I told battalion that the VC were attacking our perimeter with hand and rocket grenades and automatic weapons of all calibers. Battalion then told me that a reinforcement platoon from Charlie Company, from our sister 1st Battalion, was in the area, but the choppers carrying them were receiving fire from the southwest. From the southwest?

At 0855, I reported to battalion that three of our now four KIAs were caught in a crossfire, and we were having difficulty getting them back to a more secure area. I also told them that we needed additional ammunition, mostly M-16 and machine gun rounds. At 0914, I told battalion that we were still exchanging hand grenades and automatic weapons fire with the attacking VC and asked them to launch a Dustoff chopper for at least three of our more seriously wounded troopers. We now had four KIA and seven WIA. At 0928 a resupply chopper landed at LZ Peru with much needed ammo and other supplies, and we put our wounded troopers on board. At 0958, the first lift carrying a squad of our brothers from the 1st Battalion arrived at LZ Peru. We sent scouts to guide them into our perimeter. At 1015 and 1020, two more lifts brought in the two remaining squads of the reinforcing platoon. Thanks to Sky Soldier dedication, training, and professionalism, the whole operation could not have been smoother. The attacks continued off and on, so I decided to bring in some bigger stuff to discourage the VC. When I requested additional reinforcing artillery support, my forward observer told me that the Field Force artillery had 8 inch and 175 mm gun batteries standing by. I told the forward observer to request on-call fire for the 8-inch guns on the possible reinforcement (and egress) trails several hundred yards from the company perimeter, mostly east and northeast, targeting any VC reinforcements that were moving into or those moving out of the area. I also asked that the 175s target areas a couple of hundred meters beyond the northeast shoulder of LZ Peru.

At about 1035, I reported to battalion that after the arrival of the 1st Battalion reinforcements, we were consolidating our positions and that we had received some 60mm mortar rounds that fell short of our perimeter. We reported that we could count at least fifteen VC KIA and had seen numerous blood trails both in and around our perimeter. At 1100, we coordinated with battalion to keep all choppers from the area so we could take maximum advantage of artillery and close-air support without endangering them.

We also had to delay the artillery fire in some areas to keep them from endangering approaching support aircraft. We then carefully coordinated popping more red smoke with each platoon and the forward air controller. It was critical that the right color smoke be used in the right place at the right time to avoid friendly fire air strikes. We then set off the red smoke grenades at strategic points around the perimeter. Commanding a rifle company during intense close combat is like trying to conduct an eclectic jazz band during a Category 5 hurricane.

At 1120, we heard huge explosions northeast of our company perimeter. The air strikes were being placed exactly where we had requested. They lasted until 1135. Soon thereafter, as we requested, the artillery units began pounding around our perimeter at the staggered distances. The whole atmosphere was chaotic, ungodly loud, and terrifying. The enemy attack continued to rage, and I felt the VC were equally determined to eliminate us at all costs. The platoon leaders were requesting additional artillery support. I couldn't get them more, but I could get it closer. The brigade artillery fire missions were placed at a safe distance just outside the perimeter. I couldn't bring the bigger guns closer to our perimeter where they were needed because of the danger of making large corrections from where they were presently targeted. We normally make smaller, safer, fire control corrections while approaching friendly troop positions. Since our brigade artillery fire missions were placed at a safe but closer distance just outside the perimeter, I told the forward observer to send them a fire mission, "drop two five [25 meters] and level your bubbles." (The leveling bubbles were on the artillery aiming device.) This correction would get the incoming artillery rounds closer to our perimeter, but it also raised the possibility of getting shrapnel (hopefully spent shrapnel) inside of our perimeter. Once the forward observer sent that correction, we immediately got the ominous reply from our artillery battalion,

"Danger close." This was a pro forma response to warn that this latest correction could result in some dangerous friendly fire.

Once that required warning is sent by the artillery unit, it is up to the ground commander to decide whether to continue with the requested fire mission. I told my forward observer to acknowledge the "Danger Close" alert and then to repeat my fire correction. He radioed back and repeated the correction: "Drop two five and level your bubbles." It wasn't the most dangerous correction, but it was going to be close. It was now or never.

As I was requesting that last artillery correction, I could hear some huge explosions in the distance that sounded like 250, 500, and even 1,000-pound bombs. Those magnificent A-1s and F-100s were looking for and finding targets well outside the perimeter and were probably pummeling VC reinforcements or those trying to retrograde out of the area. The forward air controller was doing a great job of vectoring the aircraft in on the targets and possible routes of ingress and egress.

The A-1s and F-100s had dropped their bombs and were now flying low on strafing runs, raking the possible VC reinforcing units and their resupply system, and hopefully forcing the units in forward positions to withdraw. After a final huge burst of fire from our platoons, artillery, and fighter bombers, the VC finally became silent and moved away. I called for an immediate cease fire for the brigade artillery close-in fire but requested that we keep the corps artillery blasting away at possible VC remnants retreating into the distance. I could still hear the fighter bombers screaming down and continuing to bomb and strafe distant targets of opportunity. I was grateful for the total professionalism and dedication by all.

Our leaders moved around the perimeter shouting to their troopers to cease fire and adjusting their platoon and squad positions while keeping their troopers on a high state of alert for a possible reattack. I was so proud of them and all the troopers. I decided to walk around the perimeter to see how it was holding and ensure that the troopers remained on high alert. I also had to determine how many casualties we had taken and how many VC we had killed during the attack. The VC contact seemed to have lasted an eternity, and I feared the worse for our guys. I thought that we had lost fifteen to thirty troopers. As I made my tactical assessment, I was pleasantly surprised; we had suffered four KIA and nine wounded, mostly taken during the initial VC attack.

I felt that we had to wait a prudent amount of time before we attempted to move beyond the perimeter to assess additional VC casualties. Some of our wounded needed to be evacuated and treated back at our base camp or at a field hospital, but in the meantime, our wonderful company medic did the best he could to treat them and make them comfortable. We had to reform the perimeter and distribute ammo. I waited to send out small patrols beyond the perimeter. Meanwhile, I continued to move around the perimeter, talking to the troopers, giving them all a pat on the back, and reminding them to remain alert. As I made my rounds, I found one trooper sitting in his watery fighting hole, with a Detroit Tigers hat cocked on his head, nonchalantly reading a comic book called "Sergeant Fury and His Howling Commandos." Here he was, after an intense and deadly firefight, and he was reading a damned comic book! I looked out into the dark abyss beyond his fighting position and saw what looked like a disfigured, dead VC, and I could just make out some other possible lifeless shadowy forms in the jungle beyond. The resiliency and focus of the American soldier have never ceased to amaze me. As I moved further along the perimeter, I saw another mud-covered trooper burying a dead VC close to his fighting position. After he had buried most of the body, a VC foot with a sandal was sticking out of the dirt and the trooper was pushing it down nonchalantly with his mud-caked jungle boot. I thought I heard him humming while he was doing it. I initially considered his calm demeaner to be positive because it showed that he had stayed calm during and after a storm of incoming and outgoing fire. On the other hand, he could be dangerously close to being immune to the cruelty of war. Combat commanders must continuously evaluate troop actions and reactions before, during, and after each firefight. There is a fine line between a soldier's quiet, calm professionalism and an acquired callousness, which could lead to danger-laden carelessness in the heat of a battle. A leader must be able to quickly assess, recognize, and correct any degradations in a unit's tactical capability, morale, and fighting élan. These necessary battlefield responsibilities challenge each combat commander's leadership, training, experience, and even instinct to the fullest.

I returned to my company headquarters to plan our next move, which would be a final, tactical assessment of when and how to get out of there. We counted sixteen dead VC within or just outside our perimeter plus a seventeenth that the trooper had buried and a couple that I saw beyond the perimeter. As we probed further outside of our perimeter, the VC seemed to have disappeared as quickly as they had appeared. As patrols moved beyond our perimeter, they found and reported numerous blood trails and body parts. As they moved out even farther, they saw signs of mortal devastation. The artillery and close-air support missions had caused massive, almost incalculable carnage. As I assessed the damage that the artillery and the air support had caused to the VC, I realized that, in the end, we had lured the VC into our own crab trap.

As I sat in my command post planning our next move and reflecting on what we had just been through, I was hoping that the unit that attacked us was the same one that attacked our brothers in Alpha Company on the 29th and 30th and that we had delivered some deserved retribution for our fellow Sky Soldiers. After we did some final battle damage assessment, we were ready to get the hell out of there. There was nothing but further danger if we stayed in this position much longer. The VC probably figured that they had given us a blatant and deadly warning, but they still had the initiative to attack at any time. After I gave a final after-action report to battalion, they told us to move to LZ Peru to get our dead and wounded out by chopper and to resupply with ammo, water, and rations. I told battalion that from the LZ we would be planning a retrograde movement (our base camp at Bien Hoa was about 35 or so kilometers due west). For now, it looked like our trek back to base camp would be by foot. The weather again turned to a drenching and blustery rain. We knew it was going to be a soaking wet difficult slog through that dark morass. As we moved toward LZ Peru, I made sure that we put out strong flank security, and if I had found it necessary, I would have ordered flanking suppressive fire all the way to the LZ.

OUT OF THE CRAB TRAP: MOVING BACK TO BASE CAMP

We moved toward LZ Peru in the pelting rain with each of our KIA wrapped in their own ponchos and a trooper or two on each end lugging them through the heavy, wet undergrowth. Carrying dead comrades through the wet jungle is as difficult and traumatic of an experience as one can imagine. Just the thought of carrying a dead fellow trooper is mentally debilitating, and the added physical exertion of "carrying dead weight" adds to the incredibly emotional experience. The visual that hits me in the gut every time is the sight of a dead comrade's muddy boots sticking out from under the poncho he was wrapped in just a couple of hours ago when he had been a living, breathing brother-in-arms. That lamentable scene is permanently burned into the memory of every trooper who endured combat in that hellhole. The Dustoffs landed in a flurry to evacuate our dead and wounded. As I escorted them all to the choppers, I felt sadness and a brief relief knowing they were on their way back to their loved ones.

The follow-on choppers then landed, and we quickly unloaded the supplies and ammunition that we needed so desperately. We then formed the line of march on our azimuth back to our base camp, still many kilometers away. I felt that we still needed to move several more kilometers before we got beyond that "ring of fire." We were now into the mission's fifth day and had been cutting and slashing through the jungle all day without incident. I had an uneasy feeling that we were still being closely watched and followed, but that was a constant feeling in the jungles of Vietnam. That night we moved into a company defensive perimeter, and I continuously made sure everyone was still on a constant high state of alert. No one had had much sleep, and the constant grinding pressure creates a situation where one small mistake can cost precious lives. Fortunately, that night was uneventful, and we broke our perimeter at first light on July 4. As we moved into our company tactical line of march for our sixth day, I felt that we were out of immediate danger and moving closer to being out of the "ring of fire." We still had some difficult terrain and treacherous areas ahead to get through, but we all looked forward to reaching our base camp after three more days of tough slogging.

As we were cutting through the thick bamboo and underbrush, a scourge of small arms fire raged from concealed positions and sounded like the end of the world. No matter how much you experience a close-in firefight, you never get used to the absolute terror that you feel hearing the initial sound of incoming fire. I hit the ground, crawled, and hugged the nearest tree (not really knowing which side would be the best, but it felt so good and secure) and tried to get a quick initial assessment from the platoon leaders. I heard rounds chipping away at the tree just above my head. Our troops on the flank poured out return fire. After a couple of minutes, it all stopped, and we were left with an eerie but comforting silence. Unfortunately, one of our troopers had been KIA. As we secured the area for a possible reattack, it was difficult to assess how many VC there were, whether they were ready to pounce again, or if had they moved out taking their wounded or dead with them. The rain pounded us in earnest and as we broke out, the ground was so slick and the undergrowth so thick that it took four fellow troopers to carry our fallen comrade wrapped in his poncho. I called ahead to battalion and reported that we had a KIA and requested that they send a Dustoff to evacuate him. They quickly responded that a chopper would be on the way in about ten minutes and that I needed to give them a coordinate for pickup. Not being in a cleared area and not knowing whether there was a potential LZ ahead, I quickly gave them a coordinate just ahead of our line of march. When we got to that point, unfortunately, there was no clearing we could use as an LZ. I had some scouts move out in all directions to see if they could find a suitable LZ, but they just found more thick, unyielding jungle. The only way we could get our dead trooper out would be to blast a semblance of an LZ out of the jungle by wrapping detonation cord and some C-4 explosive around a circle of trees. We set out a 360-degree perimeter around the newly identified LZ. After about ten or fifteen minutes of blasting a large enough hole in the jungle, we radioed for the waiting evac chopper to approach the makeshift LZ. Our troopers all pitched in to move the large, heavy jagged logs and branches out of the way, so that the chopper could get at least close. We popped white smoke for proper identification as the evac chopper approached our position, but he had to hover just above the stumps. The chopper pilots in Vietnam were incredibly brave and invaluable to morale, especially the intrepid Dustoff pilots. As the chopper hovered lower and lower, the downward blast of the rotor blades whipped wet, freshly cut branches and wood chips everywhere, with some ripping into those of us waiting on the ground. The chopper crew dropped a stretcher down and we placed our dead trooper on it then secured him with some rope. The crew was then able lift him up and in for the trip back to our base camp and eventually back to his loved ones. Once we knew our fellow Sky Soldier was taken care of, we reconstituted the company tactical line of march and trudged back into the dark, wet quagmire of the jungle.

We still had at least a couple more days until we could reach the perimeter of our home base camp at Bien Hoa. We cut and moved through dense walls of jungle throughout that day. Cutting through the jungle normally happened at an agonizingly slow pace as our point man and closely following troopers would cut through the undergrowth with machetes. At times we could only move through bamboo-laced, triple-canopy jungle at about a hundred yards or less per hour. We also had to rotate the physically and mentally exhausted troopers "walking the point," every twenty to thirty minutes (depending on the thickness of the bamboo, it was sometimes less). As we rotated the point out, their jungle fatigues were ripped to shreds from cutting through the brush and thick bamboo. We normally had our shirt sleeves rolled up, and as we cut through the bare, brittle bamboo our arms would be constantly cut and welted. Much of the foliage had been sprayed with Agent Orange and other herbicides, which further burned our raw arms and set us up for possible health issues later in life. The brave troopers who continuously volunteered to walk the point became instant heroes to the rest of the company. We always wondered whether they had a death wish, were dedicated to saving the lives of their fellow troopers, or just lived for the excitement of the challenge.

At the end of that day, we set up our defensive perimeter, deployed some listening posts, and settled into what would become another uneventful night. The following day, we slashed our way slowly through a particularly gnarly growth of bamboo and finally that afternoon broke out of the jungle thicket and into a rice and vegetable farming area dotted with small, thatched huts. This relatively open area was certainly easier and faster to move through, but it presented with a new set of problems of security and our ability to react. We were now out in a more exposed area and had to be extremely alert and increase flank security as we moved forward. The platoons set in for the night by digging fighting positions in a company perimeter. At least they could spend the night in dry spider holes. We were dangerously out in the open, but we also had great observation and fields of fire. We put small listening posts out toward the edge of the jungle to ensure we were not surprised by enemy attacks springing out of the surrounding jungle.

We located a small, unoccupied dilapidated hut where we set up company headquarters for what would hopefully be our last night before reaching base camp. I finally dozed off at about 0200 only to be startled awake an hour later when a bark of small arms snarled from behind the hut. I woke in a daze, cleared my head, and slithered toward the area of activity. I called out to the field first sergeant, who had crawled out ahead of me. He reported that there were one or two suspected VC just outside the back of the hut; the close-in security posts heard sounds sifting through the light brush in the rear. After a brief and strange silence, I heard some frantic scurrying, then two sharp resonating cracks. One of the NCOs reported that he had seen a VC moving toward the shack and that he had bloused him. He thought he was a lone attacker. When I got to the VC, I could see a small hole in his forehead and a huge hole blasted out the back of his head. The M16 round had been designed to destabilize as it entered a target and would rip horizontally through whatever it hit. We discovered from his identification papers that he was a VC reconnaissance platoon leader. He had been carrying an AK-47, detonation cord, and had some C-4 strapped on his back. He had planned to inflict as much damage as he could, likely trying to destroy our little command post.

Early in the morning of the ninth day, after moving into our preplanned line of march, we tried to pick up our pace. That increased effort did not last long as the sun blasted through with a vengeance, and we had to trudge through scorching heat and raging humidity. The excessive moisture in the air and ground caused our breathing to become incredibly laboured. We still had to cut through another stretch of thick jungle before we could emerge into the cleared area surrounding our base camp. Later in the day, we finally beat and cut our way out of a last thicket of bamboo, into the open and in sight of our base camp. The NCOs were doing their jobs, barking orders to "keep up." They growled, "You keep goin'! You keep goin'! You're not gonna get this far and fall out now!" Finally, we were within a short distance of the berm surrounding our base camp. We would have crawled the rest of the way if we had to. As we reached line of musty sandbags and rusted barbed wire on the base perimeter, we were heartily greeted by the perimeter guards yelling "Airborne." We responded in unison "All the way." Our attitude and posture went from half-bent and almost broken to braced and proud. We were "home," proud paratroopers, proud Sky Soldiers all. We could clean up, eat a real meal, have a beer, lick our wounds, and sleep in our home base for a while.

I reported to battalion and gave them a quick update. Then I made sure that the troopers got settled into their tents, got a shower, some real food, and maybe a cold beer. I then went to my hooch, took a shower, and once I was assured that the troops were being well cared for, I crashed on my cot and slept like the dead. A couple days later I recalled that I promised myself that I would personally thank the 173rd Artillery Battalion for their incredible fire support. I drove over to the artillery battalion's headquarters and had lunch with many of their officers and NCOs. They told me that during our firefight, they had almost run out of ammunition, and that the gun tubes were red-hot from firing so many rounds so rapidly. They said that almost every man in the battalion, including the cooks, carried and loaded ammunition during the intense fire mission. After lunch, I visited the various batteries and shook as many hands as I could. Everyone in the battalion said that they were not going to let us get KIA or captured. It was camaraderie in the purest form, Sky Soldiers all. I have always thanked those that helped me achieve successful missions during my career. I have never, ever been able to accomplish anything alone.

SAYING GOODBYE TO CHARLIE COMPANY

Over the next few days, we were able to rest mind and body, regain a few pounds, and maintain our weapons and equipment. I reflected on what we had been through, all the surrounding circumstances, the bigger picture of Vietnam, and on my future in or out of the army. I wrote the painful condolence letters to the families of our fallen and thought about how many difficult letters had already been written during this war and how many more would still have to be written. Writing each one was agonizing, and with every letter I wrote, I thought about the how the family would take the tragic loss of their loved one. Then this thought would always lead me to thinking of how my own mom and dad would react if I had been killed in action. Those gnawing thoughts would grow deeper as I thought of Ann hearing such news.

Ann and I had shared many letters during my entire tour in the 173rd, and she had been spending time with my parents for dinners and holidays. Before leaving Bien Hoa, I bought her a modest, yet exquisite, diamond ring from the PX and mailed the box with a note saying, "I love you. Will you marry me?" We were thousands of miles apart, and after a nine-year relationship that alternated between romantic exhilaration and stressful distancing, I was hoping that we could finally be together and married. Every day I would anxiously check the mail looking for either a letter of acceptance or the little box labeled, "returned to sender." Weeks later, I finally got a letter saying that she had shown the beautiful ring to my mom and sister at the All-Saints Day mass and all the girls at bowling thought the "rock" was beautiful. I took this as an affirmation that we were indeed engaged. A week later I got a letter that she had chosen April 15 to be our wedding day, which would be seven days after my scheduled return from Vietnam. She said she picked that date because it was tax day and I would always remember the anniversary. Although much of the wedding planning seemed trivial compared to the constant reality of combat that I faced in Vietnam, it was actually therapeutic and gave me hope that this too would pass, and I would soon be back in the real world.

MAJOR GENERAL JACK LEIDE USA (RET)

PROFESSIONAL COURAGE

A few weeks before transferring command of Charlie Company I was told that a planned major operation would eventually call for the 2nd Battalion to conduct a combat jump near the Cambodian border as part of Operation Junction City. The operational mission was to clean out some VC and NVA base camps and logistic areas that fed out of the Ho Chi Minh trail. After the combat jump, the battalion would then to act as a blocking force to prevent the NVA from returning to Cambodia as other US forces were attacking from the south. Even though I would not be part of the actual combat jump, which eventually took place in February 1967, I was still in command so would participate in a training jump. We were trucked to the Vietnamese airborne training area near Saigon to undergo a series of standard jump refresher training. As we motored toward Saigon, I talked and laughed with some of the troopers and realized how much I would soon miss them. The humor that evolved among these troopers always provided some relief from the tensions of being in a combat environment and helped break the mind-numbing stress, if only for a short period of time.

On the morning of the jump, I took my position as one of the jumpmasters and made sure every trooper's equipment in my "stick" (line of troopers in one jump order) was safe and secure. I asked my assistant jumpmaster to actually "pass" the troopers out the door; I was going to "stand in the door" (be the first out). As we approached our jump altitude, which was normally at 1,250 feet, we began to level off. Combat jumps can occur at 900 feet and on occasion as little as 400 feet with little or no chance of pulling a reserve. I leaned into the opening in the bulkhead, hands outside the door, and on command, sprung out into the strong prop blast. Once the chute popped, and I felt that hard but comfortable jerk, I was free as a bird and loving every second. I crunched into the drop zone, a vegetable field, with a slight roll and came to a dragging halt. Once we got back to base camp, I realized that I wouldn't have much time left with those wonderful troopers. I would be gone for the planned combat jump and knew they would then be inserted right into one of the most dangerous areas in Vietnam. They most likely would face hard-core NVA units. I prayed, under my breath, for their safety during that dangerous mission ahead. During the following week I had a round of farewells with the officers, NCOs, and troopers in the company and some friends in the battalion. My time with Charlie Company taught me invaluable lessons that I would use and develop throughout my career. Many of my command actions and decisions were primarily performed as a result of training, experience, and instinct. However, I would not have had the physical or mental ability to carry out my missions had I allowed the almost constant element of fear to affect my decisions. Commanders in close combat must control personal emotions, especially fear, through courage. As Mark Twain said, "Courage is resistance to fear, master of fear, not the absence of fear." I thought of that phrase during a final beer together with the Charlie Company officers and NCOs. They gave me a company guidon with all their names embroidered on it. I have that precious guidon on my wall today.

II FIELD FORCE: LONG BINH, SOUTH VIETNAM, DECEMBER 1966–APRIL 1967

The battalion S-1 asked what I wanted to do for the remaining four months of my Vietnam tour. Since I had undergone the training at Eglin to plan, task, and call in close-air support, I thought that I could find a position somewhere in Vietnam where I could use that expertise to help support the troops in the field. Fortunately, I was reassigned to II Field Force as a G-3 (Air) Operations Officer. My responsibility was to collate and prioritize all II Field Force (Three Corps Area) ground force unit requests for close-air support, primarily for air strikes in support of planned or ongoing operations. These support requests could be preplanned (for example request missions one day for the next) or immediate (as a result, for example, of an ongoing contact with the enemy). The job entailed a much more substantive contribution than I had initially anticipated and, in the end, may have been one of the most valuable responsibilities of my career for directly helping ground units. I also had to learn the limitations of close-air support in the jungle environment and the importance of preventing friendly fire incidents. The airborne forward air controllers aboard their small L-19 aircraft were critical to these direct air support missions. They provided effective strike direction and correction while having to know the locations of our units to avoid friendly fire incidents. As I got into the job more and more, I was able recognize unit and flight call signs, what type of aircraft were involved, where they were based and what types of missions they could be tasked to do. I monitored active radio transmissions, particularly between the pilots and the forward air controllers. During the time that I was in that job, I was responsible for planning, allocation, and employment of over 400 tactical air sorties each day in support of tactical combat units.

Importantly, I was learning about the intricacies and methodologies involved with joint operations in a combat environment. I had to establish and maintain continuous daily coordination for close-air support missions between air force, army, and marine assets. I would use this joint warfare experience later in my career, especially as the J-2 during Operation Desert Storm. I wrote the close-air support sections for II Field Force operation orders during twenty-three major combat operations of at least battalion-sized or above. I had experienced the value of close-air support in field combat missions, but listening to the radio transmissions between individual flights of strike aircraft and the forward air controllers provided a feel for how complicated precise coordination of bombing and strafing runs can be. For example, we had to ensure that artillery missions were stopped or continued depending on the air support flights present in the area. We had to prevent supporting artillery rounds accidentally hitting low-flying friendly aircraft. I distinctly remember listening to the transmissions between a three-ship flight of F-4s out of Phan Rang with the call sign "Whiskey."

As they were rolling in for a strafing run, I heard Whiskey 2 blurt out, "Oh shit!"—then nothing. The after-action report for the mission indicated that Whiskey 2 was shot down, crashed, and was KIA.

Talking Strategy: My Time with Harry G. Summers, Jr.

The more I kept reading and thinking about our increasingly large number of heartbreaking daily combat losses, the more I became inwardly aware and critical of some of the various tactical, operational, and strategic decisions being made during the war. Fortuitously, during my tour at II Field Force, I roomed next to Major (later Colonel) Harry G. Summers, Jr. Harry had served as a squad leader during the Korean War and, recently, as a battalion Operations officer in Vietnam. He was now serving as an Operations staff officer at II Field Force. After he retired, Harry became a well-known expert on the strategy of warfare and the author of many best-selling scholarly books on military operations, including the neo-Clausewitzean analysis of the Vietnam War titled On Strategy: A Critical Analysis of the Vietnam War. In 1988 he became the founding editor of Vietnam Magazine. During the Gulf War, he served as a colorful commentator on network television and radio. After the Gulf War, he wrote a follow-up book On Strategy II: A Critical Analysis of the Gulf War. Harry and I spent untold hours discussing the strategy in the Vietnam War, how it should have been fought, or if it should have been fought at all. He was extremely perceptive and had studied Clausewitz and Sun Tzu assiduously, as had I. We discussed that all wars are a result of complicated tenets of interrelationships. Conflicts, which may seem straight forward and logical, but in the end, can be more complicated and nuanced. I had thought about many of those intuitive concepts as well, but not as clearly as Harry did. We agreed that, for now, the real question was not whether the war should be fought. The real question was that if it must be fought, are we fighting it in the right way? After lengthy discussions, we concluded that it was being strategically, operationally, and tactically fought badly. It was said that we never lost a battle, but, in the end, it became a false, erroneous, and eventually one of the more dangerous narratives used in evaluating progress during that war. Harry and I agreed that the North Vietnamese were playing a long strategic game. Both the leadership and the people had the true dedication, infrastructure, and the patience to fight the war to its bitter end and were, in the meantime, bleeding us dry. They had a dedicated VC support infrastructure in South Vietnam that continued to inflict a constant stream of US casualties. Then, when the opportunity was tactically, politically, and chronologically right, in order to cause an almost unacceptable higher rate of casualties, hard-core NVA would strike in strength, and take a high toll in US lives as they had in the early battle of the Ia Drang Valley (and later during Tet and battles such as Hamburger Hill (Dong Ap Bia), Dak To, and Ripcord). These battles not only took a high toll in lives, but were negatively etched, particularly by the press, into the American national psyche.

The South Vietnamese did not have an efficient governmental infrastructure nor the dedication to match the North's. A series of South Vietnamese governments, over time, were so corrupt and inept, that we eventually and figuratively pushed them aside saying, "Step aside, we will fight this war for you." Harry and I just knew, through our studies of military history and how past wars had been fought, won, and lost, that this ongoing conflict was going to be, without question, an eventual unmitigated disaster. When sons and daughters are involved in a distant conflict, and our national interest in that conflict eventually becomes subject to question, the patience and patriotism of the American people would eventually wane. We talked about how the administration and in turn the military chain of command was constantly attempting to convince the American people that there was some approaching light at the bitter end of some interminable tunnel. We had settled on using the number of VC or North Vietnamese killed (body count) as a key barometer of success. Body count numbers were unrealistically and inaccurately compounding at all levels of command, and those inflated numbers were being used as the primary methodology for assessing battlefield success. Commanders and decisionmakers at all levels, including up to the President, were given estimates of progress with data that was eventually inaccurate. As a result, we were subjected to the constant and exaggerated "light at the end of the tunnel" syndrome. Inflationary reporting was occurring at all levels, and commanders and Operations officers were responsible for what was being reported to the higher ups. Success during combat command seemed to depend on a "successfully" higher body count, and human nature and the desire to move on led to an ever-increasing warping of reported successes. In the meantime, we were losing precious lives on the battlefield at an increasingly higher and eventually intolerable rate. Bottom line, we were losing a classic battle of attrition.

During those early days, Intelligence officers worked for the Operations officers and had little influence on the accuracy, balance, and conclusions necessary for the usefulness of final assessment and reporting of enemy losses. I vowed that if I would ever have the opportunity and influence, I would prevent erroneous, warped, and counterproductive enemy assessments from ever occurring under my watch, even if those in the chain of command didn't like it. It would eventually take what I would come to define as "professional courage." The troops and our national interest deserved no less.

I learned a great deal during my discussions with Harry and they contributed to my professional thinking and about my future career in the army. Primarily, I learned that you need to do what you are ordered to do, but you do not need to blindly accept the infallibility of the plan, tactics, or strategy being used or proposed. A commander wants to know "How am I doing?" and an Intelligence officer needs to provide the necessary assessment metrics to measure success or failure, no matter the consequences. Harry and I concluded that there was little in our estimate of wartime progress in Vietnam that realistically would eventually lead to a "mutually agreeable end."

(Those discussions with Harry were taking place during 1966–67. The Tet Offensive had not yet happened, and a so-called village pacification program would eventually be used as a further alternative assessment of progress. The war carried on with various fits and starts until we finally and ignominiously left in1975.) I kept reflecting on a quote from William Shakespeare: "What's past is prologue." History has and will repeat itself. We must learn from it and ensure that those lessons learned are passed on to those that follow.

Red's Promise

Once I was settled in my work at II Field Force, I found some time for other activities. I recalled a promise that a fighter pilot friend named Red had made during one of my "cultural visits" to the Bien Hoa officer's club while I was still in command of Charlie Company. He promised that if the opportunity arose, he would try to take me on a combat mission in an F-100F (The "F" model was a two-seater). I contacted Red and he said that it could happen. He would ask his boss for the go-ahead, and since I was the G-3 (Air), he thought that would help with the approval process. When I talked to my boss, he gave me an eager smile and said that he would do what he could to arrange it. I was elated. A couple days later my boss told me the flight had been approved and was scheduled for two days later and that he would get someone to cover for me. When the day of the flight arrived, I hitched a ride from Long Binh to Bien Hoa.

The F-100, our first supersonic fighter, was a sleek, gleaming machine with blazing speed and packed a potent bomb load. It was a deadly hunter. Red took me to the pilot's ready room, which was stocked with flight suits, gear, and helmets. I was briefed on how man and airplane worked together, that we would be carrying a 1000-pound bomb on each wing, and how the pressured flight vest and oxygen system worked. As we walked around the aircraft, Red did his normal preflight checks, inspected the bomb load, and kicked the tires. The crew chief directed me up the ladder and into the rear seat. He showed me how to hook up my g-force pressure vest, oxygen hose, and how to buckle up. He then pointed out an ominous-looking lever, which, when pulled in an emergency, ignites the explosive device that punches the ejection seat up and out. He pointedly barked, "Unless the pilot is totally incapacitated, do not even think about pulling this thing."

Red slipped in, buckled up, put on his helmet, and once he hooked up his pressure and oxygen systems, he began to crank it up. The engine whined progressively louder then roared into an incredibly powerful sounding blast. We were part of a flight of three and were second in line for takeoff. My heart was beating about a thousand miles an hour, similarly to when I stood in the door for my first parachute jump. We followed behind the lead aircraft and stopped and waited as he turned onto the main runway. Suddenly, the lead punched it and off he went like a bat out of hell. He disappeared down the end of the runway and shot up quickly. You could see the deep bright red, orange and yellow glow at the back of that powerful engine. We followed quickly onto the runway, Red punched it, and we lurched forward like being shot out of a cannon when he kicked it into afterburner. It seemed like we tore into the sky like a rocket ship. I had never felt anything like it before or since. As we leveled off and got into a three aircraft V-formation, Red told me on the intercom that it wouldn't be long before we were over the target, a suspected VC supply and support base. As we approached the target, he dropped to the proper altitude, leveled off for the bomb run, and just as we were passing over the target, all three pilots dropped their thousand pounders at once. The jet lifted quickly as if released from heavy bonds of weight. The flight then turned left and began to look for targets of opportunity. I thought back to fighter planes during World War II, especially North American P-51 Mustang pilots, which, after escorting bombers to and from missions deep into Germany, were then released to find targets of opportunity over Germany and other parts of occupied

Europe. Red raked some sampans (small, wooden boats) on a river, and it was both awesome and devastating at the same time. Once it appeared that he either ran out of targets or ammunition, we were on our way home. Without giving me any warning, he did a 360-degree snap roll. My eyes felt as big as basketballs. I could hear him belly laughing like a crazy man over the intercom. I called him a few select names and as we both continued to laugh heartily, then we were on our way back to Bien Hoa.

As Red smoothly landed the plane, I wondered what it would have been if like I had really become a fighter pilot, like I always wanted to be. I quickly realized that I would likely be dead. I gave Red a big hug, thanked him profusely, and told him I would be back to buy him a beer or two. The next morning, I woke with a renewed spirit, vowing to support all those great fighter pilots to my fullest.

ASSESSING THE "UNPITIED SACRIFICE": TRANSFERRING TO THE MILITARY INTELLIGENCE BRANCH

Since my return to active duty, I had been in combat during 1965, 1966, and 1967 with seemingly nothing to look forward to but continuous reruns in the future. (I did return with the 101st Airborne Division during 1969–1970, so in sum I would be in combat during 1965, 1966, 1967, 1969, and 1970.) I saw myself, for the foreseeable future, in situations where wonderful, youthful soldiers were being lost in a morass of political and military inefficiencies, all reflecting the ebb and flow of the political "whims" of the unfeeling line and block charts at the highest levels.

Just because one believes in the civilian control of the military, and I certainly do, does not mean that standing policies, plans, and directions cannot be flawed. It appeared to us on the ground in Vietnam that there was little understanding by the policymakers for what we were undergoing daily. I kept thinking of a quote from Edmund Burke: "An unpitied sacrifice in a contemptible struggle."

But, in the end, we follow because that's what we are trained to do and "they probably know a lot more than we do."

As a result of that thinking, I again struggled with whether I should I leave the army and those wonderful soldiers. I recalled those gut-wrenching letters that I and so many others had to write, all too often. My thoughts turned to my long-range career plans. Should I stay in the army? In the infantry? I even thought that, since I had a law degree, that I could apply to the FBI as a special agent. My growing personal theory concerning any career is that if you are doing what you love to do, then you will be happy in the long run and eventually successful. I told myself "Do not make the same mistake again and leave your beloved army." I then tried to think of how I could best contribute during our army's present and future conflicts and those wonderful soldiers over the long term. In my own way, I wanted to help them and those that follow them to be successful and survive the future.

I reflected more on my discussions with Harry and realized that I had developed a strong interest in intelligence and enemy order of battle during my time in the brigade S-2. I was now leaning toward transferring to the Military Intelligence Branch. I thought of my two combat tours as an airborne rifle company commander and theorized over what could have made our missions more successful and saved the lives of those wonderful troopers. I concluded that having accurate, current, and actionable intelligence would have been a big facilitator. With proactive and timely intelligence, combatant commanders could be increasingly successful in their decision-making and save precious lives. I had read scores of historical military books on major conflicts and singular battles, and it always seemed that when one side had better intelligence, the probability of battlefield success was indeed much higher. With good, sound intelligence, a commander could be proactive rather than reactive, which is what we mostly seemed to be in Vietnam. After much thought, I finally decided to transfer to the Military Intelligence Branch.

I submitted my request for a branch transfer about halfway through my tour at II Field Force and knew that it would take some time to get through the system. In the meantime, I received orders for my next infantry branch assignment to Fort Monmouth in New Jersey, the home of the US Army Signal School. My projected position was chief of the combat arms committee, which taught Signal officers how the combat arms operated and fought and how the Signal Corps could provide the most effective communications support, especially during combat operations. I sent a quick letter to Ann with a copy of the orders. In the meantime, she was making all the arrangements for our wedding and that helped keep me hopeful and positive during those last few weeks in Vietnam. As the last weeks of my tour approached, my transfer to the Military Intelligence Branch was approved. I was delighted and vowed that I would work hard to make all my assignments in my new branch as productive and useful as possible. I was now assigned to a unit called the US Army Special Research Detachment (SRD) located in the National Security Agency at Fort Meade, Maryland. (I learned during my time in the intelligence world that the more innocuous the title of a unit was, the more sensitive and classified the mission.) As I finished up my tour with II Field Force, I was more than ready for that flight back to the world and Ann. I packed my gear, went through the standard personnel out-processing, and a couple of days later boarded my freedom bird. It seemed like that flight back may have been the longest I have ever experienced, but I dozed with ease, thought of home and getting married, and of joining my new branch in the world of military intelligence. After the plane landed in Syracuse, I bounded to the bottom of the portable stairs, kneeled, and kissed the ground. Ann and I were married a week later. She was a beautiful bride, the love of my life, the wedding was incredibly emotional, and those that attended were those we loved most. We both were looking forward to our new relationship both in marriage and in the army.

CHAPTER 3
MY FIRST EXPERIENCES IN THE WORLD OF INTELLIGENCE

UNITED STATES ARMY SPECIAL RESEARCH DETACHMENT: FORT MEADE, MARYLAND, APRIL 1967–OCTOBER 1969

The first couple that Ann and I met when we arrived at Fort Meade were Captain Paul Hassett and his wife Suellen. On our first night, they graciously invited us to their quarters for dinner and we felt like we had known them forever. They were from Buffalo, and since we were all "upstaters" we bonded immediately and would become close friends for life. They helped us settle into our small apartment, across the street from theirs. Our apartment was humble, but it was ours and we were happy to be together and married.

Paul, an artillery officer, was the adjutant (personnel) for the Special Research Detachment (SRD). The unit was organized into geographically oriented intelligence analysis and production divisions. I was assigned as an analyst in the Asia-Pacific Division. I am not clear why it was assigned to me, but it likely was because there was an open position, and I was the next in line. I was responsible for creating analytical reports on China, Korea, and Japan for the Department of the Army, Component Commands, and the Defense Intelligence Agency. Little did I know that this seemingly off the wall assignment would become a big influence on my future career. My immediate boss was Lieutenant Colonel John "Chris" Christensen. A military Intelligence officer, Chris was totally dedicated to the study of Asia and its mores, and he patiently nurtured me along in my new line of work. Through his calm guidance, I became increasingly fascinated with Asia in general and China in particular. The commander of SRD was Colonel Woodrow J. Shrawder. He had convinced the army's assistant chief of staff for intelligence that the army needed a unique unit to exploit special intelligence, mostly from signals intelligence (SIGINT, the intercept and exploitation of communications and electronics in support of various army units and intelligence products). And, where else to put that unique type of unit except in the very bowels of the National Security Agency (NSA)? He had been given the highest priority for selection of army officers for his new unit, and he eventually picked some of the most highly rated officers in the new Military Intelligence (MI) Branch. I was new to MI, and I didn't know why he had selected me. Since I had just joined the MI Corps, I was way behind the branch power curve. Unfortunately, I had never been to the MI basic or advanced courses. My contemporaries in MI had the schooling and experience that I lacked, and I was also in a later year group because I had left the army for law school.

My job in SRD required compiling mass amounts of SIGINT reports and distilling them into usable intelligence products. Once I had settled into my work, Chris gave me a special mission of providing targeted SIGINT support products to some of the army's special covert and clandestine HUMINT collection units. HUMINT, human intelligence collection, or "spy" tradecraft, is one of the world's oldest professions. Frankly, in simple terms, HUMINT can be overt, covert, or clandestine. Overt collection operations would include missions such POW interrogators and open-source intelligence (OSINT) or the collection of publicly available information such as journals, newspapers, radio, and TV. Military attachés are also overt collectors. Covert collection operations are concealed and would include Special Forces soldiers inserted surreptitiously into an area to collect area intelligence without the knowledge of the local military or civilians. Clandestine human collection involves recruiting foreign nationals who are convinced to turn on their native country for whatever reason, and then they pass on, by various means, their own country's secrets to our Intelligence officers. Clandestine technical collection means, such as cable taps, sensors, and monitors, support the mission's performance and normally is undetected.

I quickly became enamored with the army's covert and clandestine HUMINT units and their varied and valuable worldwide missions. My time with SRD and its predominant SIGINT environment, however cultivated what would become my career-long belief in the incredible value of human intelligence. During that time, the intelligence community was in the throes of an ever-growing dependence on technical sources such as SIGINT and imagery intelligence (IMINT) using satellites and strategic reconnaissance aircraft such as the SR-71 and U-2 as primary means of intelligence collection. As a result, HUMINT was being relegated to playing a lesser role. I thought that diminishing the importance and priority of HUMINT was wrong-headed then and I think that it is wrongheaded now. As I collated information from various collection sources to have more comprehensive and accurate final intelligence reports, I became more and more convinced that the combined use of all-source (Human, Signal, Imagery, Open Source) information in the compilation of data and resultant analytical products would always be exponentially better than using information from only a single source. Using information from multiple types of sources in a single intelligence product is called analytical fusion. I would eventually take this idea a step further by promoting the all-source concept for use in intelligence collections. I used the term collection fusion when I applied an all-source approach to the means and systems used to gain intelligence. I would use collection fusion to great effect during future missions throughout my career, especially during Desert Storm.

About six months after I had arrived at SRD, I read that the elements of the 173rd Brigade had taken part in a series of vicious firefights near Dak To and that the 2nd Battalion had been deeply involved. Of the 3,200 173rd paratroopers taking part in the Battle of Dak To, 27 percent had been either killed (208) or wounded (645). The 173rd's rifle companies sustained 90 percent of the unit's casualties. The single deadliest day during the extended battle of Dak To was November 19, when 83 were killed or wounded. The

North Vietnamese Army (NVA) were mainly involved in the battle. As Harry Summers and I had discussed, their high impact mission was to capture Dak To and, in the battle to follow, destroy a brigade-sized unit for maximum military and political effect. The situation in Vietnam appeared to be getting worse not better, and I was devasted over the tragedy incurred by the troopers in my beloved 173rd. All I could think of was Charlie Company and the many tragic letters of condolence that had to be written to grieving loved ones. I couldn't understand nor condone what had happened then and even to this day.

As I became increasingly involved in my job, my world shifted into a brighter space when Ann became pregnant with our first child. At first, Ann was very homesick, but she finally decided that if all the other army wives could cope, so could she. Things were getting better and better both personally and professionally. We were both excited when Colonel Shrawder also told me that I had made the list for promotion to major, although he did not know when I would actually pin on my new rank.

As Chris saw my dedication to my work and, through our many conversations, knew that I developed an ever-growing personal interest in China, he suggested that I apply for a secondary specialty as a foreign area officer (FAO) for China. He was a FAO and explained that the training included language school, a master's degree in area studies, and an in-country tour to further language and area studies. I became intrigued with his suggestion, researched the career further, and then discussed it with Ann. I was considering another possibly momentous career decision and, naturally, was feeling a bit uncomfortable doing it. FAO training promised to be a challenge, especially the language training (Chinese, according to language experts, is one of the three most difficult foreign languages to learn, along with Russian and Korean), and a total dedication would be required. Ann and I discussed how it would affect my career and our future as a family. We decided to take the leap, and with her support I applied for the China FAO program. We would now again be playing the waiting game

As I became more involved in my projects, I was excited about contributing to important highly classified support missions to our army "Huminters." I was feeling more comfortable in my work with the passing of each day, when the most traumatic experience of my life took place. Ann lost our baby girl, at term. We were totally devastated, and I cried like I had never done before. Thankfully, Ann's mother was a nurse and was with her during that time and helped us get through the worst of the situation and past the pain as best as we could. Fortunately, several months later, we found that she was pregnant again, and we were happy and cautiously optimistic.

When the date of my promotion to major arrived, Ann was not allowed into the highly secretive NSA building to help pin on my new rank. If I could help it, I would never let Ann be excluded again. Colonel Shrawder, whom I deeply admired, promoted me. I learned to treat my subordinates the way Colonel Shrawder treated me. He frequently called me into his office, and we discussed not only operational but also some army-wide topics. From Colonel Shrawder, I learned one of the most important lessons of my career: to always seek information, opinions, advice, and recommendations from subordinates. Having been promoted, we became eligible for single quarters on post. When Ann and I first saw them, although they were not large, they seemed like a palace. As time went on, I continued enjoying my work, especially knowing that I was directly supporting operational army units. I never stopped thinking about "those guys out there." Throughout my career, supporting the troops and their missions always gave me a clear priority of effort at every level.

I culled information from voluminous, highly classified files that I sifted through each day and produced tailored reports for those organizations that I was supporting. My work was mostly involved in what we call special access programs. When I had collected enough information to satisfy some or all of the requested intelligence requirements, I would put my finished reports in a large leather briefcase, chained and locked on my wrist, and visit the various army covert and clandestine units that we supported. We were fully dedicated to protecting that information and the people involved in its collection, with our lives if necessary. Those who risk their personal safety in dedication to intelligence collection are invaluable to our nation and deserve no less. The army units I was supporting truly appreciated my efforts, and they frequently told me that the type, scope, level of detail, and value of information that I was providing had been sorely lacking in the past

My First Knock on the Green Door

At Colonel Shrawder's recommendation, I was selected by the army's assistant chief of staff for intelligence to lead a unique and long overdue senior study group to look into procedural changes needed to improve the tactical and operational use of highly classified signals intelligence. I was a brand-new major responsible for a study group that included lieutenant colonels and colonels, so I knew that I had to work hard to gain their confidence. During our sessions, we painstakingly developed methodologies that would provide highly classified SIGINT information more quickly to the lowest levels of command without compromising sensitive sources. For example, we devised and recommended a system where information gathered through SIGINT sources could be "covered" or have "plausible deniability or cover" by feigning being acquired by other, less sensitive sources such as interrogations.

Our main objective was to establish new procedures so we could use SIGINT-collected information being held behind the green door, down at the lowest possible level to support the deployed forces in a timely, useful way. I don't know the origins of the term green door, but within the intelligence community, green door is slang and refers to restricting access to SIGINT-collected information, collection capabilities, or unit locations. "We Green Doored them" means that the access to information was shut down. The main problem was that SIGINT acquired information was highly classified as Top-Secret SI (Special Intelligence) or Secret SI level. To release the derived information to a combat unit required a time-consuming process, and the decision of how to disseminate or how much to disseminate was made at high levels of the command structure. The procedures were bureaucratic, excruciatingly slow, and counterproductive, especially at the operational and tactical level.

Our team created practical, thorough, and compelling conclusions and recommendations in the final study version, and it was concise and uncomplicated. I felt that it was a critical effort toward breaking down that green door and to providing SIGINT obtained intelligence in a more timely way, down to the most practical level of operational units. However, once the study was completed and presented to the intelligence bureaucracy, including some representatives of the SIGINT community, it died a slow, ignominious death. I quickly learned that the traditional Intelligence bureaucracy was alive, well, and deeply entrenched. During my career, I would encounter that infamous green door again and again. I vowed to work hard, over time, to crack it open. We would finally kick it wide open during Desert Storm.

The Call of the Eagles

In the spring of 1969, as my time at SRD was coming to an end, Vietnam was still on most everyone's military mind. Career-wise, I was well behind my MI contemporaries and needed a combat tour's experience to help burnish my new branch qualifications and professional competence. The chief of staff of the 101st Airborne Division in Vietnam was Colonel "Mac" MacDonald. I knew him when he was a battalion commander when we were both in the 82nd Airborne Division. I sent Colonel Mac a message and told him that I wanted to return to Vietnam and asked him to request me by name for an intelligence slot with the Screaming Eagles. He quickly cabled back with some encouragement and said he would try his best. The chief of staff of any division carries a great deal of weight and since I had "done my time" in SRD, I was getting ripe for a reassignment anyway.

Shortly thereafter, I received orders to report to the 101st Airborne Division in November of 1969. I had mixed emotions about leaving Ann, especially since she was pregnant, but I knew that she would be comfortable and have a great support structure in Auburn. Ann was supportive of what I wanted and what I thought was best for us and my career. She would stay with her mother and have our baby in the comfort of our hometown with the support of both our families. As my time at SRD came to a close, we said our farewells to our friends and colleagues, packed up, and headed to Auburn with a tremendous pride that we had made it through our first tour together. We were happy and optimistic for the future and were hoping, by the grace of God, that I would make it through my second combat tour in Vietnam. After enjoying a couple of weeks of leave in Auburn, I got my Saint Anthony medal from mom, kissed Ann goodbye, patted her belly, and headed to the airport in Syracuse.

A SCREAMING EAGLE: 101ST AIRBORNE DIVISION, CAMP EAGLE, PHU BAI, VIETNAM

In November of 1969, after a series of bleak flights across the Pacific, I arrived back in steamy Vietnam. Since the 101st Airborne Division was in the northern I Corps area of South Vietnam, we landed in Da Nang, near our main base at Camp Eagle. As we arrived, I reflected on when I first had the Screaming Eagle patch sewn on my fatigues and the proud and valorous history of the division. In World War II, the 101st had parachuted into Nazi-occupied France on D-Day. My mind raced back to Charlie "Catfish" Bryant, who, as a young private in the 101st, had jumped at night into the great unknown in Normandy. During the Battle of the Bulge in December 1944, while under-supplied and outgunned, the 101st had held off the German Army during their valiant defense of Bastogne.

When I returned to Vietnam for this tour, the US troop strength had been reduced from a high of 536,000 to about 400,000 and was dropping at a consistent rate each month. President Nixon had just announced the "Vietnamization" of the war, and US troops were steadily being withdrawn. The 101st was scheduled be one of the last full army divisions remaining in the country. The division's important mission was to prevent large numbers of NVA units from moving south to provide the South Vietnamese time to organize, train, and equip for their fight ahead. Since the "Vietnamization" was supposed to be gradual, the 101st still had an important area of operations and a viable mission.

Instead of having to layover in Da Nang overnight, the 101st sent a shuttle "slick" to transport in-bound division newbies to Camp Eagle. As I boarded the chopper, and the clacking rotors began to cough and whirl, I had visions of ghosts of my sky soldiers sitting on the chopper floor with their feet hanging down ready to pounce. As we approached Camp Eagle, I was struck by the huge numbers of aircraft including slicks, Cobra gunships ("Snakes"), and huge transport twin-rotored CH-47 ("Chinooks") on the expansive pads below. The division was mostly airmobile, with some smaller elements still airborne. Camp Eagle was located just outside the little Vietnamese village of Phu Bai and near the ancient Imperial Vietnamese capital of Hue. That historically beautiful city had been totally devastated by brutal urban combat between our marine, army, and South Vietnamese battalions and the VC and North Vietnamese during the Tet Offensive in February of 1968.

The 101st Airborne Division was still suffering a residual pallor from the disastrous Battle of Hamburger Hill (also known as Hill 937 or Dong Ap Bia) six months earlier. The division had suffered

72 killed and 372 wounded during that ten-day battle in May of 1969.

Those in the division assiduously avoided referring to that tragedy as Hamburger Hill due to the dreadful human connotation that the term represented. The media had invented that term and related it to the equally disastrous battle in Korea called Porkchop Hill. Both were catchy newspaper-selling phrases for bloody, terrible combat disasters. During this battle, like many others, the division had been ordered to attack and occupy an NVA heavily fortified hill, which, supposedly, had little or no tactical or strategic value. Our commanders initially called the effort "a reconnaissance in force." In the end, our losses were disastrous. After our troops eventually captured and occupied that bloody place, they were then ordered to abandon it. In the three years since I was last in Vietnam, our forces had lost thousands of lives during similar missions. We were fighting for and taking military objectives and then abandoning them with little tactical outcome except an inordinate amount of casualties on each side. This was another example of what Harry Summers and I had discussed concerning the NVA creating highly visible heavy US unit losses and the press playing tragedy to the hilt. Again, we were losing the classic battle of attrition. I vowed that I would do whatever I could to help prevent more of these bloody fiascos while I was with the 101st and during any future assignments. When I got to Camp Eagle, most of the 101st's combat infantry and artillery brigades and battalions were deployed to base camps and fire support bases in or near the A Shau Valley and ringing Camp Eagle. The A Shau Valley, a rugged, remote passageway near the border of Laos, runs north and south for twenty-five miles and was a key entry point during the Vietnam War for bringing personnel and logistics in support of North Vietnamese and VC military efforts around Hue to the northeast and Da Nang to the southwest. The positioning of the 101st was intended to prevent the North Vietnamese from moving large units and logistics south.

As I jumped out of the chopper and got into a waiting jeep, I got the feeling that the huge base was relatively distant from the sound of the guns and mentioned it to the driver. I was quickly informed that the division area was ringed by enemy firing positions and the VC and NVA would periodically fire mortars, especially 122mm rockets, into our sprawling base. The troopers called Camp Eagle "Rocket Alley". The driver dropped me off at the division headquarters where I signed in, got my basic supply of field equipment, a .45 pistol, and then was shown to a four-person sleeping tent. I later put a sign over that hootch, in jest, naming it "le splendide" (the splendid). Once I finished putting my gear in the hootch, I walked over to the division headquarters and reported to Colonel MacDonald. It was great to see his familiar friendly face, and I knew Colonel "Mac" as a great guy and leader. He told me that I would be initially slotted as the chief of the division G-2 Plans.

The G-2 Plans and Order of Battle Section

During my first session with the division G-2, he told me that the Plans Section had been rudderless. He hoped that I could improve on the quality and quantity of its contributions to the division's intelligence efforts. Since this was my first non-infantry combat assignment, I felt apprehensive but also welcomed the challenge. When I first arrived in Plans, I immediately observed that the section, especially the Order of Battle Shop, had smart, dedicated young officers, Order of Battle warrant officers, and noncommissioned officers (NCOs). I immediately assessed our present procedures and missions and knew we had to change them. We had to be more concise, detailed, and timely in our assessments and more predictive in our analysis of enemy intent and probable enemy courses of action. As a former combat commander, I knew we needed to provide predictive information so that division headquarters and our combat units could be proactive, rather than reactive, in their tactical decision-making. The G-2 Plans and Order of Battle Section's primary task was to produce the intelligence annexes for all division-level operational plans and orders. We needed to provide detailed usable information on the Viet Cong (VC) and North Vietnamese forces our units would be facing in the division area of operations. We were also responsible for all division intelligence planning and the collation of collection requirements, analysis, and intelligence products. To accomplish those missions, I relied heavily on the Order of Battle Shop, which analyzed all known key enemy unit information such as organization, capabilities, locations, weapons, strengths, weaknesses, tactics, morale, future intentions, and operational tactics and strategy. I learned a great deal about the critical importance of the assessing the enemy's capabilities, strengths, and weaknesses from the Order of Battle warrant officers. Sun Tzu's theorem "know your enemy" was now becoming a priority focus for my efforts. We were responsible for providing combat units in the 101st with accurate intelligence. This intelligence would help them devise and use the most efficient and effective tactics to defeat enemy forces and save lives. This was the very reason that I transferred to MI.

I initiated some new procedures and products. We produced situational and appropriate daily order of battle reports and distributed them down to the combat brigades and battalions. We also initiated topical products such as a Booby Trap Reference Guide, which we distributed down to the squad level. Our products and contributions were being frequently acknowledged by the division leadership and brigade and battalion commanders. Except for being in Vietnam and being away from Ann, I was now becoming more and more comfortable with my decision to transfer to MI.

Operational Missions

Although we were a staff section, we developed enough credibility with the command group that they tasked us with some unique operational support missions. One such mission was the responsibility for providing tasking requirements and direction for the division rangers ("L" Company, 75th Ranger Regiment), which had been transitioned from our division Long Range Reconnaissance Patrol unit in February. We provided the rangers with missions to collect targeted intelligence on enemy unit locations, dispositions, and activity and to provide surveillance of enemy movement along trails and other lines of communications. The rangers were responsive and professional and did a masterful job every time. For me personally, our rangers provided a positive and invaluable introduction to the world of Special Operations.

Our second unusual operational mission concerned the marines. After covering for the marines move out of Khe Sanh, the 101st had replaced them in the northern area of operations in Vietnam (I Corps) when the 3rd Marine Division, redeployed out of country. The marines left behind the incredibly valuable, capable, and aggressive 3rd Force Reconnaissance Unit, and they were attached to the 101st Airborne. Division headquarters tasked us to provide them with intelligence collection missions. Their commander, a major, was an incredible combat leader. We established a close personal and professional relationship. I often visited the unit in Phu Bai where they were billeted and trained. One day over lunch in their mess tent, I told him that we had a special mission planned for them in the A Shau Valley, near key entry and exit points of the Ho Chi Minh Trail. We had intelligence that large, battle-hardened NVA units were about to move through the area for possible future combat missions further south in I Corps, possibly around Danang, or even further south into II or III Corps. We needed up-to-date information on that movement, their strength, and probable intentions.

We provided them with as much known recent intelligence, collection requirements, and area information as we could muster. We ensured that they had the necessary type and amount of equipment, weapons, and communications gear. We also provided a detailed plan for insert into the objective area and identified some potential small landing zones in the general area for eventual egress out of the area. We airlifted them to the target area in the A Shau. As they approached the thick triple-canopy jungle, there was no immediate landing zone available, and since we wanted their insertion to be as quick and stealthy as possible, they fast-roped into the target area. (Fast roping is a technique for descending on a thick rope and is useful for deploying troops from a helicopter into places where the helicopter itself cannot touch down, like into the bowels of the valley's dark, wet jungle floor.)

After they had been operating in the area for about three days and providing us with some valuable information on NVA tactical and logistical movement, they got into in a minor firefight and sustained two slightly wounded marines. Once I received the report of the contact, I felt that their position in that rat's nest had been compromised and they needed to get out of there, fast. But when I recommended a rapid extraction to the commander, he replied that he didn't think their situation warranted a withdrawal at that time and that they could probably stick it out for one or two more days. His tactical assessment may have been courageous, but it was not situationally aware. The latest intelligence I had just received indicated that his position had been fully compromised. Finally, I was able to convince him that they needed to get the hell out of there. We vectored them to a small clearing where we safely evacuated them all out by chopper. They had done a great job and provided important intelligence that probably led to tactical successes and saved lives. The memory of their invaluable contribution and dedication to a joint service mission has remained with me after all these years. I have always admired and worked proudly with the marines.

Facing that Damned Green Door, Again!

We were acquiring some of our best and most timely tactical intelligence from signals intercepts. But even when we had signals information that could tactically tip or warn a combat unit, the infamous green door obstructed the timeliness and effectiveness of the information. This was the same door that I had tried to break open, even if with just a nudge, while at Fort Meade. During this tour with the 101st, there were several instances where we had to personally obtain the corps commander's permission (a three-star general) to release the information that would either assist in a unit's mission or warn them when they were in jeopardy. If the corps commander was not available, the deputy corps commander was delegated to release the information for dissemination. The process continued to be unbelievably short-sighted. I understand the sensitivity of the sources and that the capability must be protected, but we weren't making the proper effort to provide "cover" by using other possible sources of the information. Delaying the dissemination of valuable, time-sensitive information to troop units frustrated me to no end. I thought about the critical information derived from the breaking of the German (Enigma) and Japanese Navy (Purple) codes during World War II. Those sources were very strictly held, but at times, such as during the Battle of Midway, they were critical to that successful encounter. During World War II, those sources could be strictly protected and released in a more usable, covered format due to the longer time frames ensuing between large critical battles. In Vietnam, the battles and contacts were smaller, more frequent, and occurred more rapidly than those during World War II or even Korea. During Desert Storm, because of the rapidity of action during certain phases of the operation, I, with the help of my signals intelligence staff, would break down as many barriers as we could. We would create rapid procedures and communications in support of our commander, service components, coalition partners, and particularly our Special Forces and the British SAS (Special Air Service).

Khe Sanh Revisited?

One morning I was called to the G-3's (Division Operations Officer) office to discuss a somewhat curious operational mission. The G-3 was Lieutenant Colonel Charles W. "Bill" Dyke, an intense, brilliant officer who had earned his commission through Officer Candidate School. He had recently relinquished command of a 101st Infantry Battalion and we carried on some small talk about the exigencies of the current situation, both for the 101st, and the war in general. He then turned to the issue at hand. The division had been given a warning order for a possible mission to recover the pierced steel planking that was left on the airfield at Khe Sanh once the marines had moved out. The mission had him worried, and he asked if I could help him establish whether the mission was combat feasible and worth the effort. I told him that I could do a summary estimate of the situation in and around Khe Sanh, but the best choice would be a full-blown intelligence estimate, which would be an extensive, detailed, and deliberative process that could take some time. When I asked him how long I had to do the assessment, he said that he needed it the next day around the same time. I gulped, saluted, and told him that I would see him the next day with whatever appropriate final product we could come up with. He told me to do the best I could. I felt in my bones that this operation was a bad idea, but an intelligence officer must tell it like it is, based on proven intelligence information and procedures, not personal feelings or opinions.

As soon as I got back to the Plans Shop, I did some rapid culling through our records for an example and could not find that a classic intelligence estimate had been recently produced in the division. I then took a quick look at our current enemy order of battle for the Khe Sanh area and saw that there were several North Vietnamese hardcore regiments in the area. I knew they were spoiling for a fight and licking their chops at the possibility of setting up another tactical trap. I looked up the processes and procedures for an estimate in a dog-eared intelligence manual and held a quick planning meeting with key experts in the section then parceled out various parts of the estimate to each of them to research. We worked the rest of that day and all night, gathering all available appropriate pieces of information, collating it all, and putting together a comprehensive final report. Many precious lives were at stake, and I had vowed to myself to protect those Screaming Eagles to the best of my ability. We pieced the final report together: weather, terrain, enemy order of battle, enemy avenues of approach, enemy likely courses of action, and the final summation what I thought would be the most likely enemy courses of action. The report was not as comprehensive as I would have liked, but it was the best we could do within the allotted time frame.

As an Intelligence officer, I could not suggest what the G-3 should recommend to the command group, but through our assessment, I thought we made the case that the plan was not worth putting lives at stake just to recover some pieces of planking. I gave our final report to Lieutenant Colonel Dyke who thanked me and said he would read it in full and devise what his operational presentation and final recommendations should be. He then took it with him to the command group for the decision-making session. Later, that afternoon, he called me to his G-3 hooch and said, with some intensity, "Jack, that was the best piece of intelligence work I have ever seen. I presented a summary of its in-depth information and main conclusions to the command group, strongly recommended that the mission be scrubbed, and they wholeheartedly agreed." I was delighted. Bill Dyke was known to be loath to offer praise outwardly. (I would be privileged to later work with Bill Dyke, in Japan, when he was a three-star general, commanding US Army, Japan.)

I was convinced we helped save precious lives. My experiences in the 101st reinforced my confidence in the value of focused, accurate, predictive, and cogently presented intelligence to the missions of military units or organizations at any level. When I told my team the result of the command decision, they all were proud and knew their hard work had been well worth the effort. I thanked them from the bottom of my heart. We were making a difference. Intelligence was making a difference.

Degradation of Combat Unit Capability

As I moved around the division, visiting the various fire bases, reading operational after-action reports, and talking to second-tour vets in the infantry battalions, I noticed what I thought was a degradation of the combat capabilities of divisional infantry units, especially at the company level. I wondered how that could be the case in an elite unit like the 101st. After some research, I concluded that the two main reasons were that the company commanders and especially the NCOs were much less experienced than in past years. During Vietnam, the average time a combat infantryman spent on actual combat missions was an astounding 240 days per year. (As compared to 10 days per year in the Pacific during World War II.) One main reason was the helicopter, which mobilized the infantry into combat areas quickly and often. For an officer like me, this duration of time in an infantry unit was tough, but not nearly as tough as for the infantry soldier and especially the NCOs. Officers would spend about six or seven months in a combat infantry company and then rotate out to a staff job for the remainder of his one-year tour. However, the average NCO, unless he became ill or was wounded, would normally spend his entire twelve-month tour assigned to an infantry company. During that year, they would spend an incredible amount of time in trying combat conditions. The NCO would then return "to the world" and normally, after a year, be sent back for another combat tour. It was devastating, not only to the NCOs, but also to their families. As the war continued over the years, experienced NCOs had either been killed, badly wounded, or decided after repetitive tours, that they would retire instead of putting themselves and their families through a third or fourth combat infantry tour. The experienced NCO corps was being decimated, and we now had relatively junior and inexperienced NCOs throughout our combat units.

To compound the problem, many of the company commanders had been promoted to captain after only two years in the army. They were willing, but inexperienced, and were being given command of a rifle company, which was excruciatingly challenging and dangerous without the invaluable help and guidance from experienced NCOs. Even in an elite unit like the 101st Airborne Division, the lack of experienced NCOs was a key reason for the apparent degradation of unit capability, morale, and efficiency. Experienced NCOs are the backbone of the army.

Time for a Cigar

In the latter part of January, Ann's due date was very near, and I was more than anxious. I was thankful that she was living with her mother, who, as a nurse, knew all the best physicians and her way around the hospital. One day toward the end of January, I was on my way to the mess hall for lunch when a Red Cross representative approached me and asked if I was Major Leide. My thoughts were in many places when I stammered a distant reply. I almost fell to my knees in anticipation of his next words, when he finally said that Ann had a baby boy, and both were doing fine. It was like I had lapsed into a wonderful, euphoric dream. He said he would arrange a MARS call through the Red Cross in the States for a certain time on a certain day. (MARS: Military Auxiliary Radio System was a military sponsored group of skilled civilians who were volunteer, amateur radio operators who provided connections from phones in Vietnam to phone numbers in the United States.) The call took place while Ann was still in the hospital. This would be the only time I would talk to her during that long year. Luckily, she knew the protocol of MARS calls, such as saying "over" when done talking. It was wonderful to hear the joy in her voice. She told me that our son's name was John Francis, named after her brother, a firefighter, who had died in the line of duty. After we completed our conversation, she turned the phone over to my mom who couldn't quite figure out the "over" part and the conversation got garbled and mostly unintelligible. After I hung up, I went to the PX, got some cigars and shared them with some of the guys. Ann would send me pictures of John every so often, but unfortunately, I would not see him until he was about ten months old. It's almost unbelievable how a military family makes so many sacrifices, some of which are almost unimaginable to many. Fortunately, or unfortunately, those strained situations and sacrifices can either make a military family stronger or, in many cases, it breaks them apart. Fortunately, ours became stronger.

TAKING COMMAND OF THE 101ST MILITARY INTELLIGENCE COMPANY

In February of 1970, I was nearing the end of a professionally gratifying tour in the Plans and Order of Battle Section when the G-2 told me that I had been selected to command the 101st Military Intelligence Company. This would be my third company command in combat, a real rarity, and I was looking forward to the challenge. Having the knowledge of the intelligence requirements in the G-2 Plans and Order of Battle Section, I felt confident that I could help lead the MI company in the accomplishment of its varied intelligence collection support missions.

My replacement in the Plans and Order of Battle position was an infantry major who had just left a line infantry battalion as the executive officer and had little to no experience in MI. He was a quiet, unassuming West Point graduate, Major Jim Johnson. Jim had a fantastic attitude and was very professional and anxious to learn. He worked exceptionally hard, as I worked equally hard to help Jim learn the ropes. He wound up doing a superb job and, importantly, gained the confidence of Bill Dyke and the command group.

Later in my career, I fortunately would have the privilege of working with Jim in some very challenging places and situations. Once I had officially passed the section baton to Jim, I took command of the 101st Military Intelligence Company in March of 1970.

When I arrived at the company headquarters, the first soldier that I met was chief warrant officer-1 Mike Fried. As a German Jew in Nazi Germany, Mike was six years old when he was interred in a concentration camp in Holland along with his mother and sister. They were confined for four years, under a constant threat of execution, until liberated by the Canadian Army in 1945. Mike and his family then moved to the United States in 1955. When he became eligible, Mike enlisted in the US Army. Having native fluency in the German language and understanding the national culture and mores, he was an invaluable asset to our army's intelligence and counterintelligence missions during the Cold War, especially as an interrogator and translator. He was now my administrative officer, and I relied on him more than anyone else in the company. He basically ran the administrative side of the company so I could concentrate on our operational missions. One of the proudest moments of my life was when I promoted Mike to chief warrant officer-2. Mike eventually became a rock in the Intelligence Corps, reaching the highest levels of warrant officer rank, CWO-5, and was selected for every MI Hall of Fame distinction in existence. He has spent decades of faithful and invaluable service to his adopted country, and as of this writing, he still goes to work every day as a volunteer at a MI unit near his home. Mike and I remain close friends to this day, and I am most proud and privileged to have known and worked with him.

The Importance of Military Interrogators

One of the units under my command was the Division Interrogation Section, whose mission was the combat interrogation of prisoners of war. I had been in command for a couple of weeks when one of our infantry battalions captured some NVA soldiers in the A Shau Valley. The assistant division commander for Operations, who I knew well and respected from my days in Plans, was aware of the time-sensitive value and accuracy of the information coming from recently captured prisoners. He asked about the status of the prisoners and if we had obtained any useful information from them. I recognized that valuable timely intelligence, in many circumstances, comes from prisoners of war. I reassured him that I thought our interrogators knew the intelligence requirements and that they would soon be on their way out to the field. That was a bad assumption and a big, big mistake on my part. Instead of doing a timely interrogation in the field, our interrogators waited until the prisoners eventually were brought back to our POW "cage" near Camp Eagle. They had then conducted a casual and poor interrogation. Their eventual reports were not only too late to be of any tactical use, but, as far as I was concerned, badly written.

    I was furious and vowed to investigate what had happened. From my time with the division Order of Battle Shop, I knew the importance of current and responsive information elicited from prisoners by professional interrogators. During my after-action session with the Interrogation Section chief, a captain, and his team members, I knew we had big problems, including the team's lack of expertise and sense of urgency. I talked to other members of the company, including Mike Fried, who was a trained interrogator. I discovered that most members of the interrogation team spent an inordinate amount of time sitting around seeing who could record the most music on their new reel-to-reel tape players. I vowed to quickly address this unacceptable situation and to solve it quickly. I then collected and read field manuals, lesson plans, and as much information as I could about combat tactical interrogation objectives, procedures, and techniques.

    A couple days later, and before I could solve our interrogator problem, I received a call from the G-2 that we had captured more NVA prisoners in the A Shau. I quickly put on my tiger stripe jungle fatigues, requested a standby helicopter, scooped up an interrogator/interpreter from our attached South Vietnamese intelligence unit, grabbed our duty interrogator and a couple of radios, and headed for the A Shau jungle site. Although it was more life-threatening and less convenient to interrogate in the field, especially in the A Shau, this was an integral component of a required operational mission in a combat MI unit. The key to a successful combat interrogation is to get to the prisoners quickly rather than wait for prisoners to get to you. Time is of the essence. The information we could derive during a hot interrogation could save lives and be a valuable key to a tactical unit's success.

As we headed toward the A Shau in a slick, I could not help but think of the combat air assaults into the crab trap. As the dense, mangled jungle of the A Shau Valley came into view, my mind was filled with a jumble of conflicting memories of death, fear, and wonderful camaraderie. After we landed and disembarked from the chopper, we were escorted to a small, cleared area where several North Vietnamese prisoners were being guarded by our infantry soldiers. This would be the first eyeball-to-eyeball contact I had with live NVA soldiers. I told the interrogator and interpreter to quickly get on with their interrogation. I watched closely as they talked to the prisoners (one of the POWs was an officer). Much to my amazement and horror, our interrogator pulled out a list of questions from a standard interrogation form he had copied from a field manual. I blanched as he asked a series of peripheral, almost nonsensical, questions. His interrogation was virtually unrelated to what I knew were current key divisional and unit tactical order of battle essential elements of information. As he continued the interrogation from that canned checklist, I stopped him. I took his checklist and, as I looked at the remainder, I spotted the question, "Does your unit have nuclear weapons?" I blanched, quickly pulled him from the interrogation, and personally took over. With the invaluable help of our South Vietnamese intelligence interrogator/interpreter, we approached the interrogation using essential elements of information that I recalled from my days in the order of battle shop and from what I knew of the mission of our divisional units conducting blocking operations in the A Shau. Our Vietnamese interrogator used tried and true techniques of interrogation including ways of identifying prisoners who may or may not cooperate. He decided which "approach" or methodology provided the best basis for how to ask, what to ask, and in what sequence. Luckily, two of the prisoners appeared cooperative, which was rare in Vietnam.

I provided our Vietnamese interrogator with the most salient questions to ask, and he took it from there. As he interrogated each prisoner, he relayed the important tactical information to me, especially on key NVA unit strengths, intentions, and planned infiltration routes through the A Shau. I immediately transmitted that information to division headquarters and our division ground units most affected. After-action reports showed that because of our information, our ground combat units and the air force were able to identify the infiltration routes and attack the identified units, probably killing large numbers of NVA while destroying a large quantity of weapons and equipment destined for units further to the south.

Combat interrogation is truly an art and, frankly, I had neither expertise nor experience in its practice. Fortunately, our very capable South Vietnamese interrogator had a knowledge of the NVA military situation and aims and gained a feel for each prisoner's personal, cultural, and political situations and resultant attitudes. This experience reinforced my growing respect for the capability of those with local knowledge, military expertise, and native language fluency. I knew such assets had great potential during military operations.

Once we returned to the Camp Eagle, I quickly devised a plan to make our Interrogation Section second to none. I ordered them to spend half of each day in the Order of Battle Shop to work with the analysts and learn what the key elements of information of the day were and why. The other half-day would be spent honing their interrogation skills, working closely with our Vietnamese intelligence team, using current lesson plans that we acquired, added to, or modified, maintaining their equipment, especially rapid communications gear, and collating and updating the radio frequencies and call signs for the various divisional field units. I directed the section chief to create rapid deployment teams, including an increased involvement of our attached Vietnamese unit members. I also told them to acquire and train with upgraded communications gear and to develop standing operations procedures for rapid response and reporting. From that poorly structured, poorly led, and under-performing team, they eventually became a high-powered professional and important asset to our division intelligence collection capabilities. They were good, proud soldiers who just needed the proper mission guidance, structure, and encouragement to succeed in their important mission.

Sensors: A Look Into the Future

Another company unit was the Sensor Platoon. They were charged with developing, maintaining, and deploying a new type of system technology. When employed and implanted by hand or air, this technology would sense and broadcast radio signals to indicate signs of enemy movement. We were designated by the army as a leading test bed for this potentially valuable developmental program. The main objective of use in our area was to help detect size and frequency of movement through the A Shau Valley and on certain portions of the Ho Chi Minh Trail. After some trial and error, we had some unique successes of enemy movement detection resulting in the deployment of ground units in rapid response and the use of air power targeting the pinpointed areas of enemy movement. This new technology, as far as I was concerned, had enormous potential and we continued to develop and test them in some unique ways, places, and circumstances. Unfortunately, and I don't know why, the program eventually received less and less priority and funding, but we carried on the best we could with what we had. However, I believe that the much of the development of the modern "network-centric warfare" is an outgrowth of our initial successes in the sensor program in Vietnam. This would be my first real experience with a "new" category of intelligence collection, which we eventually would call MASINT, or measurements and signatures intelligence. I would later become intimately involved with MASINT as a major responsibility. Those early efforts led to the eventual development of today's Unattended Ground Sensors.

Ripcord: A Last Hurrah

On March 12, 1970, our 3rd Brigade began rebuilding an abandoned fire support base called Ripcord. The base was deep in the A Shau Valley, in the same general area as the infamous Battle of Hamburger Hill one year earlier. Based on our intelligence summaries, I knew that Ripcord was in a remote but critical location, blocking the NVA's unrestricted movement through the A Shau to the south. My research, analysis and reporting indicated that its existence could not and would not be tolerated by the NVA. It was only reachable by chopper. When 3rd Brigade began to reestablish the base, the NVA immediately began attacking it and sporadic attacks would continue to until June 30. The NVA began a siege on the base in earnest on July 1st. The division reserve battalion was finally sent to the 3rd Brigade. However, the fear of another Hamburger Hill may well have prevented the division from continuing to reinforce, as we might have well done previously in the war. Once that battle had been joined, the fear of repeated bad press caused media coverage in the area to be strictly discouraged. After undergoing brutal attacks for over three weeks, the 3rd Brigade was finally ordered to withdraw on July 23rd, and Ripcord was then occupied by the NVA. That July battle had cost the lives of seventy-five of our precious troopers. Our chopper pilots performed incredible acts of valor evacuating our soldiers out of the base. Our withdrawal led to unrestricted movement through that area to the south by a large number of NVA troop units. During the entire period of the battle for Ripcord, beginning from March 12 to July 23, a total of 139 troopers had been killed in action. No doubt the NVA suffered huge losses during the battle caused by our 3rd Brigade infantry units, supporting artillery, helicopter gunships, and the incessant heavy pounding they took by our air force, including B-52 bombers. But politically, they could afford the losses, we could not. Our actions in and around Ripcord may have delayed the NVA's inexorable movement south by a few months. But, since the President had previously announced the "Vietnamization" of the war, the die was now cast. Ripcord would be the last recorded major battle between US ground forces and the NVA in the Vietnam War.

The conduct and result of Ripcord again illustrated the crux of what Harry Summers and I had talked about three years earlier. The ultimate use of battle-hardened NVA units were attacking singular US troop positions and inflicting an inordinately large number of casualties, resulting in the inevitable negative press coverage. As a result, due to political pressures, our decision-makers were now focused on minimizing casualties rather than closing with and destroying the enemy. It was like putting a finger in a cracking dike. Our strategic military decisions were being increasingly influenced by political timidity and the negative press. The mantra that we never lost a battle in Vietnam was now disproved by Ripcord. Not for lack of courage or battlefield capability of the Screaming Eagles, but because of those who were pulling the strategic political strings. In the end, it proved to be a continuing recipe for ultimate failure.

LEAVING CAMP EAGLE

My tour with the 101st, although certainly not as treacherous as my tour with the 173rd, was not without its life-threatening moments.

As I mentioned earlier, Camp Eagle was under an almost constant threat of 122mm rocket fire. During most days, one could hear the loud blasts of incoming rockets or mortars launched from "rocket alley" in various areas around the confines of Camp Eagle. Toward the end of my tour, while writing reports in my office, I heard a deafening explosion just outside and felt a tremendous blast that tore the screens on my windows and ripped my door half off. I ran outside and saw that one of our ¾-ton trucks had been directly hit and was obliterated into a mass of twisted metal.

As my second tour in Vietnam wound down, I again reflected at the type of "progress" we were making in the war. I had an uneasy feeling that the bureaucrats had replaced the body count metric with "winning the hearts and minds" of the Vietnamese people as measure of our success. Early in the war, we had adopted village and provincial "pacification programs." These programs were started as the Civil Operations and Rural Support Program, which had some successes. After the Tet Offensive in January 1968, pacification was given renewed emphasis. The government bean-counters created and presented countless variations of colored charts and graphs to indicate the degrees of pacification of Vietnamese towns and villages in hopes to show progress. It just was another effort to quantify success. Initially the program may have been a good idea, and it did have some successes, but in the end, pacification became as futile as the body count debacle. We were spending time, effort, money, and ending precious lives so that a select group of number crunchers could convince the powers that be and the American people that there was some newly discoverable, various colored lights, somewhere, at the end of the same innocuous tunnel. During the entire pacification effort, about 50 percent of the people of South Vietnam were either driven out of or moved from their family homes. How can that help win hearts and minds? As Harry Summers said, we were focusing too much on the hearts and minds and not focusing on destroying the source of the insurgency, North Vietnam. Vietnam was becoming more and

PROFESSIONAL COURAGE

more a bureaucrat's war. With our last big battle having taken place at Ripcord, and the "Vietnamization" of the war leading to a new phase of the end game, we were grasping at imprecise methodologies for progress. During my tour with 101st, US in-country troop strength had dropped by another 150,000 and counting. I kept wondering how it all would end and concluded that it could only be ignominiously. All I could think about was the incredible travesty of those precious lives lost for a cause now seemingly going up in smoke and mirrors.

During my tour with the 101st Airborne, I learned how my newly learned intelligence craft could contribute to the success of military operations, especially in direct support of deployed combat units. I developed an important base of knowledge and procedures that I would use later in my career, especially during the intelligence challenges to come during Operation Desert Storm. At this point in my career, I was now fully convinced that possessing the professional courage to do and say what is right, no matter the circumstance, should be the bedrock of any intelligence officer's career objectives.

Before I left Vietnam, I received word that I was accepted into the army's FAO program with China as my specialty. Upon my return to the States, I would be assigned to the Army Language School in Monterey, California for a 52-week course in Chinese Mandarin. I was more than ready to get back to the world and spend some time with Ann and our son John, who was now ten months old and whom I still had not seen except in photos. I packed up, said goodbyes to my great division colleagues, and hitched a ride to Da Nang. It rained in buckets just before they loaded the plane and all my packed gear was soaked, but I could not have cared less as I boarded the plane and was on my way back to the world.

On the long flight home, I closed my eyes and reflected on my incredibly valuable experiences this past year with the 101st Airborne Division. Timidity was bad, professional courage was good. During my tour, I had learned a lot and eventually had made important strides in the understanding, preparation, and execution of the myriad of combat roles involved in my new field of intelligence. As I looked into the future, I concluded that MI could be, without question, a major force multiplier on numerous types of battlefields. I was now convinced that I wanted to dedicate myself to the development, deployment, and employment of intelligence and its critically important combat capabilities. Before I fell into a deep sleep, I smiled to myself as I thought of a quote by Mark Twain: **"The two important dates in your life are when you are born and the day you find out why."**

PROFESSIONAL COURAGE

CHAPTER 4

INVALUABLE CAREER-EXPANDING EXPERIENCES: 1971-1980

My post-Vietnam leave in Auburn with Ann and our young son John was a wonderfully different feeling of family. We enjoyed a new togetherness, which was what we had always hoped for. I knew that the days of Corvettes and GTOs were over, so I had ordered a Ford LTD Station Wagon while still in Vietnam. We would be driving cross-country from Auburn, NY to Monterey, CA. During the early part of our trip out West, we stopped in Little Rock, AK, to visit close friends from Auburn, Mike and Faith Donovan. After a couple of days in Little Rock, we continued our long trip toward California. We had just crossed the Oklahoma state line when John threw up on Ann, the car seat, and floor. This very long trip appeared to be getting longer, and I decided not to put Ann and John (and me) through the remainder of that cross-country adventure. I drove the LTD drove back to Little Rock, gave Ann our credit card, and suggested that she and

John fly to San Francisco while I continued the drive to California alone. After the long and lonely drive, I finally arrived at Fort Ord, on Monterey Bay. I signed into the language school and put our name on the waiting list for quarters. A couple of days later, Ann and John flew into San Francisco, and we eventually moved into some rather nice quarters on base with a distant view of the beautiful Monterey Bay.

MY EXPERIENCE WITH CHINESE LANGUAGE BEGINS: UNITED STATES ARMY LANGUAGE SCHOOL, MONTEREY, CALIFORNIA: NOVEMBER 1970-DECEMBER 1971

My classes for Chinese Mandarin began about a week after our arrival. I was thirty-five years old and was the senior officer in a class of young, sharp, enlisted soldiers who had been selected because of their foreign language aptitude. I attended daily classes at the US Army Language School at the Presidio of Monterey. For my studies at home, I put a small desk in our kitchen pantry and studied before and after school each day, including weekends. I studied hard, harder than I had ever studied for anything before.

This basic language training was the initial step in my education as a Foreign Area Officer (FAO). The FAO Program recruits officers to train as regionally focused experts who will go on to serve as defense attachés, security assistance officers, or political-military staff officers and advisers at all levels of the army and the Department of Defense. I would eventually be scheduled for follow-on advanced language and area-study training. We were tested on our academic progress every other Friday, so the weekends after testing were sometimes free. On a rare weekend, Ann and I would find a babysitter and sneak off for a meal and a couple of drinks at a great buffet at the Naval Postgraduate School at the Presidio. However, recreation during that year was not on my priority list.

During my time at Monterey, I got to know one of my more competent army classmates, an E-4 (Corporal) named Larry Wortzel, and we formed a friendship. One day, he asked if I would promote him to sergeant; I was proud to do so. Incredibly, in later years, I would also promote him to colonel. Larry would play important roles during some critical challenges in my later career.

Happily, we learned that Ann was pregnant again, and we looked forward to a new addition to our little family. Ann's mother, Fanny, came out to help through the last weeks of pregnancy, and our second son, Jeffrey, was born on November 4, 1971. Several weeks after Jeff's birth, and after much hard work and mental exhaustion, I was pleasantly surprised to find out that I had passed the course with a final grade of 90, but I was still not satisfied with my expertise in Chinese Mandarin.

ENTERING THE JOINT ARENA: THE ARMED FORCES STAFF COLLEGE, NORFOLK, VA: DECEMBER 1971-JUNE 1972

Following my tour at Monterey, I had been hoping to be nominated for the army's Command and General Staff College but was surprised when I had, instead, been selected to attend a seven-month course at the Armed Forces Staff College in Norfolk, VA. (Now known as the Joint Forces Staff College). Ann and I were excited to be in such a historic area in Virginia, and we hoped that John and baby Jeff would grow happily there.

The Armed Forces Staff College was created in 1946 to train officers from each of the military services, along with some select US civilian and foreign military students. The primary objective of the course was to teach and develop planning and execution processes at the operational level for joint, multinational, and inter-agency operations. This would be my first real experience working on a variety of joint projects with members of the other services while also dealing with interagency and coalition members during high-level concept and planning scenarios. Much of the knowledge and experience I would find during my time at the Armed Forces Staff College would be meaningful and helpful during some of my most challenging joint and combined operational responsibilities later in my career.

I enthusiastically embraced the curriculum and enjoyed working with a diverse group of fellow students. During the course, I was personally assigned two major projects/missions. The first was to research and produce a program containing twenty-three hours of counterinsurgency instruction for a Joint Chiefs of Staff-Level Planning Exercise. I researched and compiled an extensive staff exercise plan using Special Operations Forces as the primary military element in the tasked counterinsurgency operations scenario. After I submitted my report to Washington, I later received a Letter of Appreciation from the Joint Staff stating, "The contents of your program were successfully used in the most recent exercise and would be a firm basis for those in the future."

Second, during the extensive final and most major end-of-course planning exercise, I was tasked with playing the operational level J-2, Intelligence officer during an armed conflict scenario. I initially would call on the experience I had gained as G-2 Plans and Operations officer in the 101st Airborne in Vietnam and then evolve that tactical-level experience into the operational level for the exercise. For my effort as the exercise J-2, I received a Commandant's Commendation and high praise both from commandant and the school faculty. During my final academic report, they recommended that my "greatest potential was in the field of intelligence interpretation and action planning." I was discovering the basic tenets of intelligence work at all levels. Refining and adjusting to different scenarios is the challenge but also is the ultimate secret to success. Straightforward and steady communication, despite contrarian desires and opinions, even in exercises, became a major force in my procedural thinking on intelligence processes. In my final evaluation, the faculty recommended that I "be given the opportunity to further my experiences in the field of the study and analysis of China." My entire experience at the Armed Forces Staff College reinforced to me that I had made the right decisions when I transferred to military intelligence and applied for the FAO Program. I thought that I was now in my most potentially prolific career elements and hoped I could make valuable contributions in future positions of greater responsibility in the army, the joint arena, and in coalition operations.

Toward the last weeks of the course, I received orders for the next advanced phase of FAO language training in Mandarin Chinese, at the US Department of State School of Chinese Language and Area Studies in Taiwan, Republic of China. Our little family of four was in for a surely challenging, and somewhat unknown, adventure in an overseas environment.

ADVANCED LANGUAGE AND AREA STUDY

United States Department of State Language School: Taichung, Taiwan, June 1972–May 1974

We arrived on the island of Taiwan just after a major typhoon had struck. We were picked up military van with a Taiwanese driver at the airport and drove to the Roma Hotel in Taipei where we would spend the next couple of days until we moved south to Taichung, home of the language school. Many roads were flooded and the electricity throughout the island was on and off, mostly off. As we arrived at the Roma Hotel, the electricity was out, and we found that our rooms were hot, with humidity you could cut with a knife, and rife with gigantic, tropical mosquitos. But, once we were in our rooms and saw the beds, we didn't care if we were at the end of the earth; we all crashed. A couple days later, we were picked up by the US Defense Attaché Office driver and vehicle and driven south to the central-island city of Taichung, where we moved into designated quarters in a small American compound. The school provided us with an initial starter set of furniture and some basic amenities. Our house was next to a small recreational area with a swimming pool and a softball field. Three other army FAOs were at the school. As a major, I would become the senior officer in the group.

Back to School: Survival of the Fittest

I was scheduled to take 1,317 hours of advanced Mandarin at the State Department School of Chinese Language and Area Studies. I wore shorts and flip-flops and rode my bike to and from the school. My classmates included military and civilian US governmental agency students. Most classes were one-on-one sessions with incredibly capable and experienced Chinese teachers and were very rigorous. At first, I had some real challenges with comprehension, but after some hard work with patient instructors, my spoken Mandarin began to improve. I continued to feel that my comprehension, reading, and writing were not nearly where they needed to be.

The school arranged cultural trips in Taichung and its vicinity for briefings on local organizations, factories, religious sites, governmental organizations, and even a brewery. Ann would come along on many of the tours; she found them enlightening and enjoyable. As the senior FAO officer, I planned seven area-study trips into various cultural and historical areas of Taiwan. We army FAOs and one or two of our selected civilian classmates, guided by our favorite teacher, would take those trips to various areas around the island. We even ventured across the newly built Southern Cross-Island Highway, which was very difficult to transit. We drove over rough back roads, trekked into the mountains, stayed in primitive hostels, and ate simple local foods. We ventured into areas of Taiwan that still reflected some strong lingering Japanese influence after about fifty years of Japanese occupation, which had ended after World War II.

The main thrust of our study, however, remained focused on the Chinese language. Initially, the books and newspapers we were tasked to read were written in ancient complicated classical Chinese characters and format, including four-character couplets called Chengyus, which made an already difficult translation effort even more difficult. We were told that the Chinese Mandarins, who had historically controlled the country, intentionally made the reading and writing extremely difficult and virtually impossible to understand for the common people to keep them basically illiterate and therefore easier to control.

In all, there are about 40,000 Chinese characters, which is phenomenal when one thinks about it. We were told that the average person could get by well enough if they learned "only" 4,000 designated basic, important characters. The number of characters was somewhat daunting, but the inclusion of those Chengyus of characters that change the individual meaning of the characters by themselves makes the language even more challenging. Plus, each character or couplet has a tone (four in Mandarin, nine in Cantonese) so the same character can have a different meaning, depending on the tone. Fortunately, as our time in Taiwan progressed, the local Chinese newspapers began using "simplified characters" consisting of a version of the traditional classical characters but with a lesser number of strokes. They became much easier to recognize and use. Additionally, instead of using complicated classical phraseology and progression in their writing, the newspaper articles were written in casual spoken word format.

During my research into Chinese history and culture, I found a Chinese proverb that I thought was perfect as a guide for rest of my career. I asked my favorite teacher if he would paint two wall hangings with this brilliant proverb. On one side it read "The more you sweat in peace" and the other side read "The less you bleed in war." He painted it beautifully, and I have taken the wall hangings with me everywhere. I tried to adhere to the thrust of that proverb during my entire army career. Although I physically couldn't have those wall hangings with me during Desert Shield and Desert Storm, the tenets they represented had been well seared into my mind by that time. After successfully completing the course at the language school, I left Taichung as a much better Chinese linguist, but as far as I was concerned, I knew I still could learn much more. We were looking forward to our year in Taipei.

A Year of Many Countries

We moved north to the capital city of Taipei for our second year in Taiwan and settled into another set of government quarters, not far from the center of the city. I quickly and directly came under the wing of the army attaché Colonel Lynn Murray. Colonel Murray, an experienced senior China FAO became one of my career-long mentors. He and I devised a plan for the second year of my tour in Taiwan. First, he asked me to initiate and create a completely new manual and a standing operations procedure for the China FAO Language and Area-Study Program. Then, since we were still not allowed to travel to China itself, he asked me to plan a series of off-island travel for the army FAOs to at least fifteen countries around the periphery of China. After I had been in Taipei for a couple of weeks, he surprised me with the news that he had nominated me to attend the Republic of China's Army Command and General Staff College. I was thrilled that he thought I was good enough to attend the school, but I was also petrified because it would be total immersion, with little to no English spoken in or out of class. I would be the first and, as it turned out, the only American officer to ever undertake the challenging curriculum. As I waited for word concerning attendance at the course, I planned our first long trip around the periphery of China with army Captain Doug Lovejoy.

Doug and I conducted our first trip from October 21 to November 11, 1973, to the countries of Afghanistan, Pakistan, India, Nepal, Burma, and Thailand. In each country, we received briefings from the local defense attaché and Department of State officers, visited local areas of interest, and learned of the country's culture and history. In Afghanistan, after our briefings at the embassy, we toured Kabul then trekked through Jalalabad to the Kabul Gorge and down through the historic Khyber Pass into Peshawar, Pakistan. After we reached the capital, Islamabad, we were hosted by the army attaché Colonel Bill Gilliland, who was an experienced China FAO and would later be my boss at the US Defense Liaison Office in Hong Kong. We then motored to Taxilla, Abbottabad, and Murree, and then on to Lahore, located on the Indian border. Since we were due to travel into India, and there were no official lines of communication open between Pakistan and India because of the Indo-Pakistan War of 1971, we had to trek from Pakistan to the Indian border on foot. Once we finally passed through the Indian checkpoint on the border, we hired a van to take us to Amritsar, India. As we rode down the road away from the border, we saw truckloads of Pakistani soldiers who had been captured during the war and were now being repatriated back to Pakistan. I never saw such a happy and boisterous group as they moved along that border road back home.

From Amritsar we flew to New Delhi, where we received a series of briefings at the embassy and visited many of the political, religious, and cultural sites. We then traveled south to Agra, the home of the Taj Mahal. Just west of Agra, we also visited the "city" of Fatehpur Sikri, which had been built by the famous Mughal Emperor Shah Jahan as his new capital but had to eventually be vacated because of a lack of sufficient water supply. We then traveled on to Bombay (now Mumbai), and then on to Calcutta (in West Bengal). While in Calcutta, I chose to spend a few days with a communist family who spoke adequate English. I felt that immersing myself in the everyday life of common people would be the fullest way to experience communist and socialist ideology at the ground level and to get a feel for local politics as well. The West Bengalis are a very temperamental and, at times, volatile people who are constantly politically passionate and active. Sitting at the family dinner table and sleeping under their roof, I learned some valuable lifelong lessons. I came to understand how people can become passionate about something that they feel is tremendously unfair. I gained great insight into the various economic and social circumstances that create deep chasms between various political ideologies and the rich and the poor.

We flew from Calcutta to Rangoon (also known as Yangon), Burma (now Myanmar). We had in-depth briefings in the embassy about the ordinary people's impoverished life in a socialist, one-party system. We were able to compare the present squalor to Burma's splendid past represented by wonders such as the Sule and Shwedagon Pagodas. We then flew to Kathmandu, Nepal. After a day of briefings at the embassy, we traveled by truck to the Tibetan border and trekked part of the way to the Kathmandu Valley, Patain (now known as Lalitpur), and Bhaktapur. The following day, during the early morning, we were within sight of K-2 and Mount Everest, which was an incredible experience never to be forgotten. We traveled by air from Kathmandu to Bangkok, Thailand, where we received briefings at the embassy, then motored north to Chiang Mai and Chiang Rai. The following day, we rode a people's-level train from Chiang Rai south through Bangkok and then down through the Malay peninsula, where some communist rebels were located. We ended up in Butterworth, Malaysia and then took a ferry across to the historical island-city of Penang. After a day there, we flew on to Bangkok. We left Bangkok and arrived back in Taipei on November 11, exhausted, but filled with wonder about we had learned about our complicated world.

We took similar trips to Malaysia, Indonesia, and the Philippines. Those trips provided me with an invaluable first-hand knowledge and exigencies of the various countries of Asia, and I would call upon what I had learned during those experiences throughout the rest of my career. Between trips, Colonel Murray told me I had been accepted for attendance at the Republic of China Army

Command and Staff College. I was honored but immediately overtaken with knowing this promised to be an incredibly difficult language and cultural challenge.

Republic of China Army Command and Staff College

The Army Command and Staff College, along with Air Force and Navy Command and Staff Colleges, were part of the Republic of China's Armed Forces University, which became the National Defense University in 2000. Similar to our army's Command and Staff College, the course educates, trains, and develops leaders for land operations in a joint, interagency, intergovernmental, and multinational operational environment. It advances the art and science of the profession of arms in support of army operational requirements. A major difference from US military schools was Taiwan's inclusion of political warfare courses into the school curriculum and the presence of political commissars as students in the course. The commissar's mission is to ensure political education and control of the military.

The president of the Armed Forces University was General Chiang Wei-Kuo, the son of the legendary Nationalist Chinese leader Generalissimo Chiang Kai-shek. Wei-Kuo had been an exchange officer in the German Wehrmacht and had gained a fluency in German. He then fought in the Second Sino-Japanese War and Chinese Civil War. He also had attended the US Army Command and General Staff College, so he was relatively fluent in English as well. Before his retirement from the army, he had been the commanding general of an armored corps. During my initial interview with General Chiang, I could tell right off that he was a true soldier and a real gentleman. We discussed a plethora of interesting and complicated issues, both vis-à-vis the Chinese Communist Regime in Beijing and the complexity of international political and military relationships. He was a brilliant man, and, thankfully, we got on as professional colleagues and, in the end, friends. Knowing full well the linguistic and substantive challenge I was about to face, he was encouraging. He gave me some sage advice on how to get along in a foreign military school and said that during the course, he would assist me as much as he could.

As my time at the school progressed, we had several counseling sessions.

Instead of wearing shorts and flip-flops, as I had done in Taichung, I wore my uniform to class, and I felt like I was back in my military comfort zone. I was involved in most of the course classes, except for the few that were limited by internal political-military sensitivities such as those involving the "political commissars." Slowly but surely, I learned the more difficult military technical and operational terminologies and became more and more comfortable in the language. However, at times, I had real problems with the variety of hard-to-understand dialects spoken by some of our chief instructors, who were mostly colonels from various regions and provinces of mainland China and had crossed over to Taiwan with the generalissimo after the Chinese Civil War.

The longer I took part in the classes, the more comfortable with the language I became. Total immersion is an invaluable tool in learning fluency in a language. I eventually began to even think in Chinese. Experts in linguistics say that when you start thinking in the language, you have at least the beginning of a semblance of fluency with that language.

I continued to have "strategy" sessions with General Chiang, and, after a time, I invited him to our small home in Taipei for dinner. I was stunned and honored when he accepted. After he arrived at our house, we had pints of German beer and cooked some steaks on the grill. He was delightful, and we had a great evening together. His visit had caused a great commotion in the Chinese neighborhood due to the number of black official cars and security guards in his entourage.

As I continued to progress in the course, I was asked to give a lecture in Chinese, not only to my classmates in the Army Command and Staff College, but to the entire Armed Forces University. I gulped but accepted, reluctantly. I then had to pick an appropriate topic. After some thought, I selected "Special Operations Forces in a Counterinsurgency Environment." I did my research, both at the embassy library and at the school, prepared my presentation, made some slides with instructional topics and diagrams, all with captions in Chinese, and ran the final version by my close Chinese classmates. They provide some solid recommendations, not only on the content, but also how to describe and brief it. The presentation took place in a huge auditorium filled with an audience of Chinese officers of all ranks, from all services. As I did before my first parachute jump, I asked myself: "How the hell did I get myself into this?" I began my presentation with some hesitation and stammered a bit, but once I got warmed up, I became more comfortable and more cogently fluent. In the end, the presentation went great, the audience applauded, and I felt at that moment I was the most fluent in the Chinese language as I would ever be.

As I approached the end of my time in the course, I had a final session with General Chiang. As we said our goodbyes, he gave me a set of books on military strategy that he had written and published. The main themes of the books were the use of armor formations and how they are organized and used in several types of combat scenarios. I have harkened back to his theories on the strengths but also on the weaknesses of the use of armor. I would especially reflect on those theories during Desert Storm.

As I was nearing the end of my tour in Taiwan, I received word that I had been selected to be the Assistant Army Liaison Officer (Attaché) in the British Crown Colony of Hong Kong. That meant another three years in a foreign environment, away from our family and friends. However, as a bit of a reprieve, we would be provided some time in the US before I would have to report to Hong Kong. I would spend about six months in Washington, DC, temporarily assigned to the Defense Intelligence Agency and charged with preparing special studies and projects on China and Asia.

DIRECTORATE FOR ESTIMATES DEFENSE INTELLIGENCE AGENCY: JANUARY-JULY 1975

Ann and I had recently found out that she was pregnant again, and we were excited to have a new addition to our family. She would probably have the baby while we were on leave in Auburn, just before we would depart for Hong Kong. We moved into a rental house in Virginia for those six months. I was assigned to temporary duty as a special assistant to the chief, Far East Division, directorate for Estimates at the Defense Intelligence Agency. (Later in my career, I would become the chief of that division.) I dug into that temporary job with enthusiasm. In support of the Defense Attaché System (DAS) I conducted a great deal of in-depth research and wrote reports on some highly classified special projects and in-depth studies on the Far East in general and China in particular. Within each of those reports, I listed key intelligence requirements that needed to be answered by select offices within the DAS. I learned much about the inner workings of the DAS and was grateful to have that preliminary experience since I would be working as an attaché during my upcoming tour in Hong Kong.

Additionally, I prepared and coordinated various Defense Intelligence Agency positions on Far East and China as part of Department of Defense Joint Staff actions and during follow-up discussions concerning national policy positions with the Department of State and other governmental agencies. I was assigned a special project to write and collate a briefing book of background intelligence reports and special topics on the People's Republic of China (PRC), especially on the People's Liberation Army (PLA), for the designated next ambassador to the PRC, George H. W. Bush. (I would later welcome him during his return visit to the PRC in 1989, when he was President of the United States, and would later shake his hand during the Desert Storm Victory Parade in Washington, DC.)

I also initiated and developed one of the first rudimentary computer management programs in support of the DAS. At the time, computers were extremely slow and limited, and programming was in very early stages. With the help of some bright, young computer programmers, our final effort did, in a small way, assist in the administrative management of the large, worldwide DAS. Those six months with the Defense Intelligence Agency was a short yet busy time. I learned a great deal of substantive information and about the workings of the intelligence community, and the far east, all of which would prepare me for my liaison and collection missions in Hong Kong and beyond.

HONG KONG SOLDIER

US Defense Liaison Office, Defense Intelligence Agency Hong Kong, British Crown Colony: July 1975–July 1978

As we prepared for our move to Hong Kong, we put most of our household goods in storage and moved out of our rented house in Virginia. Ann was very pregnant, and the four of us drove to Auburn for a well-anticipated few weeks of leave before we left for our three-year tour in Hong Kong. As we approached the time for our move, our daughter Meridith was born. We were thrilled that we now had a little sister to join our boys. After a very long trip, made even longer since we had two little boys and baby Meridith in tow, we finally arrived in the British Crown Colony of Hong Kong. Our second floor flat was in Stanley Village, which was a longish drive (I had to learn to drive on the left side) from the US Consulate. It was just past Repulse Bay and its famous hotel. Our flat was in a scenic area overlooking Tai Tam Bay and just up the street from the Stanley Market. Although Hong Kong is a vibrant place and one of the most unique cities in the world, we were a bit daunted that we would have to remain in the confined, smallish area of Hong Kong (people called it "the Rock") for a full three years, but we vowed that we would make the best of it.

The US still had not established official relationships with the PRC, so our office in Hong Kong served as a primary unofficial window to China. My position in the consulate was the assistant army liaison (Attaché) officer in the US Defense Liaison Office. One of my missions was serving as the primary liaison with the British Joint Services Intelligence Staff (JSIS), and the other was that of a normal attaché: "China-watching," researching and reporting on the PRC, especially the PLA. We weren't officially designated as attachés due to the sensitivities of the British relationship with the Chinese government. We had a robust tri-service office headed by a navy captain. The navy officers (including a marine) in our office, performed normal attaché functions, but were also involved in US Navy ship visits in the Hong Kong port of call. My immediate boss was initially Colonel Dick Gillespie, an army China Hand. Later, Colonel Bill Gilliland, also an army "China Hand," would become my boss. He had previously served as the army attaché in Pakistan and had welcomed Doug Lovejoy and I when we had visited Islamabad.

My primary job, other than my liaison with the Brits, was to collect, analyze, and report on the political, military, and economic issues of the PRC. I maintained equal concentration on the PLA as I maintained military order of battle information. My time in Hong Kong corresponded to some interesting periods in the modern history of the PRC. I closely followed and reported on the important political and military machinations of the time, including the contortions caused by the political and military porridge stirred by the infamous Gang of Four during the latter stages of Mao Zedong's time in power (he died in September 1976). I then closely followed the ascension of Mao's replacement, Hua Guofeng, and how his transition to power affected the multifaceted levers of power in Beijing. Once Hua finally rid himself of the threat from the noxious Gang of Four, he began influencing and changing some interesting facets of China's internal and foreign policies. For example, he was premier when he led the second phase of the transition to simplified characters to the written Chinese language. The use of simplified characters helped the people better understand the news and gave them access to daily information, which improved general literacy. He also ordered the national anthem rewritten to reflect the latest developing pragmatic communist ideology instead of the blatant, strident political themes that evolved from the "revolution." Most importantly, in July 1977 Hua restored Deng Xiaoping to his original vice chairman posts both in the party and military commission. Hua also directed that a new national constitution be adopted. During that tumultuous and important period in China, I was neck-deep in the challenges to research, interpret, and report on the latest complicated internecine relationships in China and the importance of its direct and indirect influence on the PLA.

My Time with the Joint Services Intelligence Staff

I served as the principal office liaison with British counterpart organizations, primarily with the JSIS, which was composed of multi-service, intelligence, and line officers along with some long serving China Hand civil servants. Army Lieutenant Colonel George Redfern was a career British intelligence officer and the commander of the JSIS, and we worked closely together. I also had great relationships with other British officers such as those from the Royal Army Engineers and the Royal Army Intelligence Corps. I continued to nurture relationships with virtually all JSIS officers. My dealings with the Brits in JSIS, both working and social, were ideal, and the exchange of information was virtually seamless and, as far as I could tell, close to limitless. The Brits had diplomatic relations with the PRC, so their access and information was real, more recent and, when compared to ours, voluminous. Ann and I enjoyed traditional formal military dinners at the beautiful Victoria Barracks Officer's Club, including "Bobby Burns Nights," when the bagpipers would pipe in the Hagis.

I formed interesting and unique relationships with members of the Royal Hong Kong Police who monitored border crossers from China. Some of these border crossers were very smart and determined and had gotten past the British commanded Gurkha border security units or had used an organized smuggling system to enter the colony. The flexibility and disparity of attaché missions were not limited to just strict military relationships. Over time I developed a close working and social friendship with one of the police chief inspectors. The attaché is many things to many people: military adviser, military representative, diplomat, intelligence collector, military assistance adviser, and social coordinator. In the end, the military attaché system is an invaluable contributor to national intelligence, diplomacy, and defense. I would continue to see visible reinforcement of these many tasks as my career continued into more complicated and expanded mission experiences.

Once I had settled into a work and social routine, I enjoyed playing tennis with a few of the Brits in JSIS on the courts of the British Army's Victoria Barracks. We normally played during lunchtime, and it often was unbearably hot. One day, my boss in the US Defense Liaison Office told me that the navy was going to have a visitor who would like to play tennis and asked if I would be the visitor's tennis partner and to arrange a game of doubles.

After I happily accepted, he told me that my tennis partner would be retired Admiral John S. McCain Jr. who had been the overall military commander of the Dominican Republic operation when I was in the 82nd Airborne and then commander in chief of United States Pacific Command when I was in Vietnam during my second tour (and the father of the late Senator John McCain III). I enthusiastically set up the match with a couple of my Brit friends. On the day of the match, I picked up the admiral at the Hong Kong Hilton. He was dressed in white shorts, white shirt, white floppy hat, and was smoking a cigar. We talked about our mutual experiences in the Dominican Republic and Vietnam, and we hit it off right away and I admired his fighting spirit. We had a very enjoyable tennis match all-around. Admiral McCain would come back to Hong Kong twice more and each time we would play doubles matches with our favorite Brits.

PROFESSIONAL COURAGE

About halfway through my tour, the Chinese Red Cross offered to return the remains of two Americans who had been shot down during the Korean War and subsequently died on Chinese soil. The two sets of remains belonged to a lieutenant commander from Iowa and a parachute rigger from Pennsylvania. I had been selected to represent the Department of Defense during the handover. Driving to the China border, I reflected on the small yet sobering role I would play in accepting the remains of these two heroes as I helped send them back home to their loved ones in the United States. As we approached the border bridge, I looked halfway across at what would be the closest I had come, up to that point, to the country that I had studied so deeply. I linked up with the senior Red Cross representative and a British Royal Air Force officer on the Hong Kong side of the bridge, and we walked together toward the center. We met the Chinese Red Cross representatives at the halfway point, and solemnly accepted the two precious boxes wrapped in white linen. We thanked the Chinese for their efforts and initiative, turned around, and as we walked back toward the Hong Kong side of the bridge, my eyes teared from the gravity of the situation, escorting these two heroes on their final journey back to their families. I felt like I was in some sort of semi-lucid dream and remembered the incredibly brave troopers of Charlie Company who had given their lives for their country, as well.

At the halfway point of my tour, Colonel Bill Gilliland surprised me with the news that I made the Lieutenant Colonel's promotion list. The rank of Lieutenant Colonel in the US Army is a pretty big deal, but in the British Army it is a really big deal. When the day of my actual promotion arrived, I was proud that our whole family was at the consulate for my promotion ceremony. Ann pinned the silver leaf on my shoulder. I was happy to have her there for this ceremony, which was quite a bit different from my promotion to major at Fort Meade, when I couldn't even get her into the building. She was an integral part of not only our family but also "our" career as well. I beamed when the Brits first called her the "Colonel's Lady."

Creating a Unique Collection Program

During the three years I spent in Hong Kong, I worked hard, day and night. I often worked nights attending liaison social functions with Ann, where I would try to learn all I could about the PRC. During the second half of my tour, I developed a unique and very sensitive intelligence collection initiative that would help identify PLA troop unit designators. I began building a database with one scrap of information at a time, until the program began to grow to a point where it could be of practical use. To collect this information, I debriefed virtually every visitor I could identify who was returning through Hong Kong from the PRC. I would ask potential visitors to the PRC to look for certain indicators and, if they were returning through Hong Kong, gave them a procedure on how to provide the required information to me.

PROFESSIONAL COURAGE

This program gradually grew, but over the years, some of the serving action officers lost interest in collecting the pertinent information, and the program, at times, went fallow. But I would continue to use whatever influence I had, from whatever job that I had at the time, to help resuscitate the program again and again. The results of these prolonged efforts over the years would be invaluable during the Tiananmen Incident. I knew this database would provide important information to someone, someday, but I could not have anticipated how crucial it would be to help identify participating PLA units many years later when I was the defense and army attaché to the PRC. The information from that program provided the wherewithal for our attaché office to provide reporting of a major significance to the decision-making process of our national leaders, including the president. I was tremendously proud to have initiated and supported that program for so long, especially knowing that it did pay off when it really counted.

I kept trying to broaden my horizons by meeting new people, going to new places, and learning from everywhere that I could. One of my more memorable relationships during my tour in Hong Kong was with a China/Asia expert, reporter, editor, and author. Russell Spurr was the editor of the highly regarded "Far Eastern Economic Review." He also wrote two best-selling books: Enter the Dragon about China's war against the US during the Korean War and A Glorious Way to Die, which described the tracking and sinking of the famous Japanese battleship Yamato. Russell and I became long-lasting friends and had many in-depth discussions about China and the Far East.

As my time in Hong Kong progressed, I developed a real desire to visit the Gurkha units that patrolled the PRC border. I met the British Gurkha Commander Lieutenant Colonel Miles Hunt-Davies at a formal military dinner at Victoria Barracks. I asked Miles if he could help me go on a patrol with the Gurkhas. To my great surprise, Miles eventually arranged it. Once at the Gurkha camp in New Territories, we prepared to follow the Gurkhas on their nighttime patrol mission. As the patrols began moving into the scrub brush, Miles and I folded in behind one of them, trying to be as inconspicuous as possible—easy for me, tough for big Miles. I watched closely as the Gurkhas, each carrying their short-barreled semiautomatic rifles moved like ghosts through the thickets, initially, then along some well-worn paths, up to and then parallel to the Chinese border. Their mission was to prevent infiltration by refugees attempting to flee the economic doldrums of China to live and work in the more vibrant factories and workshops in Kowloon, Hong Kong, and even stretching to Portuguese Macau. I was filled with admiration for the Gurkhas and the amazing history they represented. Another of my lifelong dreams fulfilled: to "walk" with the legendary Gurkhas.

I continued to focus on developing my expertise by constantly reading, studying, researching, and conducting as many conversations as possible with anyone who had opinions or information on the political, military, social, and economic situation in China. I frequented local bookstores, scouring for any scrap of information that could add to our analytical database on the PRC as a whole and the PLA in particular. After culling information from multiple sources, I consolidated all of it into my personal databases and wrote numerous reports for local and national consumption. In those three years, I wrote hundreds of reports that contributed to the national database and certainly to my own personal knowledge of the PRC. To keep up with my Chinese, I took tutored language lessons provided by the consulate. Unfortunately, in Hong Kong, the Cantonese and Fukienese dialects are predominantly spoken and are very, very different from Mandarin. Fortunately, the Chinese characters are the same, so I was able to keep up with my reading and writing, which was helpful during my collection and reporting mission.

Toward the end of my tour, I was hoping to be selected for a battalion command (a battalion-level unit is normally commanded by a Lieutenant Colonel) and, hopefully, a Military Intelligence

Battalion. I received a message that I was in fact selected for a battalion command, but then was totally shocked when I was assigned to a US Army Special Forces Battalion Command position at Fort Bragg. I would revert to the Infantry Branch for the duration of that command. It was a wonderful surprise, and we were excited about living in on-base housing at Fort Bragg, "The Home of the Airborne and Special Operations."

Ann was a treasure during our Hong Kong tour. She evolved into an ideal attaché wife and grew in grace as the "Colonel's Lady." John, Jeff, and Mei (Meridith had become Mei-Mei, which is little sister in Chinese, then shortened to just Mei) had a wonderful, broadening experience during those three years. The boys had attended Hong Kong International School and matured greatly. We were pleased that they all had grown by leaps and bounds, both socially and academically. Finally, as we left Hong Kong, having enjoyed and benefited professionally, socially, and academically through those three years, I was now looking forward to a new challenge as a battalion commander with the Green Berets.

A SPECIAL FORCES SOLDIER

US Army Institute for Military Assistance, US Army John F. Kennedy Special Warfare Center and School, Fort Bragg, North Carolina: July 1978–January 1980

After we arrived at Fort Bragg, I signed into the US Army Institute for Military Assistance, which was under the US Army John F. Kennedy Special Warfare Center and School (JFK Center), and we initially moved into transient quarters. Several days later, we moved into our permanent quarters and signed the kids up for Fort Bragg post school system. I took a few days of leave to help Ann and the kids get settled into our new quarters and get oriented on and off post. When I eventually reported into the JFK Center, I was introduced to the center's commanding general Major General Jack Mackmull, who had been a driving force not only in army aviation but especially aviation support for Special Operations. He was also key to the creation and development of what would become the First Special Forces Operational Detachment—Delta, a.k.a. Delta Force. General Jack Mackmull was a great leader and eventually I would be honored to call him friend.

The major organizations within the center and school were the Institute for Military Assistance, the Special Forces Officer and Special Forces Enlisted Courses, the FAO Course, the Psychological Operations School, and the Civil Affairs School. (Civil affairs teams find local civil resources to support military operations, minimize civil interference, and help with humanitarian assistance activities.) Although the JFK Center had many moving parts, it was primarily known as the home of US Army Special Forces: the Green Berets. In 1978, the US Special Forces were only a little over three decades old. They derived their lineage from a combination of the World War II Alamo Scouts (soldiers during WWII who provided specialized reconnaissance needed to defeat the Japanese), the combined US-Canadian 1st Special Service Force (The Devil's Brigade), and operational groups of the Office of Strategic Services, the predecessor to the Central Intelligence Agency. In June 1952, the 10th Special Forces Group (Airborne) was formed by Colonel Aaron Bank, a giant in the Special Forces community and a veteran of numerous Office of Strategic Services Jedburgh missions, to conduct sabotage and guerrilla warfare in Nazi-occupied Europe. During the next ten years or so, the various services began creating their own special units such as the army Special Forces and Rangers, navy underwater demolition teams, marine corps force reconnaissance teams, and the air force air commando group. By 1961, with growing American involvement in South Vietnam, President Kennedy visited the army's Special Warfare Center at Fort Bragg and made his vision for a dedicated counterinsurgency force clear. Then, in 1962, President Kennedy again showed his unwavering support for these "unconventional warriors" by authorizing them to wear distinctive headgear as a uniform item. From then on, these unique soldiers would be known as the Green Berets. President Kennedy wrote to the Special Forces commander, "The challenge of this old, but new form of operations is a real one and I know that you and the members of your command will carry on for us and the free world in a manner which is both worthy and inspiring. I am sure that the Green Beret will be a mark of distinction in the trying time ahead."[2] By the late 1970s, the Green Berets became a dramatic symbol of excellence in the US Army; in Vietnam, a war where they exhibited uncommon valor every day and lived up to their motto, "De Oppresso Liber" (To Liberate the Oppressed), they were slowly but surely rebuilding for the future and doing it with the utmost professionalism.

My Green Beret: Smoke Bomb Hill

The day before I officially reported to the JFK Center, a group of grizzled veteran Special Forces senior noncommissioned officers visited our quarters and presented me with a new Green Beret. I was duly thankful and attempted to try it on. They all laughed and asked me to give it back to them. They then put that beret through some ritualistic, historical process of shaving off the nap, wetting it in the sink, "forming" it, and then shoving it in the oven and heating it up to whatever the recipe was for the perfect temperature and amount of time for a Green Beret. After removing it from the oven, they let it cool a bit and then put it on my head and formed it again. They then took it off my head and handed it back to me, they all laughed, saying "now you won't look like such a dork when you put it on." When I left the battalion, those same sergeants gave me that same beret that they had bronzed, and I have it in a place of honor in my home today.

Little did I know when I first set foot on Smoke Bomb Hill (an area of Fort Bragg where the center was located) that I would

---

[2] http://www.specialforcesassociation.org/about/

eventually have many years both serving with the Green Berets or in positions supporting or tinvolving their operational expertise. During my time at Fort Bragg, and in future assignments, I would be dedicated to the continued development and future improvements of the Special Operations community.

Smoke Bomb Hill seemed to harbor an infinite number of characters and giants in the Special Forces community such as Colonels Ray Maladowitz and Mike Radke, along with the famous "Charlies": Colonels "Chargin' Charlie" Beckwith, Charlie Norton, and Charlie Brewington. These legends of the worldwide Special Operations community normally gravitated, and rightly so, back into the Special Forces' womb at Smoke Bomb Hill. I was truly privileged to know and work with all of them. The commandant of the Special Forces School was Colonel Ola "Lee" Mize. He had been awarded the Medal of Honor for his actions during the Korean War in 1953. Incredibly, he had killed sixty-five enemy soldiers during a brutal fourteen-hour battle. During the latter part of the battle, and after he ran out of ammunition, he continued to kill the charging enemy with an entrenching tool (shovel). Eventually, Lee Mize became one of my lifelong heroes and a dear friend. For whatever reason, he took me under his wing. Colonel Mize and I developed an especially close relationship and spent countless hours talking about various subjects, both professional and of the latest relevant topics of the day.

My battalion command was a challenging and unique one. It included, at any one time, about 1,800 soldiers. The battalion was primarily responsible for Special Forces students who were attending the officer and enlisted Special Forces Qualification Courses: the Survival, Escape, Resistance, and Evasion (SERE) Training; High Altitude, Low Opening (HALO) Course; and the Military Scuba Diving Course. I was responsible for command, control, training, administration, and logistic support for the battalion as a whole and all in it. Interestingly, there were eleven colonels listed as members of the battalion, including the legends I named earlier.

I was delighted that one of the other colonels was none other than Lynn Murray, my mentor from Taiwan, who was now commandant of the FAO School. I spent a great deal of time talking to and learning from Colonel Murray, both at the school and at our quarters, on how to be an effective FAO and especially on how to be an effective and contributory military attaché.

During my time at Smoke Bomb Hill, I had free rein to visit all the various courses, talk to both the cadre and students, assess the viability of courses, and was encouraged to make recommendations to the various course commandants. It was a tremendous learning experience and gave me a great sense of contributing to the improvement of very important special capabilities, not only for our army but our nation's military as a whole. Special Forces teams are made up of soldiers with specific required specialties, and some can be qualified in more than one. The specialties include operations, intelligence, weapons, communications, medical, and engineering. The qualification courses are demanding, and those that graduate are considered experts in their individual specialties. One specialty that I became increasingly interested in was that of the Special Forces medic. The basic medic becomes proficient in general medical care, not only for those in their own team, but for local population of the area in which they would be operating. In discussing the curriculum with the chief medical instructor, I learned that the faculty was developing an advanced program whereby the medical course was being extended and taken to a more advanced level, including medical trauma training. That initiative would later evolve into the physician's assistant program that would become a Special Forces specialty and would later be adopted into civilian practice.

I tried to make parachute jumps with numerous classes to get a feel for the students' attitudes, morale, and get some one-on-one feedback about the training. Airborne camaraderie is conducive to serious bonding and promotes a variety of valuable discussions. As time went on, I had the required number (sixty-five or more) and type of jumps required to be awarded the Master Parachutist Wings. I gave my various types of jump records to Colonel Mize, and he sent the paperwork through for me. When I got the orders for those wings, I looked back proudly on some of my parachute experiences, such as those at Fort Bragg, in the Dominican Republic, and Vietnam. Colonel Mize pinned the Master Parachutist Wings on my chest like a proud father. Receiving that symbol of virtual airborne immortality from a legend, whom I admired greatly, was one of the most significant and emotional experiences of my career.

One Special Soldier

I had always felt that the opportunity to use linguists, especially native linguists, would help lead to ultimate success in foreign operations, liaison, and intelligence collection missions. One day, as I was reading the progress reports from the latest Special Forces Qualifications Course, I noticed that one of the students, with an Iranian-looking name, had not achieved the required qualifications for graduation and had been ultimately dropped from the course.

I asked to talk to the Special Forces Company First Sergeant Asa Ballard, who was a legend in Special Forces. The word around the Special Forces community was that Asa, a great guitarist, had written numerous country-western songs, and that one of them had been, "The Ballad of the Green Berets," which was listed as being written and then recorded by Sgt. Barry Sadler. (It was the Billboard number one single record for the year 1966.) The Special Forces sergeants who had known Asa over the years, claimed that he had written that song and should have gotten credit for it, but Asa, being a very solid soldier, never mentioned it to me or anyone else and just plowed on with his important mission.

I asked Asa if he had an idea what had caused the Iranian student to fail the course. He said that it was probably because his basic knowledge of English was poor and he found it difficult, if not impossible, to understand enough of the course of instruction to take and pass the tests. I couldn't stop thinking that this situation could be indicative of other opportunities for targeted recruitment and that we needed to pay operational attention to certain key languages and literacy for future reference-one way or the other. The 1979 Iranian Hostage Crisis was still ongoing. American diplomats were still in captivity, and I, as usual, kept thinking about the high value language capabilities, especially native fluency, during covert and clandestine intelligence operations. As for the continuing Iranian crisis, I thought that if a rescue attempt was ever planned and executed, we could need someone to fold into the local environment and help with support of the mission within Iran itself.

I asked Asa to bring that Iranian American student to my office. When the student arrived, he saluted and reported smartly. I was immediately impressed by his military bearing and his evident positive attitude. I saw a spark in him that impressed me, and he reinforced my initial opinion that he could be a tremendous asset to our overall future special operational capabilities, especially in the Middle East. I asked him if he still wanted to be a Special Forces soldier. He replied, in halting English, that he was dedicated to serving his adopted country, especially with the Special Forces. When I asked him if he was willing to do what was necessary to get his Green Beret, he enthusiastically agreed. We provided him with a tutor and put him into the special intensive English language program, which he eventually passed with amazing speed and progress. I then reassigned him to the next Special Forces Qualification Course, which he passed with flying colors. Asa and I were very proud, and we instinctively thought our new Special Forces soldier would be a valuable asset during possible future operations.

After I left the battalion in January of 1980, I maintained interest in the fate of our hostages still held in Iran. Exactly four months later, on April 24, 1980, Operation Eagle Claw, the ill-fated rescue attempt, was launched and I wondered if our young Iranian American Special Forces soldier had played any part in that operation. I talked to Asa, and he told me that he in fact did play a major role in the internal Iran support element of the plan. That experience reinforced my continued support for native linguists being major contributors to future Operations and Intelligence efforts. The important caveat in recruiting a native linguist is that it comes with a counterintelligence challenge, with him or her having a possible lingering dedication to their native country.

My in-depth experience with the various organizations involved in that battalion command was extensive and invaluable to my future assignments. In addition to the Special Forces related courses, the major capabilities of all additional Special Operations missions, including the FAO (of which I was a member) School, Civil Affairs School, and Psychological Operations School were filed into my memory bank for use in future responsibilities.

I flew with many of the HALO classes and with some scuba classes in a C-130 when they jumped into the bay (which we called Shark DZ) offshore from our scuba school in Key West, Florida. I became especially interested in the incredible importance of the SERE training program, which instructs stranded soldiers how to survive in harsh environments and evade capture. Since the SERE responsibility had not yet been assigned anywhere as an army-wide program, I strongly felt that responsibility belonged with Special Operations.

My Return to the 82nd Airborne Division

As I approached the end of my time in command, I decided to look into the possibility of a follow-on assignment at Fort Bragg. An additional assignment there would mean that the kids could continue at school on base, keep their friends, and continue with their athletic and social activities. I desperately wanted to return to the 82nd Airborne Division, but the only job possible at my rank was that of the division G-2 (Intelligence) and that position was already filled and the incumbent supposedly still had quite a while remaining before he was scheduled to rotate out of the job.

PROFESSIONAL COURAGE

I later heard that an old friend, Colonel Art Stang, had become the division chief of staff. Interestingly, about same time, I had also heard that the commanding general of the 82nd was not especially pleased with his current G-2 and may be looking for a replacement. I had a phone conversation with Art, and I drove over to the division where we had lunch in the mess hall. Art Stang was a legend, not only in the airborne community, but within the rangers as well. He had been promoted below the zone to every rank and at that time was the youngest colonel in the army. He was a renowned athlete and runner and ran every morning with a different troop unit. He was, by all accounts, a future chief of staff of the army. Art and I caught up on our careers since our days with the 173rd. Interestingly, during our conversation, he did not discount the possibility of my move to the 82nd. In fact, he seemed somewhat encouraging. Several days later, Art called me and said that the commanding general had selected me to replace the present

G-2. He gave me a report date and told me he would coordinate the move with the army and the folks at Smoke Bomb Hill. I was totally elated. I would be leaving the battalion and the center with some regret because I had truly enjoyed my time on Smoke Bomb Hill, but I really looked forward to returning "home" to the 82nd Airborne Division.

As I was about to leave, the cadre in the battalion gave us a great farewell party and presented me with two wonderful gifts. One was the bronzed Green Beret and the other was a stained-glass depiction of a Green Beret, which was exceptionally beautiful. Only two had ever been made. The first had been presented to the great Special Forces patron, John Wayne, and the other, to me. Both the beret and the stained glass are in places of honor in my home today.

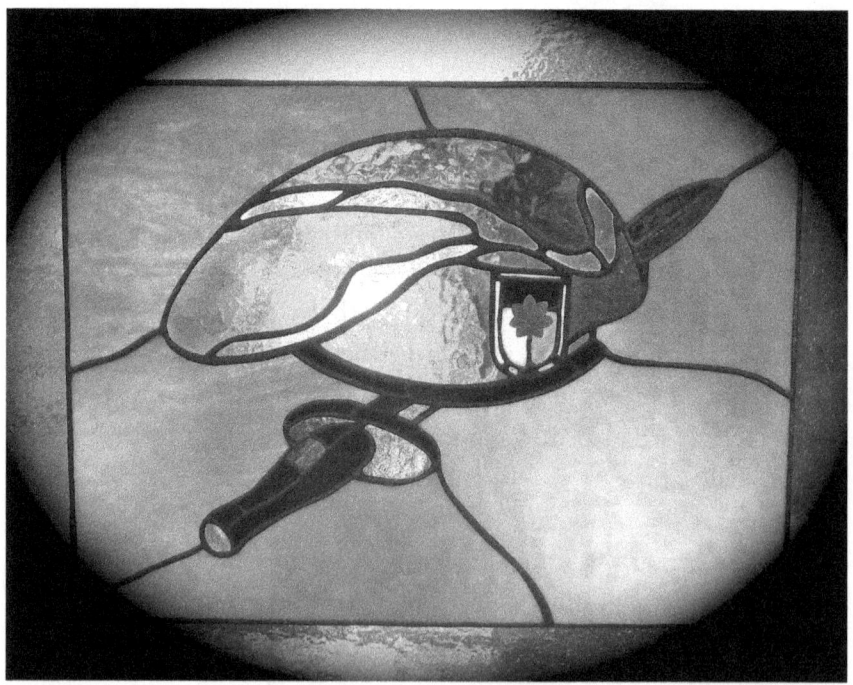

CHAPTER 5

ALL-AMERICAN! ALL THE WAY!

82ND AIRBORNE DIVISION, FORT BRAGG, NORTH CAROLINA: FEBRUARY 1980–JULY 1981

Two days after I had signed into the division but had not officially started my new job as the G-2, I heard that my friend Colonel Art Stang had dropped stone cold dead on the division street while running with one of the infantry battalions. Evidently, he had suffered a severe coronary attack. Everyone in the division, and much of the army, were absolutely stunned and devastated over the sudden loss of such a great soldier. As a result, the division commanding general (CG) ordered everyone in the division to undergo a series of physicals, physical training tests, and cardiac stress tests. He also encouraged everyone to have a proper will. Frankly, these actions and reactions were especially important to those of us in the 82nd Airborne Division. After all, the division had the mission to deploy anywhere in the world within forty-eight hours and be ready to engage an enemy immediately upon arrival.

BACK TO THE ALL AMERICANS

Once I passed all the required physical tests and completed a will, I officially reported to the new division chief of staff Colonel Rafael "Ralph" Hallada. After the chief welcomed me, we discussed his expectations for my duties as the G-2 and prepared me for a meeting with the CG. As I waited to be ushered in, I had flashes of inadequacy because I did not have the intelligence branch experience normally necessary for a job at this level. But I did have my Vietnam intelligence experience with the 101st Airborne Division, Art Stang's prior recommendation, a Combat Infantrymans Badge, and was a Master Parachutist. I was hoping those arrows in my quiver would at least give me some instant credibility with the CG. The chief ushered me in and introduced me to Major General Guy S. "Sandy" Meloy. He was a legend in the airborne community and particularly in the 82nd. He had commanded units in the division at every level, from platoon leader to division commander. Recently, he had been the commander of the 1st Brigade, chief of staff, assistant division commander for operations, and had been the CG since December 1978. Incredibly, he was so versed in airborne operations that he had personally written, in exquisite detail, several volumes describing the Division Airborne Doctrine and Standard Operating Procedures. Those volumes included an incredible number of procedures and capabilities required for an elite airborne division to function optimally in a high operational tempo.

Once the chief escorted me into the CG's office, General Meloy got up from his desk and warmly welcomed me back to the division. He seemed genuinely pleased that I was now his G-2, and we discussed what he expected from me in my new job. I was not only delighted to be back in the 82nd but also to be working directly with this legendary airborne soldier. I got up and gave him an "All the way sir" salute and left his office. I was stoked.

Not long after I assumed my job as the G-2, we were tasked to write an intelligence annex for an upcoming major operational training exercise. The final briefing for the exercise was scheduled for presentation to the CG the following week. Although, I initially didn't know the officers or troopers assigned to the G-2 Section, they all seemed bright and dedicated. After I provided my initial guidance for our input to the exercise scenario, we all worked very hard for the next several days and nights putting together the G-2 portion of the briefing. On the day of the presentation to General Meloy, I apprehensively took my assigned seat next to the chief. We had prepared notional weather, terrain, enemy order of battle, and probable enemy courses of action on our charts and maps, and I was anxiously ready to go. The G-3, normally responsible for the entirety of operational briefings given to the CG, had previously received a copy of all the various staff section briefings, including mine. He began by presenting the normal opening remarks describing the reason and content of the briefing and then had my charts and maps displayed on some easels and began to present what was my portion of the briefing (the intelligence is normally the first part of an operational briefing). General Meloy stopped the G-3 dead in his tracks and said, "Isn't Jack supposed to give this part of the briefing?" I would later learn that the CG had little confidence in my predecessor and the G-3, by default, had been presenting the G-2 portion, as well as his own. I promptly got up and began my presentation using the charts and maps that we had so carefully prepared. After I completed my briefing, I anxiously looked at the CG for some sort of reaction. He looked me straight in the eye, smiled broadly, and gave me a big airborne thumbs-up. I was relieved, happy, and off and running in the job I was so looking forward to.

As I settled into my job routine, I made a point to frequently visit various unit commanders in the division to get a personal feel for their requirements and to learn of any problem areas. I discovered that one of the airborne infantry brigade commanders was none other than my old friend from the 101st Airborne Order of Battle Section days, now colonel, Jim Johnson. We hugged like lost brothers. I would later run into Jim when he was the 82nd Airborne Division Commander during Desert Storm and again when he was the 18th Airborne Corps commander. Evidently, my predecessor had rarely, if ever, visited the various commands, and the commanders were genuinely pleased that I was visibly supporting them, especially when they were on alert, preparing to deploy on an exercise, or on an actual mission. We would discuss, for example, my experiences of having commanded airborne infantry companies in the 82nd and 173rd Airborne in combat and how frustrated I was with the lack of usable intelligence during those times. As an Intelligence officer, having the Combat Infantryman Badge, Master Parachutist Badge, and the enthusiastic willingness to provide individual and unit personal support, resulted in virtually instant credibility with the unit commanders. Additionally, I tried to jump with as many units as I could to get to know and create a bonding relationship with the commanders and troops we would be supporting.

Because of the division's on-call, "on a moment's notice" tactical, operational, and strategic missions, I had to become intimately familiar with many the army and defense department's mostly highly classified contingency war plans. They were continuously being updated and we had to make sure we passed on any important changes to the CG, the command group, and the major unit commanders.

Master Blaster On-Call

The division was always a beehive of activity and unusual challenges. I recall one incident when three troopers, including a first lieutenant battalion adjutant, were killed when their chutes failed to open. They had descended so quickly that they had no chance to pull their reserve parachutes. Initially, we didn't have enough information to determine what had caused the tragic incident. Main parachutes malfunction very, very infrequently. Additionally, during a normal main malfunction, because of horizontal chute drag due to the speed of the aircraft and the prop blast, there is usually enough time to deploy the reserve chute. But, in this case, there appeared to be a complete loss of horizontal chute drag, and the three troopers had tragically fallen almost vertically. Three radical malfunctions of the same type and at the same time was simply unheard of. After further investigation we discovered that the static lines on those three main parachutes had been cut. Word of incidents such as this travel quickly in the division. As one can imagine, great consternation and apprehension began to bubble and boil throughout. There was a concerted effort in the headquarters to keep the specific reports of and information about the incidents on close hold. The CG ordered all chutes in the division be immediately impounded into a secured storage area and physically guarded twenty-four hours a day by armed military police. Each chute in the division was then physically inspected separately by two experienced noncommissioned officer riggers. The three chutes that had malfunctioned received special forensic attention.

All chutes have a log record attached that shows the history of the chute, how many times it was used (jumped), and, most importantly to this event, which rigger had packed the chute each time. No matter how hard one tries, it's virtually impossible to restrict the information for an incident such as this as the word normally gets out and runs throughout the division grapevine. The Criminal Investigation Division conducted a thorough investigation and identified one rigger who, for whatever warped reason, was suspected of cutting the static lines while packing those specific three chutes. However, time was short because we still had our national military response mission responsibilities. We didn't have the time to do complete forensics, officially charge, arraign, and try the identified rigger, but we had to get him out of the division, and get him out fast. His defense could have been that someone else had gotten to the chutes after he packed them. The case could drag on, and because of jurisdiction requirements, he could possibly remain in the division. As a result of the initial investigation, we were able to immediately transfer him out of the division to a non-rigger job on another army post where the criminal investigation would proceed. We then had to get all our parachutes back to operational status, so every single chute in the division was again double-checked thoroughly, labeled OK, and then returned to the secured area. To ensure that all in the division would know that the problem had been resolved, General Meloy decided that all master parachutists in the division headquarters would make the first jump with the recently double-checked chutes. I, of course, was included. At Green Ramp, we donned our chutes, went through jumpmaster checks, and boarded our C-130. As we reached the jump altitude over the drop zone, we went through our jump commands and when the jumpmaster gave the "Go" command, the CG was the first to pop out the door. I was third behind him, and in a flash, I was out the door and into the prop blast. When my chute snapped open, I was more relieved than usual, and when I saw that all the other chutes had opened, and there were no malfunctions of any kind, I breathed a sigh of relief. Once the division grapevine heard that the test jump had gone well, the built-up tension left the division like air out of a balloon. I never heard about the further investigation, but at least the problem had been eliminated from the division.

A few months later, there was a push to periodically jump at a lower altitude to adjust to jumping at a combat-jump altitude, which would be between 400-900 feet depending on the impending danger on the ground. Our normal training jump altitude was 1,250 feet, but combat jumps require jumping in at a lower altitude to reduce the possibility of enemy detection and ground fire. Historically, combat-jump altitudes vary, and some have been done as low as 400 feet, but that does not give much time to pull a reserve if the main chute fails. The decision was made to compromise the periodic training jump altitude to 900 feet. When I made the training jump in Vietnam with the 173rd, I jumped from about 900 feet, or possibly a tad lower. General Meloy again called on the Master Blasters in the division headquarters to make the first 900-foot jump. We again proceeded to Green Ramp, geared up, got jump-mastered, trudged onto the C-130, and roared off. As we approached the drop zone, I felt the aircraft slow to jump speed (about 135 miles per hour) and then drop in altitude. As we reached 900 feet, General Meloy again stood first in the door, and this time I was just behind him. I punched out the door, the chute popped open after the normal four-second interval. Nothing seemed different except the ground was closer after my chute fully deployed. I thought that in a pinch, and with quick reflexes, I could have gotten a good pull on my reserve if necessary. Another airborne adventure not to be forgotten.

An Exercise in Actual Crisis Planning

After I was well settled in as division G-2, General Meloy called a select group of us into his office. The two deputy CGs, the chief of staff, the G-3, the division sergeant major, and I were present. There was an air of importance and some uncertainty. The CG had received a sensitive alert order directly from the army chief of staff, General Shy Meyer, to begin planning for an interdiction mission in the Zagros Mountains of Iran.

We were in the deep throes of the Cold War and the Soviets had been creating problems in that region of the world. The Soviets had been coveting Iran's oil reserves and attempting, as part of the Cold War, to weaken our strategic ally, the Shah of Iran. The warning order we received from Washington was to prepare an operational plan to prevent an incursion by the Soviets moving from military bases in the Caucasus, through the Taurus and Elburt Mountains, the Zagros Mountains, and into Iran proper. Although this was something we had discounted as an immediate possibility, we in the 82nd had to always be aware of a multitude of problems around the word and be prepared for a wide range of missions.

The eventual Soviet objective for the operation was to capture, occupy, and exploit the Iranian oil fields. Washington had learned of this possible military operation through top secret (at the time) intercepted communications describing the Soviets conducting extensive military exercises, which portrayed an invasion of Iran along several "fronts," including a main thrust through the Zagros Mountains. Evidently, the Soviets were attempting to take advantage of what they perceived as Iranian weakness at the time and the lack of will of other nations to come to Iran's defense.

Knowledge of our mission, for the time being, would be shared only within the group that had gathered in General Meloy's office, and he would be the only one to decide on any exceptions. The CG provided us with his initial guidance, details of the operational situation, and our objectives. The G-3 had a command post tent set up in a field across from division headquarters. The tent was surrounded by barbed wire and guarded by a twenty-four-hour armed division military police detachment. Due to the utmost secrecy of the planning phase, I would have to initially gather some of intelligence available without creating any suspicions within the G-2 Section. Fortunately, we shortly received a highly classified Intelligence package from the Department of the Army with a great deal of the valuable relevant intelligence, along with appropriate maps, sketches, and photo imagery. I began spending much of my days and of most nights in the operations tent, going through what had become my normal operational planning process: assessing the enemy order of battle including strengths and weaknesses, weather, terrain, and possible enemy courses of action. Similarly, as I had done while with 101st Airborne, when we addressed the exigencies of recovering the perforated steel planking from Khe Sanh. Based on my initial intelligence assessments, the G-3 created an operational plan that called for three airborne infantry battalions, with three more in reserve and three batteries of light artillery in support, occupying positions in the mountains and passes along the Soviet probable route of march. At first blush, our operational plan, depending on the strength of the invading force, its attendant artillery and air support, had the potential to become a vicious firefight, possibly with high casualties on both sides. After the G-3 collated all our inputs into our operational plan, he sent it by courier to the army staff. The following day, we were informed that due to the probable risk of high US casualties and resultant national and international political fallout, that there was not a lot of enthusiasm for our proposed plan in Washington. We were directed to modify the plan or go back and start over.

That night, while lying in my cot in the tent, I thought more and more about other possible scenarios. I considered that the Soviets may well initially use special operations forces (Spetsnaz) early in the operation but would eventually move their highly mechanized attack force rapidly through the passes. Our light infantry battalions would be able to slow those forces down, but, in the end, probably would not be able stop those fast-moving armor-led units advancing through the mountain roads and passes. As I scoured the map and terrain studies, I noticed the number and type of bridges along the narrowest route of march. I then thought we could deploy our infantry units to occupy and defend the bridges. I then recalled the airborne operations in Holland in 1944 and the high casualties the paratroopers incurred during Operation Market-Garden against far stronger mechanized German forces (depicted in the film A Bridge Too Far). So, defending the bridges was probable a nonstarter. I then thought that if we could destroy some key bridges along those narrow mountain passes, we could stop them cold. But I knew they had several armored vehicle launch bridges (AVLB), which are like mobile scissor bridges that mechanically stretched from one side of a chasm to the other to create a virtual instant bridge. I then thought that if we could identify and drop longer bridges that created gaps that were too wide for their AVLB to span, that would work. I thought that as an economy of force, we could destroy one or two of those longer-spanned bridges using a small number of division engineers protected by some airborne infantry.

Around 0300, just as I was finalizing my calculations and formulating the concept, General Meloy came through the tent flap.

We were the only ones inside the tent. I poured us both a cup of strong airborne coffee and we talked for a while about the challenges involved in the contingency operation we had been assigned. I asked him if I could run a concept by him and see what he thought. As usual, he welcomed my input and after I briefed him on my AVLB concept, he beamed from ear to ear and said, "Jack, run that by me one more time." After I briefed him again, he told me to finalize my concept and brief it to the rest of the select group later that morning. After my briefing, the G-3 then crafted an operational plan based on my preliminary concept. The CG then phoned General Meyer and recommended that he needed to come to Fort Bragg and be briefed on our latest operational concept. (Which we were internally now calling the AVLB Briefing.)

General Meyer flew down to Bragg the next day. After we had finished our briefing, we all were elated when he said that he liked the concept, thought the plan was sound, doable, and would provide the desired military effect and accomplish the mission with little probability of high casualties and resultant political impact. As time went on, the probability of a Soviet incursion into Iran dissipated, but the lesson I took from the exercise, was that ingenuity and foresight using intelligence can be a force multiplier, and I would later apply it in great effect during Desert Storm.

The Beginnings of Army SERE

Several weeks later, a reserve military intelligence major arrived in the division for his two-week active-duty stint with the G-2 Section. He came into my office, saluted, and barked, "Sir, Major Rowe reporting for duty." I asked him to sit down, gave him a cup of coffee, and as we talked about his military background, he said that he had been in Special Forces in Vietnam, left active duty, and was now in the reserves. He was assigned to the 82nd for his annual two weeks of active duty for training. As I kept mulling his somewhat familiar name in my mind, it suddenly hit me, he was Nick Rowe, who he had been the young Special Forces first lieutenant when captured and held as a prisoner of war in Vietnam. He had then written the book Five Years to Freedom about his capture, his many attempts at escape, and finally successfully escaping after being held captive by the Viet Cong for five years. Nick and I talked for quite a while, and we hit it off right away and the next evening he came to our house for dinner. At dinner, I asked him why he had left the army that he evidently still loved. He said that he didn't look forward to being a "thirty-year prisoner of war." After he had returned from Vietnam, the army kept sending him around the country to various posts and service organizations to give lectures about his experiences and to help train soldiers to avoid capture and how to act when captured. How they were to act, survive, and eventually escape. I asked him if I could help get him back on active duty and into a regular assignment. He told me that since his time at West Point, the army had been his life and was always what he felt he was born to do. After a couple of days, he told me that he had decided to come back on active duty. I was on the phone that day. I had recently received permission from the CG to create a much-needed embryonic Survival, Evasion, Resistance, and Escape (SERE) program for the division, and I thought during his two weeks with us, Nick would be the perfect choice to take that project on and certainly would excel at it. At that time, the air force had been designated as the Department of Defense's executive agent for SERE, but there was no army-wide program or SERE school. Because of the worldwide, short notice missions assigned to the division, I thought we at least needed to develop a basic-level, divisional, SERE program.

I provided Nick with one of our most talented warrant officers, Russ McIntyre, to help him with the project. Nick and Russ accomplished a lot during those two weeks and eventually produced a division-wide series of reports and training methods for

SERE. However, I also knew that the army-wide responsibility for SERE did not belong in a single division. I was convinced that the program would best placed under the umbrella of the JFK Center on Smoke Bomb Hill. I drove over to the center and had a long chat with my mentor Colonel Lee Mize and suggested that Nick and Russ divide their time researching and building their SERE project between the division and the JFK Center. He agreed without hesitation. The night before Nick was to return home, we went to a local Vietnamese restaurant and said our goodbyes over a satisfactory number of "33" beers. Months later, Nick called and said that he had been accepted back on active duty. I was happy for him. I called Colonel Mize and suggested that Nick be assigned to the JFK Center to create and develop a SERE program and school that would eventually become the army's core for SERE. He again wholeheartedly agreed and together we were able to help get Nick assigned to the center once he returned to active duty. When Nick arrived at Fort Bragg and was about to sign in, I had lunch with him, wished him luck with the SERE program, and told him that I was going to transfer Russ McIntyre over to Smoke Bomb Hill to help him in his efforts. Nick put his heart and soul into that program and eventually brought it to an army-wide success. He was so successful and so well thought of that to this day, Nick is considered the Godfather of the army's SERE program. The course headquarters and training area is called the Colonel James "Nick" Rowe Training Compound at Camp Mackall, North Carolina and is considered by many to be one of the most important advanced training programs in Special Operations and in the army.

Nick and I tried to get together, especially at our home for dinner, as often as we could until I left Fort Bragg. The next time I saw Nick was in 1987 when we both were attending the Military Assistance Advisory Course. I was attending prior to my move to China as the defense and army attaché. Nick, now a colonel, was on orders to the Philippines as the chief of the Army Section in the Military Assistance Advisory Group. We talked at length about what we had been doing since we had been together at Fort Bragg and where we both were headed for our next assignments. Having read about the continuing communist New People's Army insurgency in the Philippine Island of Mindanao, and knowing Nick, I suspected that he would get personally involved solving the problem. I knew that he probably would want to get into the "weeds" fighting the insurgency, but I told him that he probably should leave the down and dirty efforts to those in the field tasked with that mission. Nick nodded his head in agreement, but his eyes told me otherwise. We said our goodbyes and promised to keep in touch. In April of 1989, I was told that, while riding in a staff car leaving the Military Assistance Advisory Group housing compound in Manila, Nick was killed by automatic rifle fire. The New People's Army eventually took credit for the assassination. I found out later that Nick had been involved in the counterinsurgency, and it may have cost him his life. Nick was a great soldier and wonderful friend. I miss him to this day.

The Red Beret Caper

The beret is as emotionally and viscerally involved in the airborne tradition just as jump boots are. People often ask, what's the big deal? Believe me, it's a big deal. In 1973, the 82nd had been authorized by the army to wear the red beret. Historically, elite airborne units around the world have proudly worn the distinctive red beret. Unfortunately, after 1973 and over the next several years, many other units in the army had unofficially, and without authorizations, adopted their own versions of distinctive, sometimes crazy, headgear. Things got so out of hand, that in late December 1978 the then chief of staff of the army directed that except for the Special Forces (Green Beret) and the Rangers (Black Beret), all units would wear only the officially recognized headgear: the dastardly baseball cap.

When I left Smoke Bomb Hill, took off my green beret, and moved over to the division, I had to wear the army green baseball cap. I hated that baseball cap with a white-hot passion, and the folks in the G-2 Section were well aware of that disdain. In October 1980 General Meloy pleaded our case for wearing the red beret with the then army chief of staff, General Shy Myer. Finally, around Thanksgiving of that year, the return of the red beret for the 82nd was officially approved. (And approved for wear by those in the army on airborne status.) During a 16,000-trooper formation at our division stadium, General Meloy proudly announced that we could now officially wear our red berets again. The yells of "airborne" and "all the way" could be heard all the way to downtown Fayetteville. Once I could don a red beret, I returned to my office, placed that green baseball cap on the top the bookshelf behind my desk, and ran it through with a huge bowie knife that I had carried in Vietnam. That pathetic looking cap, with that massive knife run through its innards, stayed on my bookshelf until I left the division. As a going away gift, the G-2 Section gave me a beautiful plaque with a photo of all of us standing in front of the division museum, and in the corner of the plaque was an etched image of a bowie knife stuck in that ugly green cap.

Developing a Linguist Database

One day, while visiting the Division Military Intelligence Battalion, I was told during that they had a shortage of Spanish-speaking linguists in the battalion. As a result, when I got back to my office, I sent a high priority message to the Department of the Army requesting additional Spanish linguists. As I thought about the 82nd's worldwide mission and the possible requirement, not only for Spanish linguists but for other language speakers as well, I decided to conduct a division-wide language survey. I recalled that during some of my visits to various divisional units, I had spoken to several Spanish speakers, many with native fluency. I thought, that if we could identify the Spanish speakers already in the division, we could use their capabilities when and where we needed them. Additionally, I thought that we needed to come up with a process to identify not only Spanish speakers in the division but identify those who spoke other key languages, as well.

I tasked our planning section to create a questionnaire to send to the S-2 of each battalion-level unit in the division. The questionnaire required each unit to identify any foreign language speakers in their battalion and assess their level of expertise. As the results began to come in, we quickly learned that the division was rife with linguists in a multitude of languages, many with native fluency. I became increasingly amazed that we had such a previously unknown and untapped capability in the division. As a result of the survey, we found that we had nearly 2,500 Spanish speakers in the division (many had taken Spanish in high school), and many had native fluency. We also learned that the division had additional language capabilities that would be useful if we deployed to certain key areas of the world. Remember, this was during the Cold War. Aside from Spanish, we had speakers in such languages as Russian, Polish, Ukrainian, German, French, Italian, and even some esoteric languages like Swahili. I decided that we should first collate a linguist database for each brigade. I then tasked our plans shop to roll the results of the survey into a division-wide database that could be easily organized and disseminated to rapidly deploying brigades. Once alerted, each brigade could check its own linguist data base and if not satisfied, could use division-wide assets. Therefore, the deploying brigade could select, like a menu, the appropriate linguists available in their brigade or within the entire division. Once the data bases were finally collated and distributed, we began to use them, first in training exercises, then for contingency plans and, finally, for actual deployments. It eventually worked great, and the brigade commanders were very pleased with the system and its ultimate support when needed. Since it seemed to work so well within the division, I recommended up the chain of command that the army could use the same procedure for linguist collation and programming, but nothing that I know of ever came of it. At least we had the capability in place in the division, and our system would be used frequently and to great effect by our rapidly deploying brigades.

A BLUEPRINT FOR THE FUTURE

Being the principal Intelligence officer for an elite unit like the 82nd Airborne Division was a daunting daily challenge. We constantly updated the intelligence portion of numerous contingency plans involving key missions and areas of the world; produced daily division-wide current and periodic intelligence reports; established a SERE program for the division; and produced a series of studies on the ways, mores, and survival techniques for key areas of the world. Our most unique and useful product was titled "How to Fight and Survive in a Desert Environment." We provided General Meloy and the unit commanders with Intelligence support for six major exercises and deployments, coordinated the division map program with the Division Support Command, and created, developed, supported, and integrated a unique terrain analysis team into our intelligence capability. I continued to work on improving processes for developing collection fusion plans for use in our mission deployments, divisional contingency plans, and training exercises.

The initiatives and processes that I had developed in the G-2 Section supporting a combat-ready airborne division, and my close personal and working relationship with General Meloy would become a valuable blueprint for my later support with General H. Norman Schwarzkopf during Operations Desert Shield and Desert Storm. I continued to stay in touch with my mentor Colonel Lynn Murray at the Foreign Area Officer School. We would have friendly discussions over meals and more formal meetings in his office. During one of these meetings, he introduced me to a visiting lecturer, Colonel Lee Holland. Lee had been the army attaché at the embassy in Teheran in 1979 when protestors had taken over the US compound and held fifty-two American diplomats and citizens hostage for 444 days. He and his fellow hostages had been released in January 1981. Lee and I had lunch together and then spent some time discussing the FAO program and its importance to our representation and intelligence collection missions. He described, in scary detail, how the embassy in Teheran was overrun and he and his colleagues were captured and held hostage. Lee especially agonized over the fact that once the Iranians had taken over the Defense Attaché Office, they confiscated a tremendous amount of highly classified documents that may well have been damaging to our national interests. He was still very distraught when thinking about that chilling event.

As my tour in the 82nd was ending, General Meloy called me into his office and, like a proud father, told me that I had been selected for promotion to colonel. I thanked him wholeheartedly and he gave me a big airborne hug. Sandy Meloy was the best commander I have ever had, and we remained in contact until his death. Colonel is the rank every officer hopes to attain the minute they are commissioned in the army. With hard work and doing my very best in every job that I had, I was fortunate to reach that milestone. Sure, hard work and the right jobs helped, but some luck was also involved. Having the right bosses at the right time for the right job is like playing Russian roulette. One unfortunate circumstance and one bad efficiency report can limit a career drastically. Most important is having a loving spouse who understands the attendant hardships and sacrifices and appreciates the incredible privilege of a life in the army. An army spouse needs to be understanding of the constant uncertainty, constant displacement, long hours of waiting, and the ability to accept unpredictable demands with a singular quiet grace. Ann was my rock. I was fortunate, by the grace of God, that my life was not snuffed out in combat before I could marry Ann, have a wonderful family, and continue with my life-changing career.

Adding to my incredible experience in the 82nd, and making the colonel's promotion list, I learned that I had also been selected to attend the National War College in Washington, DC, for a year beginning in the summer of 1981. I would probably be promoted to colonel while at the National War College. During my last few months in the division, General Meloy was replaced by another great soldier, Major General Jim Lindsay. Even though I only spent a few months working for Jim Lindsay I enjoyed my time with him and learned a lot. As my time wound down, Ann and I resigned ourselves to the sad fact that we would be leaving the division and Fort Bragg, but we also looked forward to beginning the next episodes of my army career in Northern Virginia.

CHAPTER 6

TO THE PENTAGON AND BACK, AND A WHOLE WORLD IN BETWEEN

My year of study at the National War College (NWC) at Fort McNair was filled with an incredibly stimulating academic environment and wonderfully talented classmates, many of whom would eventually reach the pinnacle of their respective services. The student body at the NWC included officers from the ground, sea, and air services, including the Marine Corps and Coast Guard. Additionally, about a third of the students were drawn from the Department of State and other federal agencies, along with some international fellows. The NWC is a university-type school, rather than a service school, and provides an academically challenging environment for future leaders in preparation for high-level policy, command, and staff responsibilities. The curriculum emphasizes joint and interagency perspectives through senior-level courses in theory, development, and assessment of national security strategies.

Shortly after I arrived at the NWC, I was promoted to colonel. Ann pinned an eagle on one shoulder and the commandant pinned on the other. Promotion to colonel gave me particularly deep satisfaction as it represented my prior dedication and hard work. I had finally arrived at an intersection of my own personal interests, academic study, and service to country. Once I settled into the daily academic routine of the NWC, I was surprised with another honor: The faculty and my peers had selected me as their seminar leader.

Within such a challenging and encouraging atmosphere, I dove headlong into as much of the various aspects of the complex arena of national security policy formulation as I could. I researched and wrote reports on topics such as "Regional Strategies," "The War Powers Resolution," "Arms Sales to Taiwan," and a long, detailed thesis on "US Strategic Options in Asia." It all seemed worth the effort when the commandant told me that one of my reports had received special recognition from the National Security Council for "a detailed and insightful paper on the People's Republic of China-Taiwan Situation that is perhaps the most exhaustive review of the topic in existence today."

The highlight of my tour at the NWC came when I was designated to lead the first-ever military academic research trip to the People's Republic of China (PRC). I would be accompanied by two other classmates, one army and one navy. I was excited to finally venture into China, the country about whose history, people, military, government, and language I had studied so for so long. While on the trip, I was hoping to be able to do some recalibrating on my Chinese language skills. During the trip we visited various People's Liberation Army (PLA) headquarters, schools, and units. The trip highlight was a visit to the PLA's 197th Infantry Division where we were briefed on their unit missions and organization and later observed troops conducting skills training and firing weapons on the range. I would reflect on this trip later in my career. I have always considered my studies and experiences at the NWC incredibly formulative and worthwhile and I have always cherished my time there.

CHIEF, CHINA/FAR EAST DIVISION, DIRECTORATE FOR ESTIMATES, DEFENSE INTELLIGENCE AGENCY, WASHINGTON, DC: JUNE 1982–JANUARY 1983

After graduation from the NWC, I was assigned as chief, China/Far East Division in the Directorate for Estimates for the Defense Intelligence Agency in Rosslyn, Virginia.

Brigadier General Don Hilbert headed the directorate and we instantly bonded. Being fellow 173rd Airborne Vietnam vets may well have helped. This assignment promised to provide me with an extended experience in the alternate specialty that I had chosen: the in-depth study and analysis of China and the entire Far East. I was fortunate to supervise and provide substantive guidance to a talented group of senior military and civilian Asian specialists who were some of the most knowledgeable and expert scholars throughout the analytical community. While in Estimates, I was given a rare opportunity to contribute to national policy deliberations and analysis of the Asia/Pacific region. As a result, I was being afforded a tremendous opening to learn what being a China Foreign Area Officer (FAO) was truly all about.

Shortly after I arrived in Estimates, I was named as the acting defense intelligence officer for China and the Far East. Accordingly, I was the senior representative from the Department of Defense (DOD) for all matters concerning that area of the world to all organizations inside and outside of the department. I represented the DOD at all national and international conferences on the Asia-Pacific Region. Additionally, I was the primary US contact with the Washington-based representatives of the PLA. During those prior years of Chinese language and area studies, I had naturally developed an interest in the PLA, and now I was being provided the opportunity to have face-to-face contact with actual PLA officers.

Most were assigned to the PRC embassy in Washington. When representatives of the US government were invited to Chinese embassy functions, I was normally included and attended as the

DOD representative. Ann graciously attended many of them with me. I became acquainted with virtually all the PLA officers in the Washington area. During my early discussions with the PLA officers, I quickly realized that I had lost more than a step in my Chinese language fluency, so I decided to listen to language tapes in my car on the way to and from work. It surely did help. I really enjoyed building relationships while discussing military and political topics with the PLA officers, and some of those relationships I developed at the time would be rekindled during my later tour as Defense and Army Attaché in Beijing. During my time in Estimates, I not only gained a professional insight into China and the Far East, but a greater understanding of how the national intelligence system was structured and how it functioned. I represented the DOD during the collation, analysis, and writing of national intelligence estimates and defense estimates. I took part in high-level meetings and briefings on China and twenty-one other key Asian states in direct support of military and policy planning in the DOD, other governmental agencies.

After I had been in Estimates for six months, General Hilbert told me that I had been nominated by the army to be the military assistant to the Principal Deputy Assistant Secretary of Defense (PDASD) for International Security Affairs. Filling that position had evidently become an immediate high-level requirement in the department. I was scheduled for an interview with the sitting PDASD, Noel Koch (pronounced "Cook") in two days.

On the day of the interview, I drove to the Pentagon and pulled into a reserved parking spot in the huge Pentagon lot. Parking spots close to that imposing building are like gold. After presenting my clearance badge, I passed through the security post, walked up the stairs and then through the hallways to the E-ring, which is the outer ring of the Pentagon, where most of the highest-level executive offices were located. Mr. Koch's secretary greeted me warmly and ushered me into his office. He got up from his desk with a wide grin, shook my hand, and motioned for me to sit down. We then discussed my present situation, background, and the basic requirements for the job for about a half hour. As we neared the end of the interview, he asked when I could begin to work for him. I told him that I could probably be available quickly, but it was up to the personnel gurus to decide. He didn't give any indication concerning his decision and said he would get back to me one way or the other. He undoubtedly still had other interviewees from the other services. We said our goodbyes and I went back to Estimates. As I drove back, the thought of working in the DOD at the highest level of our military was very daunting, but the more I thought about the challenge of working at that level and how much I could learn, the job became more appealing.

I returned to my job at Estimates and continued to work on the numerous important initiatives that remained on our plate. About a week later, I got a call from army personnel and was told that I had been selected for the job and would be assigned to the Pentagon as soon as the following week. I was suddenly struck with mixed emotions. I really wanted to finish some of the important initiatives that I had started in Estimates, and I wanted to continue to learn my "trade" from the talented analysts and action officers in my division. On the other hand, I looked forward to working in the Pentagon, where I could learn the exigencies on how the DOD operates and hopefully contribute to high-level strategic policy formulation and decision-making. I said my personal goodbyes to my cohort analysts, many of whom I would enjoy working with during future assignments, and presented my out-briefing to General Hilbert.

OFFICE OF THE SECRETARY OF DEFENSE, WASHINGTON, DC: JANUARY 1983–JULY 1984

I could tell during my initial discussions and experiences with Noel that it would take me a while to gain his trust and confidence. Through discussions with him and others, I learned that his former military assistant army Colonel George McGovern was somewhat of a legend in the Special Operations community. Over time, he and Noel had become very close. George, who I knew peripherally during my tenure in the Special Forces, was a renowned runner. One day, while working for Noel, he had a heart attack and died suddenly. George's death had a real emotional effect on Noel. I could tell that it was going to be difficult for me to overcome George's memory. I vowed to work as hard as I could to win Noel's confidence and, hopefully, in the end, his friendship.

Noel was responsible for several important and complicated mission areas. He was the Deputy Assistant Secretary of Defense for Africa. He managed our efforts in international security affairs for the Near East/South Asia, East Asia Pacific, and Inter-America. Additionally, he was the department's director of special planning, which included the development of Special Operations Forces (SOF) and the responsibility for the department's efforts in the field of antiterrorism and counterterrorism. He was also responsible for representing the DOD in law of the sea negotiations. The law of the sea is a body of customs, treaties, and international agreements by which governments maintain order, productivity, and peaceful relations on the sea. As I looked at all of his responsibilities, I knew that I had my work cut out for me and anticipated a steep learning curve. The following year and a half working for Noel would present challenges to my personal time and to my family. I drove to work very early in the morning, at about 0430. Noel would normally arrive about 0900, and on most days, we would work until about 1900. My days were extremely long, but fortunately my weekends were normally free for time with family, except when we were on fact-finding trips to foreign countries. My specific personal responsibilities for Noel included serving as military executive and senior military adviser, coordinator for Security Initiatives for Inter-America, East Asia Pacific, Near East-South Asia, and Africa. I was also his senior military adviser for Special Operations and Counterterrorism.

My responsibilities were many and varied. I would begin each morning by reading through message traffic pertaining to the many countries within his sphere of responsibility that were involved in US international security initiatives. I would also select and highlight those reports that pertained to his responsibilities for terrorism and Special Operations. I oversaw the intricate planning and execution for four extended trips to Europe, the Middle East, and Africa, including former British and Francophone countries. For each trip, we would use a DOD DC-9 aircraft. During the trips, we would meet with heads of state and the highest levels of defense officials in each country. Our discussions would include mutual security issues, possible security assistance initiatives, and, if appropriate, cooperation and coordination in counterterrorism and Special Operations. Each trip lasted about a month, and all were extremely successful and worthwhile, but each one left us both exhausted. As an example, during one trip in February and March 1983, we visited Germany, Spain, Senegal, Liberia, Cameroon, Equatorial Guinea, Zaire (now known as the Democratic Republic of the Congo), Kenya, Sudan, Israel, Egypt, and then a return to Germany. Each of those trips provided me with incredible learning experiences. Most importantly, I not only learned a great deal about mutual interdependence on national security issues with appropriate countries but also gained a deep understanding of the incredibly different mores, politics, and cultural idiosyncrasies that make up our complicated world. During visits to some key countries, we were able to assess and make recommendations that led to the development of bilateral contingency plans, cooperation, and liaison in the fields of counterterrorism and SOF.

Terrorism and Counterterrorism

During the time I worked for Noel, terrorism and counterterrorism were very real and contemporary national issues. Noel had worked on the after-action report for the 1983 Beirut Marine Barracks/

Embassy bombings as a full member of the Terrorist Incident Working Group led by the national security adviser, Admiral John Poindexter. I would coordinate Noel's attendance and input at the group's periodic meetings. My White House point of contact, whom I would call as often as necessary, was a young marine major, Oliver North. Ollie was knowledgeable and accommodating every time we talked.

Noel's assigned responsibilities in the field of counterterrorism included the development of US military policy for counter and anti-terrorism; assuring the adequacy of US military counterterrorism preparations, including the development of appropriate counterterrorist forces; counterterrorism training for US forces abroad; liaison with all foreign counterterrorism forces and foreign national authorities having host nation responsibility for the protection of US military personnel and their dependents; representing the DOD at the Terrorist Incident Working Group; and furthering the development of SOF.

We established contact and continued to nurture relationships with elite counter- and anti-terrorist organizations and units both at home and abroad. In the US, we oversaw the development of joint counterterrorism capabilities. The first joint unit created was the Joint Special Operations Command (JSOC), then commanded by a good friend and inspiring leader, Major General Dick Scholtes, who had been the deputy commanding general for operations for the 82nd Airborne when I was the G-2. The units subordinate to JSOC at the time were the army's Delta Force and the navy's Seal Team Six. During that time, the existence, name, and mission of those units were highly classified. They were already in the process of becoming incredibly capable units even during the early to mid-stages of their development.

Early on we visited the and still-evolving Seal Team Six. Upon our arrival at their site, we were met and escorted by the commander, Captain Dick Marcinko. Dick gave us an initial briefing on his progress forming the unit, their training regimen, and introduced us to many of his impressive SEALs. He then escorted us through their facilities and showed us some of the unique weapons, vehicles, and communications gear in their inventory and described some others they were in the process of developing and acquiring. That evening, Noel and I had a great dinner in town with Dick and several of his SEALS. Dick Marcinko was an unforgettable maverick and exactly the type of leader needed at the time to aggressively develop, promote, acquire funding, recruit highly qualified people, and acquire unique equipment while building a unit that would eventually become a national treasure. We also visited Task Force 160, the Night Stalkers, which was and still is the best aviation support unit for the most difficult and critical missions conducted by our counterterrorism and SOF. During our visit, they took us on an incredibly difficult, impressive, and dangerous night operation exercise.

Worldwide Counterterrorism Units

We visited some of the finest counterterrorism units in the world to ensure that we could count on their support in times of crisis and learn from their unique capabilities and experiences. We began our efforts in Germany with a visit to the elite counterterrorism unit, GSG-9 (Grenzschutzgruppe 9, in English "Border Protection Group 9"). Our primary liaison contact with GSG-9 was the assistant army attaché at the US Embassy in Bonn, Major Bernie McDaniel. Bernie was a German foreign area officer and had spent most of his army career up to that point stationed in Germany, studying the German language and working in various military liaison, military assistance, and intelligence positions. He spoke German brilliantly. Bernie introduced us to General Ulrich "Rick" Wegener, who was the commander of the Bundesgrenzschutz Westen (Federal Border Protection-West), and who had a close and historically special relationship with GSG-9. Rick was its commander when Lufthansa Flight 181 was skyjacked in 1977 and taken to Mogadishu, Somalia. He became an immediate German national hero after he and his GSG-9 operators, using incredible skill and daring, breeched the aircraft, killed all the hijackers, and rescued all the passengers.

Noel and I would eventually form a close relationship with Rick Wegener and the GSG-9. During our first visit to GSG-9, the commander briefed us on the workings of their headquarters, their organization, mission, training, special weapons, communications gear, and unique rescue equipment. The commander then took us to the Heckler & Koch arms factory where we were shown some new weapons that were being developed for the unit.

One evening, Rick Wegener and the GSG-9 leaders invited us to a dinner at the state guesthouse, Schloss Gymnich, near Bonn, which was the West German capital at the time. Interestingly, the GSG-9 planned a decoy scenario for the trip to the schloss to confuse any possible terrorists who may have been trying to assassinate Noel. The GG-9 used two specially armored black Mercedes sedans. Noel and I rode in one of them, driven by a GSG-9 member who had a modified Uzi stashed in a specially built-in slot in the driver's door. He drove on the autobahn toward the state guesthouse at 210 kilometers an hour (about 130 mph), weaving back and forth and changing leads with the other Mercedes to confuse any potential assassin. It was quite an impressive and unforgettable experience.

After a wonderful German dinner at the schloss, a couple of the GSG-9 officers asked me to follow them into a large banquet hall next to the room where we just had dinner. On one wall was a large curtain covering some sliding panels. When they pulled back the curtains and slid open the panels, there was what looked like a large, somewhat faded, military operational plan. They told me that during World War II, the schloss had been General George S. Patton's headquarters. I don't know if it really was Patton's headquarters, but it sure did look like an authentic military operational plan to me. Supposedly, Patton had crafted a contingency plan for the Allied Forces to push the Russians back eastward once Germany had been defeated. I had read somewhere that Patton said that "we had defeated the wrong enemy" and may have taken his theory at least to the planning stage. He evidently foresaw the future of Europe with an Iron Curtain and an international Cold War. He may have been influenced by the questionable agreements signed at the Yalta Conference in February 1945. Patton had previously been relieved of command for making aggressive statements toward the Soviet Union.

During one of our trips to the Middle East, we were able to visit elite counterterrorism units in Israel and Egypt. In Israel we spent some valuable time with their elite national counter terror unit, the Yamam whose members were, of course, highly experienced, tough, and extremely impressive. The highlight of our visit to Israel was the privilege of spending quality time with Israeli counterterrorism and counterespionage legend Rafi Eitan. Among other accomplishments in his storied career, he was in charge of the Mossad's operation that led to the tracking down, apprehension, and return to Israel of the Nazi war criminal Adolf Eichmann. Mr. Eitan spent a great deal of time talking to Noel and me. He explained his views about the intricacies and extreme importance of counterterrorism, along with covert and clandestine operations. He was a brilliant, storied, dedicated Israeli patriot and highly regarded as a hero within intelligence circles throughout the world. Because of his vast and varied experiences, he foresaw the future with great clarity. I learned a great deal during those talks with Rafi Eitan and would recall his sage advice and counsel during some later challenges of my career.

After we left Israel, we traveled to Egypt where we were given the opportunity to have a meeting with the defense minister, Field Marshal Abu Ghazala. The field marshal had been sitting next to Anwar Sadat on October 6, 1981, when the Egyptian president was assassinated during a military parade. At the time of our visit, Abu Ghazala was considered the second most powerful person in Egypt, second only to President Hosni Mubarak. We talked at length about cooperation in the field of counterterrorism and possible bilateral initiatives including foreign military assistance and sales. During our discissions concerning the importance of trust and solidarity during the fight against terrorism, we discussed the very secretive elite Egyptian counterterrorism unit 777. The field marshal gave us permission and the opportunity to visit the unit at its field headquarters. While there, we found the 777 to be highly motivated, capable, tough, and, if necessary, probably ruthless.

During our visits with various foreign elite counterterrorism units, I became convinced that close and continuous coordination and cooperation with units in key countries in the world was crucial to the combating and eventual defeat of worldwide terrorism.

Reforming Our Special Operations Forces

During my time in the Pentagon with Noel, we became more and more convinced that there was a great need to reform our SOF. The more Noel saw the continuing nagging problems of the required support relationship between the services and the SOF, the more frustrated he became. SOF were overly dependent on the services to optimally fulfill their personnel, equipment, and mission requirements. It seemed that the services were constantly either postponing or shorting the fulfillment of SOF's personnel and equipment requirements. Noel was constantly on the phone with one of the service representatives, pleading, cajoling, and, at times. even threatening them to have them fulfill whatever obligation was the topic of the day. What finally drove Noel off the edge were the difficult and frustrating negotiations with the air force over the delivery number and dates for the Lockheed MC-130 Combat Talon Special Operations aircraft. The Combat Talon provides support for infiltration, exfiltration, and resupply during operations in hostile or denied territory.

Noel asked me to broach the subject with some of my contacts in the services and the Special Operations community. As a result of those in-depth discussions, I concluded that the current situation was untenable and dysfunctional for all sides and, if allowed to continue, could lead to major problems during future operations or crises. The services, rightly or wrongly, would most likely give a higher degree of priority to their own sets of service objectives and requirements. As a result, the services and the SOF were both getting the short end of the stick. Once I finished my extended discussions and phone calls, I briefed Noel on my conclusions. I told him, what I'm sure he had already surmised: The system was broken and needed to be fixed and fixed soon. Our national interest, lives of troops, and the further development and growth of operations forces required it.

As time went on, Noel became increasingly frustrated. He felt strongly that the SOF should not be held hostage to the whims and idiosyncrasies of the various services budgetary, logistic, or personnel support. He eventually became convinced that the SOF should be split away from service dependency and be provided their own Major Force Program (MFP). The separate MFP would provide SOF the budgetary authority to obtain their own resources necessary to achieve their own command objectives and plans. Thus, Noel began to fight like a bulldog for changes within the department and on the hill. This effort was taking place during 1983. Along with Noel's SOF division director Lynn Rylander, we began writing position and informational papers in support of major reforms for Special Operations. Eventually, we were able to convince some key members in the department and in Congress that the reform of SOF was critical to future national military capabilities. Dick Scholtes provided some of the most compelling testimony on the hill when he explained how conventional force leaders misused the SOF during the operation in Granada by not allowing them to use their unique capabilities, which resulted in higher than necessary casualties among the SOF.

As the time came for my reassignment, Noel and I had become close friends. He had a farewell party at his home for Ann and me and gave us a unique farewell gift. I learned a lot serving with Noel Koch, especially a dedication to the future of SOF. After I left the Pentagon, Noel and Dick Scholtes fought continuously on behalf of Special Operations reform for the next year and a half. Even after Noel left the Pentagon, he continued supporting the initiatives and actions that we had initiated. Finally, in April 1987, Congress passed a bill that established the unified four-star-general-led United States Special Operations Command with its own Major Force Program (MFP-11). Even though they were now separate, the SOF would still fight in concert with the combatant commanders if required, but they would no longer be dependent on the services and would be free to organize, recruit, train, equip, and fight on their own. Although the decision on the SOF reforms were made after Noel and I left the Pentagon, we were proud that we had clearly identified the problem and began the early initiatives that led to SOF reforms critical to our nation's defense.

Onward, Ever Onward

Early in 1984, I was informed that I had been selected for the colonel's command list and was slated to assume command of the 500th Military Intelligence Group (brigade-level) based at Camp Zama, Japan, in July. Ann and I were pleased because the base had full grammar and high schools, which meant that John, Jeff, and Mei would be able to accompany us during that two-year command tour.

Language capability is invaluable to any mission dealing with a foreign country and is almost mandatory under certain circumstances. Prior to our moving to Japan, I attended an intense Japanese language course at the State Department Language School in Washington, DC. Initially I was concerned that that the course might conflict with my Chinese language fluency, but I enjoyed learning the Japanese language. Although I certainly never could attain the level of fluency I had with Chinese, I learned enough Japanese to at least carry on a casual conversation.

500TH MILITARY INTELLIGENCE GROUP, UNITED STATES ARMY INTELLIGENCE AND SECURITY COMMAND: CAMP ZAMA, JAPAN: JULY 1984–JULY 1986

Ann, John, Jeff, Mei, our dog and cat, about five thousand pounds of suitcases, and I arrived at Narita International Airport in Tokyo, Japan, in July. We were met by the group sergeant major and deputy group commander, Lieutenant Colonel Ralph "Red" Hampton. Red was bright and very mission oriented. He was extremely capable, and as my alter ego would keep everything in order "at home" in the group so that I could "get out and about," which was important to the accomplishment of the type of missions assigned to the group. We initially moved into the base guesthouse, where we would stay for a little over a month until a set of quarters on "the hill" came available. Ann and I were happy to wait. We finally moved the whole family into those wonderful quarters, which were of Japanese U-shaped design, with a view of the mountains so beautiful it almost made us cry. Ann and I always said that those were the best military quarters we ever had, and that our two years in Japan were the best overseas tour we ever had.

A Mission and Its People

The 500th Military Intelligence Group was a multidisciplined unit with six major subordinate elements, each with specific missions to conduct either human intelligence (HUMINT), signals intelligence (SIGINT), counterintelligence (CI), or document exploitation. The group also had a special program to plan and conduct sensitive bilateral intelligence activities with the Japan Ground Self-Defense Force. The group missions supported national and theater intelligence requirements for the Far East, the Pacific Basin, the Soviet Union, and even portions of the Middle East. We had an annual budget of about six million dollars.

Our mission required liaison, coordination, and cooperation with our Japanese military counterparts and was so important that we recruited a group of Nisei, second-generation Japanese, who spoke English well but also had the required native fluency in Japanese. They were invaluable to our mission, and I thoroughly enjoyed talking, working, and socializing with them.

Probably the most invaluable member of the 500th, and the one with the most compelling story, was in charge of our liaison office in Tokyo, retired army Colonel Harry Fukuhara. Harry was born in Seattle in 1920. After his father died in 1933, his mother took Harry and his brother back to her native Japan. Harry then went through normal schooling in Japan and after he graduated from high school, returned alone to the United States. After the Japanese attack on Pearl Harbor, Harry was interned in the Gila River Internment Camp in early 1942. While there, he enlisted in the army as a linguist in army counterintelligence. Unknown to Harry at the time, his brother had been drafted and was serving in the Japanese Army. After the war, Harry searched for and finally found his mother and brother living in their ancestral home of Hiroshima. Both had survived but were still suffering radiation effects from the atomic bomb. Harry served in the Pacific throughout the war and remained in the army, serving mostly in Japan, until he retired as a colonel in 1971. Over the years, he served in many positions with army Intelligence in Japan and when I assumed command was the considered the "crown jewel" of the 500th Military Intelligence Group.

Harry knew virtually every senior Japanese military officer and had known most of them since they were junior officers. They always treated him with some degree of deference, and he could call and ask them a question, provide access, or invite them to a function on a moment's notice and they would almost always respond favorably. His office was in Tokyo and was always a beehive of activity, including frequent nighttime card playing sessions, oft times with the senior leaders of the Japanese Self-Defense Forces.

Harry accompanied me on several fact-finding trips. The first was by train to Kyoto, Osaka, and Kobe in southern Honshu. He explained the significance of some of the most historical and important areas of Japan. He would give me incredible tutorials on Japan and its people while traveling on the train and while visiting each important sites, all invaluable information that I would be able to constantly recall during my tour in Japan and beyond. Harry was unassuming and totally professional. He lived and breathed his mission. I learned a lot from Harry Fukuhara and admired the way he always conducted himself. Treat people well, be treated well.

The 500th Military Intelligence Group's battalion-level SIGINT unit was Field Station Misawa, located on the northern tip of the island of Honshu. Its mission was broad, and its people were intelligent, talented, and dedicated. Fortunately, they were located on the Misawa Air Base along with a US Air Force F-16 fighter wing. The base was fairly isolated, and winters were long, harsh, and the snow omnipresent. One year while I was in Japan, Misawa had 242 inches of snow. Misawa had been a key Japanese base prior to and during World War II. During my initial orientation at the field station, as I was in the process of being shown around the office complex, they pointed out a winding staircase and asked me to climb up. When we arrived at the top, we entered a small cupola. They then asked me to turn around and look with a 360-degree view. They pointed out that the building was built in the shape of a large navy ship. Evidently, the Japanese had created excruciatingly detailed plans for their attack on Pearl Harbor. The shape of the point and harbor near Misawa were similar to those at Pearl Harbor. For realistic training, the Japanese built what was now our headquarters building in the shape of a ship to use during training for bombing or torpedo runs in anticipation of their attack on Pearl Harbor. As I looked out over the horizon, I could picture "Zeros" and "Val" dive bombers and "Kate" torpedo bombers zooming in high and low off the water, practicing penetrating attacks on this shadowy looking "ship."

Several months after I had assumed command, we had a visit from my immediate boss at Intelligence and Security Command, Brigadier General Chuck Scanlon. He was a great supporter and a no-nonsense boss. Chuck had commanded the 66th Military Intelligence Group in Germany and had a good feel for our mission. I briefed him on several of our new initiatives and showed him a few high evaluations we had received from those who were using some of our new and inventive procedures and products. He seemed pleased with what we showed him. I was trying to move the group into the computer age with automatic data processing applications for intelligence collection management and objective targeting, along with the programming of fiscal and administration systems. Although computer hardware and software were still, by today's standards, in the embryonic stages of development, we were trying. Chuck and I would later work closely together, especially in the HUMINT arena, until we both retired from the army.

Three or four mornings a week we held physical training (PT) formations where we first did calisthenics then followed with group two-mile runs. One day after we had completed our PT program, Red got a call from someone in the deputy commander's office who bleated out that there was someone in our physical training formation that morning who was out of uniform. For PT, we all normally wore our gray "Army" T-shirts and black shorts. Some of the group, at times had worn socks with stripes on them, as did soldiers in other units on post. The folks in United States Army Japan (USARJ), evidently trying to find a reason for existence, decided that that all units doing PT on base would wear only white socks. We all had faithfully complied. During that phone call, they reported to Red that there was a soldier in our morning formation who had worn striped socks. They wanted him identified and to have him report immediately to the deputy commanding general (a one star general) along with his immediate supervisor. Red, with a sly smirk on his face replied that the soldier who wore the striped socks was Major General Ed Soyster, the commander of INSCOM (my big boss), who was visiting us at the time. Red with a slight twinkle in his eye and in his voice, asked if they still wanted the violator to report to the deputy commander. Red was grinning from ear to ear at the stunned silence from the other end.

General Soyster had asked me to plan a trip for the both of us—an orientation trip to some select countries in Asia. Since I was a China FAO, he was especially interested in going to China with me. I arranged our trip to match his areas of interest, especially to China and to the countries where he had subordinate units: Korea and Thailand. We had very worthwhile visits to Korea and Thailand, and when we arrived in China, we visited the embassy and interesting sites in the Beijing area. We really bonded both as soldiers and friends. Ed Soyster has always been a good friend and would become a supportive rock for the remainder of my career. He would be especially helpful as the director of the Defense

Intelligence Agency during my pressure-packed responsibilities in Desert Storm.

Six Phases of Afterburner

During one of my command visits to Misawa, I had a dinner with a group at the club. I sat next to the commander of the F-16 fighter wing stationed at the air base, Colonel Mike Ryan. Mike and I talked at length about our respective units, our missions, and the operational challenges we all faced. He was gregarious and looked like a recruiting poster for fighter pilots. His father had been the chief of staff of the air force, and there was no doubt in my mind that Mike would follow him into the same job. (In fact, Mike would later become the chief of staff of the air force.) I told Mike of my lifelong dream of being a fighter pilot and about the incredible experience of my F-100F combat ride during my first tour in Vietnam. After hearing that I had previously volunteered for a combat mission, he knew I was serious. Mike asked me to call him the next time I planned a visit to Misawa and said that he would arrange a ride in the back seat of an F-16B Fighting Falcon. I almost kissed him, but at the time I couldn't afford to lose my security clearance.

The next time I was scheduled for a visit to Misawa, I gave Mike a call and learned that he was still serious about the offer. I was pumped. After I arrived at Misawa, I spent the morning at the field station, getting update briefings, and after lunch, I went over to the base-side and had a chat with Mike in his office, especially about the F-16. The F-16 was the first aircraft purposely built to pull incredible 9-G maneuvers, and although we would not come close to stretching the G-Force envelope, I was required to undergo a pressure test to determine whether I could take the G-Force without passing out or getting sick. I passed the test with flying colors. I then went to the pilot's preparation area where I was provided a helmet, oxygen mask, pressure vest, and a parachute to strap on. Then, the pilot and I talked about the flight procedures and safety precautions and the crew chief made sure I knew, among other things, where the emergency ejection lever was so that I wouldn't yank on it accidently. I crawled into the back seat behind the pilot and the crew chief checked that I was strapped in correctly and that my "G" vest and oxygen hose were all connected correctly.

I felt secure in the seat and had a surprisingly good view out of the bubble canopy. Once the pilot got the thumbs up, he cranked up the powerful F-100 engine and eased out of his parking spot toward the runway. We were just a one-aircraft mission. As we reached the takeoff end of the runway, he hesitated for a couple of seconds like a snake ready to pounce, and then he kicked it in. As we roared down the runway, he pushed it into what seemed like six phases of afterburner. We almost went straight up and got to altitude very quickly. He leveled off just above a large white cloudbank over the Sea of Japan. It was an eerie sight, literally like riding on top of a cloud, and it was super quiet. When he asked me if I would like to take the controls, I agreed, without hesitation.

Prior to takeoff, he had shown me the armrest-mounted, joystick controller, which looked to me like a one from a complicated video game. After I took the stick and began to "fly it," I felt like I was in part of a wonderful dream. The F-16 had a fly-by wire control system so the computer wouldn't let me do anything truly stupid. I flew the plane horizontally over that huge white cloudbank, so I didn't get much of a feel for height or distance. Once the pilot took back the controls, we peeled off to the port side back toward Misawa. As we broke through the clouds, I looked out toward our headquarters building and it indeed looked eerily like the outline of a naval ship. The pilot landed the plane as smooth as glass. Another dream come true.

Off to the Cold North

Harry Fukuhara planned a liaison trip for us to Northern Japan. During our first stop we were scheduled for a meeting with Lieutenant General Masuoka, the commander of the Japanese Ground Self-Defense Forces' Northern Army. After that meeting, we were scheduled to visit his subordinate 9th Infantry Division Headquarters near the coastal city of Sendai. At the end of the trip, we were scheduled to travel to Sapporo, on the island of Hokkaido for a military coordination conference with the Japanese Self-Defense Forces. Major General Kuga, the G-2 of the Japanese Ground Self-Defense Forces sponsored and made the arrangements for our trip and would accompany us throughout. General Kuga was our primary contact with the Japanese military, and during my time in Japan, he would open many doors for us. He would also become a good friend whom we invited to our home at Zama many times. General Masuoka's mission was primarily the ground defense of Japan's northern borders. Our session with him was informative and cemented a relationship that eventually furthered our Japanese American political and military relationships throughout the rest of my tour.

Harry had thought that it would be useful for us to get a good feel for what a Japanese infantry division looked like, its mission, and how well it functioned. We were given an informative unit briefing from the 9th Infantry Division commander. The division's organization was similar to one of our standard infantry divisions and seemed to fit well into the overall mission of General Masuoka's Northern Army. All of what we saw and heard during our visit with the division impressed on us that the soldiers, leadership, capabilities, and professionalism of the Japanese Ground Self-Defense Forces were of a very high standard.

General Kuga, Harry, and I then went on to Sapporo for a military cooperation and planning conference and while there visited the famous Sapporo Snow Festival. The presentation and proposals that we made during the conference were hailed as the definitive contribution to the conference. We, in turn, learned a great deal how cooperation and coordination with the Japanese military was important to our mutual national security. And importantly, we were able to continue to strengthen our bond with General Kuga. A few days after we returned from that important and very worthwhile trip to Northern Japan, I received an official memo from the USARJ G-2 (Intelligence), who was an army colonel. The memo charged that the "trip to the 9th Infantry Division was in violation of your authority, responsibility, and charter." It went downhill from there and was so inane that I felt it did not even deserve a response. I had been trying to explain our relationship to him for the last eleven months. He was an army military Intelligence officer and should have understood my mission charter and command relationship (none with his headquarters). We were not under the command of USARJ and had a tenant support agreement only. Frankly, if he had a scintilla of professional sense of mission, he should have been doing all he could to help us advance our important mission and relationship with the Japanese military. After reading that myopic and inane letter, Red was furious and spoiling for a fight. I told him that I would handle this one personally. I am normally slow to anger, except when I feel my mission is being interfered with or my troops are being screwed with. I spent some real quality time crafting an absolutely fiery response. I showed my friend and neighbor, the USARJ G-3 (Operations), the poison dart I was about to send to the G-2 and another that I was going to send back to Washington. As a result, the next day I received a memo from the G-3 stating that the G-2's correspondence had been summarily withdrawn. This sort of posturing and warped criticism in ignorance of mission was senseless and counterproductive. Little did I know that I would experience the same type of myopic attitude during other key missions later in my career.

Toward the end of 1985, the USARJ commander, Lieutenant General Alexander Weyand, left and his replacement was none other than my Screaming Eagle friend, Lieutenant General Bill Dyke of 101st Airborne fame. We greeted each other like long-lost brothers, and I enjoyed his support and friendship for the rest of my tour. One of the most worthwhile relationships that I had while in Japan was with an army attaché at the US Embassy in Tokyo, Lieutenant Colonel Wayne Fujito. The USARJ commanders, especially Bill Dyke, relied heavily on Wayne to assist with formal and informal relationships with Japanese military leaders and organizations. He spoke excellent Japanese, was well-wired personally with key leaders in the Japanese Self-Defense Forces and had a great relationship with Harry as well. One day as I was talking with Wayne at the US Embassy in Tokyo, I asked him if he could arrange a dinner with the Chinese defense attaché, Colonel Xu Huizi. A few weeks later, Wayne told me he was able to arrange the dinner. Ann and I hosted a great dinner in Tokyo with Colonel Xu, Wayne, and Harry along with their wives. Colonel Xu seemed appreciative of the invitation and was pleased that I was so interested in China, knew much about its history and mores, and that I spoke the language. Some weeks later, Colonel Xu reciprocated with a dinner invitation of his own. We met a few more times over the next several months until he returned to Beijing.

Toward the end of my tour in Japan, I got word that I was on orders to the Pentagon and assigned as the director for foreign intelligence in the office of the Deputy Chief of Staff for Intelligence, Department of the Army. I would be working directly for Lieutenant General Sidney T. "Tom" Weinstein, with whom, over the years, I had developed a close relationship and admired greatly. Although my family had truly enjoyed our tour in Japan, we were looking forward to returning to our home in Fairfax, Virginia.

OFFICE OF THE UNITED STATES ARMY, DEPUTY CHIEF OF STAFF FOR INTELLIGENCE, THE PENTAGON, WASHINGTON, DC: JULY 1986–MARCH 1988

As we moved back to the Washington, DC area, we hoped that our family would thrive in an American-centric lifestyle. During my time as the director for foreign intelligence, I would work very long hours, again getting to work in the dark and getting home in the dark. I would arrive at work, normally just before General Weinstein, at about 0400. As I read my large stack of daily intelligence reports, I would hear his footsteps coming down the hall. He often stopped by my office, and we would have a cup of coffee together. He called me "Jake." I would brief him on selected foreign intelligence reports I thought he should immediately know about. Additionally, we often discussed other important topics, such as the missions and organizations of army intelligence elements around the world. I learned a great deal on how to approach and deal with Intelligence missions and how to treat and lead people from General Weinstein. He was the best of the best.

In my new job, my missions were incredibly varied, and my experiences there would prove invaluable. I was charged to direct and coordinate the activities of three major army Intelligence staff divisions. The first was to provide indications, warning, and current intelligence to the army staff and subordinate organizations. Second, I provided intelligence assessments for various army policy and developmental processes. Third, I had to provide scientific and technical intelligence used during the development of army systems and counter systems. My directorate also provided threat scenario integration for the Defense Planning, Programming and Budgeting System, the Army Program Objective Memoranda, Defense Guidance, Force Modernization, and other appropriate army staff actions.

I also established policies and validated intelligence production for all army intelligence production centers and established, validated, and approved threat data for use in war-gaming exercises at all levels in the army. I provided timely and accurate worldwide intelligence assessments to the army secretariat and staff. Frequently, I was required to brief current intelligence to leaders at the highest levels of the army including the secretary.

On Wednesday mornings, in the Army Operations Center, I would brief worldwide current intelligence to General Weinstein and another general officer, Lieutenant General H. Norman Schwarzkopf, the army's deputy chief of staff for Operations. My boss, General Weinstein, and General Schwarzkopf were not only good friends but also West Point classmates and professional soul mates. I was impressed by the way they discussed many of the worldwide issues in a factual, cordial, and constructive way. Witnessing the army's Operations and Intelligence chiefs working closely together in a practical and nonconfrontational way made a deep impression on me. The intelligence officer holds a place critical to the success of any operation. In fact, during wartime, a commander assumes much of the responsibilities of the operations officer leading to a direct and personal link to his Intelligence officer. As I saw the professional interaction between Generals Weinstein and Schwarzkopf, I reflected on the nightmare of Vietnam, highlighted by the body count and village pacification program fiascos. I vowed then and there, that if I was ever pressured to provide the commander warped or inaccurate intelligence because it was what he wanted to hear, or to not provide accurate intelligence because it was what he did not want to hear, I would resign from my position and probably from the army. Our national interest and the troops in whatever contemporary "Crab Trap" they were in at the time, deserved no less.

During one of those Wednesday briefings that I gave to General Schwarzkopf and General Weinstein, I described an Iraqi air attack against the Iranian oil facilities on Kark Island using the Iraqi version of the French Mirage F-1 fighter. General Schwarzkopf asked how the F-1 could have flown such a long distance without refueling. I explained the F-1 itself didn't have the "legs" to reach Kark Island from their home bases without refueling in-air or upon landing at an intermediated staging base to refuel. I told him that the Iraqis did in fact do both during the full attack and recovery missions. I explained that during the attack leg, where time and surprise were critical to the success of the mission, they did what we called a "buddy" refuel operation, where one or some F-1s had been specially configured to be used as refuelers for the attack on the southward leg of the mission. After I completed my explanation, General Schwarzkopf nodded and smiled in seeming satisfaction.

During this tour, more than any other, I learned a great deal about how the army's intelligence procedures, organizations and capabilities fit into the joint and national intelligence systems. I visited the army's technical and analytical support centers, providing guidance, assessing their capabilities and how I could help improve their mission development. As the army representative, I took part in all major national intelligence actions and procedures, such as the National Intelligence Estimates, and as the army's (General Weinstein's) representative on the Military Intelligence Board.

During this time, our son John was determined to attend West Point. Ann and I dedicated our efforts to help him in his pursuit. My status as an active-duty colonel in the army had little to no influence toward his selection. He had to earn it on his own, hopefully, with our guidance. We even built a small PT area around our house for him to train for the test required by West Point. Fortunately, in the end, he had achieved high standards academically and physically, while participating in the right extra-curricular activities to eventually receive an appointment. We all were thrilled. But due to a minor physical problem, the academy wanted him to first attend the United States Military Academy Preparatory School at Fort Monmouth, New Jersey, for a year. Attendance at the prep school was tantamount to being accepted the following year, and frankly I thought year at Monmouth would, in fact, prepare him more than anything for his transition to the challenging life at West Point.

As time passed, I heard that the general officer selection board had been "sitting," and I was hoping that I would at least be one of the eligible military Intelligence colonels being given some serious consideration. Several weeks later, General Weinstein called me into his office and told me that I had made the brigadier general's promotion list. It was an absolute dream come true. The hard work and dedication that continuously drove me since I had returned to active duty had really paid off. A couple weeks later, General Weinstein told me that I would be assigned to the Defense Intelligence Agency with duty as the defense and army attaché at the US Embassy in the PRC in March of 1988. Hopefully, the untold intense number of hours of study, experience, and preparation pertaining to China, its people, government, culture, and language would prove invaluable during my tour.

However, the move to China would prove difficult for our family. Both boys could not come with us and would be leaving the nest for the first time. John would be attending the West Point Prep School, and Jeff would be staying with my mom and dad because his high school grade level was not available in China. Fortunately, Mei would be able to come with us.

I tried to learn as much as I could about the organization, mission, and situation for our attaché office at the US Embassy in Beijing. But I still had an important responsibility as the director for foreign intelligence in the Pentagon, and I continued to put my best effort forward to keep that mission as my highest priority until I left. This was a complicated but wondrous time for my family, and we looked forward to an adventure that should be an interesting, satisfying, and challenging assignment; we didn't know just how challenging it would become.

CHAPTER 7

INTO THE MIDDLE KINGDOM

DEFENSE INTELLIGENCE AGENCY: UNITED STATES EMBASSY, BEIJING CHINA, MARCH 1988–JULY 1990

I received orders to report to the US Embassy in the People's Republic of China (PRC) in March of 1988. I welcomed the challenge to use all my studying, education, and language classes to fulfill the ultimate military responsibility for my alternate specialty as a Foreign Area Officer for China: Defense and Army Attaché to the PRC.

I was still a colonel and not scheduled to be officially promoted to brigadier general until sometime during the summer or fall of 1988. To provide the proper rank credentials to the People's Liberation Army (PLA) when I arrived in Beijing, the then director of the DIA, Lieutenant General Lenny Perroots, requested that the army promote me to brigadier general before I began my work in Beijing. The army agreed to the request, and I would be promoted to brevet brigadier general on March 1 by my mentor Lieutenant General Sidney T. "Tom" Weinstein, who was still the army's deputy chief of staff for Intelligence. I was being promoted by a great friend and military Intelligence legend, and my mom and dad were driving down to Washington, DC, for the occasion. They had not been present for any of my promotions or award ceremonies since I was commissioned as a second lieutenant at my Georgetown graduation in 1958. I was proud to escort my mom and dad through the Pentagon for the promotion ceremony. As they walked through the halls they looked as if they thought they were on Mars. General Weinstein graciously gave a speech about me, my career and dedication to duty, and then he pinned a star on one shoulder while Ann pinned one on the other.

THE BEGINNINGS IN THE MIDDLE KINGDOM

As a newly selected and promoted brigadier general, I was required to attend the capstone course at Fort McNair in Washington, DC. Capstone is a six-week course for newly promoted flag officers of all services and focuses on planning and employing the US forces in joint and combined operations. The curriculum examines major issues affecting national security decision-making, military strategy, joint/combined doctrine, interoperability, and key allied nation issues. Since a course would not be starting right away, I was instructed to move on to my job in Beijing and then choose a six-week period during my tour to return to the United States and attend the course at Fort McNair.

I left for China in early March 1988 and would spend the first several months there alone as Ann waited at home until John, Jeff, and Mei finished the school year. I was greeted at the Beijing airport by the defense attaché office Operations coordinator Chief Warrant Officer Duane Deacon, who got me through passport control and customs easily due to his relations with the customs people and the fact that I had a black diplomatic passport in hand.

The next day, Duane drove me to the US Embassy, which was not impressive. It was the former Pakistani Embassy, and in those days, diplomatic facilities were very limited, even for a relatively important country like the United States. I had seen some beautiful embassies over the years, but this one appeared to be a real clunker.

When compared to attaché offices around the world, ours was one of the largest in size. We had eight military attachés, with three army (including me), three air force, one navy, and one marine in the navy section. We also had nine support staff from various services. I had a role in the selecting some of attachés after I had been designated as the next defense and army attaché in Beijing.

During the months before Ann and Mei would arrive, I tackled the inner workings of our office and assessed all aspects of the job: personnel, morale, structure, procedures, how we fit into the embassy structure and, most critically, how we related to the PLA. I frequently met with key elements of the embassy staff, including the ambassador, the deputy chief of mission, along with the political, economic, and other embassy sections or offices with missions and interests similar to ours. I also began to move out and meet attachés from other countries and to cultivate important working relationships and friendships, many of which would last throughout my twenty-six-month tour.

After my first couple of weeks in country, I was scheduled to make my first formal visit to the PLA Foreign Affairs Bureau (FAB). This organization was the only coordinating office that provided the official dialogue, liaison, and other arrangements between the PLA and the various attaché offices or any other foreign military organizations. We called them the "barbarian handlers". By a stroke of luck, the Chinese defense attaché who I had befriended during my tour in Japan, Colonel Xu Huizi, was now a major general and the chief of the FAB. Evidently, when he saw that I was scheduled to visit, he arranged to welcome me personally and greeted me warmly as an old friend in front of the "handlers." This personal and friendly greeting by the boss would undoubtedly help ease my future access to various organizations and areas in the PLA and with other elements of the Chinese government as a whole.

The US ambassador during my first months in Beijing was Winston Lord, who had an impressive civilian and governmental pedigree and was influential within international academic communities. He was best known for accompanying Henry Kissinger on his secret trip to China in 1971 and had established working relationships with Mao Zedong and Deng Xiaoping in the 1970s. The ambassador had immediate charge for how all sections at the embassy operated on a daily basis, and he held a mission meeting every morning where each section reported on their latest actions and decisions that could affect the mission's activities, especially with respect to Sino-US relationships. I made a concerted effort to ensure that our office was viewed as an integral part of the embassy family. I acted as Ambassador Lord's senior military adviser.

As I worked daily guiding the defense attaché office (DAO) office into a cohesive functioning team, I also had to learn how to work with my many "masters." Aside from being the senior military adviser to the ambassador, I represented the views and policies of the secretary of defense, the chairman of the Joint Chiefs of Staff, the commander in chief, Pacific, and the director of the Defense Intelligence Agency in reference to all things China and the PLA. Additionally, I, along with our other service attachés represented the service secretaries and chiefs of our respective services. Due to the complexity and various demands of this reporting structure, I was required to balance multi-faceted missions and objectives such as diplomatic, liaison, intelligence, representation, and security assistance on a daily basis. It took a constant awareness, professionalism, and diplomacy to ensure that my daily actions were in concert with my varied bosses. Additionally, the DAO was tasked to administer a multi-million-dollar security assistance program with the PLA. We were helping them develop and install new military systems for the PLA and PLA Air Force. Normally, with large military assistance programs such as ours, there would be a separate in-country military assistance advisory group, but, due to the Chinese government constraining the number of our personnel, we had to support the initiative directly from the within the DAO.

The Family Plan

After those first several jam-packed months in China, I returned to the United States to help Ann pack and to make arrangements for John, Jeff, and Mei. As we always did prior to a stateside or overseas move, Ann and I thought through how this tour would affect us all. John, once he graduated from high school in June, was on his way to the West Point prep school in New Jersey. Although he was not going to be with us in China, he was at least going to be taken care of and would be in a good place. Beijing International School had not yet developed into a full-fledged high school and only accommodated the first two years. That meant that Mei, who was going into the eighth grade, could come along with us to China, but Jeff was going into his junior year, so we had to find him somewhere to stay to finish high school. Fortunately, my mom and dad graciously volunteered to take Jeff in for the two years.

Ann and I were both struggling with the finality of both John and Jeff leaving the nest for the first time. Although these kinds of challenges test the mettle of a marriage and family, we seemed to always emerge stronger as a family. As I loaded the boys and their suitcases in our van and drove away, I looked back at Ann and saw that she was devastated, knowing that we probably wouldn't all be together again for at least two years. When we arrived at the airport, we quickly unloaded their gear and I choked out, "If you guys don't want to see a grown man cry, you'd better get in there, now!"

Ann and I finished organizing for our trip and helped Mei get ready for the two years abroad. We then loaded our suitcases, our beloved Schnauzer and our cat into a friend's van and then headed to Dulles Airport. After the long, tedious trip, we arrived in Beijing.

Duane picked us up and drove us to our flat, which was on the eleventh floor of a large Chinese apartment building. We were expected to do quite a lot of official entertaining, so we were provided a larger living space and one that would be more accessible to our guests. Most other embassy personnel were quartered in a large, gated compound in Beijing, called Jianguomenwai, which also housed other international diplomats and press corps. By mid-September of 1988, Ann and Mei were getting more accustomed to the Beijing environs and I dove into my job full swing. Mei entered eighth grade at The International School of Beijing and seemed to enjoy the worldwide comradery in her new school environment. Ann kept herself busy with our social/business schedule and work with the American Employees Association located at the embassy's separate administration building.

AN UNPRECEDENTED TRIP TO THE UNITED STATES

At the end of September, I heard that General Xu Huizi, who had warmly greeted me at the FAB a few months earlier, had been promoted to lieutenant general and would hold the position of chief of operations for the PLA. He was now in a very powerful and influential job, so I proposed a meeting with him to further promote our relationship with him and in turn with the PLA. We had recently delivered the promised military systems, so I felt our present military-to-military relationship was improving and in good-standing.

I recommended to Ambassador Lord that we should escort General Xu Huizi on a trip to the United States to visit several our headquarters, troop units, and observe some of our important military systems. The ambassador agreed that a guided visit would go a long way to help our country's military and political relationships with China. Although we had many missions, our main objective at the time was to improve our relationships with the PLA. After going through the necessary military channels to DIA and in turn the Pentagon, all approved the plan with much enthusiasm. This visit would be unprecedented and extremely helpful in forwarding our relationships not only with the PLA but with the Chinese government as well.

After presenting General Xu with the preliminary invitation and a proposed itinerary by way of the FAB, we were delighted to learn that he, and his senior leadership, had approved the trip. As far as we knew, such a high-level PLA delegation had never visited the US and had not been given such unique access to some of our headquarters and units. Our plan was that army Major Larry Wortzel and I would accompany him on this truly unprecedented trip. I always depended on Larry for a plethora of tough missions and had personally asked for his assignment to our office in Beijing. I had promoted Larry to sergeant when we were both Chinese language students at Monterey. (I would later promote to him colonel, and eventually assign him as the Army Attaché in Beijing.)

We were told by the FAB that General Xu would be accompanied by two of his subordinate generals, both of whom spoke little English. This trip would challenge our Chinese language skills to the max and hopefully we would make our language instructors proud. We planned a two-week trip during early October of 1988. Our trip began in Hawaii, where we visited Pacific Command and some of their various subordinate naval, army, and marine units. We then flew on to Washington, DC, where the leadership at the Pentagon graciously met with General Xu and provided him unprecedented access to some of our command-and-control centers and offices. We then took him to various military bases to observe various troop demonstrations. During one visit to Fort Stewart, Georgia we were able to watch a Ranger unit take part in a night combat jump. We also flew up to West Point for an official visit, and the army arranged to bring John up from the prep school at Fort Monmouth. I introduced John to General Xu, who smiled broadly, acknowledging the pride that he knew I felt. We even took General Xu to a Dallas Cowboys game with the support of the local Texas National Guard unit. The Cowboy's cheerleaders greeted us in our skybox and made quite an impression on him.

Larry and I spent every waking moment with General Xu, and we really bonded with him and his subordinate generals. We had long, fruitful discussions during those two weeks and I hoped, as a result that he would use his influence to help us promote our critical military-to-military relationships upon our return to Beijing. This was just the kind of experience and result I had hoped for when I joined the China FAO program. At the end of General Xu's visit, as we waited for our flight back to China, I asked him if there was anything else we could do for him. He smirked and laughingly asked for a green card.

AN AIRBORNE ADVENTURE

After our trip with General Xu, our military-to-military relationships improved markedly. Since arriving in China, Larry Wortzel and I had been lobbying our contacts in the PLA to jump with the Chinese airborne, so we deftly slipped in that idea during our trip with General Xu. We had already received permission from our bosses at DIA and the army to make a jump with the Chinese. This was not just a personal lark. One of the missions of a military attaché is to develop professional relationships with the host country's military. Unlike ours, their airborne units are not part of the army but are subordinate to the PLA's Air Force and were mostly based near Wuhan in Hubei Province. In February 1989, Larry and I were ecstatic when we finally got permission from the PLA to jump with the Wuhan-based units.

We packed our fatigue uniforms and boots and hopped on a plane to Wuhan City where members of one of the airborne regiments met us at the airport. After we arrived at the regimental camp, we had a Chinese box lunch and then were taken to the chute-packing and equipment area. I anticipated that they would give us detailed instruction on their elements, parachute equipment, version of jump commands, and how to exit the aircraft. But they just took our blood pressure and then asked us to pack our own chutes. The chutes were like ours, but not the same. Fortunately, they led us step-by-step through the process. We then were taken out on one of the runways and were shown the jump airplane we were going to use. It was a Russian model bi-plane, the Antonov AN-2 "Colt." It appeared bigger in-person than I had remembered when I had studied photos of the plane over the years. With the help of a Chinese jumpmaster, we donned our chutes and reserves and then waddled out to the plane. As we approached the plane, I asked how one exits the AN-2, and they said to just keep an eye on the test parachutists (we call them wind dummies).

As Larry and I sat in the plane, its huge radial engine roared to life and the plane began to shudder. We were wearing PLA parachute helmets with a red star on the front, which looked and felt strange. Engine roaring, we sped down the runway until we lifted off almost vertically. With the lift of those huge wings, it didn't take long before we quickly surged to jump altitude and leveled off into a smooth, horizontal flight path.

To test the wind and altitude, two PLA privates would be the first to jump. The wind dummies hooked up their static lines and then backed up to the bulkhead opposite the huge jump door. Then, one-by-one, they suddenly lurched toward the door and dove out just like they were diving into a pool. Once the Chinese jumpmaster had a good visualization of how fast and in which direction the wind dummies were floating toward the drop zone, he beckoned to Larry and me to stand up, then hooked up our static lines. We had been told that each Chinese paratrooper used a static line for their first three training jumps and afterward, they mostly did free fall jumps. When the jumpmaster gave me a signal to exit the aircraft, I ran haltingly, with my boots banging across the metal floor of the aircraft, until I approached the huge door opening. I leaped out into the prop blast and swooshed behind the plane like a rag doll until the chute snapped open. I let out a huge sigh of relief when I looked up and saw the chute had fully deployed and then prepared to enjoy the trip down. As I looked below, I could see that the drop zone was a flat farming field, with some low fences around it, so all I had to do was to make sure I avoided them. I landed with a halfway decent parachute landing fall and was certainly happy to be back on the ground and in one piece. Larry bounded down not far from where I had landed, and we gave each other a big smile and thumbs-up. The regimental commander held a small ceremony on the drop zone and, after we signed a presentation paper, gave Larry and me PLA parachute qualification certificates. We were told that they had been in constant contact with PLA headquarters in Beijing with progress reports on our jump. The PLA wanted to know that we had landed and everything was OK. They evidently were worried about an international incident if one of us had burned in. As we shook hands with our fellow paratroopers, we were all in a good mood and, like paratroopers all over the world, we shared a camaraderie that was unique and almost religious.

We then trucked back to the regimental barracks and prepared for a dinner in their mess hall. A small group of us gathered in a special dining area, where I sat next to the regimental commander. The dinner was filled with of all sorts of special Chinese delicacies, and afterward we all sat back enjoying glasses of Chinese wine. We made some relaxed paratrooper small talk, and then I remarked, in my best Chinese and with a thankful sound in my voice, that it was good thing that the Chinese government had forbidden Mao Tai to be served at official social affairs. Mao Tai is very strong liquor, like white lightning, made from sorghum wheat and is expensive, which is why, supposedly, the government had forbidden serving it at public functions. After my fateful remark, the officers around the table began laughing and glancing at some ominous-looking bottles, evidently filled with Mao Tai, on a high table over my shoulder. As we clanked our glasses filled with the potent stuff, the regimental commander remarked with pride and, in a way that I would never forget, "Paratroopers made it, and paratroopers are going to drink it." We all got pretty well smoked that night, and Larry and I hit the sack, seriously buzzed, with a great feeling of satisfaction. We had accomplished a dream and felt comfortable in the international paratrooper womb.

Later that month, I also made another liaison trip with the assistant naval attaché, Marine Lieutenant Colonel Bill Given, and spent a couple of days with the Chinese Marines on an island off the southeast coast of China. Although I decided that they were not as professional as our own marines, they were damned good. Our relationships within multiple facets of the PLA were really progressing and important positive relationships were being built.

THE INTERNAL SITUATION IN CHINA BECOMES SERIOUS

February of 1989 ended with a visit from President George H.

W. Bush, who had been the head of United States Liaison Office in China 1974-1975, during the early days of our reestablished Sino-US relationship. President Bush was still thought of very highly in China, so we all expected a very positive and productive visit. The DAO was tasked with several missions of logistic and substantive support. During the visit, I personally escorted and supported General Brent Scowcroft, the national security adviser. I developed a good relationship with General Scowcroft and enjoyed our discussions as we went to and from various meetings. We attended a reception at the Great Hall of the People where I shook hands with the legendary Chinese leader Deng Xiaoping, who, after Mao's death in 1976, eventually began his leadership tenure of the PRC in 1978 and held three powerful positions until the end of 1989. All who took part in the meetings agreed that they had furthered a positive relationship between our two countries.

After President H. W. Bush's successful visit and as we approached the middle of April of 1989, the atmosphere in Beijing began bubbling and boiling like I had never seen in my decades of studying and observing China and the Chinese. Although there had been constant rumors of problems within the leadership, and some minor protests had been sporadically occurring since 1986, we had little initial indication that a larger, more serious situation was brewing. As a defense attaché, one of my primary missions was to monitor and promote relationships with the PLA. Many of the political leaders, especially at the top, were also members of the very powerful military commission.

On April 15, 1989 student protests suddenly sprang up after the former Chinese Communist Party (CCP) Secretary Hu Yaobang's death. Hu had been seen as the one Chinese leader who had been supposedly incorruptible, and the people, especially the students, workers, and peasants related to that much admired personal trait. Despite being a close comrade of Chinese leader Deng Xiaoping, Hu had been dismissed from his position and it may well have been due to his sympathy with the students, their demands, and protests. China's political and economic policies were seen as progressing, but some in the CCP leadership were dissatisfied with a perceived "opening to the west." Earlier, after an extended period of student demonstrations in 1986, Hu Yaobang was criticized for his handling of events. Hu, along with a group of CCP leaders, including Zhao Ziyang, had argued that economic reform should proceed with other political reforms, including an expanded role for labor unions. Hu's main critics in the CCP were a group of party elders and conservatives, including Premier Li Peng. As a result, in 1987, Hu was dismissed from office and replaced as General Secretary of the CCP by Zhao Ziyang. Hu Yaobang's critics eventually formed the core group of CCP conservatives (more orthodox Maoist, Marxist-Leninist party members) who would, in the end, determine the ultimate course of events during the future demonstrations.

On the day of Hu Yaobang's death, April 15, many flags were flown at half-mast. Large posters were displayed by students at universities around Beijing with slogans like, "A Great Loss of Democracy and Freedom," and "The Star of Hope Has Fallen." By the next day, April 16, several hundred people placed wreaths honoring Hu at the Monument of the People's Heroes in Tiananmen Square. The students seized on the death of Hu as an opportunity to vent their pent-up emotions concerning corruption and lack of the citizen voice in their government. The people had never stood up in large numbers to plead with the government about their dream for a better China. Citizens were seemingly acting out of love for their country and continued to unite as they came together in one cause. Chants such as, "There is no crime in loving your country" and "We will defy death to defend Beijing" spread throughout the capital and into smaller peripheral towns. On April 17, students and teachers from Beijing's universities gathered in Tiananmen Square shouting, "Long live democracy, down with corruption, and down with bureaucracy."

The following day, April 18, around 6,000 students gathered at Tiananmen Square, but after the day's demonstrations were over, about two hundred decided to remain in the square. The CCP leadership seemed in disarray and in disagreement over how to respond to further general unrest and even the eventual possible consideration of martial law. As we continued to observe the early, but possible serious signs of an apparent festering discontent, I knew this could grow into a crisis, and that we should prepare our DAO team for what may lie ahead. I thought back to my days in the Dominican Republic, Vietnam, as G-2 of the 82nd Airborne, and other tours where I had always tried to anticipate what could or would happen next and what we should do in preparation for those possibilities. Anticipate, always anticipate.

We in the DAO began by coordinating our activities with our fellow attachés in Hong Kong, particularly with Lieutenant Colonel Mike Byrnes, the assistant army liaison officer, who made some preplanning visits to Beijing. (In later years, Mike would become a brigadier general and eventually become the defense attaché in Beijing.) The protests continued to grow leading up to Hu Yaobang's memorial services on April 22. I decided that this growing crisis was going to take a full measure of planning and execution with focused support to the US ambassador. Our initial primary objective, to improve our relationship with the PLA, now had to be redirected. Our priority had become developing the ability to inform our regional and national leadership concerning the current situation in China so as events developed, they could make knowledgeable, critical decisions in response.

I initially established an embryonic "command center" that we could tailor and expand if necessary. We first devised a plan that called for our attaché's moving out into key areas in and around Beijing, mostly in pairs, to get a feel for what was actually occurring on the streets. Our attachés were now focusing on the actions and activities of the demonstrators, the Peoples Armed Police (PAP), and the PLA. In anticipation of probable future requirements, we booked rooms in hotels in key areas to cover the growing activities of the demonstrators and possible reactive movement by the PLA. We set up these "observation posts" in key locations in the western suburbs and the Northeast.

I then anticipated that communications would become especially critical as we spread out into the peripheral areas of the city and the countryside. We needed to be able to have constant communications between our attaché teams and our established command center located in the embassy. We contacted both DIA and Pacific Command and requested that they provide us with needed communications equipment in the form of handheld radios on an extreme priority basis. Additionally, it appeared this crisis was growing citywide and may well spread into the peripheral areas. During that period, it also appeared that PLA units were on the move. We began to receive reports that military rail convoys were taking up most of the traffic on the railroad lines. At the same time, we heard claims that as many as 20,000 troops from the PLA 38th Group Army, based near Beijing, had been moved closer to the Beijing environs. On April 26, the official party newspaper, People's Daily, printed a crucial editorial titled "We Must Take a Clear-Cut Stand

Against Turmoil." This editorial was the first public statement that communicated the party's position of zero tolerance toward student protesters and their sympathizers. It was based on a Politburo Standing Committee meeting chaired by Deng Xiaoping, which portrayed the student movement as anti-party and creating an unlawful turmoil aimed at bringing down the CCP and its top leaders. The students viewed the editorial as a misinterpretation of their movement, which they defined as a patriotic and lawful protest. Zhao Ziyang, who evidently was sympathetic to the protesters and was pushing for the People's Daily article to be retracted, was summoned to a party meeting on the subject. When Deng Xiaoping called for a vote on the theme of the editorial, the result was a 16 to 2 vote in favor of the editorial calling the student movement a riot.

On May 2, our new ambassador Jim Lilley and his wife Sally arrived in Beijing. He was just the experienced leader we needed as the situation heated up between the Chinese leadership and the demonstrators, especially the more strident students. Ambassador Lilley had been born to American parents in China and lived there until his parents moved back to the US prior to World War II. He was fluent in Chinese. After a short tour in the army, his life and career led to him evolving into the ultimate China Hand. He used his expertise in Asia serving with the CIA for thirty years before moving to the diplomatic corps, eventually serving as the director of the American Institute in Taiwan from 1981-84 and ambassador to South Korea from 1986-1989. While with the CIA, he had been the national Intelligence officer for China under the then Director of the CIA, George H.W. Bush. When the ambassadorship for China needed to be filled, and President Bush nominated Jim Lilley. I quickly became very comfortable with him as our ambassador, especially as we approached a seemingly critical time in China and for future Sino-US relationships.

On May 15-16, US Navy ships were scheduled for a port visit to Shanghai, and the sailors aboard would be allowed shore leave.

Ann and I, along with Ambassador Lilley and Sally, and some other embassy functionaries, flew to Shanghai. We were scheduled to board the command ship and have a dinner with the admiral in charge, along with the ship's captain and officers. In the meantime, the demonstrations that had begun in Beijing were spreading to other areas of China including Shanghai. We witnessed huge sympathetic marches on the streets. As Ann and I walked through the teeming streets, we noted that they seemed to be different in tenor from the intense stridency we had seen in Beijing. In Beijing, the demonstrations appeared more serious and threatening. In Shanghai, there were large numbers of people, from all walks of life, conducting the demonstrations and marches, but they appeared almost celebratory. Although the marchers were less threatening, they were still creating a turmoil in the city that would eventually become a problem for the ship visit, especially having the sailors out on shore leave among the local demonstrators. The ambassador and I, along with others went out to the 7th Fleet flagship, the USS Blue Ridge, and held discussions with the commander, Vice Admiral Hank Mauz. Later that day, Ambassador Lilley received a briefing from the embassy in Beijing describing the possibility of the regime in Beijing declaring martial law. He decided that we, including the navy, should cancel all activities in Shanghai. Shortly thereafter, the sailors were recalled, our ships sailed, and we all returned to Beijing on the next flight.

Once I arrived back in Beijing, I sensed the situation was getting worse and more out of hand. As soon as I got back to our office, Duane told me that we had received communications equipment from the Pacific Command. A few days later, we established a network as our attachés moved out into key areas of protest and areas of possible reaction by Chinese PAP and the PLA.

Adding tension to the uneasy situation and continuing demonstrations, Soviet Union General Secretary Mikhail Gorbachev was scheduled to begin a "very important" official state visit to China on May 13. Also, on this date, the students in Tiananmen

Square had begun a hunger strike and refused to leave the square, which led to increased concern over the loss of face for the leadership. Numerous journalists were in China at the time to cover Gorbachev's visit, and the demonstrators took full advantage of the increased media coverage. The Sino-Soviet Summit was scheduled to be held in Beijing from May 15-18, 1989 and was the first formal meeting between Soviet and Chinese Communist leaders since the Sino-Soviet split in the 1950s. Both Deng Xiaoping and Mikhail Gorbachev claimed that the summit was to be the beginning of normalized state-to-state relations. The subsequent meeting between Mikhail Gorbachev and then General Secretary Zhao Ziyang was hailed as the "natural restoration" of party-to-party relations.

The ongoing protests in Tiananmen Square had forced the cancellation of the original plans of receiving the Soviet delegation with a grand ceremony in the square. Instead, the delegation was given a relatively small welcoming ceremony at the airport. This apparent lack of control of the Beijing environs was certainly an embarrassment and may well have hardened Deng's resolve concerning the protesters. Deng supposedly had viewed the summit as his last chance to assert his personal influence over Sino-Soviet relations. However, Gorbachev left Beijing on May 18, and in the end, the two sides agreed that the two nations would not yet establish further developed bi-lateral relationships but would "share information and experiences."

Meanwhile, the situation in Beijing was getting increasingly tense. As a seemingly last resort, 3000 students were now on a hunger strike in Tiananmen Square to influence the government to hear their issues. An increasing number of civilians aligned with the students and formed picket lines, created protective barricades, and provided food to any student who accepted. There was a faction within the CCP, led by General Secretary Zhao Ziyang, that was seemingly sympathetic to the students. It appeared that a resultant division within the party paralyzed action for or against the demonstrators.

Inside the Command Center

With the situation worsening, we transformed our spaces into a 24-hour command center. I decided to sleep in my office for the duration of the crisis, however long that would be. I continued to stress the need to rapidly report our observations, and I would continue to add new capabilities as time went on.

The DAO continued to write reports and transmit them verbally or in writing to headquarters and organizations on our primary distribution list.

Throughout the crisis, I was on the phone line with the command center in the Pentagon. They would alert me when they were going to brief the chairman, the secretary of defense, or the president, so that I could provide them with our latest real-time assessment of the situation. Additionally, when we had enough pertinent information, we initiated immediate updated reports to our regional and national decision makers.

Our attachés were also acquiring and providing some very valuable "current situational feel" from frequent personal discussions with average citizens on the street. Our DAO attaches observed various areas of the city. The observation teams included army, air, and naval attachés. All were doing invaluable, but extremely challenging and dangerous work.

When Ambassador Lilley would make a personal telephonic report directly to the president or secretary of state, he would ask me to stand next to him to provide him up-to-date information on our political assessment and military troop movements and dispositions that we continued to develop, and to answer any follow-up questions that they might have. Ambassador Lilley and I also met with the anxious American business community to brief them on what we thought was the present situation, and we tried to calm them and keep them informed as the situation developed. Our contact with the American business community and other groups of American citizens during these very tenuous times would become increasingly important as the situation deteriorated.

THE CRISIS GOES RED

On May 18, 1989, a televised meeting occurred between Premier Li Peng and eleven student representatives. Li Peng entered the dialogue with the primary agenda of ending the students' hunger strike, not as a negotiation between two sides. Student representatives brought up the People's Daily editorial and demanded a retraction and an acknowledgment of the student movement as patriotic and that the students and citizens were acting out of love of country. The students were allowed to express their opinions, but the Li was not inclined to answer their questions and, in the end, a dialogue of equal standing with the students was unachievable. The meeting ended with Li Peng pointedly criticizing the students and basically telling them to cease and desist from their subversive activities. The students now realized that they, and the citizens, had little to no voice, and that the CCP would likely do anything to defend their current power. The People's Daily had branded the protesters as enemies of the state and counter revolutionary rebels. There was no compromise or retraction, and the situation was looking bleaker by the day.

On May 19th, Premier Li Peng delivered a long, impassioned speech, and at the conclusion, he declared martial law. Although Deng Xiaoping appeared to be attempting to stay above the fray, Li's speech and the declaration of martial law would probably not have happened if it had not been sanctioned by Deng. Additionally, on that day, Zhao Ziyang went to Tiananmen Square to the warn the students that he could no longer protect them and pleaded with them to end the protest. That would be the last time Zhao

Ziyang would be seen in public. He was politically purged and placed under house arrest for the rest of his life.

Still, the Chinese senior leadership appeared to be in the throes of an internal political struggle and stalemated as to what to do next. The leadership continued to debate possible options to deal with the demonstrations. In the meantime, they ordered the local 38th Army Group to stand ready, and by May 19, they had ordered additional units from outside Beijing to deploy to the Beijing area.

As additional PLA units poured in, they formed a ring around Beijing with what would eventually total between 150,000 and 200,000 troops. Our attaché office became increasingly active on May 19 after the BBC reported troop movements to the north and west of Beijing. Our attachés scoured the streets and roads, discovering, identifying, and reporting troop, police unit movements along with the latest activities of the demonstrators in various strategic areas in and around Beijing. As they reported back to us, we kept Ambassador Lilley informed and continuously sent reports back to Washington.

Martial law was finally implemented on May 20, and PLA units initially attempted to enter the city from several directions; however, for the most part, they were blocked by residents in support of the students. An entire convoy near Muxidi, likely from the 38th Group Army, was halted by residents, but the confrontation was peaceful, with residents speaking to soldiers and the unit took no further action to move into the city. The 38th was a local unit and had close connections to the population of the capital. Many of the students had served in the 38th before attending university, and many had done summer training with the unit as reservists. Initially, the commander of the 38th was reluctant to use force against the students when martial law was declared. (The 38th was later in a tense standoff with the 27th Army and other "outside" units occupying the city during the crackdown). The commander of the 38th Group Army chose to check into a hospital rather than obey the martial law order and was subsequently relieved of command.

One evening, during the latter part of May, I took Ambassador Lilley in my personal car to show him the areas just beyond the center of the city. There were people in the streets everywhere. We saw burned out buses, trucks, and other vehicles, along with mountains of trash that were being used as barricades to deter troop movement, especially in areas where armored vehicles might move through. The people manning the barricades looked fiercely motivated and satisfied that they had, so far, successfully defied the government and the "invading" troops. As I looked at their determined faces, I hoped against hope that they would be successful in the long run. But I knew how the leadership was reacting, and my knowledge of Chinese history gave me extreme doubt as to the demonstrators' odds of success. After we got back to the embassy, Ambassador Lilley and I talked at length about the situation, how we thought it might play out, how we had organized and developed our efforts, and what we might have to do under certain contingencies. We both agreed that this was probably not going to end well. As we talked, the ambassador was calm and in control. He was dressed casually and wore a baseball cap, and his demeanor reassured me that we had a leader we could count on. I was reminded of some of my early morning discussions with General Meloy and General Weinstein. We were very, very lucky to have Jim Lilley with us during that critical and tense time.

On Wednesday May 30, a large statue that had been constructed by students from several of the local art academies appeared in Tiananmen Square. It was a rough copy of our Statue of Liberty, which they called the "Goddess of Democracy." The statue's appearance seemed to cause a frenzy of activity, and the crowd in the square increased to about one hundred thousand. Tens of thousands of curious Beijing citizens gathered around or walked by the square to catch a glimpse of the thirty-foot statue. The following day, one of the embassy political officers and I drove past Tiananmen Square on our way to a meeting with some local liaison officers. When I saw that imposing statue looking directly across the way at the massive picture of Mao Zedong hanging on the front of the Forbidden City, I knew it would resemble a sharp stick in the eye to the leadership. The situation continued to progressively worsen over the next two days. By this time, an estimated one million Beijing workers joined in support of the students, and they all appeared dedicated to the cause but still pledged to act peacefully.

Although the real crisis came to a head on the June 2, much of what happened that day, and thereafter, was strangely influenced by an unfortunate, little reported incident the day before. On June 1, in the Muxidi section west of Beijing, a PAP unit lost control of a vehicle and swerved into a crowd, killing three cyclists and injuring a fourth. The locals converged on the area to discover what had happened and eventually gathered around the scene of the accident in large, enraged groups of all ages. Evidently, unaware of the incident, the Chinese leadership decided to try one last desperate attempt to clear the square peacefully, and at 2200 that evening, a column of foot soldiers, followed by buses and vans tried again to enter Beijing's city center. As fate would have it, they had chosen to enter through the western Muxidi approach, where a large crowd had gathered in sympathy for the three slain cyclists. The agitated citizens attacked the column and eventually forced them to retreat. Importantly and probably sadly, had the troops decided to enter the city from the eastern approaches, they may well have made it to the square with less resistance and possibly been able to peacefully clear it, since at that same hour there were less than a thousand demonstrators in the square. Forces that were occupying the Great Hall of the People would have been able to join them to clear the square, possibly with little bloodshed. It seems that the vaunted CCP intelligence, reporting and decision-making system had failed at the most critical time of the crisis.

Later that night, the troop units that had tried to break through earlier from the west, circled around and finally tried to enter the city from the east, but by then, due to word of mouth, the crowds in the eastern area had increased to over one hundred thousand. Once again, a "peaceful" military effort was stymied, and the troops were again in retreat.

In the meantime, Larry Wortzel and Bill Given were initially in the northwestern reaches until they ran into a blocked rail convoy. They then switched to the eastern and southern regions and continued making observations, calling in reports, and carrying on discussions with the leaders of some of the units. Later that day, they observed units moving into assault formations around the Nanyuan Airfield and saw convoys preparing for movement toward Beijing proper. Some of these units included elements of the 15th Airborne Army that Larry Wortzel and I had jumped with a few months prior. As they were observing two units of the PLA heading toward Beijing from the Nanyuan area, Bill Given became violently ill with a severe kidney stone attack. The ever-reliable Larry Wortzel drove him through a column of armored personnel carriers, bribing and cajoling the troops as they made their way through back to the embassy clinic. Bill was rushed to the airport and flown to Hong Kong where he was successfully treated and remained until all was clear in Beijing.

On the morning of June 2nd, air force attaché Colonel Larry Mitchell and I took a ride through key areas of Beijing and out along the ring road into the periphery of Beijing. Some areas seemed chaotic, others were calm and normal. We discussed whether the Chinese soldiers would fire on their own people, and recalling my studies of Chinese mores and history, the only conclusion I could reach was "They always have, why would this be any different?" I was hoping that I was wrong, but I had that gnawing feeling in my gut that things were about to implode. Larry and I knew that Deng and the rest of the CCP leadership would try to hold on to power at any cost. The people were also realizing that the government's deadly hold on power was tantamount, despite the sense of unity and hope that was fueling protesters. We drove back to the embassy. I went inside and Larry Mitchell ventured back out into the morass.

On June 3, the PLA made a final attempt to move troops peacefully toward Tiananmen Square. That morning a regiment attempted to move toward the square unarmed. They were turned back at the second ring road by citizens and students. Events escalated quickly after that as troops were moved into their final assault positions early in the morning. The armed movement toward the center of Beijing by the PLA began in earnest. Even after two weeks of political indoctrination, the civil-military split was still in evidence: Units from the 28th Group Army turned weapons over to demonstrators, and their armored personnel carriers and trucks were burned by the crowd. In the west, a three-army group force, including the 38th, 65th, and 27th moved toward the Muxidi area using armored personnel carriers, followed by tanks. They were not being timid this time and were reportedly using deadly force as they moved toward the square. We learned that the final instructions for martial law issued on 3rd were:

1. The operation to quell the counterrevolutionary riot would begin at 2100 (June 3rd).
2. Military units should converge on the square by 0100 on June 4.
3. Square must be cleared by 0600.
4. No delays will be tolerated.
5. No person may impede the advance of the troops enforcing martial law.
6. The troops may act in self-defense and use any manner to clear impediments.
7. State media will broadcast warnings to citizens.

On June 3, at 2000, the 38th Army began to advance from military compounds in the west toward the square to the east. This army with 15,099 soldiers included tank and artillery units, began encountering demonstrators, and at about 2200 opened fire on protesters about 10 km west of square. They eventually got bogged down again in Muxidi. The crowds were stunned that the army was using live ammunition and reacted by hurling invectives and projectiles.

The people seemed in a state of shock when they realized their government was out to kill, not to just frighten. We heard from some Chinese doctors that the PLA, especially those moving into Western Beijing were reportedly using internationally banned "expanding bullets," which create larger-than-normal wounds after impact. Beijing citizens continued to try to block troops from moving forward toward the square. Students and others were blocking military vehicles with their bodies as tanks rolled forward, and the sounds of shooting constantly echoed throughout the Beijing environs. During the early hours of June 4, a few thousand protesters were still in Tiananmen Square when all the lights were turned off. Shortly before dawn, the lights came back on and the tanks that had surrounded the square began to roll in. The 27th Army Group was using deadly automatic weapons and firing directly at peripheral demonstrators. The 27th passed through other army group units along the periphery and finally broke through to the square about 0300 on June 4. By the time they reached the square, most of the demonstrators had already gone. They had seen the writing on the wall and their leaders had recommended that those who stubbornly remained finally abandon their efforts and move out of the area. Military trucks loaded with troops backed up the tanks and eventually toppled the Goddess of Democracy statue.

The attacking forces joined with more units that came out from the Great Hall of the People, with other troops emerging directly onto the square from underground facilities. We heard that one of the units emerging from the underground was the same airborne unit that Larry Wortzel and I had jumped with. Together with the troops from the 27th Army Group, they cleared the square by 0400 The tank units that attempted to enter the city from the east beginning at 2100 on the evening of June 3 did not reach the square until 0500 on the morning of June 4, after the square had been all but cleared by the troops coming out of the west. Later, other units coming from the south would move in and reinforce those already at the square.

A Quick Run to the Airport

During this most dangerous period of time, I had asked Duane Deacon to make sure that Ann and Mei were safe and to keep in touch with them frequently to see if they needed any help. He reported back that they were fine. During our constant reporting to Washington, walking the streets with Larry, and being surrounded by sporadic gunfire, Ann and I got word that our son John, who was on leave from West Point, was on his way to Tokyo to catch a flight to Beijing to visit us. Although most flights from Tokyo to Beijing had been canceled, I wanted to make sure that he stayed in Tokyo and was being taken care of. I called the DAO in Tokyo, provided them with John's flight schedule, and asked them if they would send someone to Narita Airport and instruct John to cancel his trip to Beijing. After they checked with the airlines at Narita Airport, they said that John's original flight had been canceled, but he was able to change to another flight and was already on his way to Beijing. They also told me that a young daughter of a Beijing Embassy officer, who was in the US at the time, had connected with John and was on the flight, as well. When I informed her father's office in our embassy that she was on her way with John, they asked me to pick her up, as well. The flight was scheduled to arrive in Beijing, after dark, that evening.

    I grabbed my old faithful Larry Wortzel, took one of the DAO cars, and we began a journey that would take us through the large number of PLA units lining the highway all the way out to the airport. Larry drove slow and focused, headlights off, weaving through various troops and vehicles that lined the roads, and at times even driving off road when blocked by military vehicles. The PLA troops looked like green ghosts in the night as we slowly moved through their ranks and appearing not to know how to respond they just seemed to glance at our car as we passed by. We expected them to stop us at any time, but we tried to act calmly and kept moving on, although our guts were grinding. After what seemed like an eternity, we finally made it through the military morass and approached the airport. I still couldn't believe that John had made it through until I saw him and the girl standing outside the airport. I gave him a big hug and didn't mention that he should have stayed in Tokyo.

We stashed their bags in the trunk, told them to lie on the floor in the back, and rolled down the windows in case there were concussions from weapons being fired at us. Larry eased the car back into the night toward Beijing. My fears and apprehensions on the trip back were magnified now that John and the girl were with us. Again, after a long, slow tortuous haul through the darkened ranks of soldiers and vehicles, often within a few feet, we finally reached the end of the troop formations and were able to speed up our journey back to the center of Beijing. We delivered John's friend to her parents' quarters, took John to our apartment, and Larry and I drove back to the embassy. Once there, I went into the DAO command center and Larry again forged back out into the Beijing night.

THE CITY QUIETS

Even after the square had been cleared, units of the 38th and 65th Army Groups were still bogged down in the Muxidi area. Between 0600 and 0700 on June 4, they began to abandon many of their armored personnel carriers and trucks, which were being torched by the people in the area. We reported some soldiers actually helped the people burn some military vehicles. But, once the word finally spread throughout the city that square had been taken by the PLA, the mood and situation around the city quieted down considerably.

There are numerous differing historic opinions and reports on the number killed during those tumultuous days. Most reporting promoted the mistaken impression that the major killing field was within Tiananmen Square. In fact, according to our attaché and other reporting, the major civilian casualties took place on the approaching routes into the city proper. When our Assistant Air Attaché Ken Allen went through the Muxidi area after the firing had subsided, he observed that the walls along the roads, at shoulder height, were pocked with a near continuous line of bullet holes. We estimated that between 1,000 and 1,500 people may have been killed in the Muxidi area. Another 500 probably were killed south of the city at a bridge where soldiers had to force their way through with bayonets. Another 500 probably died to the east as a tank unit from Tianjin moved toward the center of the city. We estimated that only about 100 demonstrators died in and around the area of Tiananmen Square that day. After June 4, 1989, the CCP claimed a death toll of 200, saying that only thirty-six were students and that twenty-three members of the PLA and PAP were killed. We learned that on June 4, 1989, that the combined death toll was around 2,600.

After the square was cleared, and the first-aid post on the square was abandoned, it is likely that the few injured demonstrators who were left in the vicinity may well have been eliminated by the armored personnel carriers belonging to the units charged with tearing down the symbols, memorials, banners, and other remnants left behind by the demonstrators. Between June 5 and 7, we estimated that all of the dead had been removed to the crematoriums. The PLA and PAP were still arresting, interrogating, and even shooting in the vicinity of the universities to make sure all demonstrations were finally quelled, and the leaders were neutralized. Even after the violence on the night of June 3-4, the streets of Beijing were filled with sporadic gunfire from the PLA for days. The Tiananmen incident was now seemingly over, but it created both immediate and long-term effects. The DAO in particular, and local US interests in general, were about to feel those effects within the next forty-eight hours.

CHAPTER 8
POST TIANANMEN: DESTROYING CLASSIFIED AND EVACUATING CITIZENS

The square had been quickly cleared of people, barricades, tents, posters, and trash. After several days, we began to receive reports that the Chinese government had immediately begun to round up and punish its own citizens, based on the surveillance footage that had been recorded during the previous weeks. According to some reports, many students and other citizens were taken from their homes and killed while many more deaths were reported and recorded as "accidental." By June 7, the Chinese Communist Party (CCP) leadership had mostly established control of their citizens and streets. The international press and diplomatic missions were reporting negative, but mostly accurate, information of the horrific events of the previous week. The Chinese leadership needed to show that they were still in total control. They realized that the Tiananmen "incident" had tarnished their reputation internationally and within their own country. During the latter part of the uprising, hundreds of thousands of citizens of almost all sectors of society around Beijing and other areas, such as Shanghai and Canton, had also been demonstrating. The regime probably thought that there was a real risk of being brought down. After the "incident" on the square, some residual uncertainty and anger was still festering in the country. So, to prevent further political conflict both internationally and within the citizenry of China, the regime began to promote denials of their bloody crackdown. The international press began describing the Chinese regime's propaganda as the Big Lie. The propaganda promoting that big lie included: "The incident never took place." Chinese citizens and the international community were continuously told that "troops never invaded the city," "hundreds of students never died," and the "reports of gunfire and use of tanks were false." The accounts of dead and wounded in hospitals were denied. The Chinese government was also promoting stories of soldiers being viciously attacked by rioters with weapons furnished by "overseas reactionary political forces." The government also stated that the troops exercised maximum self-restraint but were compelled to open fire. They added that nearly 100 soldiers and policemen were killed while putting down the "counterrevolutionaries," and that citizen casualties totaled no more than 100 dead and 1000 wounded. Those were elements of the official story coming from the leadership, who apparently believed that if they repeated the lie enough, it would become the truth. Citizens outside the capital, with limited access to other sources of information, for the most part, accepted the government's version of events. As time passed, the big lie was perpetuated by spreading photos of captured "hooligans" with shaved heads, hands bound, and with signs of crimes hanging around their necks. Citizens who informed on the alleged renegades were praised in the media. Additionally, the regime started to focus on discouraging and criticizing key diplomatic missions, possibly to simply confound, frustrate, distract, or even pressure them to leave the country.

Fang Lizhi

Fang Lizhi was an astrophysicist and long-time, well-known Chinese dissident. Though Fang and his wife, Li, did not actively participate in the protests, they had discussed Chinese politics with some students at Peking University who became student leaders of the Tiananmen Square protests. On June 5, 1989, feeling unsafe during the post-Tiananmen atmosphere, Fang and Li entered our embassy grounds and were granted asylum by the US. They were then placed on the top of the Chinese government's most wanted list of people who had been involved in the protest. Fang and his wife became an international cause célèbre. The Chinese became obsessed with Fang and his presence on our embassy grounds. Fang and Li were kept as "guests" in a large shed that had been converted into a guest house at the rear of the ambassador's residence.

THE JINGUOMENWAI INCIDENT

On the morning of June 7, 1989, shots rang out around the Jinguomenwai diplomatic compound, where most of our embassy personnel and the press corps were housed. At the time, Ambassador Lilley and I were holding a meeting in the snack bar with a group of embassy staff and dependents. The ambassador and I were providing our assessment of the current situation and trying to calm the tensions that had developed over the past week and a half. An anxious uncertainty was roiling among the embassy personnel and their families. During these "emergency" meetings with the American business community or with embassy staff and dependents, Ambassador Lilley requested that I always wear my uniform as a "sign of confidence, strength, and stability."

This particular meeting at the snack bar, however, was not normal, nor a coincidence. Approximately twelve hours earlier, we received a late-night phone call at the embassy.

The caller warned, "I know where your apartment is. Do not be in there after 10:00 in the morning [that would be on June 7, 1989]. It will be dangerous to be there."

The caller repeated the warning. After hanging up from the call, we passed the substance of the call to Ambassador Lilley. The ambassador emphasized that we would take the warning seriously. He then instructed the regional security officer to summon all embassy dependents and staff members to the cafeteria for a meeting and to keep them out of their apartments during the time frame that Larry had been warned about. At approximately 10:00 in the morning, the PLA opened fire on the Jianguomenwai diplomatic compound, with rounds raking many of our apartments, including Larry's.

I was still in the snack bar as those shots raked through the compound. I also heard what sounded like some additional gunfire in the vicinity of the embassy. I immediately recognized the distinctive cracking sound of incoming fire from AK-47s, which, of course, brought back dark memories. My immediate concern was for Ann, who was in the embassy annex providing up-to-date information to concerned American citizens. I rushed toward the embassy front door and found Ann in the hall by my office. She was understandably worried but remained calm and wanted to help where she could. I tried to be calm as well and asked her with a wry smile, "Are we having fun yet?" Ann rushed into my office and called Mei at our apartment and told her and John to stay where they were. I gathered whomever we had available in the office and told them to stay put. I instructed them to phone their families to be sure they were OK and to be prepared to take emergency measures, such as defending the embassy compound and protecting classified materials. I reported back to Ambassador Lilley at the cafeteria and tried to help him calm those that were still there. I then rushed to the embassy and held a meeting with the marine guards.

I was determined to plan for any contingency and to help wherever we could. Larry Wortzel, who was still at the embassy, loaded a couple of marine guards in an office van and drove to the gate in front of the Jianguomenwai diplomatic apartments, where he was stopped by a PLA sentry. Larry identified himself as an assistant military attaché and stated that he was there to assist the US dependents who were able to leave. The sentry initially refused Larry entry to the diplomatic apartment, but he demanded to speak with the company commander, who eventually permitted him access. Larry was allowed to evacuate any American dependents he could find but was banned from helping allied dependents (such as British and Australians).

A short time later, I left the embassy and drove to Jianguomenwai. Once I gained entry into the compound, I entered the building and climbed the stairs toward our group of apartments. I counted thirty-two bullet holes in the balcony of one of our other attaches. From the balcony, I looked down to the street thinking that maybe some stray troops had fired indiscriminately into the compound. As I studied the shape of the bullet holes in the balcony walls, I realized that they must have been fired horizontally and not at an angle if fired from the street. I spotted a large, seven-story gray concrete apartment building, which was under construction directly across the road. Construction equipment was parked all around it. It appeared to me that the shots may have come directly out of the upper floors of that building. My initial reaction was that the shootings were likely premeditated.

I then went into the embassy doctor's apartment and could see a series of bullet holes including some that had penetrated several books stacked on shelves in his living room. I took one of the books containing a bullet hole and stuck a pencil in the hole. By the angle of the pencil, I saw that the bullet had come into the apartment horizontally, not from down on the street below. I would later show Ambassador Lilley this book and pencil as proof of the premeditated attack. I reported the incident back to Washington with a description and picture of the book with the pencil attached. Our opinion at the time was that this was orchestrated by the regime as a stern warning. Later, when I eventually was able to talk to a PLA officer about the attack, he claimed that it was probably some renegade soldiers firing from the road. I showed him a picture of the book and pencil. Case closed. We would later discover that the soldiers who fired on the diplomatic apartments were from the 38th Army. Supposedly, as they were moving from the east side of Beijing, they "sprayed" bullets at the diplomatic compound. They claimed that they were trying to get a "sniper" off the top of the roof, but we found this to be a specious claim. We later determined that they had fired directly into the compound using armor piercing rounds. This incident appeared to be a calculated move to either intimidate or force the diplomats and members of the press out of the compound, and possibly out of the country. The regime was trying to decompress this situation in their own way and on their own time. We became increasingly convinced that the decision to fire on the apartments had come from higher authorities. Additionally, the regime had already pulled the plug on the CNN correspondents and wanted all other foreign correspondents to leave as well. Some correspondents had been beaten up and thrown in jail. The government was attempting to reduce any influential foreign presence and criticism through intimidation so that they could have the upper hand in this extremely sensitive situation.

Once I finished checking out other areas of the compound, I rushed back to the embassy. I was constantly thinking of the numerous, detailed conversations I previously had with Colonel Lee Holland, who had been the army attaché at the embassy in Teheran in 1979 when protestors had taken over the US compound and held fifty-two American diplomats and citizens hostage for 444 days. He had shared the details of the absolute terror of the situation and how the militarized college students had taken over each portion of the embassy and not only captured hostages but also took large amounts of critical classified documents. Once I arrived at the embassy, I reported our findings from Jinguomenwai to the ambassador and then, through our channels, to Washington. Prior to that incident, evacuation from China was voluntary, but once we had reported the firing incidents to Washington, the National Command Authority (the president) through the State Department made evacuation of US citizens mandatory. That order would probably include Ann, Mei, and John. When I got the word that the embassy would organize a capability to evacuate all American citizens in China, I nominated Larry Wortzel the defense attaché office (DAO) representative for the total embassy effort. Larry and I attended the initial meeting called by the consular officer, who was in charge of the evacuation effort, and it did not go well. She had little knowledge or experience how to even begin to organize such a large, complicated, and daunting effort.

Initially, the consular section had planned to set up convoys to go out and pick up stranded American citizens. But identifying and locating our citizens in China and then identifying contact points and transportation assets was a massive, if not seemingly impossible, task.

DESTROYING CLASSIFIED

Due to the rumors of troop movements around the embassy and the continued reports of sporadic rifle fire in and around Beijing, I became increasingly concerned about the vulnerability of our office personnel and our large inventory of classified documents. Later, we also received reports that the Chinese might enter the embassy compound using a SWAT team to arrest Fang Lizhi and his wife. I kept going over in my mind the discussions I had with Lee Holland at Fort Bragg: Our national interests would be severely damaged if our security was somehow breeched and we lost highly classified key documents. Other US embassies had been attacked and ransacked, not only during Lee's experience in Teheran, but also in Islamabad, Pakistan, and Libya. The bottom line was that we had highly sensitive material that needed to be protected. From my early days at Fort Meade, I was constantly aware, trained, and made cognizant of the necessity to protect classified information not only from even US citizens without a clearance or need to know, but especially from foreign elements.

Since I knew we could, in time, reconstitute our files, I decided to begin destruction of the most highly classified and sensitive documents first and then, given time, the remainder. The decision to destroy classified documents is not taken lightly and is normally only done under certain dire circumstances. I took a deep breath of professional courage and then gave the order to begin the destruction. I immediately sent a message back through our reporting channels, "Destroying Classified." We then fired up our shredder. That report back home must have really gotten everyone's attention, and maybe disbelief, but no one questioned it. The shredder groaned on throughout the night and into the next day. When it overheated, we would shut it down. We eventually brought in fans to cool it.

With ominous mounds of shredded paper and bags everywhere, I had to start planning for the next possible and even worst scenario. I sat down at my desk and wrote out a contingency plan for coordination with Pacific Command (PACOM) just in case they were ordered by Washington to make what we call a military forced entry into China to rescue threatened or detained American citizens and official US personnel.

PACOM at least needed a heads-up and up-to-date information to craft what would be complicated and dangerous contingency plans. As always, I made a concerted effort to anticipate any possible future scenarios and their impact, big or small, good or bad, probable or not.

THE EVACUATION CHALLENGE

In the meantime, Larry Wortzel was in the early stages of planning and organizing for the evacuation of American citizens, which seemed an almost insurmountable task. The key problems included knowing how many citizens were in China at that time, where they were, how to get to them, and how to get them out. The consular section provided us with as much information as they could muster at the time. It was virtually impossible to get an accurate number of US citizens in a country so vast as China. There were tourists, academics, students, scientists, military exchange officers, businesspeople, and other esoteric visitors such as archaeologists and paleontologists. US citizens living or travelling abroad are encouraged to register with the nearest embassy or a consulate, but many do not. We could only attempt to evacuate those US citizens in the Beijing environs and the consular section gave us what they claimed was an imprecise number that were in the Beijing area of 1400. Larry and his group then located, confiscated, and organized the use of as many US government vehicles, especially vans and buses, as possible. The consular section set up a 24-hour robust emergency phone bank, which included volunteers like Ann, to answer citizen questions. Callers were provided information on how to proceed and where they should go, which included instructions for Larry's designated pickup points. The embassy was receiving a flurry of calls from not only local US citizens but also concerned relatives and friends from all over the world. About 2,000 telephone calls were coming in daily to the main switchboard.

As he gathered additional information, Larry and his group began conducting their evacuation efforts at designated pickup points. Larry, as usual was all business and suffered fools badly. When he arrived at one of the pickup points, I believe a tourist hotel, the gathered US citizens suggested that before they would comply with his orders, they would like to have a sit-down question-and-answer session. Larry responded in his ever-efficient manner, "Get your asses in the vehicles or you're on your own." Larry has always had a way with words.

Larry and I encountered some blowback from Chinese officials during this effort on behalf of our government and its citizens. They would say, "What's the 'big deal'? "Why are you pulling out?" "This is a safe country." "There are no bodies in Tiananmen Square." "You're exaggerating this situation." We knew that this all was a continuation of the big lie. We simply replied that Washington had ordered an evacuation and we are carrying out that order. We continued our search for US businessmen and their dependents, along with others such as students and the many tourists supposedly in the area. We also had to deal with some recalcitrant American citizens. For example, as we tried to identify and move American students out of the universities, many of them resisted. However, once Larry and his group confronted them with the possible alternatives, most changed their minds and decided to leave after all. To complicate matters, some of the students told us that they didn't have any money, so we had to find a way to provide some embassy emergency funding for them. Additionally, there were a number of Chinese Americans, some of whom had been living in China for up to twenty years, who suddenly decided that they wanted to leave, as well. With their US passports in hand, many informed us that they were taking their grandchildren with them as well. As the remaining press helped to get the word of the evacuation out, the embassy's administration building was swarming with people requesting assistance and information.

At least we could order any American military member we knew of working in or visiting China to leave without question, which we did. Only once did Larry encounter resistance from a medical corps major, who said that she didn't think there was much danger in what she was doing or where she was doing it and that she was staying put. She wouldn't listen to Larry or to reason. Larry called me and reported the situation, and I asked him to put her on the line. Once she was on, I identified myself and told her that the evacuation order had come from Washington and that if she was looking for additional options, there weren't any and she was to do as she was ordered or face a court-martial. Eventually, she did comply with Larry's directions.

Larry did not have enough vehicles to transport everyone, so he had to round up additional US government and other vehicles while continuing to conduct further reconnaissance for possible alternate evacuation routes. He even met with two Soviet military attaches who had been classmates of his at the National University of Singapore and they provided some buses to collect and drop US students at our collection point. Others in the embassy continued checking hotels, communicating with American companies, hospitals, exchange students, and any other locations of Americans. We were mostly responsible for those American citizens located in the Beijing area, while US officials in other areas of China were checking into other possible hot spots. Due to the continued visceral sensitivity, actions, and strong declarations of the Chinese leadership, evacuation of American citizens from the Beijing area became an ever-higher priority. As far as we could tell, there were still no known casualties among the estimated 1,400 citizens in the Beijing area. We considered that to be a very imprecise number, but it was the only one we had to go on. We continued to work our designated pickup points and routes of evacuation to the airport where the embassy had arranged for charter aircraft to evacuate the citizens and others, including embassy dependents that had been picked up by Larry's group.

The consular section informed me that Ann, John, and Mei were scheduled to leave on one of the chartered flights on June 9. Ann continued to work the embassy phones until she had to return to our flat to do some emergency packing. Her plan was that she and Mei would eventually travel to Auburn and reunite with Jeff. She would have to leave our dog and cat behind until I could send them on after the emergency flights had been completed. When she called to say goodbye, it was very emotional but, again, we had become accustomed to such goodbyes as part of being an army family. When they got back to the states, Ann and Mei went to Auburn until I was able to leave China as well. John stayed in Auburn for a couple of days and then took a bus back to West

Point. I didn't see them until I would return to the United States later that summer.

We continued to work the evacuation effort until we located all the American citizens possible and eventually moved them to the airport and out of China aboard the chartered aircraft. All in all, we in the DAO were able to contact, meet with, and evacuate more than 700 US citizens, mostly from the Beijing area. There is little information about the evacuation from other areas of China, especially Shanghai and Canton, but citizens in those areas were under relatively little threat compared to those in the Beijing area. Many may have gotten out through Hong Kong by boat or train.

At the height of the Tiananmen crises and immediately thereafter, our DAO had to respond to a variety of crisis situations that directly affected the well-being of our families and US citizens, while ensuring that all pertinent information was being reported and our classified documents remained secure. Creating such plans, executing them in an urgent timeframe, and maintaining clear and accurate communication are skills an attaché can learn in training, but such skills are perfected mostly through unique and challenging experiences. During a relatively short and unanticipated window of time, our DAO responded with: extensive and timely crisis reporting, concluding with actual destruction of classified documents, initiated contingency planning with PACOM if a military forced entry into China was necessary, planned a mutual defense of the embassy, and safely evacuated thousands of American citizens. Observations were constantly being reported. I was also always supporting Ambassador Lilley during his briefings to Washington and his high-level diplomatic negotiations with the Chinese. These situations and actions can and should be included in the curriculum of any attaché course, but crisis situations will always differ. By nature, they are subject to great change, and many events of a crisis are nearly impossible to anticipate. Teaching and simulating a variety of crisis scenarios is very difficult. Experiences such as ours in Beijing 1989 are just one of many unique attaché situations that must be documented, compiled, and taught. Languages and culture can be taught, strategy can be studied, commitment can be built, procedures can be learned, but preparing to act in an unanticipated crisis requires a type of thinking that can only be built from learned individual traits and experiences.

BEYOND TIANANMEN

As a result of Tiananmen and its aftermath, President H. W. Bush suspended military sales and visits to China. Additionally, the PLA cut off all communication with the DAO making our normal liaison mission virtually impossible to pursue. The streets of Beijing were still eerily quiet, and we had to conceive a plan on how to proceed with our various charged missions under much different circumstances. I rode my bicycle daily into many accessible parts of Beijing to get a feel for the current situation and atmosphere. I talked to the citizens and shopkeepers. They seemed relieved that the crisis was over but were still very unsettled about their immediate future. The city was still very quiet, and it was not yet back to being even close to normal. I saw a break in the chaos and knew that conducting our day-to-day mission would be difficult for the foreseeable future, so I decided that this was a good time to return to the US to finish the required General Officer Capstone Course at Fort McNair that I had put off.

In early July, I returned to the states and took a few days of leave in Auburn to pick up Ann and Mei and just to have some relaxed time visiting with Jeff, mom and dad, Ann's mom, and the rest of our families. I really needed this time away, and although I did not fully realize it at the time, it was very therapeutic, not only for me but for Ann as well. I needed to be with and focus on the people that I loved so I could try to purge my recent experiences in China temporarily out of my mind. That time away helped me to process all I saw that spring and summer in Beijing, but, in the end, I would never get it totally out of my psyche.

Ann, Mei, and I drove to Washington DC and settled into our temporary apartment so that I could attend the capstone course at Fort McNair. The course was intense, helpful, and engaging, but an unexpected highlight for me was touring the Vietnam and Korean War Memorials. I had avoided going to the Vietnam Memorial for twenty-one years, fearing the pain I would feel seeing the tens of thousands of names on that wall, especially those of Larry Britten and those troopers that fell while I led Charlie Company. But the moment I scrolled my finger on each of their names on that wall I felt a deep sense of awareness of what was on the other side of that finger, and I never prayed so deeply in my lifetime. I quickly realized that I should have visited the memorial much sooner because it was indeed a cathartic and almost healing experience, although the scars will always remain. We also visited the Korean Veterans War Memorial later in the day when it was getting dark and hard rain had started. The spotlighted scene of nineteen Korean War veteran statues patrolling in their ponchos and walking among juniper bushes in that rain was incredibly inspiring. I thought back to when I was a second lieutenant at Fort Dix and how the Korean War infantry veterans in my platoon would describe the incredible hardships, especially during the brutal cold weather, they faced during their trying combat experiences. It reinforced my deep feelings about the tremendously unique hardships faced by the infantry soldier in combat.

BACK TO BEIJING

After the completion of the course in mid-September 1989, and Ann, Mei, and I returned to Beijing. The summer of 1989 in Beijing has been described as The Summer of Discontent. Chinese civilians had seemingly lost hope in their government and trust in their leaders and even in the much of the rest of the world. The United States had been virtually closed out of normal relationships with the PLA, so we assessed and reassessed our day-to-day situation as best as we could and reported our findings to Ambassador Lilley and to Washington. My priority was still trying to find ways to promote US-China military relationships. Prior to Tiananmen, the DAO had friendly lines of communication with the PLA, and I personally had numerous friendly relationships among many levels of the Chinese government, including within the PLA and the People's Armed Police. But after the Tiananmen incident, the US was accused of being one of the "influences" blamed for the uprising and therefore was a "reason" for the negative reaction of the Chinese military. Our relations were strained and my contacts with the PLA were very limited at first, but slowly, even through chance meetings, we chipped away at getting back to some semblance of normalcy.

A Date with the Russian

Traditionally, each fall the PLA would invite the military attaché corps to the Chinese arms manufacturing plant on the outskirts of Beijing to shoot the locally made weapons on their range. But in the fall of 1989, the US attachés, and a few from the other countries that had come down hard on China as a result of Tiananmen, were not invited to attend that year. However, later that fall I was invited to the PLA range on a private visit as a guest of a Russian assistant military attaché. He had been an assistant military attaché in Washington, and I had met him previously at the opulent Russian Embassy in Beijing when I had met with the Russian defense attaché, a major general. On the day of the visit to the range, the Russian picked me up at my flat in mid-morning and we drove out into the countryside. Our discussions during that drive were on the light side.

He had arranged to have us fire the Chinese version of the Russian AK-47 and the Tokarev pistol. Although a little rusty, I shot pretty well, and I enjoyed not only the shooting but also the opportunity to step away from the Beijing environs and embassy for a bit. As he drove us back, we decided to stop at a small Chinese restaurant where we ordered some fried noodles and dumplings along with a couple of the normal Chinese quarts of beer.

This was an opportunity to forge a friendship with a Russian officer who would go far in his military career because he was bright, multilingual, and very professional. I hoped we would meet again in the future. We unfortunately, never did. This was one of my favorite challenges of the attaché profession: Being alert and tough and taking advantage of all the opportunities that came with it, be it intentional or accidental.

A Special Relationship

I had spent much of my military career building relationships with all sorts of people from all over the world. I was always able to find some unifying personal or professional connection, even if not shared by a common language. During my tour in Beijing, I formed a unique, interesting, valuable, and satisfying relationship with the Vietnamese defense attaché Colonel Nguyen Lu. I found him very low-key, self-effacing, and with a fascinating background. He had attended the Chinese PLA officer candidate school in Kunming, China but after graduation returned to North Vietnam to fight in the same war as I had, but of course on the opposite side. During the war, he served as an infantry battalion commander in the North Vietnamese Army while I was an airborne infantry company commander. After the war ended, he remained in the army, learned to speak Russian, and eventually was dispatched to Moscow as a Vietnamese military attaché. In all, he spoke Vietnamese, Chinese, Russian and had a halting grasp of English.

I first met Colonel Lu at a foreign embassy reception. I spotted him, in his uniform, standing in a corner of the large room by himself, looking somewhat uncomfortable and detached. I decided to walk over to him and introduce myself. At first, we carried on a somewhat awkward conversation in both Chinese sprinkled with some English and quickly began discussing our historically inimical backgrounds. We talked at length about both of our careers and families. It felt strange, but we seemed to hit it off right away. After that initial meeting, we met several more times at various venues and eventually became sincerely good friends. The name "Lu" was more of a Chinese name, not a standard Vietnamese name.

I thought maybe that the Chinese had given him the name "Lu" when he attended officer candidate school and for whatever reason, he retained it. During a subsequent conversation, I learned that on his way from Hanoi to assume his defense attaché position in Beijing, he had taken a circuitous route, stopping in Moscow. That greatly piqued my interest. During that period, one of the highest priorities of our government was to know about and understand the Sino-Soviet negotiations that were about to take place because of Secretary Gorbachev's recent visit to China. I felt that Colonel Lu might be able to provide some learned insight into the new developments between those two strategically important countries and I thought that he might have some personal insights. I invited him to several lunches and dinners. During our discussions, Colonel Lu seemed to have a clear and very cogent personal views about the various phases of the growing Sino-Soviet relationships. Although he spoke somewhat haltingly at first, as time went on, he would provide logical personal opinions and assessments concerning the ongoing negotiations taking place between China and the Soviet Union. Colonel Lu's knowledgeable insights inevitably provided an invaluable piece to our national understanding of those important negotiations and relationships.

Fortunately, Colonel Lu and I continued to share numerous varied discussions and social meetings together throughout the remainder of my tour in China. As I was approaching the end of my tour, we had a delightful farewell lunch at an international restaurant, and we talked about how strange but wonderful it was that old enemies could eventually develop into such close friends. As we walked out of the restaurant, we looked at each other, hugged like brothers. He gave me a small gift and we parted, friends forever.

I will never forget Colonel Lu, his sincerity, and, most of all, his friendship.

Several years later, I was talking to a friend who was going to Vietnam on business and was going have direct dealings with the Vietnamese military. I asked him to inquire about a Colonel Lu who had been the defense attaché in China in 1989-90. I asked if he could locate him to please pass on my best regards. Some months later my friend called me and said while in Hanoi, he had asked about Colonel Lu. He was told that "Lu" was indeed not his real name and that he was one of the two highest-ranking officers presently in the Vietnamese military. I was told that the General (Colonel) "Lu" had passed on his best regards to his dear American friend and invited Ann and me to visit Vietnam as his guest. Unfortunately, we had not been able to go, but the thought of doing so has always remained intriguing.

Another Presidential Visit

In late October, Former President Nixon made a return visit to China at the request of President H.W. Bush. In a return to the site of his historic diplomatic triumph when in 1972 he made a surprise visit to China to initiate the normalization of relations between our two countries. President Nixon was still held in high regard by the Chinese people and the Chinese leadership, and we were hoping his visit would help improve our strained relationships. President Nixon was first scheduled to visit our embassy. He was gracious and mingled comfortably with the embassy staff and dependents. When he spotted me in my uniform, he approached me and asked if we could talk privately about my opinion of the current situation. I provided him with my assessment of the past and present political-military situations and our current relationship with the PLA. I detailed the attack on the diplomatic compound and described the relatively large number of PLA guards at the embassy gates now armed with intimidating AK-47s instead of the pistols they had carried previously. He seemed pleased with the information I shared. All in all, he was interested and knowledgeable about the current situation in Sino-US relationships. I then escorted him over and introduced him to Ann and Mei, and they talked for quite a while. He was incredibly gracious throughout.

That evening, Chinese foreign minister hosted a dinner in honor of President Nixon at the Great Hall of the People. During dinner, the Nixon spoke bluntly to his Chinese hosts about the hurt and damage the actions of their government had caused during the Tiananmen incident and thereafter. He also expressed deep concern over the AK-47 PLA soldiers guarding our embassy. The president firmly stated that the inordinately large number of soldiers and their AK's should be removed. In the end, his visit proved to be very worthwhile indeed. It seemed like the tensions toward our embassy were lessened, the large troop presence around the embassy was diminished, and the AKs disappeared. For whatever reason, a couple of weeks later the AKs did, however, reappear. Most importantly, however, after President Nixon's visit, martial law was slowly lifted.

Fang Lizhi Revisited

One evening, Ann and I had been invited to a dinner party at Ambassador Lilley's residence. As the event was coming to an end, the ambassador asked me if I could provide a ride to the Beijing Hotel for another guest who was a Korean friend of his from his days as ambassador to South Korea. I gladly agreed. As we left the ambassador's residence with the Korean gentleman and his wife in our car, we could see several black cars parked along the street in both directions. I was sure they were there to keep an eye on the residence and to ensure that the Fang Lizhi was not being spirited away. As we drove away, two of the black cars pulled out behind us and followed us closely all the way to the hotel. As we let the Korean gentleman and his wife out, one of the cars peeled off, stopped, and two men wearing black leather coats followed them into the hotel. I'm sure they checked and double-checked the ambassador's Korean friend thoroughly and probably left him wondering "what the hell just happened?"

Our driver pulled away from the hotel and we were on our way to our flat. The second black car followed us all the way to our apartment building. After Ann and I got out of the car and started toward the building's entrance, the black car pulled up right behind ours and two sinister looking men got out, quickly looked inside our car, and then demanded that our driver open the trunk, which he did. As we watched, we could see that our driver was justifiably petrified, but in the end, they found nothing and then indignantly signaled that he was cleared to leave. He looked incredibly relieved, but still visibly shaken as he left for home. Fang and Li remained in the US compound until June 25 of 1990 when the Chinese authorities allowed them to leave on a US Air Force plane for the UK.

MY TIME IN CHINA WINDS DOWN

The remainder of winter and spring 1990 in China were relatively uneventful, certainly when compared to the summer of 1989. Our DAO relationship with the PLA was becoming less and less strained, but we didn't know how long or at what level the icy relationships at the government level would last. Our administration, represented by Ambassador Lilley, was holding a diplomatic hard line with the Chinese regime. During this most sensitive period, Ambassador Lilley asked me to accompany him, in uniform, to several high-level meetings with People's Republic of China (PRC) officials. Throughout these exchanges, the ambassador emphasized in the strongest terms the negative consequences that the Tiananmen incident had on China not only domestically but internationally.

I recall one call Ambassador Lilley and I made on the deputy chief of staff of the PLA, the legendary and irascible General Xu Xin. Their "discussion" was like a couple of heavyweight boxers going toe to toe and was incredible to watch and hear. At one point in the conversation, the ambassador asked me to chime in with my opinion of the situation, atmosphere, and consequences from the military point of view. I gulped. Using my best Chinese, I carefully told Genera Xu how I thought the situation had evolved to this point and detailed my recommendations on how to better our military-to-military relationships going forward. Surprisingly, after I finished, General Xu crafted a slight wry, almost tortured smile and nodded in what appeared to be reluctant agreement. It was an experience I would never forget. An attaché must be very flexible. In the late spring of 1990, as my rotational date approached, I received verbal alert orders to Fort Belvoir, Virginia, to assume duties as the deputy commanding general for the army's Intelligence and Security Command (INSCOM). It sounded like a great next job. Ann and I were excited to return to the Washington, DC area but we also could choose to either move into our house in Oakton or live on post at Fort Belvoir. Prior to receiving official orders to INSCOM, I received a call from my assignments officer who told me that General Max Thurman, then commander in chief (CINC) for Southern Command, had asked that I be assigned as his director for Intelligence, J-2, in Panama. I respected General Thurman very much. I had some dealings with him when he was the army's vice chief of staff, and I was the director of Foreign Intelligence for the army's deputy chief of staff for intelligence and again during my time as defense and army attaché in China. General Thurman was interested in US Army-PLA relationships and had a successful short visit to China during my early days in Beijing. He had recently led the successful Operation Just Cause in Panama and still had some lingering operational challenges in the area. General Thurman knew that my family had a trying time during our stay in China, and he passed on that he would certainly understand if I decided against becoming his J-2.

After some serious introspection, with mostly family in mind, I decided to decline General Thurman's offer. A couple of weeks later, I received my official orders to INSCOM. Ann and I were planning a move into our new home and were looking forward to my working at Fort Belvoir. A few weeks went by, and I received another phone call from my assignments officer. He asked if I would be interested in being the J-2 at United States Central Command (CENTCOM) at MacDill Air Force Base in Tampa. I was told that General H. Norman Schwarzkopf, the CINC, had asked for me by name. Evidently, his good friend and classmate General Tom Weinstein had recommended me for the job. As with General Thurman's request, I was flattered that another combatant commander had asked for me, by name, to be the J-2 on his primary staff. Frankly, the more I thought about it, the more I really became torn between stability for my family and a yearning to be a director for Intelligence, J-2, for a warfighting CINC. I asked for some time to think about it. General officer assignments don't normally provide much leeway for refusal, if any, especially for such an important position as a J-2 at a combatant command. I really don't know why, but I think because of what I and the family had just experienced in China, maybe I was given some allowance.

I felt like a free agent, but after agonizing over the decision, I eventually turned down General Schwarzkopf's offer as well. I would later learn that General Schwarzkopf was not an easy man to turn down, especially if his mind was made up. He normally got what he wanted, either through an exquisite charm he could turn on with great effect or with a degree of intimidation which was second to none. A couple of days after I had declined the CENTCOM J-2 job, I got a harried call from Lieutenant General Chuck Eichelberger, the then army deputy chief of staff for Intelligence. He sounded quite agitated but was civil. As we talked, he added a surprising dimension to the J-2 situation. He stated, somewhat frantically, that Military Intelligence had, for whatever reason, lost credibility with CENTCOM as a whole and, more importantly, with the CINC in particular. He pleaded for me to "go down there and reestablish our good name." I did not know what the specific problems were, but he sounded frustrated and urgently stated several reasons why he thought that I would be the right guy to "fix things" with CENTCOM. I always had respected General Ike's judgment, so I told him that I would talk to my wife and get back to him. Ann, as she always had done during our almost twenty-five years as an army couple, understood the situation and my desire to be a J-2. In the end, we decided that I would accept the assignment to CENTCOM.

I had known General Schwarzkopf from my days as the director of Foreign Intelligence, on the army staff in the Pentagon. As mentioned earlier I had given weekly briefings to then Lieutenant General Schwarzkopf and to my boss, Lieutenant General Tom Weinstein, in the Army Alert Center. Generals Schwarzkopf and Weinstein were very close, and I always admired how they, as the army's G2 and G3, worked so well together. They had the kind of optimal synergistic relationship that I have always advocated between Intelligence and Operations officers. They also were true friends who had bonded as classmates in the West Point Class of 1956. During my contacts with General Schwarzkopf during those briefings, he always struck me as a brilliant and thoughtful soldier. Once my assignment to CENTCOM was assured, I got a warm welcoming message from General Schwarzkopf saying that, among other things, "I would enjoy having fun in the sun in Tampa" during my assignment and that I would be able to "chill out from China."

Ann and I then planned our move from Beijing to Tampa. We had our household goods packed up and forwarded, went through a number of farewell events, said goodbye to our cohorts in the embassy, to the great DAO folks, Ambassador Lilley, our close foreign attachés, and to some of the friends we had made in the

Chinese military. After our very eventful two-year tour in China, Ann and I both were looking forward to that "chill out time" in the Florida sun that General Schwarzkopf had promised.

During my last few days in Beijing, I, personally, was given an award, and the DAO was given two unexpected awards. The PLA surprised me individually with the highest military award given to foreigners. I am as proud of that medal as any I have ever been given. No matter the circumstances, China and its people have had a special place in my heart for a long time and still do to this day. An officer from the Foreign Affairs Bureau officially delivered the award to the embassy. I think General Xu may have been personally involved in the recommendation and approval process. The citation read:

> American Defense and Army Attaché John A Leide, from April 1989 to June 1990, during his service to China, for an unremitting effort in undertaking the duties of promoting US-China relations.
>
> And for that he is awarded the Ba Yi [8/1] medal of the Chinese People's Liberation Army to commemorate his efforts. June 20, 1990.
>
> [Note:"Ba yi" or "8/1" represents August 1, 1927, when the PLA was formed during the Nanchang Uprising against the KMT.]

Additionally, just a couple of weeks before I left Beijing, we were informed that the DAO had been awarded the "Defense Meritorious Unit Citation" by the Department of Defense for our actions during the duration of the Tiananmen incident. We were all very proud and humbled. It was a rare award presented to a Defense Attaché Office. As we read the award citation, tears welled up in our eyes and we hugged with sincere respect and admiration for one another.

We were also gratified that the citation recognized our singular effort in the evacuation of 700 US citizens to safe havens during the crisis.

The Defense Meritorious Unit Citation read as follows:

> The United States Defense Attaché Office, Beijing, People's Republic of China, distinguished itself by exceptionally meritorious achievement from 19 May 1989 to 10 June 1989. During this period, the Defense Attaché Office organized the evacuation of American citizens under martial law conditions in the city of Beijing. Over forty major significant information reports were submitted, providing timely and accurate eye-witness observations and judgments about Chinese actions, events, capabilities and intentions. These reports were a principal basis for national level policy decisions by the United States Government. Moreover, at considerable personal risk, members of the Defense Attaché Office, along with other United States Embassy successfully implemented the evacuation of over 700 United States citizens from the Beijing area to safe havens. By their exemplary performance of duty, the members of the United States Defense Attaché Office, Beijing, have brought great credit to themselves and to the Department of Defense.
>
> Given under my hand this 4th day of May 1990
>
> Signed,
Dick Cheney
Secretary of Defense

MAJOR GENERAL JACK LEIDE USA (RET)

CHAPTER 9

INTO THE GATHERING STORM: OPERATION DESERT SHIELD

Ann, Mei, and I decided to make a stop in our hometown of Auburn, New York on our way back from China. We reunited with our son Jeff who had finished his senior year while living with my mom and dad. This visit to Auburn was the relaxation we really needed, and I was grateful to be together and in harmony with my family. John was at West Point, but I was assured that he was happy and was where he was meant to be. Being in the army is never easy on a family; it either tears a family up or makes them stronger. Ours became stronger.

In mid-July, Ann, Mei, and I drove south and arrived in steamy Tampa, Florida. We were on our way to Central Command (CENTCOM) at MacDill Air Force Base and were trying to get our bearings on the area. After I signed in on base, we were told that there were no living quarters available for us at MacDill until the incumbent J-2 at CENTCOM moved out. We moved into a small two-bedroom apartment and planned to be there for at least the next several weeks. Jeff drove down days later and joined us, and that small apartment became very cramped. Although this is not what we really had expected when we had planned our move to MacDill, Ann, Jeff, and Mei took it all in stride. They were, as always, great troopers.

UNITED STATES CENTRAL COMMAND, MACDILL AIR FORCE BASE, JULY 1990

As I began my orientation sessions in the CENTCOM headquarters, I immediately became aware of the real-world growing crisis with Iraq. Saddam Hussein had been continuously fanning the flames and threatening his neighbors over border disputes and oil production. On July 17, 1990, he warned in a televised speech that he would attack Kuwait if his demands were not met. On July 19, 1990, the chairman of the Joint Chiefs, Gen. Colin Powell, and the CENTCOM commander-in-chief (CINC), Gen. H. Norman Schwarzkopf, began contingency planning for the defense of Kuwait and Saudi Arabia against an attack by Iraq.

As I moved around the headquarters, I talked to as many people as I could to get a feel for activities in the J-2 section and the command relationships and headquarters in general. Eventually, I was escorted to the J-2's office. His greeting was surprisingly sterile, and I tried to carry on pertinent conversations with him, but he was uncomfortably distant. I had phoned him while still in Beijing when I knew I would be relieving him. He was also somewhat reserved on that call as well and told me that his executive officer, Army Major Frank Bragg, would take care of me. We had a good working and personal relationship from our days at Fort Bragg when I was a battalion commander in Special Forces and G-2 of the 82nd Airborne Division, and he was at 18th Airborne Corps, so our communications should have been more positive.

Since I was due to officially assume the position of J-2 in a few weeks, I planned to follow him around and learn until that transition. As the director for Intelligence, J-2, I would have the staff responsibility for all intelligence and counterintelligence matters within the command. I also had overall responsibility for the collection, analysis, production, and dissemination of intelligence necessary to support the command's missions. I would be responsible for the management of all assigned intelligence resources, which, in number and kind, would eventually become unprecedented. I knew that, in a combat environment it would be a real challenge to meet the high demands required of the J-2. I also figured that the current J-2 would provide me with the requirements for the position's responsibilities, how to deal with them, and especially what the J-2 relationships were with General Schwarzkopf, the deputy CINC, the chief of staff, other primary staff officers, and the various service components. Unfortunately, I would be sorely disappointed. During my initial meeting with our chief of staff, marine Major General Bob Johnston, he suggested that I fly up to Eglin Air Force Base to get a feel for the process and procedures of a military exercise that was going on at the time and to meet the CINC. As mentioned previously, I first met General Schwarzkopf during my tenure as director of Foreign Intelligence for Lieutenant General Weinstein in the Pentagon during 1985–1986.

Exercise Internal Look: July 1990

Exercise Internal Look was scheduled to be conducted during the last two weeks of July. This exercise scenario which included an invasion of Saudi Arabia by the country to the north (Iraq) and was originally the brainchild of General Schwarzkopf. It was prescient and turned out to be an invaluable exercise for future challenges of planning and eventual deployment. After we landed at Eglin, Ed Valentine, the DIA representative to CENTCOM, met me at the tarmac. I asked Ed how the exercise was going and was taken back when he told me that there were significant problems within the J-2 that needed to be fixed. First, the J-2 section had not put together an acceptable comprehensive picture of the battlefield for the CINC, based on the flow of the exercise reporting. This had only been remedied by Ed's red team (enemy forces) inputs to the blue team (friendly forces), which allowed them to get through the exercise. Second, the J-2 analysts had little expertise on how to derive and present battle damage assessment (BDA) from the intelligence scenario that had been provided during the exercise. Two crucial missions that suffer during wartime are BDA and collection management because they are practiced far less in peacetime-especially for large operations. Lastly, Ed said that he had crashed the message center by simulating thousands of reports from the various intelligence collection systems. Additionally, the J-6 (Communications) had no idea of the magnitude of message traffic and communications that would be needed to support the J-2 during various fast-moving, high activity scenarios and, frankly, neither did we. In fact, when we returned to MacDill after the exercise, I learned that the J-6 had not received any combat requirements for communications support from the J-2. This lack of anticipation and preparation was a real potential disaster in waiting. We had to fix it, and fast.

An air of anxiety and a strange tension was hovering around this command post exercise and was different from any I had taken part in previously. It may have been the aura of reality being breathed into the exercise's scripted scenario by Saddam's activities, or it may have been the larger-than-life presence of General Schwarzkopf, or both. After some preliminary briefings and introductions, I was scheduled to meet the CINC at his trailer, which served as his living quarters and office. I met with his executive officer, Colonel (later General) "BB" Bell who was a solid professional and helped me a great deal during some trying times. He was basically the CINC's gatekeeper. BB showed me into the CINC's office, and General Schwarzkopf greeted me in the familiar gregarious way as he did during those sessions we had with General Weinstein in the Pentagon. As we shook hands, he patted me on the back, told me to sit down, and asked me about my family. He took special delight that our oldest son, John, was at his alma mater West Point. When I accepted the role to be General Schwarzkopf's J-2, I knew I would be facing a challenging assignment. However, I did not anticipate the immediacy for developing a wartime J-2 organization, system, and capabilities. The tense situation between Iraq and Kuwait was becoming more ominous by the day. During that early conversation with the CINC, he said, "If you're right 50 percent of the time I'll be happy." I cringe in retrospect. I think of how possibly disastrous it would have been if, in fact, we were right only 50 percent of the time. I certainly would not have been satisfied with that sort of success or failure rate, and he would not have been either. The rumor that General Schwarzkopf was a gruff and demanding commander, was not apparent at that first meeting in his trailer. One of the first questions he asked me was whether I played golf. He was not a golfer, but he felt that many of the staff officers in the headquarters spent too much time playing golf or tennis in the wonderful Tampa weather. I spent most of that first meeting just listening so I could begin to formulate what the CINC really needed from me. Not one to mince words, he quickly moved on from the small talk of weather and golf to some problems he was having with my old boss, the director of the DIA, Lieutenant General Ed Soyster. In his force projection scenario, General Schwarzkopf had presented the seriousness of a threat scenario and the level of physical military threat in his area of operations to be much higher than what the DIA was projecting. He knew that General Soyster and I were friends and I promised to help mend the fences. In the end, those disagreements with General Soyster eventually went away and he would be incredibly supportive throughout the war. The CINC had a photographic memory or something akin to one. He had read huge amounts of historical materials, particularly on the Iran-Iraq War, and had a repository of intelligence on the Iraqis in his own personal databank. I knew intelligence would be used assiduously during his decision-making, and I would have to go out on a limb during some critical assessments.

Once I was assigned as General Schwarzkopf's J-2, I knew I would be facing a challenging assignment. However, I did not anticipate the immediacy for developing a wartime J-2 organization and intelligence system. The tense situation between Iraq and Kuwait became more ominous by the day. Within days of that first meeting in the CINC's trailer, CENTCOM had installed a mobile tactical air control center in Abu Dhabi. On August 5, 1990 President H.W. Bush had announced his willingness to use military force against Iraq, and Kuwait was seemingly bowing to Saddam's demands to cut oil production. Saddam's volatile, warlike posturing and his venomous blustering vis-à-vis Kuwait was something we needed to take seriously and to watch very closely.

I had to quickly dig into the guts of the Internal Look exercise because it was moving towards reality, and I had to become aware of any resultant situations and problem areas. I had to ramp up my knowledge on Iraq, its leadership, intentions, and military capabilities very quickly. Frankly, I had to move at lightning speed from being a senior China military analyst to being a senior Iraqi military analyst for a warfighting CINC.

Exercise Internal Look continued at Eglin and went on as planned, as the real crisis continued to heat up. Our latest intelligence reported 100,000 Iraqi troops and 300 tanks had moved closer towards Kuwait's border. Every evening, I attended the briefings scheduled for the CINC and his component commanders (army, navy, air force, marines). During my initial attendance at the evening briefing, I took a seat behind his chair. After he sat down, he then turned around, smiled broadly and welcomed me aboard. The briefings that were presented to the CINC each evening included two different versions: the exercise scenario and a real-world briefing on the burgeoning Middle East crisis being created by Saddam. The briefing room was normally hushed and very somber, but I initially chalked it up to the looming crisis. That may have been part of it, but the other part, which I would find out later, was that the CINC was not easy to brief and satisfy, to put it mildly. As the briefers moved into the real-world, substantive part of the presentation concerning recent Iraqi activities, I felt an uneasy sense of ineptitude that I had not felt in a long time, if ever. This would be the beginning of a torturous, complicated and most difficult experience of my military career.

Fine Tuning Our Working Relationships

While still at Eglin, I dedicated much of my time to building communication and a trusted working relationships with the rest of the CENTCOM staff and component commanders and their staffs. I tried to carry on conversations with the outgoing J-2, but despite his normally low-keyed demeanor, he acted distant and harried. Sadly, he had the aura of a dejected man. I had known him as a good officer and had been looking forward to learning from him. I heard that General Schwarzkopf had, unfortunately, lost confidence in him, and that was virtually the kiss of death. However, during the exercise, I saw the J-2 action officers briefing the CINC, and they appeared to be professionally efficient and to have a good handle on the burgeoning situation.

Upon my return to MacDill and prior to my assumption as the J-2, and I spent at least 18–20 hours a day in the J-2's Current Intelligence Center reading reports and talking to analysts and contacts in Washington and elsewhere. The indicators of an Iraqi threat to Kuwait were looming stronger every hour. Saddam had spent much of his national treasure during the eight years of the Iran-Iraq War and borrowed huge sums of money from Kuwait and other countries in the Middle East to pursue his senseless war with Iran. He had a large standing army, plus his elite Republican Guard divisions, that he wanted to keep active and supportive to back up his continued bluster and threats. He then blatantly moved three

Republican Guard divisions, even further south into western Iraq and the pressure of the situation grew significantly. As we saw the signs and signals of a possible threat to Kuwait, we ramped up our information flow into our briefing maps and charts, knowing full well that we would have to brief General Schwarzkopf numerous times each day.

The pressure to prepare briefings and provide incisive analysis to the CINC and other "J" staff sections grew. The J-2 officers were intelligent, well informed, and came up with some excellent initiatives and analyses, but from what I could see, they lacked a logical intelligence analytical flow that would lead to accurate conclusions on Saddam's capabilities and intentions. When the staff made their required, analytical conclusions and recommendations to the J-2, he was slow to make requisite decisions and to provide the necessary firm, positive guidance in return. The analysts, who were working extremely long hours each day, appeared frustrated that they weren't getting the necessary cogent direction and guidance from their boss. I saw that our mission, in turn, was suffering without the requisite intelligence analysis that the CINC and his staff needed. I knew that we had to come up with some different approaches to how we were going to develop our situational assessments, intelligence processes, and briefings.

I sensed that the J-2 needed and probably wanted to move on. I still respected him and wanted to do what was best for him and, most importantly, for the mission. I decided that during the present burgeoning political and military crisis, our mutual situation was unacceptable. Following a meeting in the J-2's office, and after the analysts and project officers left the office in frustration, I sat across from him and said, "Look, you're retiring but I'm going to have to live with this crisis for the duration, so I'm going to assume the job early, like right now. I suggest you go home, take care of your family, and get on with your well-deserved retirement." He likely saw the fierce determination in my eyes. I told him that I would assume the responsibility and would take any heat from the chief of staff and the CINC for the decision. He nodded in a resigned agreement and appeared somewhat relieved. He later cleaned out his office and left the headquarters.

The following morning, still several days before I had been scheduled to officially take over the position, the staff was preparing for General Schwarzkopf's usual morning briefing. I quietly took a seat in the J-2 chair in place of the "former" J-2. When General Schwarzkopf arrived and sat down at the head of that long table, two chairs from mine, he looked over at me and said, "Jack, what are you doing here?" I looked at him seriously and squarely in the eye and said, "Sir, I've got the conn." He gave a wide smile and said, "Good, you've got it—welcome." Later in his book, he would preserve this moment: "Meanwhile our Intelligence section, already the best in the Middle East business—got a brain boost with the arrival of its new chief, Brigadier General Jack Leide. A Far East specialist who had been America's military attaché in China at the time of the Tiananmen Square massacre, Leide had come to Central Command expecting a well-deserved respite. But when the crisis broke, he jumped in and taught our young staff how to be effective under a crushing workload."[3]

One of the initial command members I met in late July 1990, before I took over officially as the director for Intelligence, was the CIA special adviser (SPAD) to the CINC. He supposedly was a very experienced field operator in the CIA and had numerous overseas assignments and he was on his last tour before retirement. SPADs were supposedly given "special" tours, either as a reward for past service or just to get them out of the way, especially the crustier ones. It was common knowledge at CENTCOM that the SPAD was not a team player and prided himself on upstaging the J-2 at every opportunity. He loved to constantly travel throughout CENTCOM's vast area of operations as a semi-dignitary alongside

---

[3] General H Norman Schwarzkopf, *It Doesn't Take a Hero* (Bantam Books, 1992), 294

the CINC but was seldom found around the headquarters after the CINC's morning briefing. He was nicknamed the "ghost" by CENTCOM J-2 staff veterans because he was seldom found when and where needed, but he could probably be found on one of the many tennis courts in the area.

The SPAD was known for giving the CINC "privileged" information and not sharing it with the J-2. This practice was especially galling to the J-2 folks, and a virtual disgust was visible at the mere mention of his name. This was not the way to evolve a vital partnership going into a crisis and very possibly a war. It appeared that he may even have been seeking information that would contradict military intelligence reporting and then would give it to the CINC privately. The SPAD was evidently not coordinating or sharing his reporting with my predecessor, the J-2, and the SPAD's divisive activities may have been a factor in J-2's eventual corrosive relationship with the CINC. In addition, I was told by J-2 veterans that actions by the SPAD may have been a primary reason for the strained relationship between the CINC and Lieutenant General Ed Soyster as well.

I was determined to fix the situation and to help unify the intel effort throughout the various government organizations during this crisis. I always had friendly, fruitful relationships with various CIA colleagues throughout my career, both in the United States and abroad. My past work with the CIA had earned me several accolades from the agency.

However, it seemed during this period that the CIA's relationship with the military in general, and with the combatant commands in particular, were not optimal. We had evidently allowed a bureaucratic chasm to evolve when our military needed a willingness to help from all in our governmental structure. A disconnect and parochialism among services, agencies, and departments during a time of crisis could potentially damage the vital interests of the United States.

PROFESSIONAL COURAGE

While still in Florida, I made a quick visit to Washington with Ed Valentine and was able to convince the SPAD to coordinate a visit to the CIA headquarters. Those meetings at CIA were outwardly cordial, but some of the meetings were not very productive. What struck me during these discussions and briefings at the CIA was that the SPAD did not accompany me to all of the meetings and, surprisingly, when he was present for discussions on the crisis, he showed little in-depth, substantive knowledge of the important issues in our area of responsibility, especially relative to Saddam Hussein and Iraq, even though he had spent at least two years at the command

As the crisis increased and Saddam's forces were on the move, we were working closely with the Joint Chiefs of Staff J-2, DIA, and the service intelligence organizations, establishing a seamless and close relationships that would continue throughout the war. But my worst premonitions about the SPAD materialized when he continued to provide the CINC with key intelligence reports without showing them to us in the J-2. Finally, out of total frustration, approached him and demanded that we be included in the intelligence he was providing to the CINC. Select portions of that CIA reporting may have been critical to the full all-source analyses that we were providing to the CINC. The SPAD replied that his reports were very sensitive and that I was not cleared for much of it. I was incredulous and said that I would mention to the CINC that I should see all relevant intelligence reporting. The SPAD seemingly demurred and said he would let me see portions of the overall CIA analyses, but there would still be parts that I would not be able to read.

During one pressure-filled day, hectic and with critical intelligence collection and analysis requirements, I asked one of our watch officers to find the SPAD, who had been seen only sporadically since the crisis began. I was still in disbelief that he was exhibiting such little sense of urgency. The watch officer growled, "As usual, he's not in the headquarters building; the SOB is probably playing tennis." About fifteen minutes later, the watch officer came in with a contorted look of frustration on his face and exclaimed that he had found the SPAD at the tennis courts and the SPAD had told him, "If Leide wants to see me, have him ask me himself."

I had a major international crisis on my hands, and everyone I ever knew, or even didn't know, was calling and asking how they could help. I was totally shocked that I would get a response like that from the SPAD. I can hardly remember seeing him during the following critical days of growing crisis. I was hoping against hope that this negative relationship with the SPAD was not an omen of things to come once we became involved in a possible conflict. The most unbelievable part of this sad tale is that when we all deployed to Saudi Arabia for the coming conflict, the SPAD decided that he was not going to join us, and he remained in Tampa for the duration of the war.

A Prediction Fulfilled: WATCHCON 1

In the final days of July, I was working virtually around the clock in our Indications and Warning Center still trying to organize and encourage the J-2 Directorate into a semblance of an effective operational combat intelligence staff. Iraq, Kuwait, and Saudi Arabia attempted to reconcile differences, but those talks had failed. I provided guidance to the J-2 staff on ways to determine whether the Iraqis would invade Kuwait and what Saddam would do once he consolidated his military position in Kuwait. Such assessments were crucial to determine how we should approach the Saudis if tasked to defend the kingdom. Anticipation and assessment of enemy intent and capabilities are key to how intelligence contributes to future missions.

As we approached August 1, I had the feeling deep in my gut that Saddam was going to actually invade Kuwait. I pursued that feeling with my analysts and I told them to assess what the Iraqis were now doing and determine if anything was different from past exercises they had held in western Iraq. I told them to look at the forward movement of artillery, especially self-propelled artillery, any inordinate kinds of logistics buildup, and if there were any differences in the presence or increases in medical and engineer personnel and other special units from those past exercises. After going through a priority collection and analysis, they determined that there were, in fact, historical idiosyncrasies in the logistic buildup and that there was an apparent increase in medical support units. They also determined that the Iraqis had also moved self-propelled artillery forward. If it was just an exercise, a large increase in logistic, artillery, and medical support units would not have been seen as appropriate priority measures.

By August 1, as a result of our priority collection efforts, we estimated that there were eight Republican Guard divisions (two armored, one mechanized, one Special Forces, and four infantry) between Al-Basrah, Iraq, and the Kuwaiti border. Some of those units had moved as far as 700 kilometers from their home bases. I quickly tasked the analysts to collate our latest information and analysis and probable invasion warning signs that we had had seen into a Special Intelligence Summary and to distribute it immediately to the intelligence community. We then went on the highest intelligence alert, WATCHCON 1 (Watch Condition 1), and published a warning of imminent invasion into Kuwait.

One of the initial decisions I made was to try to get some boots on the ground. I felt that we needed some human intelligence eyes and ears in Kuwait. We sent one of our best officers, army Major John Feeley, to report from our embassy in Kuwait City. We made sure that he had good satellite communications equipment so that he could provide us immediate updates on the looming situation.

On August 2 the Iraqis attacked Kuwait in strength. The initial invasion force consisted of four divisions of the elite Iraqi Republican Guard as well as Iraqi Special Forces. At about 0400, John Feeley called and asked to talk to me immediately. He was hearing gunfire and explosions and it looked like the Iraqis were attacking into Kuwait City itself. I quickly rushed into the war room and told General Schwarzkopf, "The Iraqis are in downtown Kuwait City!"

The invading Iraqi forces had come from land, sea, and air and captured Kuwait City and the remainder of Kuwait in about two days. They had moved to take control of all airports, military compounds, and airbases. The Iraqi Air Force, using mainly helicopters quickly took control of Iraqi airspace. The Kuwaiti military, although outgunned, initially fought valiantly but was in disarray because of the rapidity of the Iraqi onslaught. To Saddam's great disappointment, the Kuwaiti royal family had escaped to Saudi Arabia. The invasion was complete, the scene was set, and all awaited the reaction of our government and the international community. I now had to provide General Schwarzkopf the intelligence he required to brief the national leadership on the situation and to plan his recommended military response.

After the Iraqis attacked into Kuwait, our intelligence analysts provided me with my initial briefings and gave me what seemed to be a fairly accurate picture of what the Iraqis had done in the past twenty-four hours. I waited for what I thought should be the rest of the story, but I soon realized that there was no "rest." I then asked in rapid order, "What do those Iraqi actions mean? Why did they take those actions?" and "What does that mean for what we think the Iraqis will do in the future?" I initially received blank stares. I knew they needed further guidance and leadership in the heat of the situation. I told them that from then on, whenever they provided me, the CINC, or any other decision-maker analyses on the enemy activity, they always needed to add their own learned analysis of what it means and what they think it means for the future. I impressed on them that they knew more about the Iraqis than any analysts, anywhere, and that they should not hesitate to give their views and recommendations. I also assured them that I had their backs. There are certain times when you must give your subordinates the opportunity to fail, or they will be loath to be honest and will not have the professional courage to tell it like it is. There were many times that the CINC would ask me what I thought the Iraqis would do and I had to give him my best assessment, knowing full well that what I told him could lead him to making decisions where the mission and many lives were at stake.

I tasked the analysts to provide the CINC the most accurate predictive analyses as possible. We had to tell him what we thought the Iraqis would do during the next twenty-four hours and then what we thought Saddam Hussein would do during the next twenty-four to ninety-six hours. I instilled in and required from the analysts the following analytical process each time they constructed an enemy activity intelligence report and gave assessments to the CINC, me, or anyone else:

- Here's what the enemy did in the past twenty-four hours.
- Here's what that enemy activity means.
- Here's what that means for future enemy activity.
- Here's what we think the enemy will do during the next twenty-four hours.
- Here's what we think the enemy will do during the next 24–96 hours.

Predictive analysis is one of the most critical functions the intelligence officer contributes to the commander's decision-making and mission planning functions. With cogent predictive analysis in hand, a commander can make a series of tactical, operational, and strategic decisions to direct his forces to either counter an anticipated enemy action or use initiatives to disrupt the enemy. Leaders can make more informed key decisions on whether to attack, defend, reinforce, or withdraw, and predictive analysis can be the ultimate key to a successful decision. One of the inherent problems I saw within the intelligence community as a whole prior to Desert Shield and Desert Storm was a shying away from an Intelligence officer's most critical duties of providing his commander with that predictive analysis. We had over time become loath to provide analytical predictive analysis because it is, above all, fraught with danger: the danger of being held accountable for actions by decision-makers when the prediction proves to be wrong. Looking for someone to blame politically or militarily for disastrous results on the battlefield is nothing new and blaming those results on faulty intelligence has been historically easy to do. The intelligence officer constantly puts not only himself and his reputation on the line, but most importantly the lives of soldiers, sailors, marines, and airmen as well. I always instilled in my people the fact that we needed to be professional, but most importantly, to always have professional courage. Accurate predictive intelligence is the key so that the commander can be proactive in his actions and orders rather than be reactive to the enemy's actions. These basic but critical tenets were key to how we would eventually function during the boiling cauldron that would become Desert Shield and Desert Storm.

Preparing to Deploy

We prepared a series of daily briefings for General Schwarzkopf during the lead-up phase prior to our deployment to Saudi Arabia. We also prepared briefings for his meetings with President H.W. Bush, Secretary of Defense Cheney, and the chairman of the Joint Chiefs of Staff General Powell. We gave the CINC our absolute full and up-to-the-minute intel on Iraqi military deployments and intentions for his important mission to Saudi Arabia with Secretary Cheney on August 6. Their mission was to impress upon the Saudi King of the need to station US troops on Saudi soil; first to preempt an invasion of the kingdom by Saddam Hussein's forces and to eventually eject those forces from their neighbor Kuwait. I would use my small situation map board at planeside with the CINC before he boarded his aircraft to attend these critical meetings and immediately when he landed upon his return. In his book he remembers these planeside and other briefings: "Leide's intelligence officers were bringing me hourly updates not only on Iraq but also on Iran and the other Middle Eastern countries whose intentions were still unclear."[4]

In response to the Iraqi invasion of Kuwait, Secretary Cheney, under the direction of the president, and with the eventual permission of King Fahd, ordered the initial deployment of US forces to Saudi Arabia. Those forces included F-15 Eagle squadrons; maritime prepositioned squadrons two and three based on the islands of Diego Garcia and Guam; two carrier battle groups; the ready brigade of the 82nd Airborne Division; and an Airborne Warning and Control System. The US response and the subsequent defensive build up in the Persian Gulf was dubbed Operation Desert Shield. Desert Shield and the follow-on offensive Operation Desert Storm would become the largest US military deployments since Vietnam and the largest single divisional-level battlefield since World War II. Operation Desert Shield's mission was twofold: to defend Saudi Arabia from further Iraqi aggression, and to demonstrate to the Saudis and the rest of the Arab world that the United States would not back down from its commitments to its allies in the region. Given the multidimensional global-political machinations attempting to solve the crisis, the solution to which resided in the mind of a megalomaniac, I knew that our deployment to Riyadh, Saudi Arabia was inevitable.

We all were issued our deployment gear, including two items that I would keep on my person constantly, inside or outside: my weapon (a pistol) and my gas mask. I recall packing my duffle bag in our small apartment and saying to Ann that "we would probably be back in a couple of weeks," but thinking to myself that this could take a long, tortuous time. I was about to be off to what would become my fourth combat tour, but this one could be much different. For the first three tours, I was a company commander responsible for the lives of a couple hundred troops, and, yes, those were extremely difficult and very dangerous tours, and I came close

---

[4] Schwarzkopf, *It Doesn't Take a Hero*, 299

to "buying the farm" many times. This time, I would be presenting the CINC the intelligence that he would use to make decisions where possibly hundreds of thousands of lives would be at stake. That feeling would gnaw at my gut throughout the conflict and even to this very day.

We departed MacDill on the CINC's military command 707 aircraft on August 22. I left behind a residual staff segment that would be able to support us from the rear. Some would eventually deploy forward when our forward J-2 staff section was able to be increased. I had a strange feeling of trepidation as we boarded the CINC's command aircraft, but the flight to Saudi Arabia would be relatively more comfortable than the other times I flew to war. I sat across from the CINC on the plane and we talked not only about the crisis at hand, but I think we also made small talk just to relax. It was almost surreal, and I think our minds and bodies were telling us that we needed to rest in order to charge up for what was to come. We refueled during the flight and eventually an unexpected deep sleep overcame all of us. The next thing we knew, the crew awakened us for some breakfast, just before our arrival in Riyadh. As we approached Riyadh, I had a similar pained feeling in the pit of my stomach that I had as I was flying into my three other combat tours, but this time was quite different. This could likely turn into a terribly ugly scenario with chemical and biological weapons and with large numbers of forces on both sides and a huge number of lives at stake. I held the Saint Anthony medal that mom had given me and said to myself, "Here we go again, don't screw this up." As the door opened, a blast of hot, dry air hit me and almost took my breath away. As I walked down the stairs, I had a feeling of walking into a real unknown.

PREPARING FOR WAR: RIYADH, SAUDI ARABIA

When we first arrived in Riyadh, most primary staff officers were put up in a hotel for a week or so and then were moved to rooms at the Ministry of Defense and Aviation (MODA). We were provided a command operational area deep in the bowels of MODA headquarters. A walk down a set of stairs took us through some thick, antinuclear blast doors and then into an elevator that brought us below to our new "home." CENTCOM headquarters was a series of small rooms and one larger room that was used as our briefing room, which we euphemistically called the war room. I had a small office near the war room where I constantly devoured intelligence reports and operational traffic, gave guidance for and edited the morning and evening briefings that we prepared and gave to General Schwarzkopf. He had sleeping quarters in three separate areas, including one near the war room. I was assigned a driver, air force Sergeant Troy Clifton, who was nothing short of phenomenal. We nicknamed him "Brother Deals," and he protected and took care of me and our mission like a junkyard dog.

I now had sufficient time and experience in the job to address some of the important lessons learned from Exercise Internal Look. I was hoping that we could develop a system to accomplish what we call "intelligence preparation of the battlefield" and its attendant analysis to assist the CINC during his decision-making processes. First, we had to develop an "intelligence architecture." This should have been addressed and solved long ago in anticipation of situations such as this. But due to lack of foresight, intelligence data, reporting, analysis, and products were scheduled to be dispatched throughout the theater without sufficient communication resources. I looked at the problem with the utmost priority it deserved and asked our DIA representative Ed Valentine to help develop an architecture well beyond the traditional C3I (command, control, communications, and intelligence). I determined that we needed to quickly generate an in-theater intelligence architecture more akin to what is now known as C4ISR (command, control, communications, computers, intelligence, surveillance, and reconnaissance). Ed told me that it would be possible to provide at least a rudimentary architecture within a relatively short period of time.

I assigned a talented young air force officer, Major Eben Trevino, to help on the project. Ed and Eben worked night and day and finished the study, which documented and produced a rudimentary, but eventually constructive, depiction of the what the intelligence architecture in Kuwaiti theater of operations should look like. It appeared almost unparalleled from past attempts and consisted of over 155 disparate intelligence-related systems, along with their closely associated communications and computer hardware and software. We then used the study to coordinate and help fill requirement shortfalls, such as communications capabilities with other key elements such as DIA, our J-6 (Communications), and our service components.

Our Diplomatic Partner

During Desert Shield and Desert Storm, Charles "Chas" Freeman served as our country's Ambassador to Saudi Arabia as the president's in-country representative who worked closely with the military commander. As a career diplomat, Chas was somewhat of a legend, and I knew him as a close colleague. He was not only one of the premier Sinologists but also a high-level Arabist in our system. He was in the class just before mine at the State Department Chinese Language and Area Studies School in Taiwan. He was legendary for being brilliant and the ideal Chinese scholar/student and was set out as an example for all of us to emulate. Burnishing his legend in the China field were his duties as President Nixon's principal interpreter during the president's historical first visit to the People's Republic of China to negotiate the normalization of relations between our two countries. During Chas's later diplomatic tours, he had served in various areas of the world and evolved as a multi-lingual capable officer including expertise in Arabic language and area studies. General Schwarzkopf asked me if I knew him, and I told him that we were friends and that we were fortunate to have a polished and supportive career diplomat instead of an inexperienced political appointee. I met initially with Chas to establish a smooth and functional working relationship with CENTCOM, and the CINC worked with him as well. We established a great relationship, and Chas was extremely valuable when critical issues arose that involved political mores. Even during the times when the military aims and objectives clashed with those of the chief of mission, or during the intense pressures of combat, Chas was always a professional and supportive partner.

The Scud Threat

A little documented set of occurrences took place in early December 1990, well before the launch of Desert Storm. The Iraqis launched a series of SCUD missiles from a large military base south of Baghdad toward the country's northwest border. When our infrared sensors detected a launch and alerted our Scud defense systems, the ominous sirens were sounded. Once we learned the time and point of launch, our knowledge of direction was critical to the troop and coalition alert system. Those early Scud launches occurred three times over the period of two days, and all three missiles detonated around the same area over Iraqi territory, just short of the Syrian border. Additionally, they all detonated at about the same place and same altitude of an average of 7.5 miles above the earth. Upon my inquiries, the consensus among our science adviser and national analysts was that these were test launches.

The Iraqis had imported the Scuds from the Soviets and were trained in their use by Soviet military support teams over the years. Having studied the Soviet uses of, and defenses against, short-range ballistic missiles, especially during the 1962 Cuban missile crisis, I asked our analysts both in Riyadh and MacDill to look at the possibility that these tests could have been a precursor of the possible use of Iraqi use of biological or chemical submunitions. The conclusion of some analysts and scientists was that these missile launches might well have been a test for chemical or biological submunitions release. Detonation at a high altitude could result in a much wider dissemination of biological or chemical agents. Although no chemical or biological agents were aboard these missiles, the ballistic characteristic of the "predetonation" was an ominous sign of a possible chemical-biological munitions use in the future.

If Saddam were serious about using biological or chemical submunitions, one of his primary targets would probably be Israel, but he also must have known that the Israelis would have transformed Basra and Baghdad into glazed parking lots in retaliation. To attack another Arab country with weapons of mass destruction would almost be anathema to Saddam, politically, militarily, and religiously. But the possibility of Saddam employing chemical or biological weapons during the war never left my mind.

We knew the Scud threat would be a thorn in our side months before launching any operations. The Iraqis had 600 missiles of three different types. The basic model was the Soviet Scud B, although the Iraqis had modified several Scud Bs to create two additional models with more extended ranges: the Al Hussein and the Al Abbas. The range of the standard Scud B is 280 miles with an accuracy of no better than a half mile. They developed the Al Abbas (also known as the Scud C), with a range of 375 miles, which we believe was the variant launched against Tel Aviv. A third variant, known as the Al Hussein, with a range of 560 miles, was initially at fixed launch sites in western Iraq near the oil pumping stations and were primarily aimed at Israel. Those redesigned and elongated models tended to break up upon reentry into the atmosphere.

During the war, I personally inspected one of those modified missiles that had crashed into Riyadh proper. The Iraqis had cut the missile fuel tank into two parts, extended it by using a piece of sheet metal to make it longer, and then riveted the two parts back together again. The additional sheet metal panel was thin and more fragile than the rest of the missile construction. As I looked inside the mangled missile, I saw where they had to extend the control wires to accommodate the stretched length of the modified missile. They simply spliced an extra length of wire where needed and then used black electrical tape to wrap the splice. As I further inspected the missile, it appeared to have wobbled upon reentry and broken up as it reached maximum pressure.

Despite their modified weakness, these missiles were still a formidable threat due to their mobility. They were carried on a Soviet model MAZ-453 vehicle or on modified truck beds. The vehicles could move out of hidden sites, fire their missile, and move back to their hide area in a matter of minutes. I estimated how many Scuds and what types the Iraqi's had, as I formulated an attempt to somehow preempt their launches. I asked my analysts to study the missile "life cycle" so we could target and destroy them at the point of manufacture, movement to deployment sites, in storage sites, movement to firing sites, on the launcher, or enroute to their targets. I knew they were going to be an incredible problem both militarily and politically. A total of eighty-eight Scuds would be fired during Desert Shield and Desert Storm. Forty-six of them were launched at Saudi Arabia and forty-two at Israel.

A Report Conundrum

One important CIA assessment produced during the lead-up to our attack into Kuwait and Iraq was an assessment of specific chemical and biological agents that Iraq might employ. As I read it, I was looking for the pattern of conclusions that should have been concise and clear. I carefully read the entire report that afternoon then laid it in front of General Schwarzkopf. I purposefully did not share my opinion with him. I just suggested that he read it, then I went back to my seat and watched him as he read it. I could tell that he was getting agitated, and his neck was getting redder and redder. After he had finished it, he slammed the document closed, came over to my desk, and threw it down. He gruffed, "They wrote this with so many caveats so that they would be right no matter what happens. It's useless to me." He was furious and rightly so. These often-noncommittal national intelligence products drew many secondary conclusions that were written were simply vague and wavering. One of the conclusions within their assessment was that "Iraq was likely to use chemical weapons in a defensive ground war with the coalition."

Blood Chits

One day in the war room, one of my action officers came up to me and said, "I don't believe it sir; we are responsible for blood chits." I feigned naivety and replied, "Who the hell is blood chits?" Of course I knew what a blood chit was from my tours in Vietnam, but my attempt at levity only left him more overwhelmed. The US military began to use blood chits in the China theater of operations for the American Volunteer Group or the "Flying Tigers" under General Claire Chennault in 1941-42. We can remember that their "blood chits" were stenciled on the back of their brown leather flight jackets in Chinese with the American and Chinese flags. Blood chits were used during World War II in the tens of thousands and continued through the Korean and Vietnam wars. After Vietnam, the system was disestablished, but we were now reestablishing the program for Desert Storm.

I turned the responsibility of developing, ordering, and distributing the thousands of blood chits to one of my sharp officers in the map section. The map support folks were good when given almost an impossible task and I was confident they would be able to handle this. Besides, if just one of those thousands of blood chits would help get back just one of our pilots or special operators, it would be worth every effort that we would make. We decided that instead of a piece of paper we would print it on silk, so a pilot, for example, could carry it easily in his flight suit or gear. We would print the chit in Arabic, Persian (Farsi), Turkish, Kurdish, and English. Each chit had a specific serial number and when issued was related to that pilot only. The chit had a large American flag on the top, and in each of the languages, the chit said:

> I am an American and do not speak your language. I will not harm you! I have no malice toward your people. My friend, please provide me food, water, shelter, clothing, and necessary medical attention. Also, please provide safe passage to the nearest friendly forces of any country supporting the Americans and their allies. You will be rewarded for assisting me when you present this number and my name to American authorities.

Information on the program's effect, then and now, is classified to protect any involvement by us or "them." This was another job that we were asked to do that was not normally within the realm of intelligence support and was a little known but potentially important program.

PREPARING FOR BATTLE: OUR ARAB ALLIES

Not to denigrate any cultural or religious differences, but there are in indeed differences, which at times seem ever so minute, but can create political, operational, cultural, and even religious discords. These normal frictions are magnified during time of war. In the Middle East, these differences are magnified to an almost intolerable extent and could add immeasurably to the "frictions of war."

Our Saudi Connection

The most important politico-military relationship was with our principal host, Saudi Arabia. The first notable problem we encountered with the Saudis occurred before the main body of CENTCOM deployed to the Middle East. We sent a small liaison group to coordinate and work with the Saudi Ministry of Defense and Aviation (MODA). I designated an army military intelligence colonel as our team leader and included a young, talented female army captain in the group as well. A couple of days after our team had arrived in Saudi Arabia, I received a frantic phone call from the colonel. The Saudis were refusing to allow our female captain entry; no female had ever stepped foot in the MODA headquarters building. I told the colonel to pass on to the Saudis that if she was not allowed in the building, none of our team would enter. Seeing the critical need for an intelligence liaison during the crisis, they reluctantly agreed. As time passed, women military members were seen throughout the kingdom, and performed magnificently, but I could tell that the Saudis were never comfortable with their presence. Although this insensitivity to women is abhorrent to us, we had to be culturally sensitive to their differences from our views of the roles for women.

Upon arrival in Riyadh, our initial challenges included finding workspace, organizing for war, establishing communications, and just trying to discern which Saudi organizations and key personalities we had to deal with. We needed desperately to establish proper and beneficial relationships with our Saudi hosts. Their country was at great risk, and we had pledged to defend it. Although the Saudis had built an incredibly large and sophisticated (at least in appearance) command and control center in the MODA building, the space they allocated to CENTCOM's warfighting headquarters was terribly limited and constricting. Especially since we had to task the fighting of a major operation and control 541,000 troops. We in the J-2 (initially 43 people) were given a small space in which we had to accomplish all collection, analytical, and targeting elements of the intelligence cycle, run secure communications, and make our small patch into a secure facility.

Our next objective was to establish a relationship with whatever Saudi intelligence leadership was in place at the time. As we proceeded with our initial conversations, I discovered the Saudi J-2 didn't have much of a clue about nor interest in tactical or operational intelligence. His main interest over the course of the campaign focused on Saudi internal security. The Saudis are no different from many other countries around the world. The primary use of their national intelligence structure is for internal security and regime preservation. I had periodic meetings with the MODA J-2, who was basically focused on possible terrorist/sabotage activities by Iraqi or Iraqi sympathizers. Possible targets included a wide variety of varied threats, from the poisoning of the Saudi water supply to the contamination of cans of Coke. As time progressed and we came closer to the initiation of Desert Storm, I pushed the MODA J-2 hard to increase security at all levels, including physical security of key headquarters and bases. The Saudi system was very capable when performing internal security, and even during the crisis we worked closely with the "religious police" or Mutaween. An understanding of Saudi cultural-religious dicta and priorities throughout the campaign would be a critical key to success. That concerted effort was strained to the breaking point with the arrival of "infidels" and particularly "infidel women." Since we had many headquarters, troop cantonments, logistic bases, harbors, lines of communications, and numerous key airbases, we needed to work with the Saudis as closely as we could to prevent sabotage, assassination, and terrorism.

Eventually, we would deploy many counterintelligence (CI) agents from all services to the theater. Much of the work our CI agents did was in concert with our coalition partners, particularly the Saudis. Again, anything to do with internal security received the Saudi's attention and therefore priority in their cooperative effort. The first counterintelligence mission was the standard prevention of enemy foreign collection processes from gathering information on our capabilities, weaknesses, force structure, and intentions.

Second, the CI agents were involved in counter and anti-sabotage/terrorism. Third, we gave the CI system, both in-theater and around the world, the sensitive and critical responsibility to track the foreign hostages ("guests") Saddam was holding in Iraq and our embassy personnel that had been initially trapped in Kuwait.

Fourthly, I tasked them with researching and creating a database on Iraqi intelligence and counterintelligence organizations, missions, and capabilities around the world.

The Saudis evidently did not have a dedicated, robust system for operational or tactical intelligence. We were stretched by sheer numbers of requirements. Under normal circumstances, we would need two sets of intelligence collection, analytical, and dissemination experts to work 12–18-hour shifts, but we had to provide four different sets of analysts. We had two shifts in our own Joint Intelligence Center and one in our Joint Intelligence/Operational Center, and we had to put assets, albeit a smaller group, in the combined (Saudi-US) Command, Control, Communications and Intelligence Center (C3I). On top of those demanding organizational requirements, we had to adjust to the Saudi work ethic; they normally would arrive at work around noon and work until late in the evening.

Through some of those seemingly insurmountable situations, certain elements of the Saudi military forces did themselves proud. The Saudi Air Force performed brilliantly throughout. They were totally integrated into the Air Tasking Order and worked with our air force almost seamlessly. They had worked and trained with Central Command Air Force for years, had similar F-15 aircraft, and had developed a professional and integrated cadre of leaders. The pilots and crews were well trained, and we understood each other well, at least operationally. The key to success in coalition warfare is that countries should not wait until a crisis to get to know their allies and to establish an effective working relationship. Another successful Saudi military organization during the campaign was the Saudi Army National Guard (SANG). Our Military Assistance Advisory Group had been working closely with the SANG for many years. The SANG has been strongly supported by the Saudi royal family and is considered by some as the palace guard. Therefore, it has been well funded over the years. On the negative side, the Saudi regular army units did poorly and were not a real factor in our total effort.

General Schwarzkopf's Arab "Counterpart"

Lieutenant General Khalid bin Sultan was the son of Defense Minister Crown Prince Sultan and the brother of the Saudi ambassador to the United States, Prince Bandar bin Sultan. Khalid was chosen to lead the Arab Coalition Forces even though there was already a Saudi command structure in place. He may have been chosen because of his education and language skills, which were excellent. He graduated from the British Royal Military Academy at Sandhurst, studied at the US Army's Command and General Staff College, graduated from the US Air Force's Air War College, and held a master's degree from Auburn University in Montgomery, Alabama. He also had prior positive relationships with the US and British military. Khalid's job at the time was as commander of the Saudi Air Defense Forces and was in charge of the Saudi/Chinese CSS-2 medium-range ballistic missile force. Khalid had been deeply involved in the purchase of the new missile systems. He eventually became a very valuable "co-commander" within the coalition and would be key to the formation of the Arab Corps and the ultimate military successes that they had during critical times of the campaign.

The Saudis had formed an operational headquarters under Lieutenant General (Prince) Khalid, and I constantly inquired whether General Khalid had a J-2 but received little to no information. When we held combined briefings in Saudi command center and briefed all the intelligence issues of the day, there was no offer of contribution from the Saudis. I was constantly frustrated over the how information seemed to only go one way, with little input from our Saudi counterparts. After one briefing, I was sitting next to a Saudi major general, and I introduced myself and asked his name and what job he had. He said that he was the J-2 and then replied that he was General Khalid's J-2. Finally, I had thought I found a Saudi tactical and operational intelligence officer in the Saudi military infrastructure. But as we talked, I quickly discovered that he was totally clueless when it came to tactical and operational intelligence. I would see Khalid's J-2 at various meetings and briefings, and we would exchange pleasantries, but we had little, if any, conversations of substance. I don't believe he even knew what questions to ask and may have been embarrassed by his almost total lack of intelligence expertise and information. To this day, I haven't the foggiest idea why he had been assigned as a wartime J-2.

At some juncture in the early planning phase, the CINC decided to do some military "bonding" with Khalid and chose to conduct some one-on-one sessions with him in a smaller war room. General Schwarzkopf asked me to come up with a scenario to present to Khalid for our first session together. He wanted the scenario to be a realistic Iraqi attack into Saudi Arabia to make his teaching points to Khalid very calculated. My J-2 section had already crafted a realistic possible scenario in which the Iraqis would attack on three axes with a certain number of brigades on each axis. The CINC wanted me to do the briefing personally because he wanted to make the scenario as realistic as possible. Since I would be briefing his boss, I decided to include Khalid's J-2, who I knew as being a friendly guy but not an effective intel officer. Since we would be briefing both the CINC and his boss, Khalid, I broached the subject with the Saudi J-2, but he appeared not to have much of a clue what to present or how to present it. I suggested that I would give the most substantive part of the briefing and he could do a portion that would make him most comfortable: Saudi weather and terrain.

At the time of the briefing, I brought in maps, charts, and overlays showing the attack scenario with the attack axis arrows. The Saudi J-2 showed up with nothing but a pointer. I gulped and suggested that he could still brief on his country's weather and terrain. The CINC and Khalid came into the designated war room, and they were in a relaxed mood, bantering back and forth like long-lost friends. The CINC nodded for me to start my briefing. I began with a contingency that we had prepared for a real possibility: "At 0300 hours tomorrow morning the Iraqis will attack along three axes into Saudi Arabia with two armored and one mechanized brigade along axes one, two, and three." I gave as much realistic detail as I could. As I continued my description, Khalid and his J-2 both seemed very tense and uncomfortable. I suddenly realized that I was being so realistic in my presentation, that they may have thought that I was giving them a real assessment of Iraqi plans. The tension was so high in those final days that almost any realistic threat could send anyone into a tailspin. I assured them that although possible, this was just a scenario. You could see the tension visibly ease from their bodies. The Saudi J-2 then moved to the map and gave a faltering, terribly useless briefing on the weather and terrain. He really didn't know what kind of specific information a commander needed. His capacity in English was not great and he tried hard, but his performance was dismal. I felt for him and kicked myself for trying to include him in the briefing. After we left the briefing room, I politely thanked him and walked away. I decided that, unfortunately, I could not waste my time dealing with him in any substantive way in the future. He was clearly out of his element and would not be a factor as far as I was concerned for the rest of Desert Shield and Desert Storm. The CINC and Khalid spent a couple of hours discussing the scenario and how to fight the fight. The CINC had several more friendly sessions with Khalid throughout the various stages of the campaign, especially as we approached the launching of the ground offensive. It appeared to be similar to what we in the army called "footlocker counseling."

An Important Relationship with the Egyptians

When we discovered that the Egyptian president Hosni Mubarak announced strong support for coalition efforts and followed through with the pledge of forces, we developed a close relationship that lasted throughout the war and into the aftermath. As with all our other coalition partners, we had some cultural, even some doctrinal, differences with the Egyptians, but the transition to war requires close, seamless relationships and we worked to make it fruitful. I needed to establish personal relationships with the key Intelligence officers in our area of operations, and this was not an easy task. The director of Egyptian Military Intelligence was Major General Omar Suleiman, and President Mubarak had great trust and confidence in him. (In fact, after the war, Suleiman was transferred from director of Military Intelligence to the director of General Intelligence, the Egyptian CIA equivalent, but with more power. After President Mubarak was deposed, Suleiman became the president of Egypt for a short period of time.)

When the CINC had arranged his first meeting in Riyadh with General Suleiman, he wanted me to attend, so I met General Suleiman at the main door of the MODA building and escorted him to the CINC's office. I was immediately impressed with his professional and friendly attitude. The CINC, who suffered fools badly, appeared to show immediate respect for Suleiman, and they conducted a lengthy and relaxed conversation. I was brought into the conversation by both, and I felt comfortable with the relationship right from the beginning. I had already been working with his initial small planning contingent, which had arrived in Riyadh earlier, and was equally impressed with their professionalism and planning acumen. Compared to my initial experiences with the more ill-prepared Saudis, the Egyptian planners were like a breath of fresh air.

THE SAGA OF JSTARS

The Northrop Grumman E-8 Joint Surveillance Target Attack Radar System (Joint STARS or JSTARS) is a battle management and command and control aircraft system. It tracks ground vehicles and some aircraft, collects imagery, and relays tactical pictures to ground and air theater commanders. The E-8C is a modified Boeing 707-300 aircraft that carries specialized radar, communications, operations, control subsystems, and also includes ground station modules for communications between the aircraft and units on the ground. The two key missions of the JSTARS are basically surveillance and targeting of enemy units and systems. JSTARS evolved from separate but parallel US Army and Air Force programs to develop, detect, locate, and attack enemy armor at ranges beyond the forward line of troops. Congress ordered the two programs to merge in the 1980s and the air force became the lead agent of JSTARS. A joint program office was established, and both army and air force operators flew onboard and continued the development of the system.

In August, I had asked my collection management team to look into the viability and availability of JSTARS. As we moved into Desert Shield and toward Desert Storm, there was a growing controversy pertaining to the deployment of the two existing JSTARS prototype aircraft to the theater. The army and air force each had a different perspective of what mission it was meant for and where it would be most useful. Air force operators looked for immediate targeting data for attack aircraft and could track moving targets in real time. Army operators manipulated the data differently to look at changes through time to predict and analyze enemy ground movements and resultant intentions. Evidently, there was dissension brewing between the army and the air force on whether the system should be deployed to our theater and whether it could be used for what it was designed. At almost the same time, I got a call from an old friend at army, Major General Paul Menoher, asking that I help the army get the JSTARS deployed to our theater.

The system was still in a developmental stage, and it appears that the air force did not think that it was ready for prime time. It seems that the army was aware of the air force's position and worried that the JSTARS demise for use in our mission had already been decided. I received a heads-up from Ed Valentine and contacts in the army that CENTCOM had previously sent out a closely held back-channel message to the Joint Staff in the Pentagon that said that "Desert Shield is not suitable in time or place for the introduction of JSTARS." I was told the air force had convinced General Schwarzkopf that the JSTARS system was not yet ready for prime time and asked the CENTCOM J-3 (air force) to send that message. Because JSTARS had a surveillance mission, I should have been informed of, and signed off (concurred) on that important message.

I was furious at this breach of a normal staff action requirement, and I could not let this go. My strong opinion was that there were 541,000 troops in possible peril during the upcoming operations, and the JSTARS had the unique capability of "seeing" deeply and providing a real-time picture into the enemy force disposition and activities. The JSTARS could greatly aid us in determining the reaction that the Republican Guard and other reinforcing divisions would have to our initial attack scenarios. It was critical for us to know if they would stay in place and wait for us to come to them or if would they react quickly to counterattack our attacking forces either head-on along high-speed avenues of approach or in a flanking movement. We had no other system that could look and see that deeply with a near real time intelligence capability. This was not the time for parochial decisions. Our mission needed everyone contributing and operating jointly on a multi-service basis.

In September 1990, the JSTARS team had conducted a successful Operational Fielding (Feasibility) Demonstration for both American and allied personnel in Europe. They had successfully located and targeted three 25-vehicle convoys moving at night.

Additionally, Lieutenant General Freddie Franks, the VII US Corps commander, had used the JSTARS in January of 1990, during the REFORGER (Return of Forces to Germany) exercise. He was impressed with the result and had become a vocal supporter throughout. Despite these proven capabilities, the air force was in a coordinated effort to prevent the JSTARS deployment to the theater, and we were told that it came from the very highest levels.

Back in Washington, the Military Intelligence Board, chaired by the DIA Director Lieutenant General Ed Soyster, was meeting with its full membership including representatives of the service intelligence chiefs. The JSTARS program and its possible deployment was a key topic on the agenda. Fortunately, our DIA representative, my right-hand man, Ed Valentine was back in Washington attending the meeting and representing our interests. He explained to General Soyster what the potential risks were to our forces on the ground, due to the gaps in our collection posture, if the deployment of the JSTARS was not approved. He also pushed the point to General Soyster that the intelligence board should be above the parochial squabbling of the services. He emphasized that the mission of the board and, in turn, the DIA, was to honestly broker and provide whatever could be made available to assist the operational commander in the field to assure mission success. General Soyster approved the immediate deployment of the system to theater. He would continue with his full support throughout the crisis. Unfortunately, even with General Soyster's support, we still had the problem of the CINC-approved negative message.

During my discussions with Paul Menoher, he said that a JSTARS briefing team was standing by to launch to Riyadh. The JSTARS project members, both air force and army were evidently proud of their efforts in development of the system and were supportive of a deployment and welcomed the opportunity to show what the system could do in support of our most difficult and critical missions. I was trying to find an opportunity to broach the benefits of JSTARS with General Schwarzkopf, but since he had already agreed to the September back-channel message that the JSTARS was not needed in-theater, it would be a touchy discussion to initiate. A fortuitous opportunity occurred one Sunday when the CINC gave us an afternoon off to relax in our rooms at the MODA officer's club. When he saw me walking down the hall, he invited me into his room. He was wearing his West Point bathrobe and slippers and was the most relaxed that I had ever seen him. As we sat in his "living room," he offered me a Coke and we initially talked about family and other mundane, but relaxing, topics. He then asked me what I thought of our situation with the war and what I thought I needed to help our effort.

I talked to him about two issues. The first was how much we could have used the Lockheed SR-71 Blackbird reconnaissance aircraft and its great capability to provide quality imagery and more importantly, synoptic (wide area) coverage of our huge area of operations. He nodded knowingly and understandingly and knew that it had been a mistake for Congress and the Department of Defense to have retired the entire SR-71 fleet. Having gotten that point and the frustrations involved out of the way, I decided to go for the jugular on JSTARS. Knowing the answer, I asked him what his highest priority for intelligence information would be once our ground forces breached the frontline traces into Kuwait and Iraq. He replied that he would want to know what the Republican Guard divisions would do in reaction to our initial ground incursion. The Republican Guard divisions were far to the north but could move quickly to threaten our forces once they "breached the wire." I told him that I had nothing that could reach that far to the north to keep track of the movements of the Republican Guard, other than possible communications intercepts. I told him that if we could get the JSTARS in-theater, and it worked, we could have a capability to reach the present locations of the Republican Guard divisions. We could then dynamically see if and when the Republican Guard were moving forward into a counterattack mode, retreating, or staying put in position. I could that see he fully understood the problem and knew that JSTARS may well be a valuable and viable solution to his most important information requirements at the most critical time of the ground campaign.

Once I told him that a JSTARS team was standing by to come to Riyadh to brief him, he looked at me with a firm determination and said, "Get them over here to brief me as quickly as possible." Once I got back to the war room, I contacted Paul Menoher and suggested that he launch the JSTARS team to the theater.

As the word of the request for the JSTARS team's impending visit spread, there were still some signs of opposition. I stood firm, and whenever a question arose, I replied that "there is too much at stake not to give it a shot." Days later, the JSTARS team arrived. The Air Force-Army Joint Briefing Team gave their presentation to General Schwarzkopf, key commanders, and staff officers. The team explained what the system was designed to do, how it had progressed to that point, what the problems were that they had run into, and that they had two developmental aircraft, one of which was close to being fully functional. General Schwarzkopf took the briefing quietly and asked a few nonconfrontational questions. I had a feeling that those around the table were loath to present strong points in support or against the system deployment because no one ever knew how the CINC would come down on their comments. At the critical decision time, all were waiting for the CINC to speak, but then he looked at me and asked, "Jack, now tell me again why we need the JSTARS in-theater." After presenting my more developed positions on the Republican Guard and other positioned Iraqi divisions, my bottom line was that the probable positive capabilities far outweighed the possible negatives. The CINC seemed at peace with himself and said that he wanted the system deployed to the theater without delay.

Any discord among operators smoothed over to focus on the mission, and Paul Menoher personally worked within the Department of Army to get a provisional JSTARS detachment manned, equipped, and trained in time for deployment. By January 14, 1991, JSTARS was flying its first mission. It could not yet do targeting and intelligence collection at the same time. (In later development, it could). JSTARS eventually would successfully locate and track enemy units, especially those along the Iraq and Kuwait borders with Saudi Arabia. Throughout the course of Operations Desert Shield/Desert Storm, JSTARS flew forty-nine consecutive, successful missions, mostly at night, tracking and targeting fixed and mobile enemy forces and Scud missile launchers for coalition forces. The JSTARS was critical during the first ground engagement near Khafji in Saudi Arabia. Most importantly, it was invaluable, tracking Iraqi reactions to our ground offensive. After the war, both the army and air force agreed that the JSTARS proved its worth: My good friend and incredibly talented and supportive colleague Brigadier General John Stewart, G2 for Army Central Command, stated, "The JSTARS was the single most valuable intelligence and targeting collection system in Desert Storm."

LEAD-UP TO THE AIR CAMPAIGN

During days leading up to the launching of the air campaign, General Schwarzkopf spent most of his time in the war room. He sat in the middle of the main table that faced the operational and intelligence charts and graphs, and I sat directly behind him. I had to be ready at any moment to answer the CINC's questions. On his left was the chief of staff, Major General Bob Johnston, USMC, and on his right was his deputy, army Lieutenant General Cal Waller. During the morning and evening briefings, others would attend. His British counterpart, Lieutenant General Sir Peter de la Billiere, and his French counterpart, Lieutenant General Michel Roquejeoffre would usually attend the evening meetings. General de la Billiere had a background and command in the British Special Forces, the SAS, and I was able to relate to his interests and tasking. I previously had built strong and enjoyable working relationships with some other British cohorts, such as Lieutenant Colonel George Redfern, during my time as liaison with the British Joint Services Intelligence Staff in Hong Kong (1975–1978). I now bent over backwards to provide the SAS units presently in theater all the intelligence and mission support I could for their cross-border missions. Our working relationship became close, and they often expressed their appreciation for my supportive efforts to the CINC. I also developed a close relationship with Major General (later General) Wayne Downing; we both had been rifle company commanders in the 173rd Airborne Brigade. He was coordinating the in-theater Delta Force special operations effort. I initially developed four specific intelligence and targeting missions for special operations units. All involved challenging deep cross-border and potentially very dangerous operations. First, I needed to know if the area in western Iraq was trafficable for our heavy armored forces. It was critical that we not get bogged down in loose sand as our planned Left Hook charged toward the north/northeast. Second, I asked them to find and destroy any mobile Scud missile launchers in Iraq and try to capture any Iraqi soldiers that they found. Third, I asked them to locate and cut the coaxial and fiberoptic communications cables, which were probably buried along the railroad line in northern and western areas of our projected area of operations. And fourth, I tasked them to destroy any microwave towers they found along specific target areas of Iraq. Wayne would brief the CINC in a private room before each of his missions and I would attend each meeting. After a couple of those briefings where he described his targeted missions and how he planned and was prepared to accom-plish them, the CINC turned to me and flashed a reassured smile and said, "At it again, huh Jack?"

I continuously studied the Iraqi order of battle, and my J-2 team produced a handbook on the Iraqi weapon systems. We distributed it widely within the headquarters and sent copies to our subordinate commands and to intelligence organizations of interest worldwide. I studied it assiduously. One day while I was sitting at my desk in the war room, the CINC was talking to General Khalid about some of the Iraqi missile threats. The CINC suddenly turned to me and asked, "Jack how many FROG [acronym for "Free Rocket Over Ground"] missiles do the Iraqis have in their inventory?" I was able to tell from rote memory how many there were originally, how many were left at that moment, what their effective range was, and what warheads they could carry (including chemical). The CINC looked at me and smiled with pride and relief then resumed his conversation with Khalid.

On January 16, 1991, CENTCOM announced 425,000 US troops were in the theater and were supported by the ground forces of nineteen nations and the naval efforts of fourteen nations. A few days earlier, UN Secretary General Javier Perez de Cuellar had met with Saddam and concluded there was little hope for peace.

CHAPTER 10

WE ARE AT WAR: OPERATION DESERT STORM

RIYADH, SAUDI ARABIA: JANUARY 17, 1991

As we approached the early hours of January 17, 1991, General Schwarzkopf came into the war room, followed by B. B. Bell carrying a small tape recorder. My gut was in the same heavy grip that I would get every time I boarded a chopper for an air assault in Vietnam. The J-3 (Operations) action officers had prepared large sliding briefing boards with each air and cruise missile sortie laid out in various colors for a variety of strike missions. Lieutenant General Chuck Horner, as the Joint Forces Air Component Commander (JFAC), would be directing an immense daily air tasking order for all air force, navy, marine, and coalition missions. CENTAF was about to unleash a stunning amount of air combat power including cruise missiles launched from both ships and high-flying bombers.

The CINC sat in his chair in the middle of the long command table; a hushed air of inevitability permeated the room. He then read aloud a message that he had sent to the to all the troops basically stating that we were now at war, and that it was just war. He then asked B. B. to play Lee Greenwood's "Proud to Be an American" and as the song reverberated in those close quarters, even among all of us hard-boiled combat veterans, I don't know if there was a dry eye in the room. After asking the chaplain to say a prayer he then said, "Now we all know what to do. Let's get on with it." The air campaign had been under intense planning for many months, and we all felt deep pride that it was finally coming to fruition but were also gripped with dread for the pilots who would carry out those dangerous strikes. We were especially concerned for pilots of the F-117 stealth fighters that were targeted against critical Iraqi military and civilian infrastructure targets in downtown Baghdad.

Aircraft from numerous airfields and aircraft carriers had already been launched toward their eventual targets. The navy Tomahawks were also on their way to their targets and would not be recalled. The never-before-used AGM-86C Conventional Air Launched Cruise Missiles had also been launched from B-52 bombers, which had flown all the way from Barksdale Air Force Base, Louisiana, launched thirty-five cruise missiles against high-value Iraqi targets, and then immediately returned to Barksdale. They completed a 14,000 mile, aerial refueled, thirty-five-hour, nonstop mission, making it the longest strike mission in the history of aerial warfare. Earlier that evening at 0212, just forty-eight minutes before the air campaign was scheduled to begin, Air Force Pave Low (Special Operations navigational helicopters) and Army Apache attack helicopters crossed into Iraqi airspace and successfully struck and neutralized a key Iraqi radar site. Then, at 0300 on January 17 (7 p.m. Eastern Standard Time on January 16), Desert Storm began its roar in earnest. The coalition air forces would launch 750 attack sorties and the US Navy would launch 228 combat sorties from six aircraft carriers in the Red Sea and Arabian Gulf.

Friendly casualty estimates for that day were relatively high due to scheduled strikes on high-value targets, such as Iraqi Air Force headquarters, key military command and control headquarters, communications centers, telephone exchanges, power facilities, and other important military, political, and economic targets. Iraqi defenses were and would remain at their highest threat level until we could systematically degrade their air defense systems and command and control headquarters. We were reluctantly expecting the worst while praying for the best. General Schwarzkopf described in his book:"At 0310:'PHONES OUT BAG': General Leide, whose Intelligence staff monitored TV and radio broadcasts, reported that most correspondents in Baghdad were off the air, which indicated to us that the telephone exchanges had been destroyed."[5]

Post-strike reports from General Horner's headquarters were coming in from the returning aircraft, Tomahawk and cruise missile missions. We were all elated to see that there were unbelievably high survivability rates, especially since all of the F-117 stealth fighters had returned safely from their incredibly dangerous missions. General Schwarzkopf was beaming as he heard the F-117 strike mission reports. He turned to me and smilingly remarked, "Amazing, 100 percent returned safely." Among the almost 1,000 attack sorties that night, only three aircraft were shot down: An F/A-18 with the pilot lost, an A-6 with the pilot and weapons systems officer Jeffrey Zaun surviving but captured by the Iraqis, and the third was an F-15E where the pilot and his weapon systems officer were both lost. Zaun's swollen face would be on the cover of Newsweek magazine in February 1991.

General Horner's air campaign plan was beginning to bite, and bite hard. The CINC naturally wanted initial assessments of our attack objectives and began asking the J-3 for additional results,

---

[5] Schwarzkopf, N. *It Doesn't Take a Hero* (Bantam Books, 1992), 415.

or battle damage assessment (BDA) for the strikes. The J-3 had initially presented multicolored sliding briefing boards and charts reflecting the multitude of strike missions on that first day. Initially those charts could not be quickly updated to reflect any meaningful BDA, and this would become a persistent challenge throughout the campaign. Few results were reportable in that short period of time except for some generic descriptions such as "target or targets hit." The CINC was now being more persistent and asking more in-depth questions on the results of the strikes, but because he was not being given satisfactory answers, he became more and more frustrated. After the original relief that the vast majority of the strike aircraft were back safely, he began to drop some challenging heat on the J-3. The CINC wanted more specific answers on the strike results, and he wanted them sooner rather than later. He needed meaningful BDA. This form of heat from the CINC came in many forms and would be encountered by all of us for the rest of the campaign. After taking the CINC's initial queries and blasts, the J-3 slid his sortie charts away, never to be seen again. BDA would now essentially become the responsibility for us in the J-2 and we would have to meet it head on. We would need to acquire, collate, and analyze after-action data collected from all operational and intelligence sources and provide the CINC what he needed to know for his follow-on decision-making.

THE DYNAMIC DEVELOPMENT OF BDA

As the U.N. deadline for Iraq's withdrawal from Kuwait passed on January 15th, and the Air Campaign was scheduled to launch, the CINC and I had discussed what criteria to use if we had to publicly assess our progress during the campaign. We looked each other in the eye and said almost in unison, "No body counts." We knew it was an inherently inaccurate method of gauging successes on the battlefield in Vietnam and would be equally the same here. In the end, body count became almost the end-all for Vietnam; not only did it not work, but it became counterproductive as the administration reported these convoluted measures to the American people to create a veil of perceived success.

Now in Riyadh, as we entered the critical air campaign, I had to decide how to integrate all of the disparate intelligence methodologies historically used for assessment of enemy capabilities and weaknesses. We still had to provide conventional enemy order of battle, daily theater intelligence summaries, and other special intelligence assessments, such as the SCUD missile and weapons of mass destruction threats. However, I knew from the first day that much of the CINC's daily key tactical and operational decisions would be based on BDA. All commanders want to know not only what the enemy is doing, but "How am I doing?" in order to make follow-on tactical or operational decisions. I stressed from the beginning that we needed to calculate not only physical damage, but functional and psychological damage in our assessments. During peacetime, we hadn't trained or exercised with the strike volume and rapidity realistically so initially we didn't know how to fully concentrate or organize our efforts. We would have to learn as we progressed through the four phases of the CINC's Campaign Plan: The Air Campaign, the Isolation of the Kuwaiti theater, the Preparation of the Battlefield, and the Ground Campaign.

Many factors would complicate our BDA demands. During the air campaign, air and Tomahawk land attack missile sorties were scheduled to occur daily in unprecedented numbers. Additionally, our challenges included the vast geographical areas involved, the huge numbers of the Iraqi targets, restrictions by operational security, reliability of equipment, time constraints, political influences, the dangers of public release by uninformed sources, and our ability to package our BDA assessments and products in formats that the CINC and his operational commanders could use to make timely and knowledgeable decisions.

In anticipation of the tremendous number of air targets, and the need for almost real-time feedback for development of immediate retargeting, we had to develop a functional organization, along with on-the-fly intelligence acquisition, assessment, and reporting procedures. All would become a key part of deliberative planning and execution processes by measuring battlefield success and failures of each combination of missions. As with other intelligence functions, true BDA is partly science but much of it is art. It reflects virtually all types of enemy damage that includes the physical but could also involve command and control, psychological and political damage inflicted on an enemy. We had to develop a system to take advantage of the fusion of various sources of intelligence (human, signals, imagery, etc.) to create a more accurate and complete intelligence assessment. BDA would eventually become a crucial daily dynamic procedure in support of the deliberative, decision-making processes of General Schwarzkopf and his subordinate operational commanders.

When conducting BDA or other key intelligence assessment of the enemy's present and future capabilities, Intelligence officers need an unencumbered ability to continuously assess and reassess operational progress or lack thereof without unneeded or unwelcome pressures, criticisms, or second-guessing. They need to be provided with the opportunity to fail and encouraged to express honest and learned opinions without continuous threats of retribution. I constantly encouraged analysts to tell it like it is and reinforced that I had their back. Timidity during combat could literally be the kiss of death. Intelligence officers must always be intimately aware what future military objectives and missions are planned so that they can anticipate and conduct required intelligence collection, analysis and production.

Since we had little guidance, expertise, or experience on how to accomplish the expected high level of BDA, we initially had to create a great deal of new procedures and inject subjectivity into many of our conclusions. We had little precedence for the huge number of projected targets and the need for speed and priority for analysis from day-to-day to almost hour-to-hour. As we approached the beginning of the air campaign, our BDA cell, which was created from a group of dedicated young officers and NCOs from all services, was cobbled together for the first time to do one of the most crucial jobs of the war. Initially, we attempted to organize along traditional enemy ground, navy, air, and air defenses, chemical and biological capabilities, and a special Scud cell was added. However, I knew that timing was of the essence. We had to first and foremost address immediate requirements, which was the evaluation of success of various objective categories of the air campaign including major target set categories that would result in the desired debilitation of targeted enemy capabilities.

Hopefully, with our newly initiated dynamic BDA processes, the CINC would be able to continuously weigh the importance of different objectives of the air campaign and prioritize actions against key objective target sets such as airfields, roads, railroads and bridges, command and control, military production, electric power grids, military units, and military production facilities.

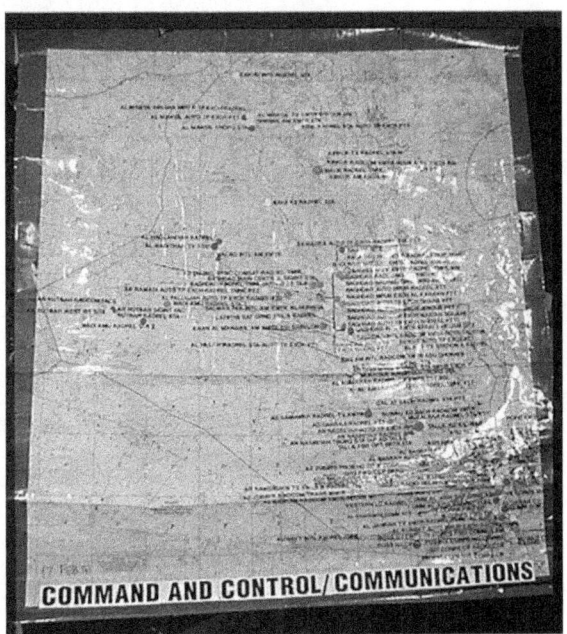

```
COMMAND AND CONTROL/COMMUNICATIONS/LEADERSHIP
              - CUMULATIVE BDA RESULTS AS OF 0300L 09 FEB 91.

OBJECTIVE: DISRUPT IRAQ'S ABILITY TO COMMAND AND CONTROL THE MILITARY
AND INFLUENCE THE CIVILIAN POPULACE.

ASSESSMENT:  ------------------------O--------X------------------------
             SLIGHT             MODERATE             SEVERE

   - IRAQ'S NATIONAL C3 CAPABILITY BADLY DISRUPTED.
     -- A FRAGILE WORKING CAPABILITY REMAINS DUE TO REDUNDANCY AND
        RECONSTITUTION.
WITHIN THE KTO:
   - NCA CONTINUES TO MAINTAIN CONTROL OVER CIVIL/MILITARY OPERATIONS.
     -- SOME DEGRADATION OF LAND LINES NOTED.
   - ATTACK OF KEY C3 NODES WILL CAUSE SATURATION OF REMAINING COMMS.
   - NCA ABILITY TO INFLUENCE CIVILIAN POP. DEGRADED DUE TO DESTRUCTION OF
     TV/RADIO TRANSMISSION FACILITIES.
   - WITHIN KTO, C3 NODES ARE CONTINUOUSLY DISRUPTED.
     -- FORCING IRAQ TO REPAIR DAMAGED COMM LINES.
     -- FORCING MOVEMENT OF SOME CP ELEMENTS FOR SURVIVABILITY.

TARGETS: 21 TARGETS ARE IN THE VALIDATION PROCESS.
```

```
COMMAND AND CONTROL/COMMUNICATIONS/LEADERSHIP
              - CUMULATIVE BDA RESULTS AS OF 0300L 20 FEB 91.

OBJECTIVE: DISRUPT IRAQ'S ABILITY TO COMMAND AND CONTROL THE MILITARY
AND INFLUENCE THE CIVILIAN POPULACE.

ASSESSMENT:  ------------------------O--------X------------------------
             SLIGHT             MODERATE             SEVERE

   - IRAQ'S NATIONAL C3 CAPABILITY SIGNIFICANTLY DEGRADED.
   - NCA CONTINUES TO MAINTAIN CONTROL OVER CIVIL/MILITARY OPERATIONS.
   - LAND LINES FROM BAGHDAD TO BASRAH AND BAGHDAD TO JORDAN ARE
     SIGNIFICANTLY DISRUPTED.
   - DAMAGE TO IRAQ'S BROADCAST CAPABILITY HAS SIGNIFICANTLY DISRUPTED
     IRAQI'S PROPAGANDA CAMPAIGN TO MAINTIAN MORALE IN THE KTO.
WITHIN THE KTO:
     -- EFFORTS TO RECONSTITUTE C3 CONTINUES.
     -- C3 IN III CORPS DISRUPTED.
     -- DESTRUCTION OF VEHICLES AND LOCs HINDERING COURIER COMMS.
     -- C3 IN II, IV AND VII CORPS REMAINS EFFECTIVE.
     -- RGFC LANDLINE COMMUNICATIONS HAVE BEEN MODERATELY DISRUPTED.

TARGETS: 6 STRATEGIC TARGETS ARE IN TODAY'S ATO.
```

Our next task was to decide how to present to the CINC the results of our daily, and sometime hourly, BDA assessments against those complicated and extensive target sets. A huge number of strike reports had to be collated and presented, using proper metrics, as he decided his following actions and orders. Various voluminous key strike results from the daily air tasking order had to be collected, analyzed, and collated for presentation to the CINC. Initially, the Joint Intelligence Center BDA cell created informative but complex depictions for each target set overlaid on a map of Iraq. They placed colored dots next to each target in the set, with each colored dot indicating the status of the damage to the target. For example, yellow would represent struck, but not damaged, while orange would represent struck and damaged, but not destroyed or rendered ineffective. Red represented struck and destroyed. We briefed the CINC every night using those intricate and voluminous charts. The CINC took them in stride and normally made little comment. I just knew in my gut that we were not giving him the key assessments that he needed in a clear and concise format to help him in his decision-making processes. I discussed the problem with Col. Chuck Thomas and the BDA cell. Together, we devised a unique concept that would present clearer and comprehensive charts for the CINC that he could actually use to make more knowledgeable targeting and operational decisions. The revised charts provided him with the most accurate information while providing more understandable daily assessments and conclusions for each target set in a more simplistic and useable format. He could then use them to proactively make daily operational assessments and decisions. For example, he could graphically see from each target set the percentage we had accomplished, how many targets remained and how many targets were planned for the next day. He could then dynamically move mission priorities within each target set or between target sets. This is an example of the constant need to improvise and adapt intelligence formats, procedures, and products to provide the commander with the information that he ultimately needs to make informed daily operational decisions that positively influence the outcome of battles. We must be able adapt to a dynamic battlefield and the commander's requirements. Aside from our air, ground, naval, and marine components and from our coalition partners, additional reporting was coming in from DIA, NSA, CIA, and open-source information from radio, TV, and newspapers. We were still establishing procedures to collect information, determine its importance and validity, then collate, analyze, and package the results into meaningful information. We were constantly improving our dynamic targeting and BDA efforts while developing critical analytical and reporting procedures for the CINC, his component commanders, and our coalition partners. Our intelligence analysis and production teams were also becoming increasingly proficient at developing creative and constructive reporting procedures. A very important and well received product was our CENTCOM Daily Intelligence Summary that reported on recent Iraqi activity, capabilities and probable courses of action each day and was disseminated broadly. After the war, while visiting the Situation Room in the White house, the watch officers and resident analysts unanimously told me that, each day during the war, the most valuable intelligence product that they received and used for their own analysis and reporting to the President and his team was the CENTCOM Daily Intelligence Summary.

As time went on, the media attempted to assess tank "kills" as a gauge of success. The number of tanks destroyed, while important, eventually became a counterproductive exercise during the air campaign, preparation of the battlefield, and leading into the ground campaign. Fortunately, we were able to fend off those calls until the latter part of the air campaign. Additionally, despite continuous clamor for at least an educated guess, we continued to ignore any pressure to use Iraqi body count during the entire campaign. Internally, however, we needed to factor in some subjective numbers of Iraqi killed in action from a variety of sources into our assessments of current unit capabilities.

INTELLIGENCE: AN INTEGRAL PART OF THE OPERATIONAL EFFORT

The CINC relied heavily on our intelligence while using his own judgment and instincts to make decisions. We in the J-2, almost by default, became responsible for the conduct of the Joint Targeting Center, traditionally the responsibility of the J-3. The J-2 and J-3 were fully integrated, and I assume, because of the fast-moving environment, we just skipped a step since the operational strike tasking was reflective of the targets we were providing. Because of our BDA processes, we instinctively and constructively knew which targets were the most critical to the CINC's strategic plan and resulting target set requirements. His strategic plan included missions to isolate Saddam, eliminate Iraqi offensive and defensive capabilities, incapacitate Iraqi national leadership, reduce the threat of Iraq to friendly nations, and to minimize damage to Iraq to facilitate post-war rebuilding.

To accomplish those elements of the strategic plan we first prioritized all of our targeting efforts based on the CINC's centers of gravity: Saddam Hussein, the Republican Guards, and Iraq's nuclear, biological, and chemical capabilities. Next, we had to target the degradation and final destruction of the strategic elements leading the effort against those centers of gravity. Therefore, we had to address specific target sets such as rail networks, roads and bridges, power facilities, command and control centers, air defense nodes, airfields, delivery systems, large military storage and production facilities, and intelligence centers. I personally concentrated heavily on planning the disruption and degradation of Iraqi military command and control and discussed my efforts frequently with the CINC. He also asked me to personally develop targets for the BLU-82 "Daisy-cutter" being dropped from C-130s by our Special Forces. Targeting priorities dynamically would shift as we had moved from the air campaign to preparation of the battlefield, and finally to the ground campaign. We had to anticipate and plan for this phased targeting effort, and it became an integral part of our planning process.

We would need to urgently organize our collection, analytical, and reporting capabilities and be selective in our reporting and procedures to meet a multitude of continuing challenges. At times, we received reported mission accomplishments or damage assessment that we could not agree with or confirm, so we had to either contradict or modify those claims, all in good conscience. I reflected back to Xuan Loc, Vietnam, in 1966 when blood trails were counted as a killed in action (KIA) and resulted in inflated kill numbers being briefed to commanders and eventually to the president. In the twenty-five years that had gone by, I still vowed that I would not let that happen on my watch; our troops and national interest should never pay the price for skewed reporting and analytical methodologies. During the course of the war, I had to disagree with or contradict positive, but erroneous operational reports. At times the CINC would become visibly upset. On one occasion, in great frustration, he barked, "You damned intelligence guys." But, I never backed down. I constantly vowed to keep our reporting as clean, truthful, and as honest as possible. In Tom Clancy's book Every Man a Tiger, one of my heroes, General Chuck Horner describes some of the heat I took in the war room:

> Often, Jack Leide takes some hits [from General Schwarzkopf]. His job is to provide estimates of what is going on in Baghdad. But, since no one knows for sure, his opinions are always open to criticism— especially when these differ from the CINC's reading of the tea leaves. Moreover, the CINC often wants answers that are simply not available. So, when he asks and Jack can't answer (nobody could except the enemy), he gets the needle from Schwarzkopf (who thinks that will make Jack work harder—an impossibility, as he is working

as hard as he can). Despite the needles, he is bulletproof and barely flinches when he is roared at. The man has style.⁶

Most importantly, despite the CINC's bluster and discomfiture with some of the intelligence we provided him, he never told me to change any analyses, methodologies, reports, or conclusions. Equally important, although he may not have liked it, he continued to use the analyses and conclusions we provided him to make daily decisions during the entire campaign. Air Force Major Rick Francona, who I had personally requested as the CINC's interpreter for Desert Storm, while writing about controversial possible warping of intelligence, referred to his time in Desert Shield and Desert Storm within the intelligence directorate:

> The Director of Intelligence at that time was U.S. Army Major (sic) General Jack Leide— airborne, ranger [sic], combat infantryman, former defense attaché in Beijing during the Tiananmen Square crisis—a no-nonsense soldier who you knew had your back. I saw him make some tough, unpopular calls, but tailoring intelligence while American forces were engaging the enemy would not have happened on his watch.⁷

The most important briefing of each day was called the "evening follies," and normally included the British (General Sir Peter De la Billiere) and French (General Michel Roquejeoffre) commanders and component commanders, normally army (Lt. Gen. John Yeosock) and air force (Lt. Gen. Chuck Horner), and occasionally marine (Lt. Gen. Walt Boomer) and navy (Vice Admiral

---

⁶ Tom Clancy with Chuck Horner, *Everyman a Tiger* (G.P. Putnam's and Sons, 1999), 461.

⁷ Rick Francona, *The Daily Journalist*, 2016. https://thedailyjournalist.com/the-strategist/intelligence-reporting

Stan Arthur). Once the air campaign began, the most important event was the daily air tasking order (ATO) briefing for the following day's targets. Normally, Brigadier General Buster Glosson and General Horner would present the briefing. As Buster gave his brief, the CINC would have me nearby and would selectively ask me if a target was a good one. For the most part, I agreed with the briefed targets; when some were controversial, we worked through them. As General Horner mentions in his book: "I drop by to talk with some of the CENTCOM staff; sometimes with Brigadier General Jack Leide, CENTCOM J-2 (Intelligence), who is really helping us."[8]

One controversial target, for example, was the Al Firdos bunker, which had been previously mostly inactive, came up on our target list after we initially intercepted its increased traffic patterns and identified it as an intelligence command and control communications center. Normally, the Iraqis prohibited civilians to be anywhere near a military facility, and we had not observed civilians inside the perimeter of the center, so the strike was given the go-ahead. The strike was reported as being successful, but before we could complete our BDA, the Iraqis were showing videos and still pictures of the devastation, including civilian bodies surrounded by weeping Iraqis. Evidently, some of the local Iraqi leaders brought their families into the bunker on the night of the strike. All hell broke loose, especially in Washington, and of course the Iraqis played it up big. At the next evening's briefing, the CINC, having felt the heat for the mission, asked General Horner and Buster Glosson for the strike details. The CINC asked me to stand behind him. After the brief was finished, he asked, "Jack was that a good target?" Without hesitation, I said, "Yes sir, it was." He nodded calmly and that was the last we heard about the Al Firdos bunker from him. But, after that strike, we were limited by Washington as

---

[8] Tom Clancy with Chuck Horner, *Everyman a Tiger* (G.P. Putnam's and Sons, 1999), 460

to what we could target in Baghdad proper. However, another target we had identified, targeted, and destroyed was a concrete river bridge in Baghdad. Again, Washington questioned why we had struck a civilian traffic bridge in the middle of Baghdad. I replied that we had studied the bridge, queried the contractors who had built it, and discovered that there were military fiber optic communications cables embedded in the bridge strands. Nothing further on that particular subject was heard from above, but those kinds of queries remained common.

PLANNING TO MEET THE TERRAIN: MAPS, TRAFFICABILITY, AND WEATHER

We in the J-2 had responsibility for theater-level mapping, including collating and coordinating requirements, then prioritizing those requests and finally requesting production of the map products with the proper scale, type, and numbers. I never questioned why the J-2, as a staff section, was responsible for providing maps to our components rather than the J-4 (Logistics). The army was the DOD executive agent for maps and had its map responsibility in the G-4. Our initial effort began with a small, peacetime-level J-2 contingency warehouse in Bahrain, with minimal staff and inventory. Now, the Map Section of the J-2 was responsible for coordinating this vast effort but were initially hopelessly understaffed and lacked dedicated communications and transportation. In both the Dominican Republic and Vietnam, I went on missions with no operational maps and, frankly, very little intelligence. We relied on the road maps we secured locally, and I learned to sketch terrain out of necessity. I then vowed to myself that I would never allow our troops to fight in an area without quality map products.

The area in which we were to operate was unbelievably immense. We needed to support possible defensive operations in Saudi Arabia (830,000 square miles), some of the Gulf States, and the objective areas of Kuwait (17,820 square miles) and Iraq

(168,000 square miles). Mapping for those areas was either nonexistent or hopelessly out of date and, because of the flat, broad, desert terrain, they were of little use, especially if the scale was as small as 1:50,000, which most of the existing maps were. We even approached the British Mapping Service, which eventually provided superb support for certain map products to fill certain scale deficiencies in our national effort. This enormous effort required close cooperation and orchestration between CENTCOM, the national-level mapping infrastructure (to arrange the transport of the immense number of map products from the continental United States and the UK to the theater), the army, and our coalition partners. We had to prioritize where mapping support would be focused geographically, the kind of maps needed and at what scale, and the chronological sequence. We also had to determine a planning sequence for distribution. Initially, our primary mission was the defense of Saudi Arabia. Its vast expanses and the lack of discernible terrain features created the initial challenge. Most of Saudi Arabia had not been mapped properly, if at all. Taking imagery to produce and provide manually gridded products was nearly impossible due to Saudi internal political and cultural sensitivities. We were able to do only a limited amount of in-theater imagery of Saudi territory as we approached the final stages of planning for Desert Storm.

I was caught in the horns of a dilemma between operational security and operational support. There were few of us who knew the operational planning for the area involved and the time frame for the ground campaign. I was one of a limited number who knew the areas from which we were to attack. If I concentrated the map requests to just the areas that would be involved, the plan could be compromised. Unfortunately, as a cover, I had to at least request some maps for selected areas where we didn't need them. After meeting with component mapping officers and factoring the many requirements and possibilities, the Map Section began to work in earnest, and achieved an unbelievable mapping effort. We eventually provided an unprecedented 118 million map products, a number represented by an equally unbelievable weight of 200 tons of maps. In order to transport this immense load quickly to the theater, we required fifty-five C-5 aircraft sorties, each of which were worth their weight in gold. Frustratingly, the maps we finally produced and distributed were either, because of limited scale and the flat desert expanses, were not terribly useful as our ground forces moved quickly into and through the desert in the attack. Frankly, in the end, our Ground Positioning System (GPS) although limited in number would eventually help a lot.

Before the CINC made his key tactical decisions leading to the ground campaign, we had to determine whether the desert in western Iraq was trafficable for large, armored formations, and the principal weather elements and their predictability. For example, General Horner began the air campaign during a period of least visibility, most hours of darkness, and the least amount of moonlight illumination. Since we had developed a night-fighting capability over the years that was second to none, we owned the night and it worked beautifully. The Saudis had little information on Iraqi terrain trafficability, but they allowed us to test similar terrain in western portions of Saudi Arabia. I also had some of our personnel question some Bedouins who moved through the desert between Iraq and Saudi Arabia, but that effort resulted in little useable information. We needed boots on the ground. I tasked our Special Operations Forces to conduct some cross-border reconnaissance missions to test the various parts of the desert over which we would maneuver and fight. I had nightmares that our armor-heavy units would get bogged down in porous sand. We also scoured resources around the world including historical oil company ground exploration documents. We eventually did receive concrete and positive reporting from one of the Special Forces teams that had infiltrated into Iraq. At last, I told the CINC that the terrain analysis team from ARCENT and air force weather team had their briefing finalized. The results were critical because if we launched those heavy divi-sions with thousands of vehicles out west and the ground was not trafficable, the whole operation could become a total disaster.

Prior to the briefing, I told General Schwarzkopf that he should basically take away two things. First, the area out west was indeed trafficable. I gulped when I said that because the lives of the attacking troops were at stake, and if they got mired in the sand, there was the possibility of them being fixed into a chemical kill zone. Second, I told him that we could predict the weather seventy-two hours out.

The Fire Trenches

The Iraqis had spent months digging extensive defense lines along the frontline trace of their defenses hoping that the attacking forces, being bogged down in the defensive fields of barbed wire, trenches, and mines, would be vulnerable to indirect and direct fire and then slowed to a bloody crawl. Additionally, they had laid oil pipelines up to and into some of the trenches and filled them with oil.. They planned to light the oil in the trenches once we began our movement across the initial trench, wire, and land-mine barriers. I tasked our analysts to consult with oil experts, both in the theater and worldwide. We learned that the oil already pumped into the trenches had likely "cured", and when lit would probably just smolder. We had to ensure that they were not filled with fresh oil. Again, with the assistance of oil experts and using satellite imagery, we identified the oil pumps that the Iraqis would use to refill the trenches. We put the key pumps and gateways on our priority target list and the air force took them out.

A Trip to Cairo

During Desert Storm, our analysts, components, and coalition partners tasked us with an enormous amount of intelligence requirements, and to help satisfy those requests, the development of a suite of intelligence collection platforms became a significant challenge due to the rapid accumulation of those collection requirements, the fast-moving environment, and needing to accomplish what we could in a relatively compressed time frame. In addition, all coalition members were almost totally dependent on CENTCOM for intelligence. For example, because of their operational methodology, the Egyptians required three sets of all intelligence materials, one of which required a courier service to Cairo by Army Major Sam Peppers, our liaison officer to the Egyptian director of military intelligence. The other two were required by separate operational commanders. In a time of peace, most of the collection requirements, including those of the Egyptians, would have been a fairly easy process, but it became a time-consuming process during an accelerating fog of war.

Prior to the beginning of the ground campaign, the CINC, Rear Admiral Grant Sharp the J-5 (Plans), and I flew to Cairo to brief key Egyptian military leaders. I brought along overlays of the templates for the divisions opposite the Egyptian sector. I married the overlays and operational maps together and displayed our unique invaluable tactical information to the assembled group, which included General Omar Suleiman, their defense minister, chief of the general staff, and chief of operations. They were experienced combat veterans and saw the immeasurable worth of those unique divisional template products on the combat scale maps. The templates were replete with exquisite detail for all of the frontline divisions, with every fighting position, weapon system, trench, obstacle, barbed wire, and avenues of approach. These unique products were produced by the Army Intelligence Agency back in the US using satellite imagery. Marine imagery analysts were also brought in to help with the effort. After that meeting with the Egyptian military leaders, I was able to break away for a session with General Suleiman and then went to dinner with his military intelligence staff. I remember the camaraderie we established, how wonderful it felt to dress like a human being again, and how a cold beer tasted like the nectar of the gods.

WORKING WITH THE NATIONAL INTELLIGENCE AGENCIES

Our national intelligence agencies provided us with assigned augmentation support teams, including the CIA's Joint Intelligence Liaison Element (JILE), NSA's Cryptologic Security Group, and the DIA's National Military Support Team. We placed those teams physically and operationally into our current Intelligence Section spaces and they became an integral part of our total analytical team. I was looking for help wherever I could get it, and we welcomed them all with open arms. Fortunately, they all arrived with their own dedicated communications. The JILE provided us with access to CIA files and the ability to instantly provide the CIA with our timely requirements for information. The JILE team members were bright and capable, but initially they were not well versed on the military situation so did not immediately identify with the requirements or the questions that needed to be asked or answered. Eventually, over the course of the war, the JILE would provide us with some invaluable information for key Iraqi production facilities and other technical information such as lines of communication, which we desperately needed while developing our targeting parameters and requirements. They provided us with full or partial answers to hundreds of our requirements, and it would have been difficult to get along without them during the entire course of the war. As the initial JILE team progressed toward the end of their first thirty-day period with us, the team chief said his team was rotating out. Evidently, it was a normal rotation policy for JILE teams to stay on deployment for thirty days and then be replaced by an entirely new team. They were just starting to fit in and play an important role in our intelligence effort, and now we would have to train a new crew. As hard as I tried to defer the 30-day limit, I had no luck. Again, I was incredulous at another CIA action that seemed so incongruous with the fact that we were at war. The NSA Cryptologic Security Group did invaluable work for us throughout the war, but, as with the CIA special adviser back at MacDill, the senior NSA representative to CENTCOM also did not deploy with us. Thankfully, the NSA graciously agreed to assign us a tactically and operationally knowledgeable signals intelligence colonel as the senior NSA representative with us in Riyadh. Last, but certainly not least, the DIA's National Military Intelligence Team, led by Ed Valentine, was with us totally before, during, and after the war. They became our life's blood throughout.

Challenging Tank Kills: An Unwarranted CIA Challenge

Just prior to the launch of the ground campaign, as we were working to help the CINC with his key tactical and operational requirements, the CIA in Washington threw a counterproductive wrench into our focused support. I received a harried message from our DIA representative, Ed Valentine, who was in Washington at the time. He informed me that the CIA strongly disagreed with our BDA figures on tanks destroyed or damaged, and they were threatening to take their counter-assessment to the White House the following day. Ed quickly sent us the figures that the CIA would present, and their estimates were vastly different from ours. As of that date, we had estimated that the number of tanks destroyed or disabled up to a certain cutoff date was around 1,200, but they were claiming that we had destroyed or disabled only about 370. When I showed Ed's message to the CINC, he went absolutely ballistic. He glared at me, belching fire as only he could, and roared, "The CIA is doing it to me again." I asked the CIA's JILE chief what he knew about this blatantly untoward initiative, and, not surprisingly, he feigned total ignorance. And, of course, there was no SPAD to ask. Ed said that the DIA would "carry our water" for us during the controversial process and beyond if necessary. The CINC directed me to draft a message to the DIA from him personally, hoping that a message of support and confidence from the commander on the ground would carry some weight with the power brokers at home. The same message would fall on deaf ears at the CIA, and they decided to take the tank kill controversy to the White House. When I informed the CINC of the CIA's final decision, he was infuriated and frustrated beyond belief. If their tank BDA numbers were so widely at odds with ours, they could have and absolutely should have brought it up with us first and long before now. Key operational decisions are not made on analytically myopic whims. Meanwhile, some of the most strident analytical elements had convinced the CIA director, Judge William Webster, that CENTCOM was wrong, that CIA was right, and that it was the judge's "duty" to take the issue to the White House. They evidently convinced him that the supposed wide disparity in the estimative figures for Iraqi tank destruction meant that a catastrophe could occur once we launched the ground campaign. This appeared to be another example of the CIA's shortsighted modus operandi during the war.

The judge and his analysts took the CIA's claims to the White House. The chairman and the J-2, Rear Admiral Mike McConnell pleaded our case and methodology to the White House arbiter, National Security Adviser General Brent Scowcroft. General Scowcroft asked where and how the CIA was acquiring their information, and they replied that they were using satellite imagery alone to analyze only one particular Iraqi division, then compared their figures to ours for that specific division, and then interpolated that disparity for that particular division to claim a parallel disparity for the entire Iraqi tank order of battle. They had concentrated on one division. We had to analyze forty-two.

General Scowcroft then asked what CENTCOM was using to come up with our figures. Our interlocutors replied that we were also using information from satellite imagery, but that it was being supplemented using large numbers of theater reconnaissance assets such as air force U-2s, RF-4 Phantoms, navy F-14 reconnaissance aircraft, drones, and a plethora of other technical collection assets. In addition, they said we were also exploiting pilot debriefing reports, mission reports, gun camera film, defector debriefings, theater signals intelligence, reports from Kuwaiti resistance, and intense analysis to increase the validity and accuracy of our BDA data base. Thankfully, General Scowcroft determined that we were getting much more accurate and timely information from a vast variety of sources and that we undoubtedly had a better feel for the battlefield requirements and the situation in-theater. I assume he realized that we had a more accurate analytical vision of the intricacies of the battlefield than a nonmilitary organization thousands of miles away counting blackened tank hulls in one division. In the end, the administration supported our CENTCOM BDA estimates and recommended, most importantly, that only the CINC was to make the final decisions and recommendations based on in-theater analytical assessments. Bottom line: tactical and operational decisions should not be made or influenced by bureaucrats thousands of miles away, but by the commander on the ground.

We learned an important lesson from this process. Those who observe and attempt to influence and dictate combat operations from afar, without knowledge of the commander's key operational requirements, knowledge, and decision-making processes, are placing a critical mission into unwarranted turmoil, in the wrong place, at the wrong time. Operational commanders base their ultimate decisions on situational awareness and a suite of time-tested military methodologies required for battlefield success. The CIA analysts were basing much of their arguments and decisions on the tank kills, but tank kills were not the key issue influencing the CINC's decisions for when and where to begin and how to fight the ground campaign. A competent commander will base critical military decisions on an analysis of METT-T or mission, enemy, terrain, troops, and time available. The CIA's untimely and myopic focus on using tank attrition as the only key to success or failure during Desert Storm was antithetical to the operational commander's time-honored military criteria for critical decision-making.

The CINC's priorities and criteria for the key decision of whether to launch a ground attack was ultimately not based on tank attrition alone.

We were confident that once we launched the ground campaign, our powerful air forces, especially the A-10 tank-busting Warthog, along with our superior tanks and anti-armor capabilities including attack helicopters of our army and marine divisions would decimate the tank-heavy Iraqi divisions. Additionally, our soldiers, their training, and our own tank's advantage in range, fire control, night fighting, and ammunition gave us confidence that the Iraqi tanks would not be a major concern to the success of the ground campaign. General Schwarzkopf's first requirement before he would decide to begin the ground campaign was to reduce the combat capability of the eighteen Iraqi divisions along the frontline trace to below 50 percent of combat effectiveness. His second requirement was to reduce the number of artillery pieces along the entire frontline trace by 50 percent and by 90 percent at the breach points. My own personal priority within the CINC's artillery destruction priorities was the 100 percent elimination of BM-21 122mm multiple rocket launcher unit capability. Not only could these rocket launcher units put out large amounts of firepower over a large area in a short period of time, but I knew that they were also capable of firing chemical munitions. Shortly before the launch of the ground campaign, Egyptian intelligence director General Omar Suleiman told me in confidence that Egypt had supported the Iraqis during their horrible war against the Iranians and that they had provided the Iraqis with large numbers of 122 mm rockets. Those rockets had warheads that could be filled with chemical agents. The Iraqis could quickly and over wide distances lay down a chemical attack with great efficacy. The Iraqis had a large number of BM-21s and probably had them focused where our attacking units would have to penetrate during any attack scenario. In sum, we would use the commander on the ground priorities to begin the ground campaign, not what some distant myopic analysts thought.

A Bright CIA Light

Despite the nagging problems that we had with the SPAD and the national-level CIA, our relationship with CIA people on the ground was virtually ideal. I had an open invitation to visit their local offices at any time and had a friendly, open, and productive dialogue with them throughout the campaign. Since we were lacking a SPAD, CIA periodically provided us with one of their senior officers in the area. They were willing but their time with us and their knowledge of our operation and requirements were limited.

The positive relationship with the CIA people on the ground was like previous other relationships I had with my CIA colleagues, all working productively and contributory. Why we had the problems with the national CIA elements, the SPAD, and the JILE is, to this day, still a mystery to me. Our aims and ultimate efforts toward the success of our military campaign should have been the same.

CONDUCTING THE COLLECTION MANAGEMENT ORCHESTRA

The problem within our collection management system was that we had not trained for controlling, planning, and tasking the vast number of assets we had available during Desert Storm. We were given priority for virtually every tactical, operational, and national intelligence collection platform and system to support our intelligence effort. I had to ensure that we used them most effectively in number and time. I drew on past experiences while developing collection fusion (the synergistic use of mutually supporting collection platforms and methodologies) during my previous tours.

I often felt like it was like directing a large orchestra. After normal initial trial and error, we eventually got really good at it.

Each day we received a large number of component and coalition collection requirements, fused them together, prioritized them by situational needs, and evolved an enormous collection management tasking plan for the following day's missions. Unfortunately, because of the enormity of the tasking and the fact that we had little peacetime experience doing it in such a large scale, it took us an inordinate amount of precious time to develop into a fully functional collection management team. Collection management requirements (targets) quickly built up massively, so that we had to increase our technical capabilities and systems all while cobbling together an efficient collection management staff. We were learning on the fly, and an incredibly large number of requirements poured in every day. Like BDA, huge collection management responsibilities and scope using an enormous amount of collection assets are not normal during peacetime. Eventually, we were responsible for controlling and tasking sixty different collection systems, platforms, or links in our area of operations and additionally had the majority of our national overhead satellite systems in support. We tasked tactical collection systems on converted fighter aircraft such as fourteen RF-4s, along with some RF-5s, and F-14s. Additionally, we had various technical collection systems including eleven U-2 high altitude reconnaissance aircraft, seven RC-135 Rivet joint reconnaissance aircraft for near-real-time intelligence collection, analysis, and dissemination, and JSTARS. Because analytical and dynamic situational requirements drive collection, we often had to continuously transition or reprogram priorities for our collection assets.

Midway through the air campaign our collection efforts and assets became increasingly prioritized towards preparation of the battlefield prior to the ground campaign. The JSTARS missions, for example, were continually changing from intelligence collection to targeting, but were almost always in support of the ground components during the preparation and shaping of the battlefield. During early to mid-February, prior to the ground campaign, I was receiving a growing number of frustrated complaints from the army and marines about air sorties being diverted from preplanned ground support missions in the air tasking order to other types of strike missions. I knew that if the CINC heard of those complaints, he would not be a happy camper. I mentioned the problem to General Cal Waller and suggested that he chair a meeting each day for the next day's ground support missions, including for JSTARS. He agreed to take it on. Air force Brigadier General Buster Glosson was doing an incredible job planning and conducting the day-to-day highly effective air campaign. Buster was totally mission oriented and a fierce proponent of air power, and he likely thought that what he was doing was the right thing at the right time. But after General Waller watched the ground force support process closely for a few days, he observed what he thought were seemingly unwarranted diversions of already preapproved ground support missions. He approached Buster and said, "Buster, If you change one more target without my approval, I'm going to choke your tongue out." I thought to myself, what a masterful approach. Thereafter, it seemed that Buster was careful not to, without very solid reasons, divert preplanned missions in support of the ground forces, including JSTARS missions.

We eventually added some British and French intelligence collection aircraft as well. We constantly looked for additional collection platforms to add to our total intelligence collection suite. We even added and bore-sighted a British Over-The-Horizon Radar (OTH) system on Cyprus. We then linked it with the JSTARS for collection tipping and reporting. Each day, I would walk along the long, complicated collection management wall charts with the collection managers ensuring that we were covering our priority collection targets and using appropriate systems and required numbers for the allocated missions. At times, we also had to cover "political" targets, such as those of Saudi high priority interest and areas in the mountains of Jordan to look for weapon systems that could target Jeddah and Medina, and certain militant elements in Yemen to determine if they were conducting cross-border operations. We had little military interest of our own in those targets, but we used a couple of U-2 missions to politically assuage Saudi concerns and eventually found nothing of interest.

Once the ground campaign had begun, it would become difficult to keep up with the fast pace of the attacking units. During the first twenty-four hours, we pretty much knew the locations of frontline and reenforcing units, but after that, we would have to rely heavily on reconnaissance from the JSTARS, other airborne platforms, SIGINT and satellites. Although we had established a unique joint imagery processing center, we often struggled to get timely, adequate imagery that was sufficient for immediate tactical targeting and retargeting. A lack of communications bandwidth for the transmission of imagery was continuously a problem. Despite the initial challenges, once our collection center was fully staffed and deficiencies rectified, our planning and systems, in concert with national and international capabilities, became highly effective and responsive to the CINC, our components, and coalition partners.

The J-3 passed another challenging mission on to us to prepare a weapon system order of battle for some of our coalition partners. The Egyptians and the Syrians had some weapon systems that were the same as or similar to the Iraqis, such as the French F-1 fighter aircraft, Russian SA-2 and SA-6 anti-air missile systems, T-72 tanks, and BMP armored personnel carriers. We coordinated our efforts with our Special Forces soldiers who were deployed with foreign component commands to help us with a list of "conflicting" weapons systems. We didn't want to inadvertently attack those systems.

We recommended that they not fly F-1s because our pilots could mistake them for Iraqi and shoot them down. We also told them not to "burn" (turn on) the target acquisition radars for their SA-2 and SA-6 weapon systems, and if they had to move their T-72s and BMPs, to fit them with well-defined, and coordinated "friendly" markings. The Syrians, however, did not cross the Iraqi or Kuwaiti borders, but remained in place in Saudi Arabia. It appeared that they were there for political show rather than for the fight. This is yet another little known but important responsibility we in the J-2 had to assume.

Unique Cultural Challenges

One of the best sources of primary intelligence on enemy units is an enemy defector or prisoner, and ever-increasing numbers were falling to US and Saudi units along the Saudi-Iraqi-Kuwaiti border areas. The air campaign was inflicting mounting tolls on Iraqi personnel, equipment, supplies, and morale. Additionally, our psychological warfare efforts were beginning to have devastating effects, especially among the conscripted, reactivated units along the Iraqi defensive front line. They in fact were akin to "cannon fodder," and we took every measure to make sure they felt that way. Defectors who crossed into Saudi Arabia were kept in Saudi detention camps. We pressed the Saudis to be involved in the interrogation process, but they stated that non-Arabs should not control or interrogate Arabs, even as prisoners of war, or as the Saudis called them "guests." To know how our battlefield preparation efforts had affected especially the frontline units, we had to quickly query the Iraqi defectors the most critical questions on the latest and best intelligence on their unit status. Real time HUMINT information is critical. With the Saudis in charge, it became painfully clear that they had little priority, standard system, or procedures for managing or interrogating the prisoners. Even if they interrogated the defectors, they were not versed in combat intelligence and they were not aware of our critical elements of information. Interrogation of defectors or prisoners of war is an art. Properly trained interrogators, armed with the critical questions, and using proven techniques can elicit current and accurate information on enemy dispositions. Saudi interrogators may have had some expertise when it came to internal security, but this was very different. The Saudis did have one advantage: native fluency in the Arabic language, and we were short of native linguists. ARCENT, which had doctrinal responsibility for prisoner of war interrogation, broached with the Saudis the idea of conducting combined interrogations with us preparing the questions and follow-up while the Saudis asked the questions and translated the answers. Those initiatives were quickly rebuffed because the Saudis, simply put, would not let non-Arabs participate in the interrogation of Arabs. The ARCENT G-2, Brigadier General John Stewart, asked for my help in getting his interrogators access to the prisoners. I understood the Saudi cultural sensitivities, but my sense of mission, safety of our troops, and the importance of the interrogations just roiled in my gut, and I was not to be denied. I tried to make our case with any Saudi connection that I had, including the Egyptians, who I felt might have a decent awareness of the problem and maybe the capability to sort through the problem and influence the Saudis. As time went on, it appeared that the Saudi's primary concern was that their Arab brothers were well cared for. I knew that proper interrogation would not be cruel, and the prisoners would be treated ethically, but most importantly, this was war. The Iraqis were the enemy. I could not convince the Saudis by using any amount of military logic, so I approached the CINC who said he would ask Prince Khalid for help. Even though the importance of the information may have been acknowledged by Khalid, the issue appeared to fall into a deep, swirling black hole. After more forceful intercession by the CINC at the highest Saudi levels, we were finally cleared to take part in the defector interrogations. We could pass the questions to the Saudis who would then ask the questions and provide whatever answers they could glean. Our interrogators could then provide follow-up questions. Although certainly not ideal, this was the best we could do. This scenario shows that even when under great danger to people and nation, cultural biases can run deep and at times can take precedence even seemingly over survival.

As the ground campaign grew near, we needed to do what we could to determine whether the Iraqis might use weapons of mass destruction, especially as our units were breaching the wire. As we considered what form of Iraqi retaliation we would encounter, use of chemical and biological weapons was always on our minds. After all, Saddam had used chemical weapons during the Iran-Iraq war. We knew Saddam had large stores of both chemical and biological agents. Iraq had used chemical agents including mustard gas, sarin, and tabun throughout the Iran-Iraq war, causing tens of thousands of casualties. Additionally, thousands of Kurdish civilians were killed and wounded in the Halabja Massacre when Iraqi aircraft dropped mustard gas and nerve gas into residential areas. This attack against the Kurds was the largest chemical weapons attack against a civilian population in history and would later be declared as genocide.

In coordination with the Armed Forces Medical Intelligence Center, we decided that blood samples of Iraqi detainees, especially any who had been in the Republican Guard, would reveal if they had been inoculated against the most probable biological agents: anthrax and botulinum. There were two primary reasons why we needed the information. The first and most obvious was to alert our troops and the civilian population to that threat, and the second was that we had limited amounts of antitoxins and needed to decide whether to provide antitoxins to troops, when and which types of antitoxins should be used and for which type units. We were tasked to obtain the blood samples. I asked my Saudi counterparts if our doctors could draw blood samples from select detainees. We needed our own doctors to draw the blood in order to keep a proper chain of custody through to the US military medical scientists. Precious time went by and all I got was silence. I eventually crafted a letter to Defense Minister Sultan, for General Schwarzkopf's signature, which stressed the criticality of the requirement. We eventually received an answer stating that the Saudis would not allow non-Arabs to draw blood from Arabs, but that Saudi medical personnel would draw the select blood samples instead and provide them to us. Again, we had no choice but to accept the Saudi's offer. We sent the blood supplied by the Saudis back to the United States and quickly got a response that none of the supplied blood samples had indications of inoculation against biological agents. Despite those results, we still remained uneasy.

In concert with a very capable J-3 (Operations) action officer and my good friend Major General Dane Starling the J-4 (Logistics), we coordinated an action plan with the CENTCOM surgeon. We sent an immediate request to the DIA and requested they gather a panel of experts to provide us with recommendations on what type of antitoxins we would need, how many doses were available and prioritize who should receive which type. The panel reported that there were limited amounts of anti-agent vaccine doses in our national inventory: 150,000 anti-anthrax vaccines and 8,000 anti-botulinum capsules. They determined that anthrax agents would most likely be used along the probable attack routes of our initially deploying forces and the botulism agents would most likely be used against our rear elements, especially command headquarters. We met with General Schwarzkopf and recommended that we inoculate as many as possible of the initially deploying ground units with the anthrax vaccine, and that we provide key headquarter personnel with anti-botulinum capsules. He looked at us and said, "Ok, let's do it." Although still greatly concerned, he seemed somewhat relieved that at least we had some capability to protect a number of the deploying troops and those in key headquarters. This was the kind of decision the CINC had to make constantly, and at times, several times a day. Washington quickly flew the antitoxins to the theater and the distribution plan was immediately implemented. Even after we in CENTCOM headquarters were given our botulinum capsules, the queasy feeling about the possible use of biological or chemical agents never left us.

Keeping Israel out of the War

We all were aware that Saddam was going to use our close relationship to Israel to try to create an untenable schism within the coalition, particularly with our Arab coalition partners. According to Saddam, Arab nations acting in concert with the United States was "an unholy alliance." Although not part of our official coalition, the Israelis were a very important piece to the operational puzzle. We knew that the use of Iraqi Scud missiles against Israel was an attempt to induce Israel to retaliate. It was Saddam's attempt to break down the coalition, especially among its Arab members. Identifying mobile missile locations was a difficult challenge. During the first hours of the air campaign, we had targeted and destroyed thirty fixed missile launch sites spread among five complexes in western Iraq. Those sites had been built for the sole purpose of creating a permanent missile threat to Israel. Iraq began launching mobile Scuds into Israel on January 18, 1991. The next day, the US delivered to Israel two batteries of Patriot anti-aircraft missiles and the US Army personnel to operate them. Hopefully, that initiative would help prevent an Israeli counterstrike. The Israelis provided us forty-four separate possible locations, which they called "targets," where they hoped we could identify and destroy the mobile launchers. We needed enormous help from all, including from Washington, to convince the Israelis that our surveillance assets had covered or were covering those designated targets. We continuously had to keep satisfying the Israelis concerns to keep them out of the war. In actuality, we already had identified the majority of the Israeli-produced target sets and even added a few. In the end, it was important to them militarily, politically, and psychologically to be convinced that we were "covering" their targets, along with ours.

Scud Hunters

During one of the most critical periods of the high-pressured Scud-hunting effort, I visited the Saudi Map Service to see if they had some maps of Iraq and Saudi Arabia in their inventory that could provide us with some key military-related information. Although they had little to offer, they did show me two map sheets of southeastern Iraq that they said the Iraqis had given them after they had finished an Iraqi countrywide military map project. It seems that the Saudis had funded an effort by the Iraqis to map their entire country. I could tell that the sheets were in fact high-quality military topographical maps. I pressed the Saudi map officer to see if they could find the remainder of the Iraq countrywide map set, but, unfortunately, they said the two sheets were all they had. Once I got back to our headquarters, I then showed the map sheets to our analysts, particularly our "Scud-Hunters" led by air force Captain Mike "Scudly" DeLuca. We all sat around a table and scoured every inch of the two maps. I then asked them to look into their database and create an overlay of past Scud launches in the geographical areas represented by each sheet. To our great surprise, the known reported Scud launch points in those areas of Iraq matched the standard benchmarks located on the maps. Benchmarks are pre-surveyed points on the ground where the exact elevation and location is known and marked with a brass or aluminum plate. Because the Iraqis abhorred our SCUD-hunters, they were fearful of taking the proper amount time to do their own pre-fire mission survey. They would use the calculations already established by the survey benchmark, then fire and scoot back into cover. We could not believe it. Now, we desperately needed the entire Iraqi military map set, not only to help with SCUD hunting but also for other important uses such as targeting Iraqi military facilities represented on the maps. These maps could be the gold standard for our effort to prevent launches or at least use benchmarks in specific areas to look for and target SCUDS with our surveillance assets. When I asked an Iraq-savvy colonel in our analytical shop, who had also been an attaché in our U.S. Embassy in Baghdad, whether he had seen any such maps, he told me that at one time they had the entire set tacked on a wall in the defense attaché office. I sent an immediate high-priority request back to Washington, especially to DIA and CIA, to locate the entire map set and get it out to us as soon as possible. Unfortunately, there was no luck anywhere in the intelligence community. Either the maps weren't sent to Washington, or if they were, they got lost in some bureaucratic hell hole. Either way, critical information needed at a critical time was unfortunately not reported or lost. Big, big, lesson learned.

It was virtually impossible to find the mobile Scuds from the air, so we also had eyes on the ground to find and destroy them or to direct air strikes. We tasked Special Operations Forces including the British Special Forces (SAS) for the mission. Late one night, when General Schwarzkopf and I were sitting in the war room talking about the Scud problem, he asked me to draw out a circle on a map of where the Scud launches toward Israel were occurring. I calculated that the area was an astonishing 27,875 square miles. I equated it to trying to find a large pickup truck in an area that was the size of three states (Rhode Island, Massachusetts, and New Hampshire). Most critics, including the Israelis, when they asked why we couldn't find the Scuds, did not understand the great areas and distances involved, or the massive and almost constant cloud cover in the area.

MOVING TOWARD THE FINAL PHASE: PLANNING THE GROUND CAMPAIGN

Prior to his making his decision on launching the ground campaign, the CINC's priority and direction was that by February 23, all of the Iraqi frontline units be effectively attritted to 50 percent combat effectiveness or lower and the second-echelon divisions would be attritted to 50–75 percent. His second requirement was that we reduce Iraqi artillery along the frontline trace by 50 percent, and by 90 percent at the breach points. We began prioritizing the targeting of the frontline trace divisions and the huge numbers of artillery units that were capable of reigning devastating fire on our attacking units during the initial launch of the ground campaign. We had to prepare the battlefield and degrade Saddam's frontline forces enough to allow our attacking forces to punch through without sustaining unacceptable casualties. Iraqi artillery was the most dangerous element in Saddam's defenses, especially if those weapons were capable to deliver chemical-filled rounds. If the Iraqis decided to use chemical weapons, our units would be severely affected, and the attack may well have been forced to a stall. Incredibly, the Iraqis had as many as 145 battalions of artillery and most were placed forward to help blunt any attack. This Iraqi defensive tactic was one that the Soviets, who were also an artillery-reliant force, had taught them well. Saddam built formidable defenses, reinforced with heavy artillery to devastate our forces when we initially were to attempt our breakthrough. He was planning to exact so many casualties during the initial coalition attacks that we would come under terrific pressure to stand down, followed by a request for negotiations. We specifically targeted those divisions and the supporting artillery. I tasked our Order of Battle Section to prioritize the dynamic assessment of those frontline divisions using all-source analysis from signals and imagery intelligence, defector interrogation, pilot reporting, and any other scrap of intelligence we could muster. In an assessment of a unit's capability, we consider its order of battle, including the degree of degradation of its organizational structure, weapons, logistics, communications and morale. In our own military, when we assess that one of our divisions is rated at 70 percent capable or below, we consider that division to be combat ineffective. As we approached the launch of the ground campaign, Col. Chuck Thomas and his folks in the Joint Intelligence Center devised a simple methodology on a chart to illustrate the current dispositions of the Iraqi frontline and secondary divisions. Each division was depicted as a color-coded block. The color green indicated divisions that were between 75–100 percent combat capable. The color yellow represented 50–74 percent combat capability, and red was 49 percent or below combat-effective. We posted this chart in the war room and the CINC assiduously looked at this small but valuable chart throughout the day, every day. The chart was dated February 21, 1991.

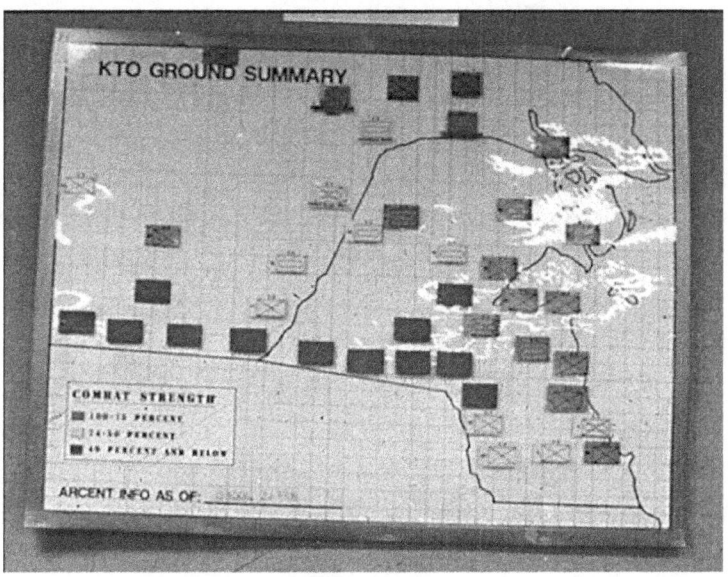

Although the chart represented thousands of hours of combat offensive action and post-action analyses, all the CINC needed was the basic information he required that was simple to read and interpret. We constantly updated that chart as the campaign progressed. A combat commander does not need to know the intricacies of the voluminous, detailed, and complicated data that is represented by very basic, but carefully conceived, charts, graphs, and depictions such as this little chart. It was used by the CINC daily to "shape the battlefield" by guiding his decisions that would ultimately weaken Saddam's frontline defenses and prepare the KTO for the ground campaign. He launched the ground campaign largely based on information provided by this little chart, which helped establish and satisfy his key decision-making requirements as we approached G-Day. The rest is history.

Back in late August 1990, the CINC had outlined the major phases of his campaign, which culminated with a ground offensive to drive the Iraqis from Kuwait. A group of bright, young officers was assigned as a special planning group under the J-5 (Plans) with the key mission of developing the courses of action for an inevitable ground campaign. That select group, led by Lieutenant Colonel Joe Purvis, was from the Army's School of Advanced Military Studies at Fort Leavenworth, Kansas. This intense education and research program was at the highest level of military art, and their course focused on the army's Air-Land Battle Doctrine to be compatible with other service doctrine, particularly the Marine Corps maneuver warfare doctrine. We called this small cell the Jedi Knights, and they worked in a small, secure space near the war room.

Only an extremely small number of staff officers other than the team were allowed in their planning room and had access to the planning sequences. I was one of the few and would visit Joe's team fairly frequently to get an update on their planning progress and to ensure that they were getting the intelligence information that they needed. At first, their scope of planning was limited by the initial number and types of units available for the ground campaign. However, on November 8, 1990, the president authorized a tremendous increase in troop levels to provide the coalition with an offensive option, and the Left Hook envelopment attack into Iraq was born. On November 29, 1990, the UN authorized the use of force to expel Iraq from Kuwait.

With the plan for his ground campaign, including the Left Hook in place, the CINC frequently asked me whether the Iraqis were moving reenforcing divisions west of Kuwait and into Iraq itself. I told him that after two or three very weak infantry divisions had deployed west of the Wadi Al Batin, all other movement had ceased, and we continued to report no increase in Iraqi troop strength into the western areas. During the whole of my career, I had always tried to anticipate what the enemy's next move should and would be and then followed on with the "why?" I tried to think through the reasons why Saddam stopped his westward deployment of troops. I came up with three possibilities: either he ran out of forces because he wanted to ensure he had enough forces in Kuwait to cause heavy losses, or he did not think that movement of large coalition forces out into the expanses of the western desert was feasible, or it was possible that he was setting us up for a "chemical kill zone" in that wide-open area out west. I informed the CINC of those three possibilities and told him that I thought because Saddam thought, if he were to survive the coming conflict, he had to pack his troops into Kuwait in hopes that a high coalition casualty rate would cause us to sue for peace. And that he may well have thought we would not move our forces into the vast western expanses. I also told him that we had not yet seen the grouping of weapon systems such as artillery, rocket launchers or scuds that could deliver chemical laydown in the area out west. I had to give him my best assessments no matter how difficult it was for him or for me. The CINC trusted his instincts and felt reassured to move the plan forward.

Desert Storm was the first war to be broadcast live from the front lines of the battle, and Saddam was an assiduous watcher of CNN. He used the continuous media dialogue to gauge the public perception for American casualties and other coalitions as well. He was well aware of America's sensitivity to a "Vietnam syndrome," and Desert Shield was the first large employment of US ground, air, and naval power since the Vietnam War. Although President H.W. Bush frequently declared that the world remained united against Iraq's aggression in Kuwait, Saddam knew that some elements in our Congress and the American public were against using our troops to force the Iraqis out of Kuwait. He had hoped to deter our offensive, create unsustainable casualties, and cause us to stall our attack, so he could then call for negotiations to "stop the slaughter." He put all of his resources into building a multi-layered defensive system in Kuwait. I don't believe he thought of his western flank as an option we would take, but he certainly should have. He probably felt that no matter what, we would have to attack into Kuwait to liberate it, as that was our designated charter via the United

Nations Security Council. He may well have been right in theory, but his strategy, operational planning and decisions would eventually fail.

IRAQ'S ABORTED STRIKE

On January 24, 1991, two Iraqi Mirage F-1s staged out of Tallil Air Base in southern Iraq and were controlled out of its Air Defense Control Headquarters. Early that morning, they were first seen penetrating with great speed toward the northern arc of the Persian Gulf. Fortunately, a Saudi flight of F-15Es was patrolling in the area and a heroic Saudi F-15E pilot shot down the two Iraqi planes. This Saudi pilot justifiably became an instant Arab hero. Initial operational reporting claimed that these Mirage F-1s were on a penetrating anti-ship mission into the gulf against US and coalition warships. Now for the rest of the story.

At the time of the shoot down, Saddam was continuously ranting about not only "burning Israel," but was also conducting retribution attacks on the Arab countries that were cooperating with the United States-led coalition. Saddam was evidently most agitated over the Saudi posture since they acted contrary to his original assessment and had also accepted large numbers of forces on its soil and then allowed that force to launch an attack against Iraqi forces. His continuous rhetoric before, during, and even after the war was to break up the coalition and to punish those who supported it. If he was successful at any time prior to the launch of Desert Storm, there may never have been a battle and he would have won the day. Even after the launch of Desert Storm, he continued to attempt to break the coalition and threaten retaliation against the Gulf States while constantly highlighting civilian casualties and the damage to historic and religious sites. At the time of the F-1 shoot down, there was still some apprehension in Saudi Arabia and some of the other Gulf States about whether they had made the right decision by supporting the coalition. Saddam was making vitriolic threats to the coalition partners. These threats included political, religious, and physical damage, but he also knew how to threaten their economic lifeblood: destroy their oil-producing infrastructure. Without oil income, these nations would be hard-pressed to support the war effort and their regimes would be in serious jeopardy.

Enter the flight of the two Iraqi F-1s on a supposed anti-ship mission into the Persian Gulf. After we attacked and captured the Tallil airbase during the ground campaign, we obtained some documents that showed plans for an attack mission with the two F1s as the striking force and using a flight of three MiG-23 air-to-air fighters in an escort role. For whatever reason, the MiGs never made the rendezvous point, and without the fighter escort, the F-1s became vulnerable to the Saudi pilots and their F-15 E air superiority fighters. What is not well known is that the objective of the Iraqi attacks, according to the captured plans, was not the coalition fleet in the Gulf, but key Saudi oil facilities, including the massive Ras Tanura oil refinery and the expansive Saudi Abqaiq oil fields. If those aircraft had gotten through and bombed those critical facilities, it would have been an Iraqi psychological coup. Most likely that Saudi pilot's success was even more valuable than originally thought. I eventually gave the captured plans to our air force who in turn gave them to the Saudis.

THE BATTLE FOR KHAFJI

During the days that followed the two Iraqi Mirages being shot down, Saddam dug in deeper. Iraq continued to pummel Israel with Scuds and sabotaged Kuwait's main supertanker pier, dumping millions of gallons of crude into the Gulf. Saddam probably had two initial main objectives in mind: to embarrass the Saudi king and to drive a wedge between the Saudis and the rest of the coalition. We also had information that Saddam met with Iraqi commanders in Basra. As General Horner mentioned in his book: "Brigadier General Jack Leide, the CENTCOM J-2, warned of activity by the Iraqi III Corps commander, Lieutenant General Salah Abud Mahmud."[9] We had observed Saddam holding meetings in a Winnebago type vehicle in propaganda tv appearances, and I had put a high collection and analytical priority on all Winnebagos observed in Iraq. After Saddam's meeting one of our collection platforms identified a convoy, including a Winnebago, returning to Baghdad. We put out an immediate targeting tasking on the Winnebago-led convoy. As far as I was concerned, he was a legitimate military high-value target. Our fighters attacked the convoy, but unfortunately, he was not killed or wounded during that attack. If we had in fact killed or severely wounded him, one wonders how it would have impacted the remainder of the campaign, or the need for our military return to Iraqi in 2003 and beyond.

We continued to report an Iraqi buildup across the border from the Saudi coastal town of Khafji, and on January 28, observation posts along the Kuwait/Saudi border reported Iraqi reconnaissance in force. All indicators pointed to an imminent Iraqi spoiling attack. On January 29, 1,500 Iraqis infiltrated into Khafji at night. Elements of Iraqi mechanized divisions followed. The operation was in fact commanded by Major General Mahmud, the Commander of III Corps. Saddam was undoubtedly worried that the continuing coalition air campaign was causing great degradation to the internal Iraqi military, civilian infrastructure, and morale. He then likely initiated the Khafji attack to accelerate the coalition ground offensive before we were ready. We discovered that Saddam's objectives to occupy Saudi territory and capture a large number of Saudis and Arab coalition prisoners were mostly psychological. Saddam had attempted to paint the original Iraqi capture of Khafji as a major propaganda victory for Iraq. On January 30, Iraqi radio claimed that they had "expelled Americans from the Arab territory."

---

[9] Tom Clancy with Chuck Horner, *Everyman a Tiger* (G.P. Putnam's and Sons, 1999), 423

As the Khafji crisis grew, General Khalid made an emotional appeal to the CINC for immediate help, especially air support against Iraqi forces in and around the city. General Schwarzkopf knew this was a critical time for the Arab force, and he insisted that the city should be retaken by Arab forces, supported by coalition air and artillery. We quickly provided the Saudis with as much support as we could and helped them with a battle plan. The counterattack included a task force led by the 2nd Saudi National Guard Brigade's 7th Battalion, composed of Saudi mechanized infantry with two Qatari tank companies attached. The task force was supported by small US Army Special Forces and Marine Corps Force Reconnaissance units. Although Saddam used over 300 tanks, the Saudi forces learned that they had a significant edge over Iraqi forces with their M-60A1 tanks, and the marines found considerable effectiveness with lightly armored vehicles by using the antitank guided weapons at relatively long ranges. The importance of our superior targeting and reconnaissance aircraft was also highlighted. It was the first major use of JSTARS to monitor Iraqi troop moves and to assist air force pilots to target and destroy large numbers of Iraqi tanks. AC-130 gunships using cannons and miniguns also provided close air support. Between January 30 and February 1, 1991, two Saudi Arabian National Guard battalions and two Qatari tank companies, aided by coalition aircraft and artillery, moved to retake control of the city. By February 1, the city had been recaptured at the cost of forty-three coalition service members killed and fifty-two wounded. Iraqi Army fatalities numbered as many as 300, while around 400 were taken as prisoners of war. With our marine artillery and air force interdiction and close air support, the Saudis and their Arab cohorts did a valiant job in beating the Iraqis back and reoccupying Khafji. It was a big morale boost for the Saudis and would stand them in good stead when the ground campaign began in earnest.

We learned from Khafji that the Iraqi military's training and doctrine was ineffective during fast-moving combat engagements, and the lack of ability to communicate and coordinate between attacking units compounded that apparent weakness. Degrading their command and control communications would certainly aggravate those operational weaknesses even further, and that had been one of my highest priorities from the very beginning. Cutting off communications between Baghdad and the corps commanders in particular would hinder their ability to receive orders from Saddam's military headquarters and they in turn would be loath to act with any appropriate level of local initiative. I had always thought that the Achilles' heel of the Soviet/Russian military was their lack of flexibility, which would be frozen by the prohibitive lack of initiative at the lower levels, especially in fast-moving environments. I have found over the years that many of the world's militaries fit that pattern. Since the Iraqi forces had been Soviet trained, their lower levels of command were inflexible during dynamic environments. I later thought that a key difference between the Iraqis and us is that even their corps commanders were reticent to make command decisions without guidance from above when it counted, while we had sergeants out in the desert performing independent actions. The Battle of Khafji showed us how vulnerable Iraqi troops would be the moment that they attempted to conduct fast-moving operations. Khafji also became somewhat of a rehearsal for coalition's air operations in the ground support role. Additionally, attack and interdiction operations during the battle for Khafji may have convinced Iraqi commanders that they would be unable to effectively move and react in the face of coalition air power. Iraqi forces did not attempt to conduct any further major actions, maneuvers, or movements during the remainder of the air campaign. After the Battle of Khafji, General Schwarzkopf asked me to give him my personal assessment about what had just occurred during the battle. I told him that from what I observed, the most important takeaway was that the way the Iraqis had planned and fought the battle was a good indicator of how they would perform when the real fight was on. After some further discussion, I looked at him straight in the eyes and summarized, "Sir, bottom line, these guys aren't worth a shit! They can't even conduct a minimal coordinated attack at the regimental level, let alone at division and above." He grinned broadly and nodded knowingly. Hopefully, I was right.

THE LANDING THAT NEVER WAS

During wartime, deception is a vital tool and assists military commanders in accomplishing their operational mission and protects the lives of their troops. During Desert Storm, we in the J-2 had an integral part in a full-throated deception plan being developed by a CENTCOM special action cell. The aims of the plan were to hide the movement of our divisions to the west in order to conduct the planned Left Hook and to hold Iraqi divisions along the Kuwaiti coast in place by convincing the Iraqi's that we were planning to conduct an amphibious operation along the eastern coast of Kuwait. The "plan" included a 45,000 marine landing force aboard navy ships off the Kuwaiti coast. We wanted him to continue to concentrate his forces along the coast and not to redeploy units to the west. Four fairly visible amphibious "training" exercises took place: two called Sea Soldier 1 and 2 in October and early November 1990 on the coast of Oman, the highly publicized amphibious exercise around November 15 called Imminent Thunder on the eastern coast of Saudi Arabia, and AMPHIBEX followed in early December. The press was well aware of the exercises, and we knew Saddam was watching. These well-publicized prewar exercises were staged to convince the Iraqis that a major seaborne assault was planned, while phony radio transmissions and other covert communications would also mask the gigantic movement of a multi-divisional allied force to the west. Also, on the first day of the ground campaign, the battleships USS Missouri and Wisconsin would fire salvos on the coast of Kuwait and seal teams would detonate explosives on the Kuwaiti coastline, all to make the Iraqis think that an amphibious operation was to follow.

I personally wanted to go deeper, beyond the overt deception of the publicized marine amphibious exercises, and I knew even more convincing deception, confusion, and disinformation could be infused by the possible use of covert and clandestine means. I thought back to allied efforts during World War II that used covert and clandestine means to place false information into the German intelligence system to convince them that the allies were going to attack in Sardinia and Greece instead of Sicily and were going to attack at the Pas de Calais instead of Normandy. I tried to think of a possible intelligence initiative in order to penetrate the Iraqi systems at the most sensitive intelligence levels. I strongly felt that the best way to deceive the Iraqis and one that would have more credibility than any other method, would be to infuse deceptive information into their overt, covert, or clandestine internal and intrinsic intelligence collection reporting and analytical system. I tasked our rear element in Tampa do an in-depth study of the worldwide Iraqi intelligence collection assets and reporting system.

After getting that report, I then asked them to assess where the most logical Iraqi intelligence collection asset was in the world in order to pass information that the marines would be conducting an amphibious operation on the coast of Kuwait. Once I scanned the worldwide locations of Iraqi intelligence assets, I selected a credible collector in an ideal location. We then tasked one of our overseas HUMINT intelligence assets to contact the selected Iraqi officer and provide him with the false information that a large amphibious operation was planned on the eastern coast of Kuwait. Once that information was planted with the Iraqi officer, we assumed, I think correctly, that his reporting of the "planned" amphibious operations was moving through Iraqi intelligence channels. I believe, in the end, that this covert reporting chain was an important factor in convincing the Iraqi command authority that we were, in fact, coming in from the sea. The Iraqis never did move troops from the coastline.

As for the media "involvement" in the plan, perhaps they felt deceived and used, but from a military perspective, the benefits clearly outweighed their blow-back. As far as I was concerned, having studied Sun Tzu and the Soviet/Russian doctrine of Maskirovka deception and "masking" are crucial components of classic military operations, especially major ones. The key to intelligence is to know your enemy while preventing them from knowing you.

G-DAY-2: FEBRUARY 22, 1991

Even though the Iraqi Army had been repeatedly pummeled from the air since January 17, they still remained relatively formidable. There were forty-three Iraqi divisions in the KTO, which originally consisted of 545,000 troops. They still had another twenty-five divisions in reserve that had not been committed to the theater. While the frontline units in the Iraqi Army had been reduced to 50 percent strength or below as the CINC had required, the reinforcing divisions behind them, although somewhat reduced in capability, were still a counterattacking threat, while the Republican Guard units, although some at about 70 percent strength, were still dangerously capable, mobile, and highly motivated.

On February 22, 1991, only five Iraqi airfields remained minimally functional, and our F-15s had recently downed fifteen Iraqi aircraft. President H.W. Bush gave Iraq a 24-hour ultimatum to withdraw from Kuwait or face a ground campaign. Saddam had used oil as a weapon when he initially had created his fire trenches and unleashed oil from a Kuwaiti refinery into the Gulf. This time, after being pounded from the air and threatened with a grueling ground attack, he ordered the Kuwaiti oil fields set ablaze. Hundreds (initially, as many as 500) oil wells were now on fire and the acrid, jet-black smoke was blanketing the sky over and around Kuwait City. Our overhead imagery picked up the absolutely astounding sight of waste and devastation. That evening at the CINC's briefing, we reported that hundreds of oil wells were on fire and there was utter devastation in the oil fields of Kuwait. After Kuwait City had been liberated, General Schwarzkopf and I flew up for a visit. As I looked down at the burning wells from the air, the area looked like a gigantic ugly birthday cake. After we got out of the plane at the airport in Kuwait City, I felt like I was taking part in some eerie nightmare or science fiction movie. It was about noon, but the amount of black smoke swirling over the city made it seem like it was midnight. We had to use vehicle headlights and large flashlights to move around the destroyed hulks of large and small military and civilian aircraft littered all the over airfield. Saddam's vindictiveness was on display, in all of its dark venom.

As we approached the launch of the ground campaign, the enormous pressures that I had endured night and day for months were wearing me down both physically and psychologically, and I suddenly felt like I was about to crack. The only other time I had that dark hollow feeling was when I was embroiled in the triple-canopy jungles of Vietnam. I got through that morass by thinking of the welfare of my troopers and sharing comfort with Father John and my patron Saint Anthony. I could not and would not let my troops down, and I felt that dedication and my prayers guided me through that ungodly quagmire. During this critically important period of Desert Storm, I was really spent and felt the pressure of constant personal responsibilities during the coming combat actions of the ground campaign. Needing to continuously satisfy an ofttime critical and demanding CINC was penetrating deeply into my psyche. General Cal Waller and our chief of staff General Johnston may have observed the signs of my turning dangerously inwards, and they probably mentioned it to General Schwarzkopf. I got a call from B. B. Bell who informed me that the CINC wanted to see me. I entered the CINC's office, saluted, and he told me to sit on the couch next to him. He at first made some relaxing small talk with me and then said, "Jack, look, we've got some critical times just ahead of us and I'm going to need you to do what you do best and help us be successful. I need you." I sucked it up, choked out a

"Yes sir, we're going to kick his ass and I want to be there when we do." I steeled myself, got up, saluted him, he smiled at me, gave me a couple of pats on my shoulders, and I walked out determined that I wasn't going to let the pressure get the best of me. My boss still believed in me, and the troops in the field needed me. I was again totally steeled to my mission.

As the beginning of the ground campaign (G-Day) fast approached, I was guardedly optimistic because our high priority intelligence indicators still showed that the Iraqi Army General Headquarters Forward in Basra had failed to pick up the gigantic movement of our VII Corps, including the British 1st Armored Division (the "Desert Rats"), XVIII Airborne Corps, and the French 6th Light Division moving to their flanking positions further out to the west. Our security, the degrading of Iraqi intelligence collection capabilities, and the deception plan were working.

G-DAY-1: FEBRUARY 23, 1991

On this fateful day, our air forces, including B-52s, were pounding Iraqi positions as the Iraqis set another 100 oil wells on fire. The total was now close to an incredible 600 wells or installations ablaze. The CINC had decided to begin the ground attack the following day based on our assessment of the degradation of strength of the Iraqi forces along the frontline trace, and the required destruction level of the forward artillery.

EMCON Suicide

As we moved closer toward the time of the ground attack, I kept racking my brain for any key targets or initiatives that might still be of value. We were using the JSTARS to help us prepare the area around the line of departure for our ground forces entering into Iraq and Kuwait. We learned from the defector's debriefing reports that the eleven BLU-82 Daisey-cutter bombs we had dropped had a definitive psychological impact on the morale of frontline Iraqi troop units. Days before launching the ground war, B-52s would hit Republican Guard positions, and the USS Missouri would knock out artillery emplacements, destroying radar sites and eliminating surface-to air missile positions along the Kuwaiti coast. I was still obsessed with fully degrading the Iraqi command and control communications and remained focused on knowing how the Republican Guards would respond if they would be able to coordinate a counterattack against our attacking forces. The Iraqis had been utilizing semi-strict control of the use of radios, radars, and other emanating systems, which we called emissions control or EMCON.

Our emissions collection systems were so sensitive and accurate that virtually every time the Iraqis turned on a radar or tried to transmit messages, we were able to identify the system and location and, very quickly attack and eliminate that emanating node. The Iraqis soon discovered that any discernible emanations resulted in a virtual kiss of death. Once they discovered the continued devastation brought on by their activations, they stopped using critical military systems such as what was left of their radars to detect attacking allied aircraft. As a result, they were not only left blind, but could not call-in fires or coordinate attacks. They were committing what I called "EMCON suicide."

As a final initiative in the hours before the ground attack, I gathered a small group of signals intelligence experts for a pre-operational meeting. I called this group my "EMCON Suicide Team." I asked what key military communications nodes were still showing signs of activity within the KTO. A very sharp SIGINT staff sergeant briefed me. He said as of that day, February 23rd, that there were a total of fourteen communications nodes (mostly divisional level) that could possibly still operate or become "hot." Ten of those unit nodes were in divisions along the Iraqi frontline trace, and the other four nodes belonged to the Republican Guard. The Guard nodes represented their forward headquarters in

Basra, and elements of the Tawalkana Mechanized, the Al-Medina and Hammurabi Armored Divisions in the northwest corner of the KTO. Some communications traffic had shown up on the lower ten nodes recently, but it had been very minimal. I had continuously spent the past months focused on degrading the Iraqi command and control communications. As for the ten nodes along the frontline trace, I felt that once our forces began their attack, they could be subject to a coordinated counterattack by the Iraqi units represented by those nodes. I quickly prioritized targeting their destruction and the air force and artillery blew them up.

Since, General Schwarzkopf's key intelligence requirement was how the Republican Guard would react once our ground units launched across the line of departure, I decided to leave the four Republican Guard radio nets in place. I figured that once our charging 7th Corps armored units set their sights on the Republican Guard Divisions, the temptation by those guard divisions under attack to break security and attempt to communicate with Basra or to provide actions and orders to subordinate units was a distinct possibility. Those would be critical communications to read and would be help our tactical advantage and operational reaction. On the other hand, with the nodes still "up," they would be able to more readily coordinate defensive or counterattack tactics against our driving armored forces. Additionally, if they transmitted in code, then it would take much longer for us to decipher the intercepts. I rolled the dice, and we left the four Republican Guard nodes in place.

THE FINAL BRIEFINGS

In preparation for the evening follies that night, we prepared a special detailed briefing, including the missions for JSTARS for all attendees, including the coalition commanders involved in the following day's attacks. Strangely, earlier that day the CENTCOM J-3 (USAF) was called to a meeting at CENTAF, where he, reportedly, was provided a hard copy briefing, including slides, for the critical JSTARS mission tasking for that first day of the ground campaign. He was to present the briefing that evening during the J-3 portion of the briefing. I was not given a heads up and we prepared the JSTARS mission brief as we had done each day previously. Before the start of the briefing, we were told, without explanation, that the J-3 would give the next day's JSTARS mission brief to the CINC. I was stunned. We had prepared a specific briefing for the JSTARS mission prioritizing indications and warning for Iraqi reactions to the next day's marine offensive. Iraqi reaction to our attacking forces was, in fact, the main reason we had convinced the CINC that JSTARS was necessary for the success of our mission, especially during initial launch of the marine ground attack and the later Left Hook. I incredulously watched as the J-3 briefing did not place priorities on Iraqi reactions as the marines broaching the line of departure into Kuwait, but rather concentrated on targeting and attacking key Iraqi positions and systems. I still truly admired CENTAF and their incredibly effective air campaign, and they, being offensively oriented, probably thought that destroying key elements of the Iraqi defenses was critically important in support of our G-Day missions and may well have been. But I still firmly believed in the absolute importance of the indications and warning mission in support of the marines for the next day. As I became increasingly concerned about the direction of the briefing and thought about breaking in, General Schwarzkopf, God bless him, asked the J-3, "Aren't the marines attacking tomorrow?" He basically implied the key question of, How will the Iraqis react? The J-3 became virtually speechless. He was like a man frozen in time.

The CINC turned to me. I told him that we had planned intelligence missions for the JSTARS with priorities for indications and warning of possible Iraqi counterattacks. He nodded his approval, and the J-3 exited with blazing speed. We then briefed our prepared JSTARS plan, which had been carefully developed by our very capable collection management team. Our plan was sound and chronologically addressed the key issues of operational indications and warning during key phases of the attack. Once we had finished our briefing, the CINC seemed pleased, and our plan was put in place. As I was about to leave the war room for a brief visit to the Order of Battle Shop, the marine liaison officer in the war room, Brigadier General Paul Van Riper approached me and shook my hand and thanked me for our continued support for the marines. As he was about to leave, "Ripper" looked me straight in the eyes and said, "We owe you one."

Later that evening we gave the CINC a very "close hold" J-2 briefing in a separate room that laid all of our intelligence cards, good and bad, on the table. He seemed very pensive and uneasy. I could see that he was feeling the pressure of the enormity of his responsibilities deeply in his gut; he was a boiling cauldron of mixed emotions. As our briefer presented the latest enemy order of battle and our assessments of Saddam's possible responses to our attacks, he showed little reaction, and just nodded. However, as we presented our final conclusions which included the possibility of the use of chemical/biological weapons, he became more and more tense and uncomfortable. The briefing was not easy for him nor easy for us.

Intelligence officers have to tell it like it is, not like we would like it to be. It takes professional courage to assist the commander in every way possible so he can make key learned decisions. Our briefer during that important final session with the CINC was Major John Feeley, who had been our eyes and ears in the Kuwaiti embassy before it was surrounded by the Iraqis during their invasion. (John was finally rescued along with the other residents of the embassy in a very daring operation including diplomatic intrigue.) John had done incredible work, then and since, and was one of General Schwarzkopf's favorites. At the end of his briefing, he said, "Sir, we had to tell you what we told you. And our honest and final assessment, in the end, is that you are going to kick his ass." The CINC forced a smile, thanked us, and left. The die was now cast.

CHAPTER 11

THE 100 HOUR WAR

"THE NATIONAL COMMAND AUTHORITY ORDERS THE EXECUTION OF OPERATION DESERT SPEAR NLT 24/0100C FEB 91. DESTROY IRAQI ARMED FORCES IN THE KUWAIT THEATER OF OPERATIONS."

FINAL PREPARATIONS FOR OPERATION DESERT SPEAR: THE GROUND CAMPAIGN

As we approached the night of February 23, 1991, the Kuwaiti theater of operations (KTO) stretched 300 miles across Kuwait and Saudi Arabia. A coalition force of 540,000 were making final preparations for a military operation that would equal the D-Day landings in scope and complexity. A few hours earlier, President H.W. Bush had directed General Schwarzkopf, in conjunction with the coalition forces, to use all available forces, including ground forces, to eject the Iraqi Army from Kuwait.

To aid the reader in understanding the full breadth of coalition undertaking as ground operations commenced, I will now switch back and forth from the activities within the war room to the situation on the ground and across the KTO.

G-DAY: FEBRUARY 24, 1991

During the waning hours of the G-Day -1, the tension in our headquarters began to rise to almost epic proportions. We were about to "cross the Rubicon." As the night wore on, we all sank into a silent shell of anticipation. My past combat experiences boiled up into a similar uneasy feeling: Soon we would launch into some deadly unknown. I left the war room and went to my office for a quick power nap. As the evening waned, I dozed fitfully for a couple of hours thinking mostly about the possible chemical and biological threat to our troops. I finally crawled out of my cot, visited the Order of Battle Shop for a quick update, and then went into the war room around midnight.

In the War Room

I slid into my desk with an air of resignation and gathered the most current information on the enemy situation to provide the CINC and the command group. As I looked at the operational maps in concert with our Intelligence charts, I could see that we were in for an incredibly eventful next couple of days. Due to the complexity and successful objectives of the air campaign, we had destroyed most if not close to all the Iraqi indications and warning systems and capabilities. As a result, we could see from our latest intelligence that the Iraqis so far had not detected any of our preoperational unit movements, especially the Left Hook out west. As I looked at the operational maps, I continued to marvel at the brilliance of the plan. The Jedi Knights, along with the army, marine, and Arab Corps planners had done a masterful job of using intelligence throughout the planning process for all of their definitive operational military staff procedures while planning the attack, envelopment, feint, and deception phases of the ground campaign.

The ground attack phase began at 0100 with a charge into the far western flank by the elements of the 18th Airborne Corps. The 101st Airborne Division and the French 6th Light Armored secured the left flank and set up a screen along that area. The 24th Mechanized Infantry Division quickly moved north into blocking positions to prevent any Iraqi movement along the Euphrates River valley. Closely following, the 1st Cavalry Division moved just west of Kuwait up the Wadi al-Batin as a feint, hopefully to convince the Iraqi's that this would show as the limit of our western flank. These movements were all done quickly and brilliantly in anticipation and in support of the main attack Left Hook by 7th Corps scheduled for the following day.

The marines, flanked by the Arab Joint Forces Command East on their right, were scheduled to begin their attack into Kuwait at 0400. The main attack by 7th Corps, supported by the Joint Forces Command north and the remainder of the 18th Airborne Corps further west were not scheduled to take place until the following day (February 25, G-Day +1) at 0600. The various unit actions appeared sound and it looked like, so far, to be going according to plan, but as we all knew, once the battle was truly joined, things could and probably would change rapidly.

In the book, It Doesn't Take a Hero, BB Bell notes:

> 0400 At G-Day, H-Hour, the following senior officers were present in the war room: the CINC, deputy CINC, chief of staff, Major General Moore, Brigadier General Leide, Major General Starling, Brigadier General Neal, and Mr. Gordon Brown. The war room was extremely quiet, with a sense that everything that could be done had been done. Brigadier General Leide moved around the room

visiting with the CINC and other staff officers, sharing intel reports. One from the Kuwaiti resistance was that the destruction of Kuwait City by the Iraqis had begun. Explosions had been reported throughout the city and in major office buildings.[10]

My immediate efforts were initially concentrated on the most forward Iraqi division, with those along the coastline, and how they would react to the attacks by the marines and Arab units into Kuwait proper. I also ensured we were able to follow the activities and movement of the more capable possible counterattacking/reinforcing units such as the 5th Mechanized Infantry and 3rd Armored Divisions, which were positioned on the high-speed roads to the west and northwest. My focus, however, remained on the Republican Guard and how they would react when we crossed our attack line of departure. Unfortunately, the early morning of G-Day started with blowing rain and sand, and these adverse weather conditions were compounded by the incredibly dense, black smoke from the inferno of burning Kuwaiti oil fields. Our key intelligence collection efforts early in the ground campaign were being hindered by these environmental conditions, so I had to prioritize key and alternative collection and analytical efforts to anticipate the Republican Guard reaction.

In the KTO

At 0400 on February 24 (G-Day) the 1st and 2nd Marine Divisions, with the 2nd Armored Division's Abrams M1A1 tank-heavy "Tiger Brigade" attached, attacked into Kuwait along with the Arab Joint Forces Command East on their eastern (coastal) flank. They moved quickly through the initial barriers and positions. As the morning wore on, they advanced relentlessly toward Kuwait City.

---

[10] Schwarzkopf, *It Doesn't Take a Hero*, 451

In the War Room

I saw General Schwarzkopf conferring with his deputy Lieutenant General Cal Waller at the command table. He appeared pleased with the initial results of the marine attack but also seemed somewhat apprehensive. He called me over and asked me how I thought the Iraqi second echelon units, especially the Republican Guard would respond to the rapid marine advances. I told him the way I saw it: the marines were moving so quickly, their left flank appeared vulnerable to a counterattack by the prepositioned reinforcing Iraqi mechanized and armored divisions, which were located on previously built, high-speed roads leading into Kuwait. As for the Republican Guard, I told him that there were three possibilities:

1) they would temporarily sit tight, set up linear defenses, and let the marine attack play out; 2) they could get into the fight and attack into Kuwait; 3) or they could assess that the battle may be lost and because of their eventual vulnerability to coalition air and ground attack, they would retrograde back to Basrah. I told him that I thought they would probably stay in place for another day or two, but depending upon the unfolding situation, could move to one of the other scenarios. You could see that he was mulling over what we had discussed. He turned to General Waller, and they agreed that the marine left flank was indeed vulnerable. He also became apprehensive that the Republican Guard could escape his high priority planned destruction. The CINC therefore decided to accelerate the time of the main attack. At about 0900, he called Lieutenant General Yeosock, the ARCENT commander, and later Prince Khalid, and discussed the possibility of moving up the main attack by fifteen hours to 1500 that same day. They were originally scheduled to attack at 0600 on the following day. After checking with their subordinate commanders and staff, both agreed that it was feasible to begin their attacks later that day: G-Day at 1500. Preparations began for the launch of the Left Hook at the agreed upon time by the 7th Corps, the deployment of the remaining

elements of 18th Airborne Corps, and the Arab Corps. The Arab Joint Forces Command North would attack northeastwards toward Kuwait on the marines left flank to block any counterattacking Iraqi divisions. The well-trained and flexible 7th Corps and remainder of 18th Airborne Corps reacted with great agility to the new attack times.

However, when the accelerated time for the attack arrived, the Arab Corps, including the Egyptians, initially did not react well. They moved slowly into and through the attack phase. The key when attacking heavily defended forward barriers is to move through as quickly as possible, but they initially moved slowly and methodically. As a result, their forward attacking units were under a continuous barrage of artillery and mortar fire. They became stalled, almost frozen in time. The CINC was not in the war room when a panicked Saudi operations officer came in with his hair on fire. Since I had delt with this Saudi officer previously, General Waller called me over. The operations officer told General Waller of the dangerous situation in the breech areas and was pleading for close air support. General Waller told him to calm down and explained the importance of rapid movement through the frontline barriers to avoid defensive fire, which is normally laid out along the frontline trace. General Waller looked him in the eye and asked if he understood and then told him to get his troops moving through the barriers, and fast. Later that morning, operational reports from the Arab Corps fortunately showed that they were accelerating their attack, eventually punching through the Iraqi frontline defenses. They were now on their way toward Kuwait City while protecting the marine left flank. The Arab forces fought valiantly during Desert Storm and should be very proud of their contribution to the fight and for the bravery of their troops.

In the KTO

At 1500, the main attack by 7th Corps out west caught Iraqi defending units entirely by surprise. All Left Hook forces moved rapidly northward throughout the remainder of the day. However, as the attack progressed, General Franks reportedly became concerned that some of his divisions were too dispersed to be mutually reinforcing and there was the possibility of blue-on-blue crossfire. Additionally, he was worried that his logistic support units, especially fuel-supply trucks in support of the gas-hungry armored vehicles, were moving too slow through the line of departure. As a result, he halted his advance only twenty-five miles into Iraq at about 1900 that evening.

On the eastern flank, by the end of the day, the marines had moved about twenty miles into Kuwait and had taken almost 10,000 Iraqi prisoners. It appeared from our latest Intelligence reporting that my original assessment of the Republican Guard remaining in place was holding true, and there were continuing indications that they were going to stay and fight.

G-DAY +1: FEBRUARY 25, 1991

In the War Room

The day progressed with apparent successes on both flanks, and the powerful 7th Corps launched its main attack. General Schwarzkopf asked me whether the Republican Guard had moved, and I gave him my best assessment. I had been tasking every reconnaissance sensor we had available and scoured all reports coming in from our collection platforms and our analysts. As the CINC wrote in his book: "Leide said that storms were still hampering our reconnaissance, so we're not sure, but we think they haven't moved. The news, if true, was encouraging"[11] Later in the evening of

---

[11] Schwarzkopf, *It Doesn't Take a Hero*, 461

February 24, the CINC then left the war room for a few hours of well-deserved sleep. Since the campaign appeared to be going well, he seemed to be in a calmer and more confident mood, but he was still anxious about how our entire attacking forces would fare during the night and into the morning. I stayed in the war room much of the night, directing our intelligence collection efforts, providing priorities, and gathering and reporting on the most current information on Iraqi troop dispositions. I was especially focused on how the Republican Guard units were responding to our approaching attacking units. These were, without question, critical hours in the campaign.

Early the next day in the war room, while I was concentrating on my priority intelligence collection and reporting initiatives, the J-3 (Operations) duty officer and good friend, marine Brigadier General Butch Neal, was keeping a very close eye on the unit operational reports and dispositions of our attacking forces. Butch and I anxiously discussed the current disposition of General Franks' 7th Corps. They had ground to a halt for the night at about the 25-mile point instead of moving forward to their planned intermediate objectives. I recalled prior strategy meetings in which the CINC told General Franks, in no uncertain terms, that his primary mission during the offensive would be to continuously press the attack on the Republican Guard and neutralize it as a combat-effective force. We knew, because of our more advanced night-fighting equipment and training, that the best time to engage an enemy force was at night. As the troops would always say, "We own the night." Previously, the CINC and I talked about that very advantage. I had mentioned to him that the Iraqis not only did not have the more advanced night vision equipment that we did, but they also did not have the advantage of Global Positioning Systems (GPS), as well.

As Butch and I stood there staring at the operational map unit stickers representing 7th Corps, we looked at each other and just shook our heads. We both knew that when the CINC came in and saw the corps in a static position and that they had not come close to reaching their phase line objective for the night, he would, to put it mildly, not be pleased. Butch constantly checked the friendly unit location status reports, particularly from 7th Corps, so that they would be totally accurate when the CINC arrived.

At 0400 on that Monday morning, G-Day +1, General Schwarzkopf rolled into the war room. He appeared semi-rested and almost exuded an air of confidence. He probably thought that this was going to be a really great day to be a soldier. When he saw the initial general elements of the reporting categories, especially the very low casualty rate for the previous day and that night, he was almost euphoric. He then moved to the large operational map with the friendly unit stickers and could see right away that the far-left flank units including the French, the 101st Airborne, and the 24th Mechanized Infantry Division had raced toward the Euphrates, eighty miles into Iraq. He could then see that, in the east, the marines and Arab forces were moving inexorably toward Kuwait City. The only thing that had slowed them down was a surprisingly large number of prisoners of war.

He then glanced over at our intelligence enemy situation map and could see that the enemy divisions along frontline trace had been annihilated by the marines. In the eastern part of Kuwait, the 7th, 8th, 14th, 18th, and 29th Iraqi Divisions had been brutally mauled and were basically combat ineffective. The two divisions that I had identified and targeted as an initial counterattack threat to our forces moving up the eastern flank, the Iraqi 5th Mechanized and the 3rd Armored Division, had been met with fury by our attacking forces and made virtually combat ineffective. Those were the two most capable main-line divisions that had worried me throughout our battlefield preparations, and now they were left to the dustbin of history.

The CINC's attention then focused on the stickers representing General Frank's 7th Corps. When he saw they had stopped their forward movement far short of their planned objective or phase line for the night, his face suddenly flushed. As I saw the telltale redness racing to his neck and ears, along with his stiffening body language, I knew that this was not going to end well. He then turned to Butch and asked him when he last got a status report of the 7th Corps unit dispositions. Butch replied that he had just recently received a complete update of the corps unit locations. The CINC gruffly told him to check again. The operations officers in the war room were scrambling around like a mound of red ants. When Butch returned with a confirmation, the CINC came unglued and immediately reached for his command phone and called the army component (ARCENT) commander, Lieutenant General John Yeosock. I could tell that the CINC was trying to control his rage, but he was failing badly. He barked at General Yeosock with a semi-controlled fury to get the 7th Corps moving and get them moving now. General Yeosock was attempting to explain the situation, and from what I could gather from the conversation, General Franks had not conferred with General Yeosock before standing down the corps for the night. The CINC then reiterated that the corps better get moving now and hung up the phone. To make matters worse, General Powell then called the CINC and asked why the 7th Corps was not at their intermediate objectives as planned. The CINC was sitting in his chair like he was on a beehive. His main operational objective for the 7th Corps, the ultimate destruction of the Republican Guard, was in danger of being dashed. During the morning, the CINC kept a keen interest in the progression of 7th Corps, and he constantly kept looking at the disposition of the Republican Guard divisions that we had visualized on our order of battle map. Later that morning, the 7th Corps was in fact moving forward, but they were not moving at the rate that the CINC thought a modern mechanized force was capable of, especially in an open desert. He now feared that if they continued at their present pace, they may well not be able to accomplish their primary mission: a full and final kill on the Republican Guard.

General Waller, sitting at the command table, was as mystified and as angry as I had ever seen him. As the day progressed, the CINC was getting angrier and angrier at what he considered a slower than warranted pace of the corps. At one juncture, when it appeared that he could no longer internalize his nagging concerns, he again called General Yeosock. The CINC demanded an explanation for the "slow" movement of 7th Corps. Evidently, whatever the ARCENT commander was telling him, General Schwarzkopf was having none of it and cut him short. With his voice almost reaching intolerable levels, he said that he didn't want to hear of any more of the problems involved with carrying out the attack plan and if General Franks couldn't meet CINC's guidance, he would find someone who could. He then told General Yeosock that unless 7th Corps moved with necessary speed and élan, that an immediate replacement (probably General Waller) was available. I looked at General Waller in the eyes and he shook his head in dismay. I could see that he was agitated, frustrated, and spoiling to get into the fight.

In the KTO

On that second day of the ground offensive, the 18th Airborne Corps continued its drive into objective areas out to the west. My former unit, the 82nd Airborne Division, commanded by my longtime friend Major General Jim Johnson, began its first sustained movement of the war. However, to the disappointment of Jim and his troops, the division had to perform a "tailgate jump" and stay on the ground. Another of my former units, the 101st Airborne established blocking positions on the Euphrates, just west of An Nasiriyah. Meanwhile, on its way to setting up blocking positions facing to the east, the 24th Infantry's Division met with and destroyed major elements of the Iraqi 26th and 35th Infantry Divisions.

The 1st Armored Division continued their assaults on their assigned Iraqi unit positions. During the night, a major storm hit the area, hindering but not stopping the attacks of units such as 2nd Armored Cavalry and 3rd Armored Division. The 1st Infantry Division (the Big Red One) continued expanding into its breach.

The British 1st Armored Division (the Desert Rats) swung to the right and were preparing to attack into the Iraqi 52nd Armored Division.

During the latter hours of that day, the final step in the amphibious landing deception plan took place when the 5th Marine Expeditionary Brigade landed on the shores of Saudi Arabia about thirty miles south of Kuwait. By that time, the attacking marine forces were closing in on Kuwait City.

In the War Room: The Republican Guard Enters the EMCON Suicide Trap

At 1200, JSTARS reported that the Republican Guard Tawakalna Mechanized Division was moving into blocking positions. It appeared to me that they were prepared to stay and fight, at least for now. Late in the day on G-Day + 1, as the forward 7th Corps elements were approaching the vanguard Republican Guard units, the Iraqis, for the first time in some weeks, began using FM radio communications. We intercepted communications from the Tawakalna Division commander ordering his units to form a defensive line oriented to the west/southwest along the Iraqi Pipeline in Saudi Arabia (IPSA) road to block our forces moving to contact. I immediately passed that important information to the CINC, and we reported it through our command intelligence network. So far, our "EMCON suicide" gamble had shown some early signs of success, and the next indications could be important ones.

In the KTO

By the end of February 25, G-Day +1, our forces had made significant gains in all sectors. The 7th Corps was now advancing quickly, and we estimated that they probably would run into forward elements of the Republican Guard divisions on the following day, G-Day +2. Over 600 oil wells in Kuwait were now ablaze. Unfortunately, and very sadly, a SCUD missile had killed twenty-eight US troops in Dharan. We then reported that Baghdad Radio had aired that Saddam had ordered Iraqi troops to withdraw from Kuwait.

In the War Room

Inside the war room, we anticipated that the culminating events of Desert Storm, especially and hopefully, the destruction of the Republican Guard, could well take place within a matter of hours. We also knew that the "elite" Guard, at least some blocking units, would fight hard, but I knew that they would be no match against our units with our superior soldiers, weaponry, training, and leadership.

G-DAY +2: FEBRUARY 26, 1991

In the KTO

Early in the day, G-Day +2, the 24th Mechanized Infantry Division drove northeast through the Euphrates River valley. Later that afternoon, they moved toward the Iraqi air bases at Jalibah and Tallil. As it continued its push, the 24th met and destroyed the Iraqi 47th and 49th Infantry Divisions and elements of the Nebuchadnezzar Division of the Republican Guard. Meanwhile, the 3rd Armored Calvary Regiment was screening the corps' southern flank. Powerful forward elements of the 7th Corps was now beginning to meet and destroy forward positions of the Republican Guard, especially those of the Tawakalna Division.

In the War Room: Iraq's Republican Guard Falls into the EMCON Suicide Trap

We were again intercepting Tawakalna Division communications that showed they were working feverishly to stiffen their defenses against the 7th Corps' leading armored spearheads. During the early hours of the 26th, a harried radio communication from either the commander or possibly the chief of staff of the Republican Guard headquarters in Basrah, angrily warned the Tawakalna Division that "they were violating communications security." The Tawakalna's division commander, reflecting both agitation and a high degree of despair, replied that "the American tank units were attacking his forward positions and that he had little security to protect."

We were now rapidly "reading" guard communications. Thankfully, since they were not encoding their tactical messages, we were able set up a what we called "flash communications" procedures. We had arranged to have standby Arabic linguists do simultaneous translations and created a rapid communication system to transmit the information derived from the rapidly translated messages back to us in near real-time. This procedure was incredibly unique, efficient, responsive, and on-the-fly. We were truly busting down that interminable "Green Door" this time.

As the Tawakalna was being pressured and continuously and attacked on G-Day +2 (February 26), further intercepts revealed that the Republican Guard headquarters had ordered the Hammurabi and the Medina Armored Divisions to move out of their defensive positions and retrograde back toward Basrah, while creating blocking positions as they moved. The Tawakalna appeared to be the sacrificial lamb to help preserve what was left of the remaining Republican Guard units. Together with timely information being plugged in from JSTARS, we were able to accurately assess the guard capabilities, intentions, and movement sequences. I was on an almost minute-to-minute time frame, handing General Schwarzkopf raw, interpreted intercepts along with near real-time JSTARS pictures of Republican Guard movements. He was then be able to coordinate the real-time actions and orders with the ground and air forces commanders. It was textbook Intelligence officer and commander interaction. I was delighted that the EMCON suicide plan had evolved and was working so well. In the end, our efforts to bring the JSTARS into theater, along with our initiative to keep the critical Republican Guard communications nodes intact for the most critical time of the ground attack phase were an incredibly successful example of our collection fusion efforts that paid off at a critical time in the campaign.

Our ground forces continued to press forward throughout the theater. As I continued to provide reports of Iraqi unit disposition and destruction to General Schwarzkopf, I had not seen him this calm and optimistic since I met him last July back at Eglin. I thought that this was exactly the way that a commander and his integral Intelligence support structure should operate synergistically. As the campaign appeared to be reaching a positive conclusion, the tension in the war room was diminishing slowly but surely.

In the KTO

The 7th Corps was now poised to swing ninety degrees due east and provide General Franks the opportunity to finally use his powerful armored "mailed fist" against the Republican Guard. In the early afternoon, leading elements of the 2nd Armored Cavalry advancing east toward Kuwait observed a line of T-72 tanks dug in at the grid line referred to as 73 Easting. They were forward units of the 12th Armored Division and the Republican Guard Tawakalna Division. The armored cavalry troops engaged the enemy tanks from long distances and destroyed twenty-nine tanks and twenty-four armored personnel carriers. Later in the day, the

7th Cavalry Regiment engaged the 9th Armored Brigade of the Tawakalna Division and destroyed six tanks and eighteen armored personnel carriers at Phase Line Bullet.

Meanwhile, after destroying the Iraqi 26th Infantry Division, the 1st Armored Division was moving northeast toward what hopefully would be a meeting engagement with the 29th Armored Brigade of the Tawakalna Division. To the south, the 1st Infantry Division and the Desert Rats were in the process of destroying the 48th Infantry and 52nd Armored Divisions. In the east, the marines were advancing ever northward with the 1st Marine Division moving northeast toward Kuwait International Airport.

JSTARS had picked up a large movement of vehicles moving northwards along Highway 80 out of Kuwait City. The retreating Iraqis were carrying an incredible amount of loot taken from the city in all sorts of military vehicles, stolen civilian vehicles, motorcycles, and bicycles. They were targeted and decimated. This became the highly publicized "Highway of Death" and was being portrayed by the media as unnecessarily cruel. The war was not over, and the enemy was trying to escape, but it was the type of scenario that the press thrives on. The media was showing nonstop footage, resulting in harsh criticism for the continuing "carnage." It felt like the reporting on the El Firdos Bunker all over again, only worse. Fortunately, or unfortunately, the media's portrayal of the hell involved in battle will continue to influence public opinion. Unfortunately, in this case, sympathy was building for the cruelest of the cruel.

By the end of G-Day +2, February 26, our forces had destroyed a total of twenty-four Iraqi divisions. During that night, from intercepts, we reported that the Tawakalna Division commander had been killed by an artillery strike. Additionally, the division was ordered to retrograde to another defensive blocking position, and elements of the Hammurabi and Medina Republican Guard divisions had been ordered to subsequent defensive positions. They were crippled, but still had the capability to put up a fight. The guard headquarter was now controlling the retrograde defense and the withdrawal of all Iraqi forces out of Kuwait and Iraq west of Basrah.

G-DAY +3: FEBRUARY 27, 1991

As G-Day +3 began, the 24th Mechanized Infantry Division was rapidly advancing eastward toward Basrah and destroying elements of Iraqi divisions as they moved. As the 24th continued their attack eastward, they captured the Tallil and Jabbah bases.

In the War Room

After receiving the news that the 197th Brigade from the 24th Mechanized Infantry Division had captured the major Iraqi Air Force Base at Tallil, I tasked Intelligence channels that any captured documents and equipment be sent back to us in the rear for exploitation. We put together a highly capable technical material exploitation team. They were to inspect the Iraqi command and control system on the base and gather all the information on both their radio communications network and, more importantly, from the hard-wired coaxial and fiber optic cable systems. Because of their extreme difficulty to intercept and exploit, the Iraqi command and control systems using hard-wired capabilities had been anathema to me throughout the campaign.

I felt that much of the critical, highly sensitive communications, especially to the SCUD launchers, had been either directed by couriers or on underground cable systems. Cable systems were difficult to tap into, especially those consisting of fiber optic networks. But, if we had time and the facility, we could at least try to place a surreptitious tap, possibly in a control or junction box. If successful, when we eventually withdrew from the base, we would have left a clandestinely tapped capability that would be worth its weight in gold during the postwar environment. I just knew in my bones that Saddam would not go away quietly.

Once I had as much information on the Tallil communication systems in hand, I held a meeting with CIA and NSA representatives. I told them that this would be a very close-hold project. I asked them to send an immediate request back to their respective agencies for a technical team, preferably from both agencies, to be dispatched immediately and I would provide them with the highest priority access to the communications facilities at Tallil. I was trying to accomplish a physical tap into the system to provide us the capability to read secure Iraqi military communications into the future.

However, in the end, I never heard a word from either agency concerning the project, and we quickly moved out of Tallil after the cease-fire. It could be that my idea never got further than the first action officer for some bureaucratic reason. Later, when Saddam began creating problems for us and those in the region again, I thought of the value that this communications tap would have had. The fact that the initiative appeared to have never even got off the ground in those agencies, illustrated some enigmatic and systemic signs of lack of urgency or inefficiency or both.

In the KTO

Finally, on the 27th, the 7th Corps was now positioned to bring ultimate devastation to the Republican Guard. General Franks' "mailed fist" included the 1st Armored Division, 1st Cavalry Division, the 3rd Armored Division, the 1st Infantry Division, the 2d Armored Cavalry, and the British Desert Rats. The two armored divisions had mauled forward elements of the Republican Guard at the Battle of Medina Ridge. Before he could make his final attack into the Republican Guard, General Franks was informed that there was about to be a cease-fire in the KTO. Unfortunately, it now appeared that General Franks would never be able to get back the time and distance he had lost from his standdown on that first night of the ground offensive.

Toward the end of February 27, the Iraqis were still maintaining some contact to hold or delay our attacking forces, while the last remnants of the Republican Guard escaped over the Shatt al Arab and other areas along the Euphrates using pontoon bridges. The Republican Guard was severely wounded but still not destroyed. In the east, the marines were now holding in place, while units of the Arab Joint Forces Command, especially the Kuwaiti units moved through them and were on their way to take their rightful place in the liberation of Kuwait City.

G-DAY +4: FEBRUARY 28, 1991
In the War Room: Cease-Fire

As we saw an apparent rapidly approaching Iraqi collapse, those in the seats of power in Washington began to think that the war should end sooner rather than later. Our troops, weapons, and operational prowess were wreaking havoc over a severely beaten enemy, and we could feel an air of pressure leading to an ultimate finality. Even though one of General Schwarzkopf's key objectives of the war, the total destruction of the Republican Guard, had not yet been accomplished, Washington argued that the United Nations mandate "the removal of the Iraqis from Kuwait" had been accomplished. Therefore, the war could be successfully terminated after a stunning victory with no possibilities of additional allied casualties. One could sense that the war was getting close to the end when General Schwarzkopf received a phone call from General Powell. The CINC seemed to be agreeing to (or at least not objecting to) what was being said, and I could see that any remaining stress and tension was lifting from his body. He told us that we would unilaterally end the conflict and demand that Saddam call an end to his military activities. It was most probable that Saddam would accept the cease fire if he wanted to stay in power. The unilateral cease-fire would begin on the 28th at 0500. The CINC told General Waller to "Notify all units that the time of cessation of offensive action is to be 0500 hours. All forces in Iraq are to remain at their current locations at that time and are allowed to continue to take those actions necessary to defend themselves and they are encouraged to destroy dangerous military equipment in their vicinity. Meanwhile, suspend all offensive operations. We will continue to fly reconnaissance and defensive air caps, provide electronic and any other surveillance of the battlefield to ensure we are in no way in danger" He then reiterated, "Remember, this is a unilateral suspension of operations on our part." He then added, "All units are to remain in place ready to resume offensive at the slightest provocation…even the slightest provocation of offensive air operations, shoot it down; we'll sort it out later." General Waller put that information out to all components. After a while, the phone rang again, and the CINC listened intently to another call from Washington, said "Yes, sir," hung up the phone, turned to General Waller, and said "Combat operations are to cease at 0800. The deputy turned to the CINC and questioned "Sir?" The CINC replied "Combat operations are to continue until 0800; we are to fight for three more hours." Cal Waller blurted, "But I just called everyone and told them to stop at 0500." Gen Schwarzkopf then said, "Well, call them again and tell them to continue combat operations until 0800." The deputy became furious and barked, "What the hell is going on? Why are we to fight for three more hours?" The CINC told him calmly 'Well, someone in the White House added up the hours of the ground campaign and discovered that if we fight three more hours, it will have been a 100-hour war." Cal Waller then unleashed, "What? Who gives a crap! Do they know what can happen in three hours? Who is going to write the letters to the parents and spouses of those who might be killed in these three hours? All because someone in the White House wants to fight a friggin' 100-hour war for the media?" He was in a sublime state of fury. After about a minute, which seemed like an eternity, the CINC turned to the Communications officer and without hesitation said, "Get the White House on the phone and tell them that General Waller wants to speak with them." Cal Waller then picked up the phone and told the component commanders to continue combat operations for another three hours, until 0800. He reiterated this was a unilateral suspension of offensive operations on our part. The CINC then turned to his deputy and said, "Thanks Cal." The final response was "Yes sir." Things again were good between them. General Waller and I, just the two of us, had dinner together almost every evening before the start of the ground campaign. Although he had a wonderful sense of humor, he suffered fools and foolishness very badly. Cal Waller was a great soldier and wonderful man.

The president announced the cease-fire during an Oval Office speech and said that Iraq must end military action; free all POWs, third country nationals, and Kuwaiti hostages; release the remains of coalition forces killed in action; agree to comply with all UN resolutions; and reveal the locations of land and sea mines. At 0800, February 28 the fighting ceased, and Iraq agreed to observe the cease-fire, attend military-to-military talks on cessation, and accept all UN resolutions regarding the conflict.

ARRANGING THE CEASE-FIRE

Once the president had made the decision to end the war at the 100-hour point, the next question was how do we, in fact, end the conflict? As we approached what looked like the end of the war, we thought that the political terms would have been prepared and sent from Washington. General Schwarzkopf could certainly set the terms of the military cease-fire, but political terms should come from Washington.

As Clausewitz postulated, "War is politics by other means." I thought about a paper I had once written about how the US historically ended wars badly. Some in the short term do not seem to end badly, but many peace deals have set up scenarios that worsened situations beyond what was supposedly preordained in whatever cease-fire was stated at that time.

After making the decision to end the war, the rest of the story was not immediately forthcoming from our national or military bureaucracies. There were those who said that if we had the wherewithal and the capability in place, we should charge up to Baghdad, occupy the city, and remove Saddam. I was dead set against getting into that quagmire. We had reports that thousands, even hundreds of thousands, of weapons had been made available to the Iraqi people to fight any invasion of their capital city. We would have lost an inordinate number of troops and the occupation of Baghdad and Iraq would be a long-lasting, complex, and very expensive undertaking in ways that were unimaginable at the time. In the end, that option was not part of any of the pertinent UN resolutions.

Leaving Saddam in place was not a good option either. He did eventually say that because he was still in power, he was, in fact, victorious against a massive coalition. I also thought that he would be vindictive enough and have a strong enough residual force to be at least a regional problem for the foreseeable future. I look back on our failure to destroy him and his Winnebago with a sense of deep disappointment and regret. Additionally, we knew where the Republican Guard and their tanks were being staged in compounds in and around Basrah. If we would have extended the war one more day, our air force, especially using the A-10 Warthog attack aircraft along with the army's Apache helicopters, would have annihilated them in detail.

SAFWAN: AN ATTEMPT AT PEACE

A cease-fire was agreed to by both sides, but we still had to make it official and set the terms. We expected that after all this time in the lead-up to the war and the period of combat, that our masters in Washington would have had a set of terms, political and military, ready for the eventual conclusion of the conflict.

I could sense some consternation in the war room about what should happen next. As General Cal Waller said, "We in Central Command were under the impression that all these smart people in Washington, including the State Department, were working on such a document and would have it ready for us, but that was not the case. Had no-one really given a great deal of thought to how the war would be ended?" When nothing substantive came from Washington, the CINC, with some frustration, took it upon himself to set the terms as far as he could determine were viable, strict, non-negotiable, but fair. The CINC chose to have the peace talks take place in occupied Iraq as a symbol of Iraq's defeat. We heard him opine with some degree of discomfiture that "Peace is going to be a hell of a lot harder than war."

After some deep thought trying to cover all facets of ending the war, the CINC scratched out notes on a legal pad and began to dictate those terms to his stenographer. As General Waller then described, "He sent it back to the Pentagon, the Pentagon changed happy to glad, we to they, and put in a few fixes, gave it to the State Department, and the State Department changed a couple of words and sent it back to us and said use this." I think that is the first time in the history of warfare that the commanding general and chief of the forces dictated the document that was used by coalition forces for cessation of hostilities."[12] As I keep reiterating, historically, we do not end wars well.

On March 3, 1991, the CINC flew to Safwan, Iraq. He had lined the road on which the Iraqi representatives would travel with M-1 tanks, Bradley fighting vehicles, and arranged for attack helicopters to fly overhead. Our troops who were escorting the Iraqi representatives said that they were "duly impressed" by the show of force. General Schwarzkopf and General Khalid sat at the main

---

[12] Waller, Frontline Gulf Oral (PBS 1996), 3.

table opposite the Iraqi representatives led by Lieutenant General Sultan Hashim Ahmed, the 3rd Corps Commander. Behind the CINC were other coalition representatives including Lieutenant General Sir Peter de la Billiere and Lieutenant General Michel Roquejeoffre. The scene was tense, and the CINC did not crack a smile throughout. He impressed on the Iraqis that there would be no negotiations, his terms were locked in stone.

The agreement included:

- Prompt release of prisoners of war by both sides and Kuwaiti civilians by Iraq with an immediate "symbolic release";
- US withdrawal from Southern Iraq, when a permanent cease-fire is agreed upon and Iraq has complied with all UN resolutions, including the rescinding of the annexation of Kuwait and accepting liability for war damages;
- Help from Iraq in finding land mines in Kuwait and sea mines in the Persian Gulf; and
- An arrangement to separate the forces in Southern Iraq to avoid further skirmishes.

The Iraqis solemnly accepted the CINC's list of demands. Then, in a surprising turn, the Iraqis requested that that they be permitted to fly their helicopters for issues such as emergency medical needs and search and rescue missions since our campaign had destroyed most of their bridges and damaged key roadways. The CINC, evidently feeling that this was an innocuous request, agreed. However, the Iraqis armed these helicopters, and along with tanks that escaped our offensive, they would be used to brutally put down the Shia in the Shia-Kurd uprising that was soon to follow. The CINC later admitted that he had been "suckered" by that request.

A VISIT INTO THE ABYSS

Throughout the first week of March 1991, sporadic fighting was still erupting, Most notably on March 2 during the Battle of Rumaila in the Euphrates Valley of southern Iraq where the 24th Mechanized Infantry Division virtually annihilated a large column of six battalions of the withdrawing Republican Guard. A few days after Iraq had accepted the terms of the UN Security Council cease-fire plan, I was in the war room with General Schwarzkopf discussing the latest situation in the KTO. We talked about Iraq releasing thirty-five POWs: nine Brits, nine Saudis, one Italian, one Kuwaiti, and fifteen US military personnel, including the second female POW. The CINC then suggested that I take a chopper ride along the friendly unit trace in Iraq and through Kuwait City to provide him a trip report of my observations. I hitched a ride on a Blackhawk and asked the pilot to fly out into and through the trace where our attacking units had driven north, northeast, and east.

As we flew through that original line of attack, there was very apparent evidence of vast destruction to both dug in and mobile Iraqi units. Ghosts of blackened hulks of armored vehicles and trucks were littered everywhere. Our tank main guns were able to hit targets from incredible distances at night, mostly in bad weather with penetrating high explosive anti-tank rounds. Blown out and rusted tank turrets and guns were scattered everywhere. We then landed at the tactical headquarters of 3rd Armored Division. I could see and feel the professionalism ingrained in the G-2 folks and a visible pride in what they had contributed during the successful combat operations of the "Spearhead" division. Next, we flew to the command post of the 1st Infantry Division where I could again see the same professionalism and pride of the troopers of the "Big Red One."

I then took a Jeep from the 1st Division command post toward Kuwait City. As we weaved down the ancillary road leading to the main road into Kuwait City. The main road, the so-called Highway of Death, was like a dystopian movie scene. Areas on and surrounding the road were strewn with destroyed Iraqi military vehicles and equipment as well as civilian cars, trucks, motorcycles, bicycles. Anything else with wheels was in pieces and charred and warped in all degrees of destruction. I saw mounds of loot taken from Kuwait City that had been stuffed into any crevice on anything that moved. As we approached and entered Kuwait City, there were residual signs of devastation but there also were displays of victory and exhilaration exhibited by the ordinary people and their Arab liberators. Although the ungodly oil well fires were still ablaze and raging, the present the direction of the winds had cleared the sky over the city. At that moment's, 605 of 732 Kuwaiti wells were a fiery cauldron. Additionally, lower-level oil lakes were also afire.

Before catching a chopper ride back to Riyadh, I had some great conversations with our Special Forces soldiers, Arab Corps liberation unit commanders, and some old acquaintances from the Kuwaiti resistance. As we flew back toward Riyadh, I reflected on the incredibly complicated set of pressured-packed personal circumstances that had led up to the liberation of Kuwait. I recounted my arrival at CENTCOM as a newbie, remembered the machinations of Operation Internal Look, and still felt the residual tremendous pressure involved in the development and execution of our intelligence support for Desert Shield and Desert Storm. I reflected on the continuous look into an unknown abyss, the daily pressure-packed ache, and the pain in the war room, and, finally, acknowledged the exhilarating sense of victory and accomplishment.

As we droned on back to Riyadh, I finally dozed off and the next thing I knew we were landing at the airfield. Brother Deals welcomed me "home" and drove me back to the Saudi Officer's Club for the night. The next morning, after he dropped me off at the MODA building, I made my morning rounds in the Order of Battle and Collection Management shops, ensuring that we did not let our guard down. I then went to the war room waiting for the CINC's arrival. Once he was seated at his table, we gave him our morning Intelligence update briefing and then after the other remainder of the briefings was complete, he asked me to sit next to him and give him a debriefing of my trip. After I described the destruction that I saw, the professionalism of the Intelligence troops I talked to, and the atmosphere in Kuwait City, he seemed pleased. He then asked me a number of further questions about my observations and assessments. After I finished, he smiled, thanked me, patted my shoulder, and I went back to my usual place just behind him.

THE SHIA-KURD UPRISINGS

Within a week of President H.W. Bush announcing the ceasefire, the historic religious conflict between the Shia and the Sunni Muslim sects was reigniting. At the seeming prodding of the administration through various methods, including especially over the Voice of America and the Voice of Free Iraq, the Shia in the south and the Kurds in the north began an uprising. The insurgency was fueled by the perception that Saddam Hussein had become vulnerable to regime change, and this perception of weakness was largely due to the apparent outcomes of Desert Storm. The Shia rebellions began in Basrah and the south during the latter part of February and early March. The Kurdish uprising began on March 5. Although the Sunnis are the majority sect in most Muslim countries, the Shia are in the majority in Iraq. Saddam and his Sunni minority had ruled Iraq with a brutal iron fist for decades. The Shia rebellion also included an eclectic group of demoralized Iraqi Shia military conscripts and a varied group of anti-regime elements. The Kurds of course have been fighting over the years for their independence in several countries, including in Iraq.

After Saddam tried to negotiate a truce, the rebels turned his offer down and he came down against them brutally. He used many of the helicopters that the CINC had allowed to fly for emergency reasons as gunships to slaughter the Shia. The Republican Guard and other units that had escaped to Basrah were also instrumental in the eventual crushing of the Shia uprising. However, the Kurdish rebellion continued, and in the end, we had to eventually use extraordinary measures and national treasure to protect them from virtual annihilation.

Although I admired President George H.W. Bush for his unwavering support during the war, we provided nothing substantial to support the uprisings that, frankly, we had played a role in instigating. We still had much of the power of the Desert Storm force in the area and could have supported the rebels and may have directly or indirectly helped bring about the final destruction of the Saddam regime sooner rather than later. But there were some very logical and important reasons why we did not intervene: it could have empowered Iran, we feared the effects of a weakened and disintegrating Iraq, and adherence to the old saw policy of nonintervention in Iraq's internal affairs. Additionally, the removal of Saddam was never officially stated as a military or political aim. Finally, and most importantly, we did not want to get pulled back into a quagmire that would last for the foreseeable future. Thus, another war that was not ended effectively to prevent future conflict. The Saddam regime never signed a peace treaty, and the war remained in effect until 2003 when coalition troops invaded Iraq and finally toppled Saddam from power.

Having studied our military history over the years, this only reinforced my view that the United States does not end wars well. Maybe it's because of our desire to get the unpleasantness over as soon as possible, or we have faith that our enemies (and allies) will do what is right in the aftermath. A look at recent conflicts and how they ended are proof of our not ending wars well. World War I ended with the Treaty of Versailles, which was so onerous toward Germany that it caused World War II. During World War II, the agreements made at the Yalta Conference eventually led to the Soviet occupation of Eastern Europe and the Cold War when the Western powers were obliged to accept Stalin's role in the territories liberated by Soviet Army. Therefore, Central and Eastern Europe would be under the exclusive control of the Soviet Union. The Korean War ended with no peace treaty, which means that North Korea and its ally China have technically been at war with US-led forces and South Korea for more than seven decades. The Vietnam War had ended ignominiously with no peace treaty. The Paris Peace Accords between the North Vietnamese and the US led to the withdrawal of all US troops and the complete takeover of Vietnam by the North Vietnamese. The Gulf War, as mentioned above, never had a peace treaty officially signed; we had to go back in and finish the job.

On April 3, 1991, the UN Security Council adopted Resolution 687, which called for a permanent cease-fire agreement. Resolution 687 also required Iraq to destroy all chemical, biological, and nuclear weapons along with any missiles having a range of more than 150 kilometers. It also stated that Iraq was to allow UN inspectors into their facilities. When I read the requirements of this initial agreement, I just knew that Saddam would be recalcitrant, not comply, and would continue to brazenly force our hand. This resolution would be the first of many. The latest "wars" in Iraq and most recently Afghanistan have also both come to unsatisfactory endings.

AFTER-ACTION REPORT

There is an old adage that says, "During time of peace it's the one (personnel) and the three (operations), but during the time of war, it's the two (intelligence) and the four (logistics)." Desert Storm gave much credence to that theory.

We took the most logical and most correct path using utmost intelligence/operational caution during the planning stage. The decision-makers, as a result, provided the cogent number and type of forces to ensure victory and to minimize coalition casualties.

Most importantly, when the CINC needed to make the final decision of when and where to launch the ground campaign and then decide the proper sequence in which to move to the next phase of the campaign, he relied on our estimate of the enemy strengths, weaknesses, and dispositions to form his key mission-order. Many of those decisions were not easy for him, and the various elements of Intelligence reporting were not easy for me to present to him. I continuously gave my best effort to not shrink under unprecedented pressure, and I refused to present less than accurate "positive" intelligence. We frequently and enthusiastically provided positive intelligence, but only as a result of our continuous honest analysis. Synergy between the combat commander and his Intelligence officer must be forged with trust and confidence. A good commander uses intelligence even though, frequently, he does not like it, and a good Intelligence officer provides the best intelligence to the commander, even though he knows the commander might not like what he is told. As various operational reporting came in each day, I had to, in some cases, contradict some of that reporting with contrary battle damage assessment (BDA) that we had independently developed. At times, the CINC would become exasperated with our less than optimistic reports, but fortunately he continued using the unvarnished daily intelligence to make his key decisions. I kept giving him the best intelligence we had developed, and that ultimate responsibility took all the professional courage I could muster. The CINC, in the end, was a tough but fair commander who led a stunning victory based on a superbly developed military force and a strategy that was continuously based on integral intelligence.

Weapons of Mass Destruction: The Aftermath

The possibility of a chemical and biological attack on our troops was a primary concern for me throughout the ground campaign. Fortunately, the Iraqis did not use weapons of mass destruction during Desert Storm. Saddam likely took notice of our not so veiled threats of catastrophic retaliation. Upon the adoption of UN Resolution 687, as we predicted, Saddam was not cooperative or compliant. He consistently interrupted or blocked UN inspection teams. Over the years, the UN inspectors and Saddam were in constant conflict. In October 1991, the UN Security Council passed Resolution 715 requiring Iraq to "accept unconditionally the inspectors." In May 1992 Iraq admitted to having a "defensive" biological weapons program. After the Iraqis allowed the UN to destroy the chemical weapons, progress was again halted in July 1992 when the Iraqis refused access to the inspection team. Finally, in late 1993, Iraq accepted Resolution 715. In 1994, the UN inspection teams completed destruction of Iraq's known chemical weapons and production equipment and "neutralized" any known nuclear program residuals. In August 1995, Iraq admitted to a more developed biological weapons program. In May 1996, UN inspection teams dismantled and destroyed Iraq's main biological warfare facility. Iraq remained recalcitrant to further inspections. In June 1997 the UN passed Resolution 1115, which called for compliance, but by the end of 1997, a continuing stalemate forced the inspectors to withdraw. On December 16, 1998, Operation Desert Fox began a three day strike on "military and security targets in Iraq that contribute to Iraq's ability to produce, store, maintain, and deliver weapons of mass destruction." In 2002 the UN, through Resolution 1284, created a new monitoring, verification, and inspection commission, and Resolution 1441 gave Iraq "a final opportunity to comply with its disarmament obligations." Saddam complied, and the inspectors found no evidence of the revival of a nuclear program. However, on September 12, 2002, in a speech to the UN, President Bush said, "We know that Saddam Hussein pursued weapons of mass murder even when inspectors were in his country. Are we to assume that he stopped when they left? The history, the logic, and the facts lead to one conclusion: Saddam Hussein's regime is a grave and gathering danger." On February 5, 2003, Colin Powell, citing evidence obtained by American intelligence, told the UN that Iraq had failed "to come clean and disarm." In a highly controversial statement, he concluded, "My colleagues, every statement I make today is backed up by sources, solid sources. These are not assertions. What we're giving you are facts and conclusions based on solid intelligence."

Eventually, on March 20, 2003, an American-led coalition invaded Iraq. Baghdad fell on April 9, and President H. W. Bush declared an end to major combat operations on May 1. Shortly after the invasion ended, the Pentagon announced the formation of the Iraq Survey Group to search for WMD. Saddam would be captured later that December. He was held in custody in Baghdad, tried by the Iraqi Interim Government, and executed by hanging on December 30, 2006. No further weapons or programs were found.

The Iraqi Combat Forces

Some of these descriptions of the Iraqis have been taken from actual interrogation reports. There are those in the media and others who have criticized our assessments. I have attempted to be honest, based on all elements of intelligence including information gleaned from Iraqi prisoners. As a result of an incredible amount of collection, study, and analysis, we understood many of the Iraqi military weaknesses such as logistics, communications, command and control, and the lack of experience and capability in combined arms operations at corps level and above. Many have considered whether the Iraqis were a greater threat because they were battle hardened or were not the threat that many made them out to be because, in fact, they were battle weary from a terrible eight-year war with Iran along with other Iraqi combat activities such as the fighting with the Kurds.

Our bottom-line description of the vast majority of Iraqi morale could be summarized by a captured Iraqi officer, who, with much emotion, asked Saddam, "Sir, I am now thirty-seven years old and still unmarried. I have fought for eight years against Iran and two years against the Kurds. Now I am here in the desert to fight Americans and their allies. Sir, will I ever have a chance to marry and lead a normal life, or do you have another target in mind?" Through interrogations such as these, we knew that the frontline Iraqis, if they had not yet defected, were demoralized by their inevitable fate, made worse by our incredibly effective air campaign.

As is the case with most complicated and important intelligence assessments, there normally is not a simple general conclusion that leads to an accurate result. Additionally, by many standards, especially when compared with other regional military forces, the Iraqis appeared formidable. Some Iraqi units were in fact relatively capable, with high morale, such as the Republican Guard and some Iraqi second-echelon divisions positioned to counterattack our attacking units. They were located on high-speed roadways or on lines of attack that had been hastily built to provide avenues of approach into the frontline cauldron. As the air campaign progressed and the air force's tank plinking was creating havoc on the mechanized units, they dug in more and more, to the point that when and if they were ordered to counterattack, they were either damaged, destroyed, or had dug in so deeply and for long periods, they could not move out of their defensive positions.

Initially the Iraqi military did have, by our count, forty-two ground force divisions in the KTO. They had a relatively capable air force, at least on paper. Their air capability was limited in support of their ground forces and had been untested in air superiority operations. We felt that their air defense system could be easily overtaxed, overwhelmed, and eventually destroyed.

For initial planning purposes, we estimated Iraqi Army combat capability at about 80 percent average for all divisions, and arrived at a total troop number, which was released publicly at 542,000. At a later date, General Schwarzkopf, for whatever reason, used the figure of over 600,000 with a 100 percent baseline for each division. These were numbers that I was uncomfortable with. If a unit is at 70 percent or below, we calculate that unit as combat ineffective.

We were facing a time-honored basic military doctrine that says to only attack when you have a 3:1 strength advantage. So, in the end, instead of using only an anticipated "Hey diddle diddle straight up the middle" attack, the main attack's Left Hook took advantage of our strengths in troops, training, equipment, and maneuverability against the aforementioned Iraqi weaknesses. The final intelligence estimates that mattered most were those we would provide to the planners who would design the air campaign, the isolation of the KTO, prepare the battlefield, and of course, design the ground campaign. Most importantly, the CINC's main criteria during the preparation of the battlefield phase was that we reduce the military capability of each Iraqi division along the frontline trace to below 50 percent, and most importantly, by 90 percent of the breach points. Those divisions, of course, were critical because they would be the first defensive units met as our ground forces crossed the line of departure, the most crucial time in any ground attack. We also needed to assess the evolving defensive bands of counterattacking armored and mechanized units that could move toward our attacking forces in meeting engagements along the second and third lines of defense. However, our focus for targeting during the isolation and preparation phases was the frontline Iraqi divisions.

In addition to the criticality of reducing the capability of the frontline units in general, the most specific and most dangerous capability to our attacking divisions was a huge number of artillery battalions (145) that could range the defensive belts. It was especially critical to destroy the Iraqi artillery because of their huge numbers of rocket and artillery tubes, especially those with the ability to deliver a chemical lay down while our forces were attempting to breach the initial defensive belts.

Prior to the launch of the ground campaign, our estimates showed that virtually all the frontline divisions were below 50 percent capability, the artillery was all but annihilated, and the second-echelon infantry and potentially counterattacking mobile second-echelon divisions were well below 75 percent. We assessed the Republican Guard divisions at about 80 percent or below. We estimated that the Iraqi Air Force's air defense system and the Iraqi Navy was rendered virtually ineffective. We also held that Iraq's critical command and control system and logistic systems, because of the air campaign's preparation of the battlefield plan, had been severely degraded and mostly rendered useless by the launch of the ground campaign.

There have been several sources of speculation and a variety of so-called analysts who have said that we at CENTCOM overestimated Iraqi strengths and capabilities. As an Intelligence officer, my first tenet is to favor overestimating rather than underestimating the enemy. This does not mean exaggerate enemy capabilities to a point of being unrealistic. I would rather overestimate and therefore eventually provide and use sufficient to overwhelming force to defeat the enemy rather than underestimate and not be provided the capability to win. As a result of the frustrations, I had experienced and our country endured during Vietnam, I was personally committed to never underestimate my enemy again.

Although the conventional assessment was that the Iraqi Army was the fourth largest in the world, we did not assess that it was the fourth best in the world. We packaged our analysis of the enemy for presentation to the CINC and other decision-makers in a way that it was contributory, accurate, and realistic to the war-fighting planning process. The analyses we provided throughout Desert Shield and Desert Storm, although at times problematic, were, in the end, sufficiently accurate so that the CINC could make the right decisions, at the right time, leading to the overall success of the operation. Those detractors who were critical of our estimates, were not under the same gun twenty-four hours a day and not subject to intense pressure and scrutiny close to the action where life and death decisions were being made every minute of every day. The presentation of intelligence assessments is partly science but mostly an art, an acquired art that had to be uniquely created and tailored to the pressure-packed and changing situations at the time.

Iraqi Casualty Assessment

Our final BDA assessments were pretty impressive and showed the absolute devastation our campaign wreaked. We shot down 38 Iraqi fighter aircraft and forced the remainder of the Iraqi aircraft (about 120) to flee to Iran. We had destroyed, altogether, 4,000 (of the prewar number of 4,550 Iraqi tanks) during the air and ground campaigns (and we knew that the remainder were lined up in a row in cantonments in Basrah and we could have destroyed most of them had the war continued for another day or so). In addition, the Iraqis lost well over half of their 2,880 armored personnel carriers and virtually all their 3,100 artillery pieces. Only five of their forty-three combat divisions remained minimally combat effective by the wars end. By the dawn of February 28, coalition forces had accumulated 70,000 enemy prisoners of war. Prior to Desert Storm, they were the fourth largest army in the world, but no more.

Were they the fourth best army in the world? No, and they were not even close now.

Starting from an imprecise information baseline, it was virtually impossible to tell how many Iraqis were killed in action (KIA) during the air and ground campaigns. We could not precisely identify casualties during a furious air campaign and a fast-moving armored battlefield over great swaths of desert. During our BDA of the battlefield, Iraqi body count had lost much of its importance as a metric. And we tried to keep it that way. Many factors led us to count damage to weapon systems and other key targets, rather than KIAs. We considered BDA of a disabled or destroyed tank, artillery piece, armored personnel carrier, and trucks as factors in our final assessments. Importantly, the degradation of Iraqi unit morale, resulting in a lack of the will to fight, was a vital category that we factored into to our dynamic objectives and assessments.

Once the war was over, questions about Iraqis killed in action persisted. Our response was the same: We don't know, and frankly any attempt to determine would be unreliable. But the pressures continued even through official channels from Washington. The CINC asked me to try to provide him our final assessment of Iraqi casualties and told me not to give it to anyone but him. I told him that any assessment would have a wide range of probable errors. He told me to give it our best shot, so I put a few of our best Iraqi military expert analysts on the project. They did the best they could from all sources including pilot reports, ground unit reports, signals, imagery, and interrogations. In the end, they came up with a rough figure of 100,000 KIA. I told the CINC that I was uncomfortable with the accuracy of that figure. I was afraid that an imprecise figure would become carved in stone as the final figure for the war. The CINC did in fact present this figure to Washington and the media, but others, such as General Chuck Horner, placed the figure at a lower level. We still can't, and never will be able to, construct an accurate or viable figure. Fortunately, in the end, it changes nothing.

Our successes during Desert Storm more than validated the passage of the Goldwater-Nichols Act in 1986, which reworked the command structure of the US military. The need for service reform had been identified during the Vietnam War. Development of the Air-Land Battle concept during the 1970s and early 1980s clearly illustrated the problems of coordinating doctrine between the services. The push for a serious look at the Department of Defense's structure came in April of 1980 with the public failure of Operation Eagle Claw. On April 24, 1980, the operation to rescue our diplomats held captive in Iran was forced to abort when confronted by serious difficulties of logistical and operational components. The after-action reports revealed deficiencies in mission planning, command and control, and inter-service operability and proved that the services were not capable of performing complex operations independently or interdependently. In October 1983, Operation Urgent Fury in Grenada finally revealed the urgent need for reform when the army and marines divided the island operationally and conducted operations in splendid isolation while lacking equipment interoperability and intelligence. Without communications capability, they failed to communicate with each other, although attempts were made using commercial telephones. Prior to Goldwater-Nichols, peacetime activities, such as procurement and doctrine creation, were tailored for each service in isolation, and wartime activities for each service were planned, executed, and assessed individually. As a result, the Senate Armed Services Committee began hearings and investigations and concluded in 1986 that changes in joint operational organization and operational capabilities were needed. The Goldwater-Nichols Act was passed in spite of sporadic overt and covert opposition from elements in the Department of Defense and the services.

The Goldwater-Nichols Act strengthened the advisory role of the chairman of the Joint Chiefs of Staff, while the service chiefs of staff were stripped of their warfighting responsibilities and charged with recruiting, training, and equipping their forces.

The chain of command would now run directly from the president through the secretary of defense to the unified and specified combatant commanders. During Desert Shield and Desert Storm, our forces were ready and fully capable to act cooperatively as U.S. Central Command assigned air, ground, naval, marine, and Special Operations assets to achieve its objectives. The Goldwater-Nichols Act increased shared procurement and required that officers could not be promoted to flag/general officer rank without having previous tours of duty in joint service positions. Despite the reduction of interservice strife, the services would continue to compete with each other for monetary budgets, and as a result this built-in service parochialism remains. Our efforts during Desert Storm fully validated the value of Goldwater-Nichols. However, the United States faces more complex and irregular threats today, and the rising cost of personnel and complicated operational missions will require a dynamic, continuous reappraisal of how we organize, theorize, and fight in the modern battlespace, or what is called Network Centric Warfare.

FROM VICTORY TO MACDILL

During March and April, we were still staying alert, keeping an eye on Saddam's activities and intentions. The Shia rebellion, in the end, had been quelled brutally, but the Kurdish rebellion remained a constant worry and eventually the Allied forces established a no-fly zone in that area that was enforced by US, UK, and French aircraft. The United Nations Security Council Approved Resolution 688 condemning the Iraqi government's oppression of the Kurds and requiring Iraq to respect the human rights of its citizens. And although Operation Provide Comfort began providing protection and humanitarian relief to the Kurds, Saddam was still indicating he would not go away quietly.

When the Saudis had agreed that we could initially station a large number of troops and equipment in the kingdom, we pledged that we would leave soon after our mission to drive Saddam out of Kuwait was accomplished. Complying with that promise, we were in the process of substantially reducing our forces, but the most visible sign that we were leaving was when General Schwarzkopf would depart the theater and return to MacDill. The UN passing and approval of the cease-fire agreement may well have been the trigger. On April 11, 1991, the UN approved the agreement, and the stage was set for our return. Washington agreed that the CINC and our primary headquarters would return to MacDill on April 19, 1991.

As I packed up what little personal gear I had at the MODA officer's club, I thought about the incredible experience I had been through these past months. I then stared at my always ever-present pistol and gas mask and was grateful that I could finally move most anywhere without them. As I left the MODA club for the last time, it was a very similar feeling to that I had after my tours in Vietnam as I anticipated the return to a semblance of normalcy in the states. Brother Deals and many of the other J-2 folks had flown home the day before. Those dedicated J-2 officers and noncommissioned officers from all services had built and developed on-the-fly critical capabilities and procedures for war-fighting intelligence cycles such as unique collection, analysis, and reporting. They worked hard and valiantly with a singular purpose. What they accomplished and how they accomplished it should be studied and emulated well into the future. When they arrived at MacDill, they were met by Ann and other J-2 spouses who welcomed them home after a job well done. I was finally going home, and it felt beyond exhilarating. The morning of our departure, I boarded the CINC's command aircraft, took my place opposite to his seat, and waited for him with a combination of relief and satisfaction. After saying his goodbyes to local military commanders and dignitaries, the CINC arrived in the command compartment, took his seat, took a deep breath, and smiled broadly. After some small talk, we all fell into our own deep thoughts. I focused on my vision of Ann, knowing she'd be waiting for me upon landing. I was hoping to be promoted and assigned to an Intelligence position at the national level. My military career had been dedicated to intelligence, and my experiences in combat and crisis had reached a pinnacle. I was hoping for ways to help develop the next generation of intelligence professionals and capabilities. I knew that new methodologies and collections systems could improve our capabilities and would be needed to support our future decision-makers, especially combatant commanders.

As we approached our landing at MacDill, we were wakened from a deep sleep. After a light breakfast, we prepared for a homecoming that none of us would ever forget. As the plane taxied toward a huge, highly animated crowd, the pilot raised a small American flag out his side window for all to see. The airfield was filled with cheering crowds with flags and welcoming signs of all kinds. A large press corps with a forest of cameras was on the field. I immediately tried scanning through the small window to catch a glimpse of Ann in the crowd, but no luck. Once the plane came to a stop and the engines powered down it seemed like the finality and sense of accomplishment of mission that I had felt previously, only the stakes this time had been much higher. As the front door clanked open and the stairs eased into place, the CINC stood up and took a deep breath. He stepped out on the top the stairs, smiled, and waved broadly to the crowd, then quickly bounded down the stairs to be greeted by his family and his huge dog Bear. After General Schwarzkopf finished hugging his family, he spotted Ann, wearing an American flag sweater. He sprinted over to her, gave her a hug, and said to her, "You've got quite a guy there." Once I reached the bottom stairs, I finally spotted Ann, ran over to her, and squeezed the breath right out of her. She was my rock, even when I was far away from her. Her presence and support never left my side; during my entire career, she was always there.

The CINC moved through that cheering and crushing crowd toward a stage set up for the welcoming ceremony. Once on stage, he beckoned to me and waved Ann, Jeff, and Mei to follow, then pointed for me and my family to stand next to him for the ceremony. As they played "The Star-Spangled Banner," I stood next to General Schwarzkopf, saluting, with a feeling of overwhelming emotion, and the satisfying finality of a mission accomplished was suddenly frozen into that one glorious scene.

People have asked if the late General Norman Schwarzkopf was truly the "Stormin' Norman" or "Norman the Terrible" of the Riyadh war room fame. Mentally, General Schwarzkopf was an extremely bright man (testing at near-genius level) with a photographic memory. His ability to recall an incredible number of facts and figures made him a very demanding task master, which often caused tension and stress among subordinates. Physically, his size was almost overpowering, and his bellowing voice raised temperatures, but when he had a twinkle in his eye and a smile on his face, he could also brighten the whole room.

Having survived two tours in Vietnam, General Schwarzkopf was determined to fight the Gulf War with every available overpowering tactic and weapon system at his disposal. Because he had been burned during the Grenada operation by breaches of operational security, he was also obsessed that we follow the strictest of security measures. Anyone appearing to impede his two-fisted approach to war was seen as an instant adversary. But behind the bear-like growls, he was a man who deeply cared for every single soldier, airman, sailor, marine, and civilian under his command—Americans, British, French, and Arabs. He was a devoted family man and was very personable in many ways. I've seen him with tears in his eyes and heard his voice crack during emotional moments. Importantly, during Desert Storm he was almost singularly responsible for forming and keeping together a critical coalition of "strange bedfellows." The leadership of the military that fought and won Desert Storm, from the chairman of the Joint Chiefs to General Schwarzkopf and his senior commanders and staff officers were predominantly Vietnam veterans. We had all worked with a singular purpose to rebuild our forces from the postwar force degradation and psychological infirmity of our military. Once the Vietnam war was over, we focused on our main threat, the Soviet Union on the plains of Europe. To cope with the challenge, the army, over time, developed a doctrine called "Air Land Battle." Because armor-heavy forces on both sides would be involved, Blitzkrieg and similar doctrines were studied and used as a basis, with close air support as a vital key component. As we evolved the doctrine, we developed commensurate

PROFESSIONAL COURAGE

new primary weapon systems, support mechanisms such as night vision equipment and GPS, logistic methodologies, rapid communications, and intelligence collection systems and platforms; all second to none. We recruited and trained highly motivated soldiers, sailors, marines, and air force personnel. The Desert Storm scenario was tailor-made for the military we Vietnam vets had built to fight and fight without recourse to losing this time. The entire campaign was planned, developed, and executed brilliantly.

CHAPTER 12

FINISHING WHAT I STARTED

In sharp contrast to my experiences in Riyadh, daily life at MacDill seemed almost euphoric. With the weight of the daily pressures of Desert Storm lifted from my shoulders, the daily operations and briefings were less strained, and we all felt a constant deep sense of accomplishment. Saddam was still creating some political-military havoc with the Shia and the Kurds, as we had predicted, and I knew that he would only continue to create additional problems in the Middle East for the foreseeable future.

MY FINAL DAYS AT CENTCOM

We still had to put work in on weekends and even holidays, but we were at home and certainly in a much less stressful atmosphere. After being called in on Thanksgiving Day to provide the CINC with our assessment of one of Saddam's latest controversial moves, I reflected and realized that from the day I arrived at CENTCOM, I had not had one relaxing full day off for well over fifteen months.

We continued to provide daily intelligence support for General Schwarzkopf, and I was proud to be working for a true national hero. Numerous military and civilian groups visited our headquarters to interview or be briefed by the now-famous CINC on Desert Shield, Desert Storm, and beyond. During these sessions, the CINC would normally have me sit next to him and ask me to chime in on talking points and responses to questions.

The CINC received invitations to testify in closed, highly classified sessions in front of the Senate Select Committee on Intelligence and the House Permanent Select Committee on Intelligence. He charged us in the J-2 to prepare a set of extensive briefing books that he could study prior to and refer to during the testimonies. I could tell from his demeaner and body language that he was uncomfortable with the prospect of testifying in front of those particular committees. Much of the intricate aspects of intelligence, especially the procedural and technical aspects, were well beyond his comfort zone. He, therefore, asked me to accompany him to Washington and to sit next to him at the witness table during the two hearings. Since he had previously only testified to congress alone, I was both astounded and proud.

We flew to Washington in his command aircraft wearing our Class A green uniforms. We first testified in front of the Senate Select Committee and the hearing was neither confrontational nor drawn out. They were very complimentary as we both answered their questions. I expected the hearing in front of the House Permanent Select Committee on Intelligence to be little more controversial in tenor. The committee chairman was Representative Ronald Dellums, who had a reputation for not being a great friend of the military nor of military intelligence. Interestingly, but not surprisingly, he was being advised not only by his own congressional staff but by selected CIA staff as well. As I looked at the CIA officers sitting behind the members, it brought back the numerous frustrating encounters we had with the CIA including the tank BDA controversy, the special adviser who stayed in Florida, the JILE rotation policy, and the struggle between our command and the CIA for planning and operational primacy for cross-border operations. To this very day, I still find many of those incidents difficult to truly understand.

During the course of the hearing, committee members on both sides of the aisle appeared friendly, made complimentary statements about our conduct of the war, and asked some detailed but mostly noncontroversial questions. The CINC deferred to me on several technical and procedural questions and issues. The committee directed one interesting question to me: "If you could have had one intelligence capability that you didn't have, what would it have been?" I answered, without hesitation, that the SR-71 "Blackbird" reconnaissance aircraft would have been incredibly useful due to its synoptic (wide-area) coverage, the quality of its imagery, and its ability to fly over our vast area of operations with impunity, before, during, and after Desert Storm. Unfortunately, the SR-71 fleet had been taken out of service by the air force in 1988. (After our testimony, and under pressure from Congress, some were brought back into service, but eventually were finally retired in 1998). I anticipated and was prepared for the highly controversial tank BDA affair to rear its ugly head during the testimony, but it never did in any form or detail. However, and not surprisingly, the final written report from the committee on Desert Storm was slanted toward the CIA's analysis of the tank kill controversy and not ours. When I first read the report, I was initially angered and frustrated by the tenor of the report; however, I knew the controversy and the report would eventually be confined to the dustbin of history by our stunning victory in Desert Storm.

On our way back to Andrews Air Force Base, the CINC was in an especially good mood. He turned to me, looked me in the eye, and said, "Jack, the thing I most admired about you during the war was that you told it like it was, even though, at times, I didn't like it." I admitted to him that when he barked at me out of understandable frustration, it bothered me. But I could not and would not change any of my procedures and assessments because I knew that what we were giving him was our best and most accurate effort. Additionally, and most importantly, no matter what, he continued to use our intelligence to make his key decisions. He never asked me to change any of our assessments, and that gave me the courage to continue to give him what I thought was the best information needed for his decision-making processes. In the end, I had to constantly rely on professional courage and present the hard facts despite his occasional wailing and gnashing of teeth. All in all, we both felt that the testimonies had gone well, and we both relaxed and enjoyed the ride back to Andrews, then on to MacDill.

Celebrating Victory and Sharing Honors

In May 1991, Queen Elizabeth II and Prince Phillip visited MacDill to present the CINC with a knighthood. Coincidently, my mom was visiting with us at that time and Ann gave mom her assigned front row seat in the limited access area so she could hear the queen's public remarks. The queen while greeting some guests, remarked to mom that they were the grand old ladies in the crowd. We were delighted to be able to provide my mom with one of the great highlights of her life. Later that day, the queen knighted General Schwarzkopf in a private ceremony in his office, and then they all moved into our operations center to meet with the primary staff. The queen greeted each of us individually. When she got to me, she asked knowledgeable and thoughtful questions about the campaign. She congratulated us on our victory and told us that we had done an extraordinary job fighting the war to its conclusion. Prince Phillip paused in front of me and asked me several substantive and procedural questions. He seemed both well informed and extremely interested in some of the details of how we had fought the war. They both were incredibly gracious and provided us with an unforgettable experience.

Shortly prior to the scheduled national victory parades in Washington, DC, and New York City, the CINC addressed the corps of cadets at West Point. Our son John was still a member of the corps of cadets and was personally and graciously invited by the CINC to have lunch with him at his table. In June of 1991, 8000 Desert Storm troops, led by General Schwarzkopf, marched in the National Victory Parade in Washington, DC. The American people seemed starved for a reason to celebrate a victory after military disasters such as Korea and Vietnam. For us Vietnam veterans, the victory parades served as a deep and satisfying catharsis. During the Washington parade, President George H.W. Bush came over to where General Schwarzkopf and the five us on his primary staff were standing at attention and shook each of our hands and told us that we all had done a great job. I was unbelievably proud of all we had accomplished and how we had done it. During the immense New York City ticker tape parade, we all felt like we were all in a wonderful euphoric dream. As we marched down the street, I thought of all of those famous wild scenes during previous parades for returning military units with heroes of every stripe. Now, I was a part of that exhilarating experience, and that honor and outpouring of gratitude would become a bright lens forever in my soul.

Before his retirement, General Schwarzkopf presented his staff with achievement medals for Desert Shield and Desert Storm. He was truly grateful for each of our roles and was generous with praise while awarding the medals. As he pinned my medal on my fatigues, he looked me in the eye and said, "Jack, I could not have done it without you." Years of dedicated blood, sweat, and tears, and the decision to make the army and intelligence my career flashed in front of me. At that moment, I knew the hard work and professional courage I had fostered throughout my career had been the keys to success.

A Change of Command

During early August, as General Schwarzkopf was nearing his retirement date. We began rehearsals for his change-of-command ceremony and anticipated a great number of VIPs to attend the ceremony. John, still a cadet at West Point, was at Fort Benning attending jump school and was due to make his final qualifying jump in August. I had initially planned to travel to Fort Benning to jump with John then personally pin his jump wings on. Unfortunately, the CINC's retirement and change-of-command ceremony would be scheduled for that very same day, a true disappointment. However, I proudly stood behind General Schwarzkopf as Secretary Cheney passed the CENTCOM command flag from General Schwarzkopf to Marine General Joe Hoar.

Was General Schwarzkopf an easy man to work for? No. Not at all. However, despite (or maybe because of) his famous bluster, he was a very successful commander at every level. He was a brilliant soldier who loved his troops and was totally dedicated to whatever mission he was given. Most importantly, for the incredible political-military leadership challenges of Desert Shield and Desert Storm, he was, without question, the right man, in the right job, during that critical time in United States' history. In the future, our army will need to and hopefully will develop similar combat leaders like H. Norman Schwarzkopf. May he rest in peace.

The rest of my tour at CENTCOM was spent working on multiple missions for General Hoar. The Desert Storm area of operations was still volatile, especially related to Iraq. General Hoar included me in almost every meeting and discussion he had with visitors to CENTCOM and with foreign leaders, both in the US and on important foreign trips to our area of operations. During my final months at CENTCOM, General Hoar told me that I had made the Major General promotion list. During the ceremony, General Hoar and Ann each pinned a two-star insignia on my shoulders. They were the same set of two-star insignia used when

General Hoar had been promoted to the same rank. He was that kind of leader: a true gentleman and great marine.

As my time at CENTCOM was coming to an end, I received orders to the Defense Intelligence Agency (DIA) in Washington as the director of the National Military Intelligence Collection Center (NMICC). Additionally, I had been personally selected to create a much-needed military intelligence capability that I strongly believed in and deeply understood: the Defense HUMINT Service (DHS). Once I received my official orders, Ann and I looked forward to this tour, which most likely would be our last before retirement. I comfortably passed the J-2 baton on to a good friend, and great intel officer, Army Brigadier General Pat Hughes who I had recommended as my successor to the CINC..

DIRECTOR FOR OPERATIONS, DIA: WASHINGTON, DC, JUNE 1992–AUGUST 1995

I was at the thirty-year mark in my career and could have still retired. But Ann knew that my service in the DIA was a role that I had worked decades to reach and was also important to our country. We both decided that I would stay in the army for three more years to see the creation of the new HUMINT service through to its ultimate creation and plans for its long-term development. Additionally, Air Force Lieutenant General Jim Clapper was the current director of DIA, and I possibly could be nominated by the army as his successor. I was headquartered in a nondescript building in the Washington, DC suburb of Clarendon and relieved not to be working in bowels of the Pentagon again. Ann, Jeff, Mei, and I (John was still at West Point) had moved into our home in Oakton, Virginia.

In all, I held three agency directorships simultaneously: director of the National Military Intelligence Collection Center (NMICC), director of the Defense HUMINT Service (DHS), and director of the Central MASINT (Measurements and Signatures) Office. I also controlled the Defense Attaché System (DAS). With the combined missions of those three directorships, I was basically serving as the DIA's director for Operations. The other major functional areas within DIA were Analysis, Science and Technology, and Support. If I had been able to provide a blueprint for the responsibilities and missions involved in the final stage of my military career, this would be it. I would be able to work on, promote, improvise, and improve virtually every military intelligence capability that I had fought for during my entire thirty-year career.

Development of the Defense HUMINT Service would become an obsession for me. I also included the further development of foreign language programs, a key to eventual HUMINT success, as one of my priorities. As the collection manager for the Department of the Defense, I continued to beat down the green door for all collection capabilities. Following the progress we made during Desert Storm, I now applied collection fusion at the highest levels. All levels and disparate types of intelligence collection functions would be eventually fused into one national intelligence collection capability and plan. I would rely on my past experiences, especially those during my combat tours, to build a system that would provide our national decision-makers and warfighters with a worldwide military intelligence collection structure needed to support analysis, products, and eventually key military decisions. During my time in DIA, I directed numerous sensitive operations in each of the positions for which I was responsible (NMICC, Central MASINT Office, and DHS) that may still be highly classified due to the sensitivity of sources and methods. Regretfully, I cannot provide specifics on many of the successful operations for which I was proud to be involved.

DIRECTOR, NATIONAL MILITARY INTELLIGENCE COLLECTION CENTER

As director of the NMICC, I provided centralized direction for the management of all-source intelligence collection. I directed all intelligence collection management, requirements, prioritization, and tasking of collection systems and capabilities for the Department of Defense (DOD), which included Human (HUMINT), Signals (SIGINT), Measurement and Signatures (MASINT), Imagery (IMINT), and today's Geospatial and Open Source (OSINT). At the national level, I attempted to replicate as much of the successful all-source intelligence collection processes and procedures that we had developed at CENTCOM during Desert Storm. We began each day by collating the huge number of daily worldwide intelligence collection requirements submitted by national-level organizations, regional CINCs, and the services and then prioritized the collated tasks. We would then decide which intelligence collection assets were available for tasking on a daily basis that could best fulfill the various prioritized missions assigned. Finally, a daily worldwide national intelligence collection plan would be crafted. The requirements were then sent to appropriate collection elements in the various services and other intelligence organizations to fulfill. However, as my responsibilities grew, I would also have direct control over the collection assets within the DHS, (including the DAS), and the Central MASINT Office. I now had direct programmatic and tasking authority over more than $500 million in national intelligence collection assets plus a large special access program budget. I had day-to-day supervision of 4,746 personnel. My responsibility included intelligence collection support to national-level decision-makers, combatant commanders, and the services while continuing to dynamically develop improved national collection postures, strategies, policies, and procedures. We continuously evaluated the value of collection systems and developed collection databases for national intelligence requirements. The task was daunting, but I continuously dedicated myself every day to the support of our troops, no matter whatever crab trap they were in.

I prioritized what were considered to be our most important intelligence collection missions, based on what DOD considered to be the most threatening adversarial countries or mission areas, such as weapons of mass destruction, around the world. I referred to these priorities as "hard targets". I dedicated a portion of my daily efforts against those specific adversaries or mission areas. Additionally, I would carve out a large part of one day every week to gather key collection managers and operators to discuss, plan, and task dedicated methodologies and systems that could be best used against those critical targets. I continuously charged the group to use ingenuity and out-of-the-box thinking to provide unique fused collection plans and directed systems for the DOD's most critical informational requirements on those threatening adversaries or mission areas. Over time, we were able to develop highly effective and unique capabilities, systems, platforms, and procedures and build them into our daily worldwide intelligence collection requirements, systems, procedures, and results. We had great success during many operations that collected key usable intelligence previously difficult or even impossible to obtain. But I did have a few frustrating efforts when political constraints would limit or deny one or more hard target collection initiatives.

DIRECTOR, DEFENSE HUMINT SERVICE

Once settled into my various worldwide collection management roles, I was officially charged by the DOD to create and develop a new organization called the Defense HUMINT Service. I had always been a firm proponent of HUMINT and during my continual readings of Sun Tsu, the Chinese military philosopher, I knew he emphasized the need for HUMINT. He wrote, "Foreknowledge cannot be gotten from ghosts and spirits, cannot be had by analogy, cannot be found out by calculation, it must be obtained from people, people who know the conditions of the enemy." There had been attempts to create such a capability in the past, but they all had gone wanting. The bureaucracy viscerally balks at change, and I knew the challenge would be daunting. But, as a result of my earlier career experiences, I had long been convinced that the human collection of intelligence is an invaluable capability and that its development was deserving of the highest effort and prioritization. I was totally driven to the task. I used our observation and reporting successes in Beijing during the Tiananmen incident as a shining example of the value of HUMINT. Technical intelligence collection systems are invaluable in satisfying much of our requirements, but they have limitations, such as being able to provide a target country's leadership's future intentions. Additionally, information collected and reported by human sources can be, at times, and under certain circumstances be more rapid, unique, and precise. Interpersonal relationships can be the critical piece to an all-source (Human, Signals, Imagery, Measurements, Open Source) collection of the necessary, viable, target intelligence that is required to support our national defense.

Over the years, there had been a continued recognition of a need for one element within the DOD that would organize, develop, manage, prioritize, task, and deploy worldwide overt, covert, and clandestine human collection assets. Although there had been some historical fits and starts attempting to organize a joint military HUMINT capability, none had ever come close to a permanent solution. Prior to this time, HUMINT collection requirements were collated in the DOD and then tasked down to the various services and other intelligence organizations where the collection assets resided. They would then select their own service HUMINT assets and methodologies to accomplish them. I was convinced that enhanced, more innovative, and more responsive methods controlled by a centralized management and tasking system would make HUMINT more responsive to the new, faster-moving challenges facing our present and future military. Additionally, we needed what I called HUMINT operational tasking authority, which would essentially give the DIA day-to-day operational control of all DOD and separate service HUMINT assets. With this new authority, the DHS could develop new, innovative, and worldwide responsive methods of collection. After much study and consultation, I led an effort to draft a HUMINT concept proposal and it was approved by the service secretaries in September 1992. The proposal consolidated all service HUMINT management and operations to better support national-level organizations and theater CINCs. Our proposal also established HUMINT support elements at every CINC's headquarters to serve as liaison between the defense HUMINT system and the theater CINCs. The proposal further posited the establishment of regional joint operational bases to provide operational control of all HUMINT collection in those assigned geographical regions. Eventually, the national intelligence community, DOD leadership, and Congress supported all elements of the proposal, and the DOD approved the creation of the DHS on December 18, 1992. This proud moment was the ultimate conclusion to a career-long effort.

Our HUMINT Blueprint

Creating an entirely new and all-encompassing DHS out of whole cloth would not be a simple task. Up to this point, the army had most of the assets and was performing the majority of service-led HUMINT operations. My greatest challenge would be the transfer of HUMINT operations responsibility and resultant personnel assets from the naturally reluctant services.

During the initial phases of my effort to create the DHS, I ran into some unforeseen problems. For example, service counterintelligence organizations felt threatened, fearing that we would eventually subsume their mission and units into the DHS as well. Army counterintelligence units, with the most to lose, were most vocal and recalcitrant. As far as I was concerned, we would always continue to require and welcome counterintelligence support, but I did not plan for their inclusion in our final DHS organizational structure. To help quell the unrest, I arranged a meeting with as many counterintelligence personnel as I could in hopes that I could provide them with details of our plans and convince them that our plans did not include counterintelligence units. Hoping that I could finally allay their concerns and resultant opposition, I arranged to brief a large counterintelligence group. Initially the tension was thick, but I eventually think I convinced them that we were not a threat to their present organizational structure and mission. Frankly, I don't think they were ever comfortable with our intentions, but they eventually supported us, nonetheless.

After a series of organizational meetings with appropriate service representatives, I hoped to eventually create a national military organization that would be efficiently and rapidly responsive to our worldwide HUMINT collection requirements and missions.

The Potential of the DAS

Through my experiences as an attaché, especially during the Tiananmen crisis, I was convinced of the great potential value of the DAS. During my time in other positions during my career, I had used valuable support provided by the DAS, so I knew of its tremendous capabilities and potential. I initially emphasized that we were observation and reporting oriented, but I ensured that I broadened my emphasis. I made it clear that every-one included in our effort knew that the representation and liaison missions of the attaché were not only important to the country to which they were assigned but to our national interest. I over-saw the function of over 100 DAS offices around the world, and I eagerly dove into their varied worldwide tasks. I daily read pertinent collection, liaison, and administrative reports, especially those from attaché offices in key countries around the world. I prioritized numerous personal visits to attaché offices and to remote special mission organizations throughout our worldwide system. As I visited each attaché office, I would hold an initial session with the defense attaché, then the first scheduled meeting would be with the office spouses. Aside from the operational mission side of the office, the situation of the families was important from the morale sup-port and security side. After each meeting, the organizational and family issues that I thought needed attention were wired back to Washington for follow-up action. The folks back at our headquarters called those initiatives and requirements that I sent back during those trips the Leide Bow-Wave. I was totally dedicated to supporting and improving the total DAS, from the selection of attachés to their training, operational direction, and in their globally critical representational and observation missions.

I continuously pushed the importance of foreign language training within the DAS and throughout the new DHS as well. I visited and supported language programs in both the United States, such as (such as in my alma mater, the Defense Language Institute in Monterey, CA) and abroad such as the U.S Army Russian Institute in Garmisch, Germany. The DAS is, without question, one of our country's greatest functioning national treasures and must be continued, continuously improved upon, and supported as robustly as possible.

DIRECTOR, CENTRAL MASINT OFFICE

Measurement and Signatures Intelligence (MASINT) is one of the least known, understood, and underappreciated critical collection capabilities within our national intelligence community. I quickly became fascinated with the MASINT mission because its capabilities are often quite obscure, unique, highly technical, sensitive, and invaluable. MASINT provides a collection of specific data that results in unique intelligence that locates, identifies, and describes distinctive physical characteristics of specific key target areas and systems.

MASINT's people and missions are often highly classified and protected. Its technical intelligence is derived from the analysis of very sensitive data obtained from identifiable features normally associated with often obscure sources such as emitters or "senders." MASINT relies on scientific and physical characteristics to obtain pertinent resultant data. Its various operational mission functional areas can be basically defined as electro-optical (interaction between electromagnetic optical and electronics), nuclear, geophysical, radar, physical materials (chemical and biological), and radio frequency disciplines. MASINT's importance has risen greatly with the evolution of highly sophisticated nuclear and non-nuclear weapon systems, esoteric vehicles, and space programs. MASINT is vital to the collection of important data throughout the world on events such as nuclear tests, directed energy weapons, and missile launches. It requires dynamic assessment, planning, fusion, and tasking of a complex combination of a variety of esoteric collection systems.

During my initial MASINT briefing, the staff officers primarily addressed a linear summary of our programs, systems, and procedures. I could see right away that we allocated funds and scheduled acquisition, deployment, and maintenance of our current systems without addressing their eventual relationship to our total mission areas. As a result, there was little methodology or consideration for the prioritization and development of future systems. I quickly scheduled an initial planning meeting with key members of the MASINT staff. I had them draw up a matrix categorizing our key mission support areas.

I then had them prioritize the mission areas and the collection systems that could be and should be used within those areas. After several long days of fruitful detailed briefings and discussions, we devised a plan that was based on our prioritized mission areas and systems. The plan included funding, research and development, acquisition, functional use, evaluation, and continuous prioritizations for each of the MASINT mission areas, and resultant collection systems. I emphasized that there not only is ever shortening technological life-cycles but we needed to look at dynamic mission area priorities as well. We established processes for continuously addressing both.

As the MASINT functional manager, I was responsible for the policy, planning, programming, and budgeting while providing continual guidance for the daily active collection missions and setting the national development, acquisition, and collection mission priorities for some incredibly valuable yet virtually publicly unknown intelligence collection capabilities. We programmed and directed a large worldwide effort, much of it through very sensitive special access programs, or as some would describe as black programs. I continuously sought to improve our collection fusion effort using MASINT, HUMINT, SIGINT, and IMINT intelligence against key targets to alert, track, and precisely identify ever more sophisticated target sets. Unfortunately, I cannot identify the many invaluable MASINT missions we conducted, especially our most successful ones. My MASINT responsibility, including its brilliant people and incredibly important contribution to the national intelligence collection effort, was one of the most fascinating and satisfying in my entire career. MASINT will play an ever-increasing role in the future, especially when adding outer space to its burgeoning mission functions.

BECOMING A HARVARD FELLOW

In the spring of 1993, I was selected by the DOD to attend the Program for Senior Executives in National and International Security at Harvard's John Fitzgerald Kennedy School of Government and National Security. The course had a well-earned reputation for high-level thought and discussion and was described as the Kennedy School's "premier program for senior-level civilian and military officials in security roles." I attended the course during August and September of 1993 and really thrived in such a challenging academic environment. The course consisted of seminars and group discussions on various challenging political-military situations and scenarios of the day. I learned a lot from those sessions and was proud to contribute opinions and experiences using lessons learned from both my wartime and peacetime experiences at home and abroad. During many of the discussions, I energetically promoted the constant need for cooperation and honest, non-confrontational, nonparochial, contributory efforts and continued dialogue between all sectors of government, especially during wartime. The seminar leader was Professor Anthony "Tony" Oettinger, an academic legend in both applied mathematics and information resources policy. Tony brought out the best in me, not only during the seminars but also in the extensive private discussions we had over the course of those weeks. After I graduated from the program in September of 1993, Tony invited me back to Harvard twice as a guest lecturer for Harvard's National Security Fellowship Program for Senior Executives. Those lectures were published as papers by Harvard's Program on Information Resources Policy and quoted during extensive interviews and lectures in the program's publications. I learned a great deal from Tony, and hopefully I contributed some useful historical insights into the critically important challenges and exigencies of war and peace. I will always cherish my experiences at Harvard, especially those private sessions with Tony Oettinger.

VISITS TO OPERATIONAL ORGANIZATIONS AND AREAS

During my more than three years at DIA, I took many operational and support trips both within the United States and overseas. In the US, I was in constant liaison with elements of the national intelligence collection and analytical structure such as the service intelligence organizations, the CIA, the National Security Agency, the Federal Bureau of Investigation, and the National

Reconnaissance Office. I would also visit technical and analytical organizations such as the Missile and Space Intelligence Center at the Redstone Arsenal in Huntsville, Alabama and the National Ground Intelligence Center in Charlottesville, Virginia.

Several months after I had arrived at DIA, it appeared that Saddam was using his semi-repaired railway system to move military units and weapon systems to the south. We had to assess his motives and what his current actions and resultant posturing could mean. During that period, I strongly suspected, but certainly did not know, that we would spend the next decade conducting active deployments to Kurdish northern Iraq, and that additional forces would be regularly deployed and redeployed to Kuwait for rapid response exercises intended to keep watch on a continually belligerent Saddam. One day, while I was attending a video teleconference session with DIA senior operations officers, the then CENTCOM J-2, and other analysts, Jim Clapper asked for my assessment on Saddam's latest movements. I posited that Saddam's actions may well constitute bluster for regional and internal consumption despite his awareness of our powerful residual military assets that remained in the area. I knew that Saddam was an egotistical and revengeful bastard, and we could not allow his recent moves to go unnoticed and not be countered. I reminded the group that Saddam's military infrastructure was still virtually dismantled, and he couldn't yet put together a viable threat to his neighbors. However, he still retained some residual military power, including what remained of the Republican Guard. He was still unpredictable and easily provoked, so his neighbors remained, understandably, wary of his future ambitions. I recommended that we put together an intelligence estimate of his latest activities and brief our key allies in the region. Jim Clapper agreed and asked me to accompany on an informational briefing trip to those countries. Our analysts provided an up-to-date assessment prepared maps and charts, and projected what they estimated to be his possible future activities. Jim and I boarded a dedicated military aircraft at Andrews and flew to the Middle East.

After arrival in the area, we proceeded to brief the key leadership in Kuwait, Saudi Arabia, United Arab Emirates, Bahrain, and Egypt. I had built friendly and trusted relationships with many of these leaders while working closely with them during Desert Shield and Desert Storm. They were all appreciative of our efforts to keep them personally informed and relieved that we would not leave them in a lurch with a still-defiant Saddam, who appeared to be in an ever-increasing belligerent mood.

During our last stop, Cairo, we were notified that President Mubarak wanted to hear our presentation personally at the Montaza presidential palace in Alexandria. Jim and I flew to Alexandria and were then driven to the palace on the Mediterranean Sea. We were escorted to a balcony overlooking the sea where initially we shared tea and small talk with Mubarak. We then provided him with our briefing, and he again expressed appreciation of our efforts in keeping him up to date. As we began discussing the leadup to Desert Storm, President Mubarak's demeanor changed. He became very agitated as he described his interaction with Saddam during the prelude to the crisis. He disclosed that Saddam personally promised that he would not invade Kuwait. President Mubarak took Saddam's words as truth and had then passed that information on to other regional leaders and to President Bush. Mubarak was furious that Saddam had deceived him. As a result, Egypt was a key ally during Desert Storm and Mubarak would continue to strongly support our military efforts to eventually defeat Saddam. Despite President Mubarak's sudden spike of anger while recounting Saddam's deceit, we would end our visit in good spirits. I traveled to more than sixty countries throughout the world, mainly to visit our attaché offices, but also to other organizations and areas in conjunction with my many responsibilities as the director of NMICC, DHS, and the Central MASINT Office. Prior to each trip, I would coordinate with key elements of the Defense and State Departments to see if there were any special missions or support functions that I could help them with during my travels. As an example, during one trip

I visited Macedonia, Albania, Cyprus, and Italy. In Macedonia I not only met with our attaché office in Skopje, but also visited with Joint Task Force Able Sentry II on the Macedonia-Serbian border to assess how we could help with their observation, peacekeeping, and reporting missions. In Albania, I met with the DAO in Tirana and later with Albanian leaders and negotiated an agreement that included their increased assistance with our efforts to transport supplies through their ports on the Adriatic Sea to our operational and support elements in Macedonia. During the Cyprus portion of the trip, the Defense and State Departments asked me to help calm the increase in tensions then occurring between the Greek and Turkish militaries on the island. During that visit, I visited the DAO and then held fruitful discussions with both the Greek military commander in Nicosia and the Turkish military commander in the north. During the meetings with both commanders, I was able to explain the problems they were creating and obtain their agreement to lower the tensions. As a result, during the following days, the situation on the ground did, in fact, calm down. While in Cyprus, I also visited the British over the horizon radar site to thank them for their support during Desert Storm. I then coordinated their continuing support for our efforts of keeping tabs on the always troublesome Saddam. During that trip to Italy, after my visit to the DAO in Rome, I held operational and support meetings with NATO and Allied Army Corps Southern Europe in Naples, Italy to assess how we could assist them with specific intelligence collection efforts. I always made a concerted effort to plan each trip to maximize our efforts of support, not only of the attaché offices, but key military organizations and missions around the world.

BACK TO MY ROOTS

In April of 1995, I was preparing for an inspection and support visit to Europe, and Italy was again on the schedule. Both sets of my grandparents had emigrated from Italy, and my paternal grandmother was born and raised in the small town of Bedonia in the Apennine Mountains. The army attaché in Rome, Colonel John Prout, had planned a fact-finding trip to Parma and suggested that we take a side trip to Bedonia since it was nearby. From studying the region, I had learned that the area around Bedonia was a hotbed for the partigiani, the Italian resistance who fought the Germans as they were retreating up the spine of the Apennine Mountains during the latter part of World War II.

After a couple of days of conducting business with our attaché office in Rome, John Prout and I drove to Parma. We had arranged a courtesy call with the president of Parma Province who wanted to take part in my visit to Bedonia. We drove from Parma to Bedonia, weaving through some of the most beautiful countryside I had ever seen. We were greeted at the city's main meeting hall by the mayor, Dr. Gianfranco Ghandi, who had arranged gracious welcoming festivities. The mayor opened the double doors to surprise us by what seemed to be the entire town gathered around tables heaped with local gifts: beautiful flowers, mushrooms, cheese, prosciutto, and candy. Smiling strangers constantly embraced me and I was quickly introduced to a cousin, who became a lasting friend of the family. The mayor asked the townspeople if they had any questions for me. One memorable question was, "How were you able to get through and survive the dangerous missions and combat tours that you experienced?" I hesitated and, using John as my interpreter, slowly replied, "It was probably because of the Saint Anthony medal my mother gave me each time I went into harm's way and also because of an infused inner strength drawn from the Bedonia mountain stock that I had inherited from my grandmother." The room fell silent, and as I thought of my grandmother, father, and mother, I started to choke up. I thought to myself in total embarrassment, "Here I am, a combat-hardened master parachutist crying in front of all these people." I haltingly looked around the room and saw that everyone else in the room was crying as well. I changed from being somewhat ashamed of my emotions to being extremely proud of them knowing what they truly meant.

I talked to many townspeople over the next few hours as we shared endless food and wine. As I prepared to leave, I remarked that it would be a shame to waste all the beautiful flowers on the tables. Someone then suggested that there was a war monument at the other end of the town built in tribute to the soldiers from Bedonia during World War I and to the local partigiani who were killed fighting the Germans. We all poured out of the hall, proceeded down the central street, and I placed the flowers in front of each of the monuments. Then I walked up the stairs and stood in front of the World War I monument, saluted, removed my military cap, and knelt in prayer. I got up, put my cap back on, and then moved over to the monument to the partigiani and repeated the salute and prayer. When I turned around and started down the stairs, I saw the whole town crying again.

Several months later, a resident of Bedonia, who spoke excellent English, surprised me with a phone call. She told me that because of my previous visit, Rome had finally approved Bedonia's nomination for the Medal of Valor, which had been written decades earlier to describe the incredible bravery and sacrifice of the local partigiani against the Germans. Little did I know that back in April, national and regional journalists were among the crowd that had gathered in Bedonia. Articles and photos of me kneeling in front of the monuments had appeared in the local press and in national newspapers, and this news brought Bedonia to the attention of the leadership in Rome. During the same phone call, I was told that the town council had unanimously voted to award me an honorary citizenship of Bedonia. I was momentarily speechless as I fully took in this rare honor. The Medal of Valor would be presented to the town in October, and the town council wanted to present me with honorary citizenship during the ceremony. I started clearing my calendar and made plane reservations.

I arrived in Rome a few days before the ceremony and again made the long drive to Bedonia with John Prout. As we settled into our rooms at the local seminary, I was surprised by a group of my grandmother's sister's relatives, who now resided in France, just over the Italian border. It was an emotional reception with lots of tears, hugs, and kisses. Later that night, John and I had dinner at the farm of another cousin, Bruno Thoma. Bruno's wife had cooked a full Italian dinner including wild boar cacciatore, and Bruno served red wine that he had bottled the previous year. The dinner reminded me of the large Italian family dinners we had at my grandparent's house when I was a boy.

The following morning, the mayor presented me with a beautiful family tree painted on a large piece of parchment that depicted my grandmother's ancestors going back to the 1700s. We then visited a one room area over a stone stable where my grandmother and her family had lived. They primarily baked bread and did other household chores for the padrone who lived in the main house. The only thing left on the wall was a worn and faded plaque with pictures of the Madonna and the Christ child, the town, and the seminary. They carefully removed it from the wall and gave it to me, and I cherish it to this day.

On the day of the ceremony, under a bright blue sky, there were representatives from the Italian government, Parma Province, and people from the surrounding towns carrying their respective town flags. A group of surviving partigiani with their tricolor scarves were in attendance along with the traditional Italian local and regional bands, a squad of paratroopers from the Italian Army, and, of course, the gracious people of Bedonia and surrounding towns. The town was also presenting an honorary citizenship to Cardinal Rossi, who had attended and been ordained at the seminary in town and had been the papal nuncio in Berlin during World War II. Cardinal Rossi began the ceremony with a remembrance mass and blessing. A representative of the national government in Rome pinned the Medal of Valor on the Bedonia town flag as the townspeople glowed with immense pride. The mayor then presented the Cardinal with his certificate of honorary citizenship and Cardinal Rossi made his acceptance speech. I was then presented with my honorary citizenship. John had crafted my speech in Italian, but I had little time to read and rehearse it. I spoke in the best Italian that I could muster; the people in the square remained silent during its entirety. As I concluded my speech with a tribute to my grandmother and her beloved hometown, the townspeople erupted with loud clapping, yelling, and of course, more tears all around.

MY FINAL DAYS AT THE DIA AND IN THE ARMY

Just prior to mid-year of 1995, Jim Clapper was near the end of a normal three-year tour as director, and I was informed by an army four-star general officer that the army would probably nominate me as the next DIA director. I was guardedly excited but had some reservations about extending my active service for another three years. As the time neared for Jim to retire, he announced that he was extending his time as director, and I was leaning more toward a sooner retirement. I was satisfied that I had made contributions in these last concurrent positions to strengthen intelligence support from the national down to the tactical level. I realized that my dedication to mission and professional courage had carried me successfully to this point in my career. As I became more convinced that I should retire, I began to plan for my army after-life.

    I interviewed for several postretirement positions, both inside and outside of government. I tried to think of my next job as an exciting experience to look forward to, but leaving my military comfort zone was going to be an unusual and uneasy experience for me. I received an offer from a large US corporation to become the president of one of their strategic business units dealing with sensitive software and hardware in support of the national intelligence community. At least I could stay in my occupational comfort zone and hopefully continue to help improve intelligence operational support at various levels. I accepted the offer and put in my request for a retirement date of August 1, 1995. I was at peace with my decision and began winding down in my job and preparing to pass the torch to my replacement. With mixed feelings, I was looking forward to what would be an emotional retirement ceremony on the parade field at Fort Myer, Virginia.

The day of my retirement ceremony began bittersweet, as I became struck with the finality of it all. As a wonderful surprise, Sergeant Troy Clifton "Brother Deals," flew up from Tampa to represent CENTCOM at my retirement. I had the most-dear people in my life beside me, with mom, Ann, our family, Ann's mom, and close friends in attendance. My only disappointment was that my beloved dad did not attend because he was ill. I knew it must be serious because he would have done anything to be there; he actually passed away later that month and it was like a dagger through my heart.

The entire ceremony was emotional and beautiful. The 3rd US Army Infantry Regiment, "the Old Guard," passed by in review formation while the United States Army Old Guard Fife and Drum Corps played historic songs. Most importantly, Ann stood at my side during the entire ceremony as she had been throughout my career, and she was justifiably recognized by the army for her unyielding love and dedication through all those years. Standing at attention, as I had done hundreds of times during my long career, I felt strangely frozen in time. Watching those meaningful, precious colors pass by, I vividly and thankfully recalled those who had been meaningful throughout my career: Colonel Woodrow Shrawder, Colonel Butch Kendrick, Colonel Lynn Murray, General Tom Weinstein, Colonel Lee Mize, General Sandy Meloy, Harry Fukuhara, Ambassador Jim Lilley, and General H. Norman Schwarzkopf. My thoughts naturally turned to Larry Britten, who, with such a bright future, had tragically given his life for his country at such a young age. I then thought of my Charlie Company paratroopers who fought and died in the Crab Trap, and the 58,000 brave Americans who gave their lives during that dark time in our history that was Vietnam. I recalled the intense experience in China during Tiananmen, almost immediately followed by the extraordinarily difficult challenges I faced during Desert Storm. Finally, I thought about the incredible number of places around the world—some beautiful, some strange, but memorable all—that I had experienced in my thirty-three years on active duty. The weather for the most part of that day had been bright and sunny, but strangely, toward the end of the ceremony, the sky suddenly darkened, and rain fell ever so softly and briefly. My mind raced back to the wet jungles of Vietnam, and I looked at that rain as some emotional symbol from those incredible paratroopers that struggled through the Crab Trap with me saying: "On this day, we were together once again and would be together to the end." My eyes began to well and I clenched my fists in acknowledgment of that almost religious and emotional bond. The rain stopped as suddenly as it began and the finality of it all struck me like a whirlwind. As I looked over at Ann with her wet hair and beautiful smile, she was a picture of the loving, supportive trooper that she was throughout our stay in the army. I still could not picture what my life would be like without her and the army that I truly loved. The most gratifying part of the entire day was that our family was together in the end, as they had been throughout those wondrous years. I thought of what Thomas Jefferson once said, "The tree of liberty must be refreshed from time to time with the blood of patriots and tyrants."

MAJOR GENERAL JACK LEIDE USA (RET)

GLOSSARY

LIST OF ACRONYMS:

ACRONYMS

ACSI	Assistant Chief of Staff for Intelligence
AFMIC	Armed Forces Medical Intelligence Center
AGOS	Air-Ground Operations School
AO	Area of Operations
AOR	Area of Responsibility
APC	Armored Personnel Carrier
ARCENT	US Army Central
ARMLO	Assistant Army Liaison Officer
ARVN	Army of Vietnam
ATO	Air Tasking Order
AVG	American Volunteer Group
AVLB	Armored Vehicle Launch Bridge
AWACS	Airborne Warning and Control System
AWOL	Absent Without Leave
BDA	Battle Damage Assessment

BOQ	Bachelor Officers Quarters
C3IC	Coalition Coordination, Communications, and Integration Center
CALCM	Conventional Air Launched Cruise Missile
CENTAF	Central Command Air Force
CENTCOM	Central Command
C3I	Command Control Communications and Intelligence
C4ISr	Command Control Communications Computers Intelligence and Surveillance
CEP	Circular Error Probable
CID	Criminal Investigation Division
CG	Commanding General
CI	Counter Intelligence
CIA	Central Intelligence Agency
CIB	Combat Infantryman Badge
CINC	Commander in Chief
CINCCENT	Commander in Chief Central Command
CINCPAC	Commander in Chief Pacific
CMMI	Command Military Maintenance Inspection
CMO	Central MASINT Office
CO	Commanding Officer
COMSEC	Communications Security
COS	Chief of Staff
CP	Command Post
CPX	Command Post Exercise
CSG	Cryptologic Security Group
CWO	Chief Warrant Officer
DAO	Defense Attaché Office
DAS	Defense Attaché System
DCG	Deputy Commanding General
DCI	Director of Central Intelligence
DCSINT	Deputy Chief of Staff for Intelligence
DCSOPS	Deputy Chief of Staff for Operations

DFI	Director for Foreign Intelligence
DGI	Director for General Intelligence
DHS	Defense HUMINT Service
DIA	Defense Intelligence Agency
DIO	Defense Intelligence Officer
DISCOM	Division Support Command
DLO	Defense Liaison Office
DMA	Defense Mapping Agency
DOD	Department of Defense
DRF	Division Ready Force
DRV	Democratic Republic of Vietnam
DMI	Directorate of Military Intelligence
DZ	Drop Zone
EMCON	Emissions Control
FAB	Foreign Affairs Bureau
FAC	Forward Air Controller
FAO	Foreign Area Officer
FROG	Free-Rocket-Over-Ground
GHQ	General Headquarters
GID	General Intelligence Directorate
GPS	Global Positioning System
HALO	High Altitude, Low Opening
HIPSCI	House Permanent Select Committee on Intelligence
HUMINT	Human Intelligence
IIR	Intelligence Information Report
IMINT	Imagery Intelligence
INSCOM	Intelligence and Security Command
IOAC	Infantry Officers Advanced Course
IOBC	Infantry Officers Basic Course
JCS	Joint Chiefs of Staff
JFACC	Joint Forces Air Component Commander
JFC	Joint Forces Command
JIC	Joint Intelligence Center

JILE	Joint Intelligence Liaison Element
JOC	Joint Operations Center
JSIS	Joint Services Intelligence Staff
JSOC	Joint Special Operations Command
JSTARS	Joint Surveillance Target Attack Radar System
KIA	Killed in Action
KTO	Kuwaiti Theater of Operations
LOC	Line of Communications
LOCSTAT	Location Status
LRRP	Long Range Reconnaissance Patrol
LZ	Landing Zone
MAAG	Military Assistance Advisory Group
MARS	Military Auxiliary Radio System
MASINT	Measurement and Signatures Intelligence
METT-T	Mission, Enemy, Terrain, Troops, Time Available
MFP	Major Force Program
MI	Military Intelligence
MIB	Military Intelligence Battalion
MIB	Military Intelligence Board
MODA	Ministry of Defense and Aviation
NCO	Non-Commissioned Officer
NIE	National Intelligence Estimate
NIO	National Intelligence Officer
NMCC	National Military Collections Center
NMIC	National Military Intelligence Center
NMIST	National Military Support Team
NSA	National Security Agency
NVA	North Vietnamese Army
OAS	Organization of American States
OB	Order of Battle
OCS	Officer Candidate School
OSD	Office of the Secretary of Defense
OSS	Office of Strategic Services
OTH	Over-The-Horizon Radar

PAP	Peoples Armed Police
PDASD	Principal Deputy Assistant Secretary of Defense
PLA	Peoples Liberation Army
PLAAF	Peoples Liberation Army Air Force
POM	Program Objective Memorandum
POW	Prisoner of War
PRC	Peoples Republic of China
PSP	Pierced Steel Planking
REFORGER	Return of Forces to Germany
ROC	Republic of China
ROI	Request for Information
ROTC	Reserve Officers Training Program
RPG	Rocket Propelled Grenade
RTO	Radio-Telephone Operator
RUMINT	Rumor Intelligence
RVN	Republic of Vietnam
SAMS	School of Advanced Military Studies
SANG	Saudi Army National Guard
SAP	Special Access Program
SAS	Special Air Service
SCIF	Secure Compartmented Information Facility
SERE	Survival, Escape, Resistance and Evasion
SFQC	Special Forces Qualification Course
SIGINT	Signals Intelligence
SOCCENT	Special Operations Command Central
SOF	Special Operations Forces
SOP	Standing Operating Procedure
SPAD	Special Advisor (CIA)
SRBM	Short Range Ballistic Missile
SRD	Special Research Detachment
TDY	Temporary Duty
TEL	Transport Erector Launcher
TO&E	Tables of Organization and Equipment
USAF	United States Air Force

USA	United States Army
USARJ	United States Army Japan
USARV	United States Army Vietnam
USDAO	United Stated Defense Attaché Office
USDLO	United States Defense Liaison Office
USMC	United States Marine Corps
USSOCOM	United States Special Operations Command
VC	Viet Cong

ABOUT THE AUTHOR

Military Biography:

In his last military position before retiring as an Army Major General on 1 August 1995, Jack was concurrently Director, National Military Intelligence Collection Center (NMICC); Director, Central MASINT Office (CMO); Director, Defense HUMINT Service (DHS), within the Defense Intelligence Agency.

CAREER HIGHLIGHTS:

Major General USA (Ret) John A. "Jack" Leide

- Served four combat tours:
    - Three as an airborne company commander
    - The fourth as Gen Schwarzkopf's Director of Intelligence, J-2 for the Gulf War
- Battalion Commander, US Army Special Forces.
- G-2, 82nd Airborne Division.
- Military Intelligence Group Commander.

- **Graduate, Chinese Army Command & General Staff College.**
- **Defense and Army Attaché to China (including during the Tiananmen Incident).**
- **Director, NMICC; Director, CMO; Director, DHS.**
- **Inducted into the US Military Attaché Hall of Fame**
- **Inducted into the US Military Intelligence Hall of Fame**
- **Inducted into the Defense Intelligence Agency's "Torch Bearers Hall of Fame"**

A native of Auburn, New York, he received a Bachelor of Science degree from Georgetown University, and a Juris Doctor degree from Syracuse University College of Law. (Where he was inducted into the Phi Alpha Delta legal honorary society). He served as a senior military fellow at the Harvard University John Fitzgerald Kennedy School of Government.

He completed the Infantry Basic Course in 1958. After holding various infantry platoon-level assignments, he graduated from the Infantry Advanced Course in 1963 prior to being assigned E Co. 325th Battle Group, 82nd Airborne Division.

After commanding an 82nd Airborne Division rifle company (B/3/325) both at Fort Bragg and the Dominican Republic, Major General Leide was selected as aide-de-camp to the Commanding General, 82nd Airborne Division and 18th Airborne Corps. During 1966-1967, in Vietnam, he again commanded an airborne rifle company (C/2/503) with the 173rd Airborne Brigade. In 1968, after transferring to the Military Intelligence Corps and joining the Army's Foreign Area Officer Program, specializing in China, he served as Chief, China, Korea, and Japan Military Branch in the Assistant Chief of Staff, Intelligence's Special Research Detachment.

In 1969-1970 he again served in Vietnam as Commander, 101st Military Intelligence Company and as Plans and Operations Officer, G-2, 101st Airborne Division.

On return to CONUS in 1970, Major General Leide studied Chinese Mandarin at the Defense Language Institute and graduated from the Armed Forces Staff College in 1972. In 1972-73 he studied at the State Department Foreign Service Institute's School of Chinese Language and Area Studies in Taiwan. In 1974 he was the first and only U.S. officer to attend and graduate from the Chinese Army Command and General Staff College.

Major General Leide then served as Assistant Army Attaché in Hong Kong until 1978 when he returned to CONUS to command a Special Forces Battalion at Fort Bragg, North Carolina. He then was the G2 of the 82nd Airborne Division until 1981 when he attended the National War College. In 1982 upon graduation from the National War College, he served as Chief, China Far East Division, Directorate for Estimates, Defense Intelligence Agency, until his selection in 1982 as Military Assistant in the Office of the Secretary of Defense, with major responsibilities in the fields of counterterrorism, special operations, and international security assistance with particular emphasis on African affairs.

Major General Leide then commanded the Japan-based 500th Military Intelligence Group, with a Pacific-Basin-wide mission, from July 1984 to July 1986. He then served as the Director of Foreign Intelligence, Office of the Deputy Chief of Staff for Intelligence, Department of the Army from July 1986 to January 1988. Major General Leide then performed the duties as U.S. Defense Attaché/ Army Attaché to China from May 1988 through the Tiananmen Square incident until assuming the duty as Director of Intelligence, J-2, United States Central Command in August 1990. He served as General Schwarzkopf's chief of intelligence (J-2} throughout Operations DESERT SHIELD and DESERT STORM. Following this assignment, he served as Director for Attaches and Operations from 15 June 1992 to 1 June 1993 when he assumed his position as Director for the National Military Intelligence Collection Center, the Defense HUMINT Service, and the Central MASINT Office, Defense Intelligence Agency.

His military awards and decorations include the Defense Distinguished Service Medal with one oak leaf cluster, Defense Superior Service Medal with two oak leaf clusters, Legion of Merit with two oak leaf clusters, the Bronze Star for Valor with three oak leaf clusters, Defense Meritorious Service Medal, Army Meritorious Service Medal with two oak leaf clusters, and the Army Commendations Medal with three oak leaf clusters. He also has been awarded the Combat Infantryman's Badge, Special Forces Tab, and is a Master Parachutist. He wears the OSD Service, Army Staff, DIA and CENTCOM badges. He was awarded the National Intelligence Medal of Achievement for his duties in China. He was also awarded the Central Intelligence Agency Seal Medallion and the National Intelligence Distinguished Service Medal.

He was presented with the "Ba Yi (8/1) Medal" which is highest award given to foreigners by the Chinese People's Liberation Army (PLA) and was also awarded the PLA parachutist certificate and badge for jumping with the PLA airborne.

He was awarded the Liberation Medal First Class by the Government of Kuwait for his duties during Operations DESERT SHIELD and DESERT STORM.

Major General Leide was inducted into the United States Defense Attaché Hall of Fame and has been awarded the Knowlton Medal by the US Army Military Intelligence Corps Association. Additionally, he was inducted into the United States Military Intelligence Hall of Fame, and into the Defense Intelligence Agency's "Torch Bearers Hall of Fame. He was the President of the National Military Intelligence Association 1995-1999 and a Distinguished Speaker at the Joint Military Intelligence College.

He was inducted into the Auburn, NY Educational Foundation's "Alumnae Hall of Distinction". He has been selected as an Honorary Citizen of Bedonia, Parma, Italy and awarded the

Christopher Columbus Outstanding Italian-American Military Service Award by the Italian Heritage Society.

He is married to the former Ann H. Searing of Auburn, New York since 15 April 1967. They have three children: John F, Jeffrey, and Meridith.

www.ingramcontent.com/pod-product-compliance
Lightning Source LLC
Chambersburg PA
CBHW031312160426
43196CB00007B/492